Dangerous Curves atop Hollywood Heels

The cover photo is of actress Gladys Walton.

Published in the USA by:
BearManor Media
P O Box 71426
Albany, Georgia 31708
www.bearmanormedia.com

ISBN 978-1-59393-605-1

Printed in the United States of America.
Book design by Brian Pearce | Red Jacket Press.

Dangerous Curves atop Hollywood Heels

The Lives, Careers, and Misfortunes
OF 14 Hard-Luck Girls of the Silent Screen

BY MICHAEL G. ANKERICH

When Night-Time Comes

When night-time comes to Hollywood,
    I think the lady moon looks down,
With kindness and sympathy,
    Upon the silent, sleeping town.

She, gently swaying in the sky,
    Bathes with the healing, silver fire,
The tired city that has wept,
    And laughed, and worked, and know desire!

And all the faiths that have been lost,
    And all the plans that went awry,
Are giving back to dreaming hearts,
    Her benediction from the sky.

For, as the wistful breezes sing,
    And as the clouds about her creep,
The lady moon is keeping guard
    Above the earth-bound stars who sleep......

Margaret Sangster

Also by Michael G. Ankerich

Broken Silence:
Conversations with 23 Silent Film Stars

The Sound of Silence:
Conversations with 16 Film and Stage Personalities
Who Made the Transition from Silents to Talkies

The Real Joyce Compton:
Behind the Dumb Blonde Movie Image
(with Joyce Compton)

*For Roi Uselton, who first introduced me to many of
these hard-luck girls of the silent screen*

*For Eve Southern, who finally introduced herself
and inspired me again.*

TABLE OF CONTENTS

"Cultivate your curves — they may be dangerous but they won't be avoided."

Mae West

ACKNOWLEDGEMENTS

As I turn the final curve and see the completion of this book before me, I'm humbled by all those who made the journey with me as I explored the lives of those featured in *Dangerous Curves Atop Hollywood Heels.*

First, I'm grateful to the family and friends of my subjects whose interviews clarified assumptions and verified facts and whose anecdotes brought my subjects to life in the 21st century: Don Gallery, the family of Wanda Hawley, Arden Keevers, Wallace McDowell, Evelyn McDowell, Raymond C. McKee, John Ricksen, Larry Ricksen, and Rupert Ricksen.

I offer a bow of thanks to those actors and actresses of the silent screen who graciously shared with me their memories of my subjects and, through their memories, took me back to the studios of the 1920s: Lina Basquette, Mary Brian, Ethlyne Clair, Frank Coghlan Jr., Pauline Curley, William Janney, Natalie Joyce, Barbara Kent, Baby Peggy Montgomery, Lois Moran, Anita Page, Dorothy Revier.

Appreciation also goes to fellow writers, researchers, and others whose insights and contributions kept me company along this journey: John Cocchi, Richard Cox, Greta De Groat, Billy Doyle, E.J. Fleming, Sharon Lane, Michael Laskin, Crystal Lentz (Washington State Library), Bruce Long, Rita Maenner, staff of the Motion Picture Academy Library, Ben Ohmart (my publisher), Brian Pearce (book designer), Jim Parish, Norma Schuh, Anthony Slide, Sherri Synder, and Keith Szarabajkas.

And, as always, how fortunate that my partner, Charlie Stulpes, and our girls, Maebelle, Ms. Taylor, and Tallulah, patiently maneuvered every dangerous curve with me as I shared, over nightly cocktails, the stories of these fascinating gals of the silent screen.

All of you made it worth the journey.

Michael G. Ankerich

INTRODUCTION

Anna Q. Nilsson had been a star for over 10 years when she was asked to give advice to young women across the country who were interested in coming to Hollywood to try for the movies. Already a seasoned veteran of over 140 films, she was freelancing successfully for the top studios, she had little reason to hold back.

"I believe that if girls generally realized the heartaches and disappointments incident to the struggle of practically every girl worker in pictures, there would be less ambition rampant along this line," she advised. "There's a Heartbreak Lane in Hollywood, leading by a circuitous path to the gates of the many studios, strewn with the wreckage of those, possibly with ample beauty, ambition, and all other qualifications, who just couldn't seem to make a go of it."[1]

Herbert Howe, correspondent for *Photoplay* magazine, gave more dire warnings to those seeking fame in pictures. The work is simply hazardous to one's physical and mental being.

"Youth enters pictures arrogantly with the idea that he's lending his charms to the camera in exchange for a fortune, whereas, in reality he is selling outright," he wrote. "My statistics prove that the limelight is as fatal to the individual as the gas flame to the bug. It destroys him. On a few occasions when I've observed a particular fine young entrant I've been moved to issue council but if you've ever tried to dissuade a moth from circling round a flame you know the only way to do it is with a fly swatter."[2]

In the early 1920s, the movie business in Hollywood was a major industry. There were over 50 moving picture studios operating in the area. The industry employed more than 20,000 people with an annual payroll of $50 million. Just 10 short years before, D.W. Griffith brought his Biograph Company and its slate of pioneers, Mack Sennett, Mary Pickford, Owen Moore, and Florence Lawrence, to Los Angeles. The Horsleys, Essanay, Kalem, Thomas Ricketts, and Al Christie soon followed and helped build the foundation of this blooming business.

Hollywood was in its infancy and still retained its innocence. Then, beginning in 1920 and for the next four years, the industry was rocked by a series of scandals that tarnished the tinsel: the suicide of actress Olive Thomas (1920); the death of Virginia Rappe and the fallout for Roscoe "Fatty" Arbuckle (1921); the murder of director William Desmond Taylor (1922); the drug-related death of actor Wallace Reid (1923); and the mysterious death of producer Thomas Ince (1924).

The dark cloud of scandal penetrated the industry, severed the veil between make believe and reality, and robbed Hollywood of its innocence. The movie capital was referred to as Sodom of the Twentieth Century and Paris of America.

Some of filmdom's leading stars, directors, and producers put their thoughts about their profession in *The Truth about the Movies* (1924). The writers, between the covers of the book, attempted to paint a realistic portrait of the industry. Part of their hope was to inform the thousands of hopeful youths who annually ventured West about the difficulty in breaking into the movies.

Frank Butler, an actor in Sennett comedies, wrote:

"From every corner of the earth they come and across the Seven Seas — borne on the tireless wings of youthful optimism. Pathetic pilgrims these, struggling on to ultimate disillusion. In most cases their assets, generally considered, amount to a one-way ticket to Hollywood (the savings of their young lives), an inadequate wardrobe, a still less adequate bank-roll, a terrifying determination to break into the movies, and (most disastrous) the rather appalling knowledge that in their old home town they were considered to be good looking.

"Of the chosen few, perhaps one in two thousand may eventually after a few years of heart-break and hard work, reach the place where they play small and infrequent parts, thereby averaging the salary of a rather badly paid dry goods store clerk. And of these, not one in twenty thousand ever attain the intoxicating heights of stardom.

"Hollywood is crowded with beautiful women and good looking men, all hammering frantically upon the iron doors of moviedom. Now and then one or two, either by good luck or persistence slip through and glimmer faintly on the horizon of fame. But of the vast majority there is no record, and by very reason of their fatal beauty they are thrust into hopeless oblivion."[3]

Dangerous Curves atop Hollywood Heels tells the stories of 14 silent film actresses who, despite the odds against them, journeyed to Hollywood and made names for themselves in moving pictures. The success they achieved varied considerably, but for a short time, they all glimmered on the horizon of fame. For each, the price they paid was considerable.

They, these hard luck girls, came from different walks of life. Many were running from dismal lives and wanted would try anything to be somebody on the screen. They were so curious about this fairyland that they talked their parents, often a rabidly ambitious stage mother, into pulling up roots and heading west to Hollywood. In the land of make believe, they reinvented themselves.

Many contrived new identities and altered their ages, backgrounds — some claimed royalty or other famous people in their linage. Some gave up husbands and children to get a taste of Hollywood. A few went from husband to husband, only to remember that they'd forgotten to divorce their mate who'd long since passed from the scene. There were the evils of narcotics addiction, prescribed by shady physicians who knew little about the addictiveness of their drug.

On the other side of fame, they had nowhere to go back to, no place to land. Many hung around the boulevard of broken dreams, but those streets turned out to be dead-end streets and reminders of how far they'd fallen and how quickly people forgot. Some escaped Hollywood and lived to tell about it.

When selecting the actresses I wanted to profile, I steered clear of those hard luck girls who are most familiar to film historians and movie buffs: Clara Bow, Mary Miles Minter, Olive Thomas, Alma Rubens, Jeanne Eagels, and Thelma Todd. Their lives had been researched, their misfortunes chronicled. I had nothing to add.

Quite frankly, I selected those I wanted to know better, those I could walk a ways with and examine what their Hollywood experiences had been and how they dealt with life after their fame was over.

I was particularly interested in how their marriages, divorces, career decisions, battles with weight, temperament, scandals, which I term their "dangerous curves," affected their lives and experience in Hollywood.

My journey with these hard luck girls began with the search for Eve Southern, a silent film actress long lost to cinema researchers. She had simply dropped out of sight after the advent of sound. Tracking back almost a hundred years, through twists and turns, road blocks and dead ends in my research and detective work, I uncovered the life and career of this fascinating actress whose career was a series of disappointments.

A few of those I selected, Martha Mansfield and Lucille Ricksen, simply died tragically, their young lives snuffed out way too soon. Juanita Hansen, Grace Darmond, and Wanda Hawley gave out along the road of success, but pulled themselves out of their downhill spiral and triumphed into old age.

Olive Borden, Marie Prevost, Alberta Vaughn, Elinor Fair, and Mary Nolan escaped into the bottle to help ease the rejection. They lived long enough to feel the chill of a cold, cruel Hollywood. It was, they learned, a hell of a place for has-beens.

Barbara La Marr, the epitome of a hard-luck girl, suffered the ravages of drink, drugs and dieting, picked and discarded men by the dozen, and adopted the son she secretly bore out of wedlock. She came to understand that her little Sonny, whom I interviewed for this book, gave her the loved she craved but could never seem to find. Her excesses took her life before the fickle public turned against her.

Agnes Ayres and Marie Prevost fought the battle of the bulge in their efforts to remain appealing before the movie camera. Sadly, they were unable to let go of their dreams and ultimately gave out trying to resurrect their careers. Natalie Joyce struggled in the shadow of her cousin Olive Borden until a sympatric director urged her to seek another profession. She left Hollywood, lost touch with Olive, and never looked back.

Uncovering their paths to and through Hollywood was a daunting task. Some had covered their tracks so well that relatives I contacted knew little of the truth about their pasts. At first glance, it seemed as though their lives began only when they walked into a movie studio. But, there they were, among the multitude of names recorded on censuses, city directories, studio contracts, birth records, and baptismal certificates.

When possible, I tracked down and worked with relatives in an attempt to piece together their lives. I poured over reviews of their films, correspondence by and about them, newspaper clippings, and fanzine articles. I viewed their available work and visited their final resting places. I was particularly interested in interviews they gave during their lives, always preferring to allow them to tell their own stories, without a lot of editorial interference.

It is my intent with *Dangerous Curves Atop Hollywood Heels* to celebrate with honesty, yet compassion, the lives and careers, however disappointing, of 14 fascinating luminaries of the silent screen.

Perhaps it was Mae Murray, the girl with the bee-stung lips, who encapsulated what life was like for those actresses who had the courage, despite all warnings to stay home, to seek fame and fortune in Hollywood.

"We were like dragonflies," Mae said. "We seemed to be suspended effortlessly in the air, but in reality, our wings were beating very, very fast."

1. Hughes, Laurence A., *The Truth About the Movies*, Hollywood Publishers, Inc., 1924.

2. Howe, Herbert, *Photoplay*, 1928.

3. *The Truth about the Movies*, edited by Laurence A. Hughes. Hollywood Publishers, Inc., 1924.

Sincerely
Agnes Ayres.

AGNES AYRES

The comeback Agnes Ayres had struggled for was just within her grasp. It was November 1936 and she'd come home to Paramount, where once, 15 years before, she'd reigned as a star. Her role in *Souls at Sea* was not a starring one, not even a supporting part. It was little more than a bit, a walk-on, but at least she was working before the camera. She was sure it was the start to her long road back to stardom.

If she had the jitters, there were those on the set who still remembered her and offered their support. Even Rudolph Valentino, her old co-star from *The Sheik*, was on hand to offer his encouragement. Agnes had her doubts that he was actually present beside her, but she'd had that assurance from some.

Since the recent publicity that Agnes was making a comeback at Paramount, a number of mediums had contacted the studio to let her know that Valentino, who'd died suddenly 10 years before, had messages for her. One medium assured her that the great film lover would be standing by her side when her scenes were filmed.[1] If he was there, fine! Agnes felt she needed all the support she could muster.

Richard Griffith, in *The Movie Stars*, gave Agnes Ayres the sad distinction of waging the "grimmest, most tenacious, and in the end most futile struggle to make a comeback via the quickies, the personal appearance route, and every other means she could think of."[2]

She'd been in films since 1915, starting at the old Essanay Company in Chicago. After years of churning out one and two reelers at Vitagraph, Agnes caught the attention of producer Jesse L. Lasky, who rescued her from the mundane and made her a star — and his mistress.

Agnes rose to stardom at Paramount with the studio's finest leading men: Thomas Meighan, Jack Holt, Milton Sills, and Wallace Reid. But it was when Rudolph Valentino carried her into his tent in *The Sheik* that her star rose to the heavens. She became the envy of millions of women.

Her association with Paramount ended when her relationship with Lasky soured. She signed a contract with Producer's Distributing

Corporation (PDC), but when the company kept her idle and off the screen, allegedly because of weight gain, she sued the company, including its vice-president, the powerful director Cecil B. DeMille.

In the middle of her legal fight, Agnes put her career on hold. She married and started a family in the mid-1920s. After the marriage ended, she set out to reclaim her place in films.

Time had passed, however. It had been nearly 10 years since Valentino had gathered her up into his arms and rode off with her across the desert. She'd once stood in the spotlight, but now, the bright light illuminated someone else. Talkies were the rage and she was seen as a relic from another time.

Not to be deterred, Agnes spent the next decade traipsing around the country playing one-night stands in cheap vaudeville houses, all the while her gaze was back on Hollywood and her ambition to work in films. She was ready to drop everything and run back to Hollywood if anyone beckoned her.

Through the desert sands in her hourglass, Agnes Ayres had plenty of time to think about the days of her life.

She was born Agnes Henkel on April 4, 1892, in Carbondale, Illinois.[3] She had a brother, Solon William, born in December 1888. It is not clear whether her father, Solon Augustus Henkel, died while Agnes was a child, or whether her parents divorced, but by 1900, Agnes' mother, Emma Slack Henkel had married Franklin Rendleman, a farmer.[4]

The family moved to Chicago when Agnes was a teenager. While early publicity indicates that Agnes had ambitions to study law,[5] in 1910 at the age of 18, she was working as a bookkeeper. She often said she had no early ambitions of becoming an actress.

By all accounts, Agnes broke into the movies as Agnes Eyre at Chicago's Essanay Film Manufacturing Company during the winter of 1914, when a girlfriend suggested they visit the studio. Agnes caught the attention of a director, who used her in a crowd scene of a Francis X. Bushman and Beverly Bayne film.

She was encouraged to return to the studio and join the ranks of extras. Gloria Swanson, another Essanay extra, and Agnes shared a dressing room.[6] They both had small roles in an early Charlie Chaplin film, *His New Job* (1915).

Agnes said later that her days at Essanay, where she played as many as four parts in a working day, were the most satisfying days of her film career. "Perhaps in the morning I would start as a school girl, hair down in curls and all that sort of thing; then at eleven suffragettes were the order, while at two the call was for enthusiastic co-ed rooters at a football game; and in the late afternoon I would put on formal clothes and attend a reception.

"During every free minute we were experimenting with makeup, waiting for a chance at real parts. It was the finest experience imaginable, days and days of just fun — with an undercurrent of real seriousness. For it meant our futures."[7]

Agnes in The Blue Book of the Screen *(1924).*

Agnes saved what money she could from her $35 a week Essanay salary. By the winter of 1916, she had enough saved to get her and her mother to New York[8], where there were more opportunities for actresses. Agnes and Emma had no contacts in the big city, so work didn't come immediately. When it looked like they might have to return to Chicago, director Frank Powell hired Agnes to appear in a number of Marjorie Rambeau films: *The Dazzling Miss Davison*, *The Mirror*, *The Debt*, and *Motherhood*, all 1917 releases.

As her career began to move forward, Agnes married Frank P. Schuker, an Army captain. The union promised to bring mother and daughter solid financial security until Agnes established herself in films. However, the two soon separated. Agnes concentrated on finding work in the movies.

It was actress Alice Joyce who, noticing a resemblance between the two, offered Agnes the role of her sister in *Richard the Brazen* (1917), a Vitagraph production. Agnes continued working for Vitagraph through 1918 and most of 1919, appearing in a series of popular shorts based on the stories of O. Henry. Agnes eventually became known around the studio and filmdom as "The O. Henry Girl." They provided excellent training ground to the budding actress.

"I have never really enjoyed anything more than those pictures," Agnes said later. "I used to love to study the heroines of the various stories and it was a joy to visualize each different one on the screen."[9]

Most of her roles at Vitagraph were wholesome heroines, with an occasional vamp part thrown in. "I was very mean, too," she said. "I said to myself as I was portraying the role, 'I hate her, and I'll do anything I can do to make her unhappy.' I always try to do that in picture acting. I try to live my part, and I find that makeup and costume really do change my personality."[10]

After almost two years at Vitagraph, Agnes turned her sights to Hollywood after producer Jesse L. Lasky turned his sights to her. He had seen her on the screen and, although he was married with children, he became infatuated with the actress. He brought her to Los Angeles, where he starred her in *Held by the Enemy* (1920).

In this Civil War melodrama produced by Paramount, Agnes played a Southern belle whose husband, whom she never loved, is killed in the war. Grieving only briefly, she is reacquainted with an old beau, who is now an officer in the Union Army. Her plans to marry are thwarted when the husband she thought had been killed shows up.

Agnes garnered glowing reviews for her work in the film. "Agnes Ayres gave a performance that was truly great. She looked wonderfully well and carried the role to perfection," noted *Variety*.[11]

Lasky placed Agnes under contract to Paramount and made it his priority to lavish his attention on her. They began a long-term affair, and he offered her the best scripts and starred her with the studio's top directors and leading men.

She confessed to a reporter not long after she arrived in Hollywood that her secret ambition was to be a success on the stage. "I had an offer to

A paycheck from Paramount, endorsed by Agnes Ayres (1922).

go into musical comedy and also a play just before coming West," Agnes said," but I didn't accept, because I really want to achieve my screen ambitions first. I feel as if I have the opportunity to do this now."[12]

Certainly with Lasky's personal attention on her, in exchange for her attention and affections, she would have been foolish to return to New York and struggle for what meager parts came along.

Before the year was out, she had leading roles in *The Furnace*, directed by William Desmond Taylor, and *Go and Get It*, under the direction of Marshall Neilan.

As she was settling into her career at Paramount, she attended to a bit of housekeeping. She set about divorcing Frank Schucker. In court, Agnes presented herself as Agnes Schucker, forgetting to tell the judge she was Agnes Ayres of the screen. Her mother testified she had supported Agnes for over a year. The judge granted the divorce on the grounds of non-support.

Soon after, the divorce decree was rescinded when the court learned

Forrest Stanley and Agnes Ayres in Forbidden Fruit *(1921).*

Agnes was a "high-priced" film star. In the end, the court ruled that she probably had good cause for divorce on the grounds of desertion. So, Agnes, as Agnes Ayres, returned to court and entered her plea.[13] The divorce was granted.

Agnes' stellar performance in *Forbidden Fruit* (1921) set her on sound footing at Paramount. Cecil B. DeMille directed her in the role of a seamstress who passes for a society lady. Agnes was stunning as Cinderella in an elaborate flashback sequence.

Variety took notice of her work. "Agnes Ayres, a young woman who has made marvelous strides since leaving Vitagraph, is given chief honors, and wears them well. She is a beautiful girl, with poise and restraint, and portrays a many-shaded character excellently."[14]

Agnes had prominent parts with the handsome, but ill-fated, Wallace Reid in three 1921 releases: *The Love Special* (a railroad story set in the West); *Too Much Speed* (an auto racing story); and *The Affairs of Anatol*, in which Reid, under the skillful direction of DeMille, saves Agnes from

Agnes on the set of The Affairs of Anatol *(1921) with Wallace Reid, Cecil B. DeMille, Monte Blue, Raymond Hatton, and Theodore Kosloff.*

drowning herself after her husband (Monte Blue) accuses her of stealing church funds.

In the summer of 1921, Agnes started work on the film for which she is remembered today: *The Sheik*. She was cast as Lady Diana Mayo, a headstrong English blonde, whom Rudolph Valentino, as Sheik Ahmed, stalks, captures, and finally seduces in his tent somewhere in the Algerian desert.

Agnes demands to know his intentions for her. He leers at her, then nods toward the inner chambers of the tent. He answers with a sneer, "Are you not woman enough to know?"

The film was a smashing success, breaking attendance records over the globe. Early critics expressed bewilderment that the script had fallen into the censors' hands and emerged a much tamer tale than the racy book by E.M. Hull.

Picture Play put it this way: "His (Valentino's) fierceness — which so delighted the gentle spinster readers — is all gone, his language and

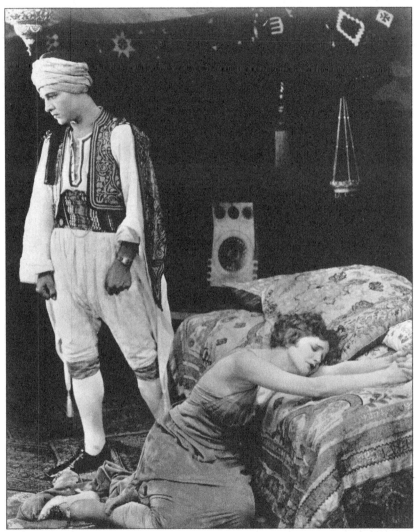

Agnes Ayres and Rudolph Valentino heating up the screen in The Sheik *(1921).*

manner are as meek as a Rollo book, and his attitude toward the kid-napped heroine is that of a considerate and platonic friend rather than the passionate, ruthless lover 'on an Arab shod with fire.'"[15]

Valentino, *Picture Play* surmised, was too young for the role. "We liked Agnes Ayres better as the obstinate beauty who shrinks from his advances, though we must say she didn't have much to shrink from."[16]

Agnes Ayres in the arms of Tom Gallery in A Daughter of Luxury *(1922).*

While *Photoplay* congratulated Agnes for playing her role "splendidly,"[17] *Variety* opined that perhaps she was the wrong actress for the role. "Agnes Ayres looks too matronly to lend much kick to the situation in which she finds herself. She has shown herself capable of much better things than this."[18]

Variety offered the same opinion of Agnes' next film, *The Lane that had no Turning* (1922), in which she played a French opera singer married to a hunchback. "As in her previous picture, *The Sheik*, Miss Ayres is relegated to a secondary position as regards to prominence by another member of the cast. In *The Sheik*, it was Valentino who outshone her, and in this release, the honors go to Theodore Kosloff as the deformed husband. Miss Ayres lends a pleasing appearance, but is not called upon to do anything out of the ordinary."

In the spring of 1922, while the shooting of *Borderland* was underway, Agnes and her co-star, Milton Sills, were asked to perform in a skit, *The*

Dumb-bell Wives, for the *First Annual Hollywood Follies*, a musical comedy show. The two rehearsed the skit, but on the night of the performance, Agnes panicked and refused to go on, claiming she had not been properly rehearsed. Sills, who was prepared for his part, was unable to perform without Agnes.

Marion Fairfaix, the show's chairperson, was furious. In a letter to Sills the next day, she expressed her frustration. When Agnes complained to Fairfax that she was unprepared for the skit, "I myself took her back into the wings for her entrance, and I did not know until after the show was over that she left the wings the moment my back was turned, or that this was what prevented your appearance. I am truly indignant that this should have happened, and that we lost the value that you would have added to the number. It seems outrageous, after you gave so much of your time as you did to be with us, that such a thing could have happened." [19]

In June, filming began on *Clarence*, her final film with Wallace Reid, who was critically ill from the ravaging affects of drug addiction. Agnes was stunned by his appearance. Larry Lee Holland, in his career article on Agnes for *Films in Review*, claims that Agnes, working on her fourth film with Reid, was secretly in love with the dying actor.

Holland writes, "He collapsed several times on the set and was sent home to recover. Agnes visited him at his home on Sunset Boulevard and would sit by his bedside for hours at a time. She claimed that she loved him and couldn't live without him, which at first amused Dorothy Reid, his wife.

"Soon, however, Wallace began to complain about her visits and Dorothy was forced to ask Agnes not to come anymore. Agnes persisted in calling until Dorothy grew desperate and, like a scene from a bad movie, threatened to throw acid in Agnes' face if she showed up again. That did it. Agnes did not return."[20]

Though she may have exhibited occasional bursts of temperament and was possibly in love with Wallace Reid, the hand guiding her career, Jesse L. Lasky, continued assigning her some of the studio's best material.

In *The Ordeal*, a society drama, she parades around in a series of stunning gowns. She plays an outcast in the modern-day story in *The Ten Commandments* (1923), her third film under the direction of Cecil B. DeMille. In the action-paced *Racing Hearts* (1923), she buys a racing car and wins the race. To promote the picture, Paramount released a story alleging that Agnes was twice arrested for speeding during the filming of picture. She spent a day on location practicing an arrest for a speeding violation, only be stopped by cops on her way home that evening.

She plays another speed demon in *The Heart Raider* (1923). While *Variety* praised Agnes as "that rare type of a good-looking athletic girl who is both (good-looking and athletic), the kind of a girl everyone likes,"[21] *Harrison's Reports* thought Agnes too old for the part. "The heroine is supposed to be of unmanageable nature and of destructive disposition, making her father pay damages on account of her speed mania. Such part requires a woman of much younger age than that of Miss Ayres. It requires too great a stretch of imagination to accept her as the young woman of the story."[22]

In 1924, Agnes did some of her best work. *Harrison's Reports* called *The Story Without a Name*, "a good melodrama,"[23] and *The Guilty One*, "one of the most gripping murder mysteries produced by Famous Players-Lasky in many a moon."[24]

Over time, Agnes grew disillusioned over being a kept woman at Paramount. She understood that, although Lasky's marriage was not a happy one, he had no intentions of leaving his wife for her. In October 1923, Agnes met a handsome, young Mexican at the home of her close friend, actress Kathlyn Williams. He turned out to be S. Manuel Reachi, attaché to the consulate general of Mexico at San Francisco. A romance blossomed, and in August 1924, the two announced their engagement.[25]

For the next month, Agnes consistently denied the two were already married. Finally, in September 1924, she told reporters the two had married in Mexico in July. She refused to explain why they had kept their nuptials secret. "We just didn't want it known, that's all," she said. The bride and groom, she explained, would honeymoon in Europe after the completion of her film, *Worldly Goods*.[26]

That fall, Agnes completed *Tomorrow's Love* (1925), the final film in her five-year tenure for Paramount. Almost immediately, she signed with Producers Distributing Corporation (PDC) for three pictures at $10,000 each. *Her Market Value* (1925) was her first PDC film, followed by *The Awful Truth* (1925), in which a series of misunderstandings between the flirtatious Agnes and her husband (Warner Baxter) lead to the divorce court. She later devises a scheme to win back her husband. *The New York Times* gushed that Agnes was "serenely delightful" in the picture and "is happily cast in this type of role. No one could or need do it better."[27]

That summer, Agnes, between pictures, invited a reporter from *The Los Angeles Times* to her home on Martel Avenue to discuss her marriage and film career.

"It is nice to be at home," Agnes said. "I am busy, usually, off to the studio early in the morning and not back again until very late. Now, I have a little time to pick my roses and get acquainted with my pets," which consisted of a parrot, a German police dog, Tino (a cat named for Rudolph Valentino), and chickens.[28]

After her long contract with Paramount, Agnes said she was looking for less "decorative" roles and a chance to make herself an "individual rather than a mere type of beauty."[29]

Agnes Ayres and Manuel Reachi at a wedding party for Mae Murray and David Mdivani. Pictured (L-R) are Pola Negri, Rudolph Valentino, Kathlyn Williams, Murray, Mdivani, Reachi, Ayres, unknown.

The next month, in July, Agnes had apparently grown bored of pruning roses and watching chickens roost. She filed a $43,000 suit against PDC claiming they had not followed though with their bargain.[30] In August, Agnes amended the suit, increasing the suit to $93,000.[31]

Part of her beef was with Cecil B DeMille, a partner in the firm, whom she said promised her better roles if she signed with PDC. She maintained that her absence from the screen had damaged her reputation with the public. In addition, Agnes was aggravated that in billing *Three Faces*

East, a film project she never made, DeMille had co-featured Agnes with an actor of less prominence, in violation of her contract which called for her to receive star billing in all her pictures.[32]

In the defendant's answer to the lawsuit, PDC claimed that excessive weight gain, a violation of her contract, was the contributing factor in not starring her in more films. Agnes was furious at the claim and was

Agnes and her husband, Manuel Reachi.

ready for a showdown in court. Perhaps the studio was not aware that Agnes was pregnant.

Two days after Agnes filed her amended suit, news surfaced that a Nora Hingley De Reachi, a resident of Hawaii, had obtained a divorce from her husband on the grounds of desertion. She asserted that she was still married to Manual Reachi when he married Agnes. Manual told reporters he was bewildered over the woman's claim. He said he had never been to Hawaii, had never been married before marrying Agnes, and had never heard of a Nora Hingley De Reachi.[33] Nothing came of the woman's accusation.

In February 1926, Cecil B. DeMille, in a court deposition, said he tried to politely inform Agnes that she was overweight. "I did not say," he declared, 'Lady, you are fat!'"

"Do you know why she has not made any more pictures," DeMille was asked.

"I remember hearing discussed the fact that the exhibitors would not take her because she had lost her appearance," he replied.

"At the last time you had occasion to see her did you speak to her about her fatness?" the court questioned.

DeMille responded, "We discussed questions quite frankly, but whether it was because she was fat or not, I don't remember."

"Did you notice any difference in her facial appearance on these different interviews?"

"She has always seemed very charming to me," DeMille answered.[34]

Agnes and her husband stood their ground. Manual told reporters, "We have authorized statements from Miss Ayres's physicians showing that she has not gained one pound of flesh for the last four years and also certified photographs to prove and uphold these statements."[35]

Agnes' attorney, Gunther R. Lessing, said the weight issue was "merely in line with other attempts to injure Miss Ayres because she dared to stand up for her rights. Since when has a bean pole become Mr. DeMille's standard of beauty? Everybody has noticed that like Caesar, he likes them fat."[36]

While the case dragged on, Agnes gave birth to a daughter, Maria Eugenia, on March 26, 1926. Pola Negri and Rudolph Valentino were named godparents.[37]

In May 1926, Producers Distributing Corporation settled out of court in favor of Agnes. They declared, "no animosity exists toward you and we hope we may avail ourselves of your services in the future."[38]

Later that month, it was announced that Agnes would appear in *The Son of the Sheik* (1926), a sequel to *The Sheik*. She would reprise her role of Diana and Rudolph Valentino would play dual roles as the father (still married to Diana) and their son.

The Son of the Sheik opened in July 1926 to adoring fans. He embarked on a nation-wide tour publicize the film. Following the opening of the picture at the Strand Theater in Brooklyn, Valentino took to the stage and spoke affectionately of Agnes and her willingness to take a small role in his film and of her devotion to her infant daughter. That evening turned out to be his last public appearance.[39]

Days later, he fell ill and died in New York of a ruptured gastric ulcer and peritonitis. He was only 31 years old. Agnes, like the rest of the world, was grief stricken.

"His death is doubly affecting to me because not only were our careers so closely linked in the struggle for picture success, but he had ever proved himself as a loyal friend," she said in a statement.[40]

Following her court settlement and the announcement of her work in *The Son of the Sheik*, the Reachi marriage fell apart. Manual Reachi left the Martel Avenue house and Agnes filed for divorce, claiming desertion and abuse.

On the stand, Agnes called her husband's treatment of her austere. On occasion, she testified, his austerity reached such a degree that she came

Agnes and Valentino during the filming of The Sheik.

out of struggles with fingerprints on her throat and nervous chills. Five times since their marriage, she continued, he deserted her, going away once to Europe without her.

"Judge, he would go into the most frightful tantrums over just nothing at all," she said in court. "Half the time, I would not have the least idea what it was all about."

Agnes Ayres and Otto Matiesen in The Lady of Victories *(1928).*

The divorce was final in June 1927. The court approved a property settlement whereby each party released the other from any claim. Reachi consented to their daughter remaining in Agnes' custody at her expense.

"I am not sorry I married because I have my daughter. And, I would marry again, because I love children," Agnes told *Photoplay*. "But if I do marry again, he will be an American. Latin men are wonderful lovers, but poor husbands."[41]

Although Agnes had invested well in real estate, she felt the need, now that she was no longer married, to return to work. In a rather sad, yet bizarre move, Agnes was cast as foil to comedian Stan Laurel in a two-reel, slapstick comedy, *Eve's Love Letters* (1927).

In 1928, she made another short and appeared in several quickies with talking sequences. From December 1928 to November 23, 1929, she appeared on the New York stage as a Gypsy Joe dancer in *Whoopee!*

Her final film of any consequence was as a dinner party guest in *The Donovan Affair* (1929), an early talkie directed by Frank Capra. Dorothy Revier, who appeared as Agnes' stepdaughter in the picture, later recalled her bumpy start with the veteran actress.

Revier remembered Ayres as being "very cool and aloof in an almost vindictive manner" at the beginning of the picture. Revier believed that Agnes was having an affair with the sound technician, and as a joke, the two of them tampered with Revier's voice test for the picture, making her voice sound distortedly high-pitched.[42]

"Frank Capra and I almost panicked before they told us it had all been in fun," Revier recounted. "Surprisingly, we became friends during the rest of the picture. I was really nice to her and started flattering her, saying how great she was in *The Sheik* with Valentino. Soon after that, she began inviting me to lunch and we became friends."[43]

Variety, in its review of the picture, noted their voices were "okay, but that Agnes Ayres seems to be putting on flesh." [44]

Following her appearance in *The Donovan Affair*, Agnes' personal and professional lives were set adrift. She lost her fortune in the stock market crash of 1929 and found herself in dire straits.

In late 1929 or early 1930, she began an affair with director Lewis Milestone, who was in the middle of shooting *All Quiet on the Western Front* (1930). In early April, Louella Parsons reported in her column that, "Mr. Milestone set out to win Agnes and apparently, he has succeeded, for their wedding will take place sometime in June."

Details about Agnes' on and off relationship with Milestone come from an unsigned draft of a letter in his personal papers at the Academy of Motion Picture Arts and Sciences Library. The writer of the letter is a Milestone insider, perhaps an agent or accountant who handled Milestone's affairs. Apparently, at Milestone's request, the writer attempted to paint a realistic picture for Agnes of Milestone's feelings for her and to bring some stability to Agnes' life following her loss of fortune.

"The big house[45] is rented for $250.00 a month and all of them have moved to the Orange Grove Avenue house.[46] She got a wire last week asking if she would accept a New York stage engagement.[47] She came to me to ask what to do and I told her that as she was making her own living to do what she thought best, but to at least get an advance from the people. Wires have been popping back and forth all week and they sent her an advance which she is leaving with the mother[48] to tide her and the child over. She now has a fair income — about $350 a month — and as long as she works, it will be more. Everything that could be done for her has been done and she is entirely satisfied with everything."

The insider then urges Milestone to refrain from the games he has played with the emotionally fragile actress.

"For the love, let sleeping dogs lie. Don't get into communication with her in any way whatever. Every time this matter is opened up, it becomes harder to fix and having Mischa[49] go to her and talk romance just makes it tougher for me. If you want her, alright, go to it, but on the other hand, if you do not want to get married, just keep away and do not communicate with her in any way shape or form. If you do, and then try to get out from under, it is going to cost a hell of a lot of dough, time and trouble."

Before the writer could mail Milestone the letter, a despondent Agnes called. "Hell broke loose again," the Milestone acquaintance wrote in an addendum to the original letter. "Someone told Agnes about an interview that you gave out in New York saying, 'I never had an intention of marrying. I was never engaged and have no plans for the future in that line. Whatever you have heard is just a lot of gossip.' She was sore as hell over the phone and I told her I would be up at noon. I met her at noon and at 4 o'clock had her quieted down again and she agreed not to pay any attention to anything. I told her I would not handle her things and get them into shape if she did not behave herself and as I have been successful so far in fixing her income so that she at least has enough to live on. Don't talk about her to anyone so that it gets back to her because each time she is told something she gets madder and madder."

In New York, Agnes concentrated on her forthcoming play, *Jungle Love*, in which she would appear with Ninion Bunyea and Herbert Rawlinson. *The New York Times* announced it would open in Atlantic City on June 9 before coming to Broadway.[50] The play never made it to New York.

Louella Parsons, in an April 1931 column, announced that Agnes would make a comeback to the screen in producer Bryan Foy's first feature film, *Half Way to Hell*.[51] The film apparently never materialized.

Back on the stage in October, Agnes appeared with Victor Jory in *On the Spot*, at the Westchester Theater in Mount Vernon, New York.[52] In December, she supported Lou Tellegen in *Cortez* on the Philadelphia stage.[53]

The next May (1933), Agnes appeared in Syracuse, New York, in a series of personal appearances in which she discussed the motion picture industry. She told the audience that silents were superior to talkies, certain studios deliberately destroy the box office value of star to avoid paying salaries commensurate with their drawing power, movie-going audiences are inclined to forget those whose hair is graying, and there will never be another Valentino.[54] Part of her stay in the city included an appearance in the children's department of a local department store.

Later that month, she joined the cast of *Hard-Boiled Angel*, starring Lenore Ulric, at the Grand Opera House in Chicago.[55]

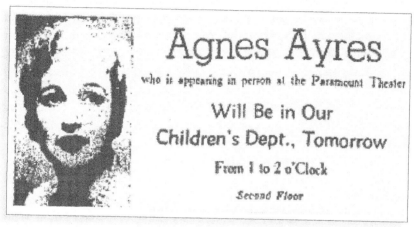

Agnes Ayres

who is appearing in person at the Paramount Theater

Will Be in Our
Children's Dept., Tomorrow

From 1 to 2 o'Clock

Second Floor

Advertisement for Agnes' beauty demonstration (1934).

In late 1933, Agnes worked in a Hollywood revue with Babe Kane, James Hall, and the Rose sisters. She talked about the past. Cecil B. DeMille, she said, "is a man of infinite charm who was a man's man." In speaking about *The Sheik*, she said she was "just a youngster trying to make good." Again, she said there would not be another Valentino. "Most assuredly, there will not. He was a charm distinctly his own. Neither Clark Gable nor George Raft can take his place." Of her role as Diana in *The Sheik*, Agnes proclaimed, "I should like to play it again and do not believe the role would be any less alive today than then."[56]

While doing beauty care demonstrations at a beauty salon in New York in October 1934, Agnes spoke with a reporter about her struggle to make her way back to Hollywood fame.

"Honestly, I haven't grown bitter, nor disillusioned or catty, I hope, but I know my old public would still want to see me and still talk about me. It's not the public's fault that a person like myself wouldn't be given a chance now.[57]

"When they'll take an untrained peasant girl,[58] spend $2,000,000 on her, and won't dream of signing someone who once had a name and public, you can't help but ask: Why?"

In January 1935, while Agnes was scraping by with what little work she was getting, her brother, Solon, was admitted to a psychiatric ward in Los Angeles after he made threats against Cecil B DeMille, whom he blamed for "spoiling" Agnes' career. Their mother, Emma, told reporters her son was a victim of shell shock during World War I.[59]

Agnes put together an all-girl dance orchestra and toured the East and mid-West in the spring and summer of 1935. The group, Agnes Ayres and her Hollywood Debs, were invited to take their show to Europe, however, Agnes nixed that idea, preferring to remain the States and reacquaint herself with her "old public."[60]

The long string of one-night stands began taking a toll on Agnes' physical and emotional health. In 1936, threatened with a nervous breakdown, Agnes returned home to Hollywood. That February, her comeback to films was announced. She played a bit role in *Small Town Girl* (1936).

Determined in her fight against obscurity, Agnes joined scores of other former film personalities to help herself and other old-time entertainers continue working in their industry. In August, the group held its first annual "close-up" show. J. Stuart Blackton, once the head of Vitagraph, presided. Leon Janney, Leo White, and Rupert Hughes were the masters of ceremony. Agnes, along with William Farnum, Lionel Belmore, Maurice Costello, Bryant Washburn, Creighton Hale, Florence Turner, and Alice Calhoun, were named officers. [61]

Despite her best efforts, Agnes was offered little more than bits roles in such 1937 releases as *Morning Judge*, *Souls at Sea*, *Midnight Taxi*, and *Maid of Salem*. She insisted she was not disheartened by the brevity of the parts.

"I'm still young," she told the *Los Angeles Times*. "I know more than I did, and I think I'm a better actress. Above all, I have my feet on the ground, which is rather unusual in this town. And, I see no reason why I can't get to the top again."[62]

She also saw no reason why her daughter, Maria, now aged 10, shouldn't be working in films. "Almost since she could talk, Maria has played at being a movie star, and so I'm going to give her an opportunity."[63] Agnes was able to secure a small role for her daughter in *Maid of Salem*.

To support herself and her family, Agnes opened a small real estate office and tried her hand at selling real estate.

She was able to keep her name in the press with the 1938 revivals of *The Sheik* and *The Son of the Sheik*. In June, it was announced that Agnes and Jean Acker, Valentino's first wife, would embark on a 20-week public appearance tour with *The Sheik*.[64]

The stress of the tour proved too much for the already fragile actress. In October 1938, Agnes suffered a nervous breakdown. After months of recovery, she spoke about her long struggle to again make a name for herself. "It cost me a half million dollars to learn the value of a nickel, but I wouldn't trade the experience for all that money back again.

"Making a comeback has been a tough nut for me to crack, but I did it once and I'm sure I can do it again," Agnes said. "The doctors say I'm just about fit and there are two or three grand things in the offing. I'm just keeping my fingers crossed that they'll break, and meanwhile, everybody in Hollywood has been swell to me."[65]

In November 1939, Agnes voluntarily relinquished custody of her daughter to her former husband, Manuel Reachi, for a period of 13 months.

"I have been ill during the best part of the last year and I think it best that my daughter go with her father until I recuperate," Agnes

A mature Agnes Ayres.

told a commissioner in the local Domestic Relations Court. Maria soon left for Mexico City to live with her father.[66]

On Christmas Eve 1940, Agnes suffered a cerebral hemorrhage at her home and was taken to St. Vincent's Hospital. She died Christmas Day without ever regaining consciousness.

In a simple service at Pierce Brothers chapel several days later, a soloist sang Agnes' favorite song from *The Sheik*: *The Kashmiri Song*, known also as *Pale Hands I Loved*. Her ashes were placed in a niche at a mausoleum at Hollywood Memorial Park, just down the street from Paramount Studios, where almost 20 years earlier, she'd reigned as a star.

Hedda Hopper devoted a column to her old friend. "There'll be many sob stories written about the passing of Agnes Ayres on Christmas Day at the age of 42.[67] When I made a picture with Agnes many years ago she was on top of the heap and her success was comparable to that of Lana Turner, Ann Sheridan, and the late Jean Harlow. She had everything a woman could want, but as she said herself, it came so fast, and she'd had no previous training for taking care of the trust and the great responsibility success imposes on one."

"She was a sweet girl — Agnes — and her passing should make a deep impression on the stars of today. And if it does, many of them may stop, look and LISTEN."

1. "Valentino Still Inspires Fan Mail," 7 March 1937.

2. Griffith, Richard. *The Movie Stars*, Doubleday and Company, Inc., 1970.

3. Her death certificate lists 1898 as her year of birth. The 1900 U.S. Federal Census lists April 1892 as the month and year. Early publicity suggested 1901.

4. The 1900 U.S. Federal Census indicates that Frank and Emma Rendleman had been married for five years.

5. Dean, Daisy, "News Notes from Movieland," *The La Crosse Tribune*, La Crosse, Wisconsin, 17 January 1917.

6. Swanson, Gloria, *Swanson on Swanson*, Random House, 1980.

7. "Gorgeous Lady Loves Her Home," *The Los Angeles Times*," 7 June 1925.

8. Emma had divorced Franklin Rendleman.

9. Schallert, Edwin. "A Chameleon in Filmland," *The Los Angeles Times*, 25 April 1920.

10. Ibid.

11. *Variety*, 1 October 1920.

12. Schallert, Edwin. "A Chameleon in Filmland," *The Los Angeles Times*, 25 April 1920.

13. "Agnes Ayres Sues for a Divorce," 21 July 1921.

14. *Variety*, 28 January 1921.

15. *Picture Play*, January 1922.

16. Ibid.

17. *Photoplay*, January 1922.

18. *Variety*, 11 November 1921.

19. Marion Fairfax Collection, Motion Picture Academy Library, 22 April 1922.

20. Holland, Larry Lee, *Films in Review*.

21. *Variety*, 7 June 1923.

22. *Harrison's Reports*, 9 June 1923.

23. *Harrison's Reports*, 11 October 1924.

24. *Harrison's Reports*, 21 June 1924.

25. "Agnes Ayres to Marry Mexican Official in S.F.," 6 August 1924, unknown newspaper clipping.

26. "Agnes Ayres Secretly Weds," *Los Angeles Times*, 11 September 1924.

27. *The New York Times*, 2 July 1925.

28. "Gorgeous Lady Loves Her Home," *Los Angeles Times*, 7 June 1925.

29. Ibid.

30. "Suit Begun Over Films by Actress," *Los Angeles Times*, 17 July 1925.

31. "Ayres Damage Plea Doubled," *Los Angeles Times*, 18 August 1925.

32. "Suit Begun Over Films by Actress," *Los Angeles Times*, 17 July 1925.

33. 'Wife in Hawaii Denied by Mate of Agnes Ayres," Associated Press, 20 August 1925.

34. Wooldridge, Jack, "Movieland," *Oakland Tribune*, 28 February 1926.

35. "Fat as Film Ban Up to Court," *Los Angeles Times*, 17 February 1926.

36. Ibid.

37. "Daughter Born to Agnes Ayres," *Oakland Tribune*, 26 March 1926.

38. "Ayres Suit Settled on Wage Basis," *Los Angeles Times*, 8 May 1926.

39. Ellenberger, Allan R., *The Valentino Mystique: The Death and Afterlife of the Silent Film Idol*, McFarland and Company, Inc., 2005.

40. Ibid.

41. *Photoplay*, May 1930.

42. Ankerich, Michael G., *Broken Silence: Conversations With 23 Silent Film Stars*, McFarland and Company, Inc. 1993.

43. Ibid.

44. *Variety*, 1 May 1929.

45. On Martel Avenue.

46. The smaller home Agnes bought when first coming to Hollywood.

47. *Jungle Love*.

48. Agnes' mother, Emma.

49. Mischa Auer, the actor.

50. "Theatrical Notes," *The New York Times*, 31 May 1930.

51. Parsons, Louella, "Agnes Ayres Will Appear in Bryan Foy's First Film," 14 April 1931.

52. "Theatrical Notes," *The New York Times*, 30 October 1931.

53. "Theatrical Notes," *The New York Times*, 7 December 1931.

54. Bahn, Chester, "Silent Films Better, Says Agnes Ayres," *Syracuse Herald*, 5 May 1933.

55. "Agnes Ayres in Collison Play," *The New York Times*, 16 May 1933.

56. "Movie Stars Head Big Paramount Bill," 22 October 1933.

57. Soanes, Wood, "Curtain Calls," *Oakland Tribune*, 4 October 1934.

58. Anna Sten was the "peasant girl" Agnes referred to.

59. "Ex-Film Player's Brother is Accused of Making Threats," *The Modesto Bee*, 31 January 1935.

60. "Agnes Ayres and Girl Band Engaged for Lakeside," *The Democrat*, 18 July 1935.

61. "Associated Stars Stage "Close Up" for 560 Veterans," 25 August 1936.

62. "Agnes Ayres Back in Films," *Los Angeles Times*, 2 March 1937.

63. "Hollywood Roundup," 16 March 1937.

64. Mann, May, "Going Hollywood," *Ogden Standard Examiner*, Ogden, Utah, 20 June 1938.

65. *Lowell Sun*, Lowell, Massachusetts, 23 August 1939.

66. Maria Reachi died July 5, 2009, in Los Angeles.

67. She was actually 48 years old.

FILMOGRAPHY

1914

The Masked Wrestler (short) (Essanay) D: *E.A. Calvert.* Francis X. Bushman, Beverly Bayne, Bryant Washburn, Rapley Holmes, Paul Raas, Agnes Ayres, Ruth Stonehouse.

1915

His New Job aka *Charlie's New Job (Essanay)* D: *Charlie Chaplin.* Charles Chaplin, Ben Turpin, Charlotte Mineau, Leo White, Robert Bolder, Charles J. Stine, Arthur W. Bates, Jess Robbins, Charles Hitchcock, Billy Armstrong, Agnes Ayres, Gloria Swanson.

1917

A Family Flivver (short) (Vitagraph) D: *C. Graham Baker.* Edward Earle, Agnes Ayres.

The Renaissance aka *The Renaissance at Charleroi (General Film Company)* D: *Thomas R. Mills.* J. Frank Glendon, Eleanor Lawson, Agnes Ayres, Webster Campbell, Marguerite Forrest, Ethel Northrup.

The Bottom of the Well (Vitagraph) D: *John S. Robertson.* Evart Overton, Agnes Ayres, Adele De Garde, Ned Finley, Herbert Pryor, Robert Gaillard, Alice Terry, Bigelow Cooper.

The Furnished Room (short) (Vitagraph) D: *Frank Gordon.* Agnes Ayres, J. Frank Glendon.

The Defeat of the City (short) (Vitagraph) D: *Frank Gordon.* J. Frank Glendon, Agnes Ayres, Frank Chapman, Mrs. Fisher, Frank Heath, Alice Rodier, Virginia Spraggins.

Richard the Brazen (Vitagraph) D: *Perry N. Verkoff.* Harry T. Morey, Alice Joyce, William Frederic, Franklyn Hanna, Robert Kelly, Agnes Ayres, Charles Wellesley, William Bailey.

The Dazzling Miss Davison aka *Who Is She? (USA) (short)* D: *Frank Powell.* Marjorie Rambeau, Fred Williams, Aubrey Beattie, Agnes Ayres, Robert Elliott, Winifred Harris, Frank A. Ford, Lillian Paige, Ruth Byron, Dore Flowden, Bert Starkey, T. Jerome Lawler, George Paige.

The Mirror (short) D: *Frank Powell.* Robert Elliott, Marjorie Rambeau, Irene Warfield, Paul Everton, Aubrey Beattie, Frank A. Ford, T. Jerome Lawler, Agnes Ayres.

Hedda Gabler (Mutual) D: *Frank Powell.* Nance O'Neil, Aubrey Beattie, Lillian Paige, Einar Linden, Ruth Byron, Alfred Hickman, Edith Campbell, Frank A. Ford, Agnes Ayres.

Paging Page Two (short) (Vitagraph) D: *C. Graham Baker.* Edward Earle, Agnes Ayres.

The Debt (Mutual) D: *Frank Powell.* Marjorie Rambeau, Henry Warwick, T. Jerome Lawler, Paul Everton, Nadia Gary, Anne Sutherland, Agnes Ayres, Robert Elliott.

Mrs. Balfame (Mutual) D: *Frank Powell.* Nance O'Neil, Frank Belcher, Robert Elliott, Agnes Ayres, Anna Raines, Alfred Hickman, Grace Gordon, Aubrey Beattie, Elsie Earle.

Motherhood (Mutual) D: *Frank Powell.* Marjorie Rambeau, Frank A. Ford, Robert Elliott, Paul Everton, Aubrey Beattie, Agnes Ayres, Ruth Byron, Lillian Paige, Anne Sutherland, Frank Frayne, Robert Eaton, Lorna Volare.

The Venturers (Vitagraph) D: *Thomas R. Mills.* Jack Ellis, J. Frank Glendon, Agnes Ayres.

His Wife Got All the Credit (short) (Vitagraph) D: *C. Graham Baker.* Agnes Ayres, Edward Earle.

He Had to Camouflage (short) (Vitagraph) D: *Wesley Ruggles.* Edward Earle, Agnes Ayres.

His Wife's Hero (short) (Vitagraph) D: *C. Graham Baker.* Edward Earle, Agnes Ayres.

1918

Their Anniversary Feast (short) (Vitagraph) D: *C. Graham Baker.* Edward Earle, Agnes Ayres.

A Little Ouija Work (short) (Vitagraph) D: *C. Graham Baker.* Edward Earle, Agnes Ayres.

Seeking an Oversoul *(short) (Vitagraph)* D: *C. Graham Baker.* Edward Earle, Agnes Ayres.

A Bird of Bagdad (short) (Vitagraph) D: *Kenneth S. Webb.* Agnes Ayres, Edward Earle, Arthur Donaldson, Frank Norcross.

Springtime à la Carte (short) (Vitagraph) D: *Kenneth S. Webb.* Edward Earle, Agnes Ayres.

Mammon and the Archer (short) (Vitagraph) D: *Kenneth S. Webb.* Edward Earle, Agnes Ayres, Herbert Fortier, Estar Banks, Jane Jennings.

One Thousand Dollars (short) (Vitagraph) D: *Kenneth Webb.* Edward Earle, Agnes Ayres, Florence Deshon, Templar Saxe, Anne Brody.

The Girl and the Graft (short) (Vitagraph) D: *William S. P. Earle.* Edward Earle, Agnes Ayres.

The Enchanted Profile (short) (Vitagraph) D: *Martin Justice.* Agnes Ayres, Evart Overton, Nellie Parker Spaulding, Adele DeGarde.

Coals for the Fire (short) (Vitagraph) D: *C. Graham Baker.* Edward Earle, Agnes Ayres.

A Four Cornered Triangle (short) (Vitagraph) D: *C. Graham Baker.* Edward Earle, Agnes Ayres.

The Purple Dress (Vitagraph) D: *Martin Justice.* Evart Overton, Agnes Ayres, Adele DeGarde, Bernard Siegel.

A Ramble in Aphasia (short) (Vitagraph) D: *Kenneth S. Webb.* Edward Earle, Agnes Ayres.

The Rubaiyat of a Scotch Highball (short) (Vitagraph) D: *Martin Justice.* Edward Earle, Agnes Ayres.

Sisters of the Golden Circle (short) (Vitagraph) D: *Kenneth S. Webb.* Edward Earle, Agnes Ayres, Alice Terry, Frank Kingsley, Danny Hayes.

Tobin's Palm (short) Vitagraph D: *Kenneth S. Webb.* Edward Earle, Agnes Ayres.

Transients in Arcadia (short) (Vitagraph) D: *Kenneth S. Webb.* Edward Earle, Agnes Ayres.

Surprising Husband (short) (Vitagraph) D: Kenneth S. Webb. Edward Earle, Agnes Ayres.

Their Godson (short) (Vitagraph) D: *C. Graham Baker.* Edward Earle, Agnes Ayres..

Sweets to the Sour (short) (Vitagraph) D: *C. Graham Baker.* Edward Earle, Agnes Ayres.

1919

The Ghost of a Chance (short) D: *Kenneth S. Webb.* Edward Earle, Agnes Ayres.

Sacred Silence (Fox) D: *Harry Millarde.* William E. Russell, Agnes Ayres, George MacQuarrie, James Morrison, Tom Brooke.

The Gamblers (Vitagraph) D: *Paul Scardon.* Harry T. Morey, Charles Kent, Agnes Ayres, Helen Ferguson, Eric Mayne, George Majeroni, George Backus.

In Honor's Web (Vitagraph) D: *Paul Scardon.* Harry T. Morey, Gladden James, George Backus, Agnes Ayres, Myrtle Stedman, George Majeroni, Bernard Siegel, Robert Gaillard.

The Buried Treasure (short) (Vitagraph) D: *Kenneth S. Webb.* Edward Earle, Agnes Ayres.

The Guardian of the Accolade (short) (Vitagraph) D: *Henry Houry.* Edward Earle, Agnes Ayres.

A Stitch in Time (Vitagraph) D: *Ralph Ince.* Gladys Leslie, Eugene Strong, Charles Walton, Cecil Chichester, Earl Schenck, Charles Stevenson, Julia Swayne Gordon, Agnes Ayres, George O'Donnell.

The Girl Problem (Vitagraph) D: *Kenneth Webb.* Corinne Griffith, Agnes Ayres, Walter McGrail, William David, Julia Swayne Gordon, Eulalie Jensen, Frank Kingsley, Harold Foshay.

Shocks of Doom (short) D: *Henry Houry.* Edward Earle, Agnes Ayres.

1920

A Modern Salome (Metro) D: *Léonce Perret.* Hope Hampton, Sidney L. Mason, Percy Standing, Arthur Donaldson, Wyndham Standing, Agnes Ayres.

The Inner Voice (States Rights) R. *William Neill.* E. K. Lincoln, Agnes Ayres, Fuller Mellish, Riley Hatch, Walter Greene, Edward Keppler.

Go and Get It (First National) D: *Marshall Neilan.* Pat O'Malley, Wesley Barry, Agnes Ayres, J. Barney Sherry, Charles Mailes, Noah Beery, Bull Montana, Walter Long, Lydia Yeamans Titus, George C. Drougold, Ashley Cooper, Charles West, Samuel G. Blythe, Myles Lasker, Ring Lardner, Irvin S. Cobb, Arthur Brisbane, Robert Edgren, Fred L. Wilson.

Held by the Enemy (Paramount) D: *Donald Crisp.* Agnes Ayres, Wanda Hawley, Josephine Crowell, Lillian Leighton, Lewis Stone, Jack Holt, Robert Cain, Walter Hiers, Robert Brower, Clarence H. Geldart.

The Furnace aka *Breach of Promise (Realart Pictures)* D: *William Desmond Taylor.* Agnes Ayres, Jerome Patrick, Theodore Roberts, Betty Francisco, Milton Sills, Helen Dunbar, Fred Turner, Mayme Kelso, Lucien Littlefield, Robert Bolder, Edward Martindel.

1921

Forbidden Fruit (Paramount) D: *Cecil B. DeMille.* Agnes Ayres, Clarence Burton, Theodore Roberts, Kathlyn Williams, Forrest Stanley, Theodore Kosloff, Shannon Day, Bertram Johns, Julia Faye.

The Love Special (Paramount) D: *Frank Urson.* Wallace Reid, Agnes Ayres, Theodore Roberts, Lloyd Whitlock, Sylvia Ashton, William Gaden, Clarence Burton, Snitz Edwards, Ernest Butterworth, Zelma Maja.

Too Much Speed (Paramount) D: *Frank Urson.* Wallace Reid, Agnes Ayres, Theodore Roberts, Jack Richardson, Lucien Littlefield, Guy Oliver, Henry Johnson, Jack Herbert.

The Affairs of Anatol (Paramount) D: *Cecil B. DeMille.* Wallace Reid, Gloria Swanson, Elliott Dexter, Bebe Daniels, Monte Blue, Wanda Hawley, Theodore Roberts, Agnes Ayres, Theodore Kosloff, Polly Moran, Raymond Hatton, Julia Faye, Charles Ogle, Winter Hall

Cappy Ricks (Paramount) D: *Tom Forman.* Thomas Meighan, Charles Abbe, Agnes Ayres, Hugh Cameron, John Sainpolis, Paul Everton, Eugenie Woodward, Tom O'Malley, Ivan Linow, William Wally, Jack Dillon, Gladys Granger.

The Sheik (Paramount) D: *George Melford.* Rudolph Valentino, Agnes Ayres, Ruth Miller, George Waggner, Frank Butler, Charles Brindley, Lucien Littlefield, Adolphe Menjou, Walter Long.

1922

The Lane That Had No Turning (Paramount) D: *Victor Fleming.* Agnes Ayres, Theodore Kosloff, Mahlon Hamilton, Wilton Taylor, Frank Campeau, Lillian Leighton, Charles West, Robert Bolder, Fred Vroom.

Bought and Paid For (Paramount) D: *William C. DeMille.* Agnes Ayres, Jack Holt, Walter Hiers, Leigh Wyant, George Kuwa, Bernice Frank, Ethel Wales.

The Ordeal (Paramount) D: *Paul Powell.* Clarence Burton, Agnes Ayres, Conrad Nagel, Edna Murphy, Anne Schaefer, Eugene Corey, Adele Farrington, Edward Martindel, Shannon Day, Claire Du Brey.

Borderland (Paramount) D: *Paul Powell.* Agnes Ayres, Milton Sills, Fred Huntley, Bertram Grassby, Casson Ferguson, Ruby Lafayette, Sylvia Ashton, Frankie Lee, Mary Jane Irving, Dale Fuller.

Clarence (Paramount) D: *William B. DeMille.* Wallace Reid, Agnes Ayres, May McAvoy, Kathlyn Williams, Edward Martindel, Robert Agnew, Adolphe Menjou , Bertram Johns, Dorothy Gordon, Mayme Kelso.

A Daughter of Luxury (Paramount) D: *Paul Powell.* Agnes Ayres, Tom Gallery, Edith Yorke, Howard Ralston, Edward Martindel, Sylvia Ashton, Clarence Burton, ZaSu Pitts, Robert Schable, Bernice Frank, Dorothy Gordon, Muriel McCormac.

1923

The Heart Raider (Paramount) D: *Wesley Ruggles.* Agnes Ayres, Mahlon Hamilton, Charles Ruggles, Frazer Coulter, Marie Burke, Charles Riegal.

Racing Hearts (Paramount) D: *Paul Powell*. Agnes Ayres, Richard Dix, Theodore Roberts, Robert Cain, Warren Rogers, J. Farrell MacDonald, Edwin J. Brady, Fred J. Butler, Robert Brower, Kalla Pasha, James A. Murphy, Johnny Wonderlich, Eddie Hefferman.

Hollywood (Paramount) D: *James Cruze*. Hope Drown, Luke Cosgrave, George K. Arthur, Ruby Lafayette, Harris Gordon, Bess Flowers, Eleanor Lawson, King Zany, Roscoe Arbuckle, Gertrude Astor, Mary Astor, Agnes Ayres, Baby Peggy, T. Roy Barnes, Noah Beery, William Boyd, Clarence Burton, Robert Cain, Edythe Chapman, Betty Compson, Ricardo Cortez, Viola Dana, Cecil B. DeMille, William DeMille, Charles De Roche, Dinky Dean, Helen Dunbar, Snitz Edwards, George Fawcett, Julia Faye, James Finlayson, Alec Francis, Jack Gardner, Sid Grauman, Alfred E. Green, Alan Hale, Lloyd Hamilton, Hope Hampton, William S. Hart, Gale Henry, Walter Hiers, Mrs. Walter Hiers, Stuart Holmes, Sigrid Holmquist, Jack Holt, Leatrice Joy, Mayme Kelso, J. Warren Kerrigan, Theodore Kosloff, Kosloff Dancers, Lila Lee, Lillian Leighton, Jacqueline Logan, May McAvoy, Robert McKim, Jeanie MacPherson, Hank Mann, Joe Martin, Thomas Meighan, Bull Montana, Owen Moore, Nita Naldi, Pola Negri, Anna Q. Nilsson, Charles Ogle, Guy Oliver, Kalla Pasha, Eileen Percy, Carmen Phillips, Jack Pickford, Chuck Reisner, Fritzi Ridgeway, Will Rogers, Sennett Girls, Ford Sterling, Anita Stewart, George Stewart, Gloria Swanson, Estelle Taylor, Ben Turpin, Bryant Washburn, Maude Wayne, Claire West, Laurence Wheat, Lois Wilson.

The Marriage Maker (Paramount) D: *William DeMille*. Agnes Ayres, Jack Holt, Charles De Roche, Robert Agnew, Mary Astor, Ethel Wales, Bertram Johns.

The Ten Commandments (Paramount) D: *Cecil B. DeMille*. Lawson Butt, Clarence Burton, Noble Johnson, Edythe Chapman, Richard Dix, Rod La Rocque, Leatrice Joy, Nita Naldi, Robert Edeson, Charles Ogle, Agnes Ayres, Viscount Glerawly.

1924

Don't Call It Love (Paramount) D: *William C. DeMille*. Agnes Ayres, Jack Holt, Nita Naldi, Theodore Kosloff, Rod La Rocque, Robert Edeson, Julia Faye.

Bluff (Paramount) D: *Sam Wood.* Agnes Ayres, Antonio Moreno, Fred Butler, Clarence Burton, Pauline Paquette, Jack Gardner, Arthur Hoyt, E. H. Calvert, Roscoe Karns.

When a Girl Loves (Associated Distributors) D: *Victor Hugo Halperin.* Agnes Ayres, Percy Marmont, Robert McKim, Kathlyn Williams, John George, Mary Alden, George Siegmann, Ynez Seabury, William Orlamond, Rosa Rosanova, Leo White.

The Guilty One (Paramount) D: *Joseph Henabery.* Agnes Ayres, Edward Burns, Stanley Taylor, Crauford Kent, Cyril Ring, Thomas R. Mills, Catherine Wallace, George Siegmann, Clarence Burton, Dorothea Wolbert.

The Story Without a Name (Paramount) D: *Irvin Willat.* Agnes Ayres, Antonio Moreno, [Frederick] Tyrone Power, Louis Wolheim, Dagmar Godowsky, Jack Lionel Bohn, Maurice Costello, Frank Currier, Ivan Linow.

Worldly Goods (Paramount) D: *Paul Bern.* Agnes Ayres, Pat O'Malley, Victor Varconi, Edythe Chapman, Bert Woodruff, Maude George, Cecille Evans, Otto Lederer.

1925

Tomorrow's Love (Paramount) D: *Paul Bern.* Agnes Ayres, Pat O'Malley, Raymond Hatton, Jane Winton, Ruby Lafayette, Dale Fuller.

Her Market Value (Paul Powell Productions) D: *Paul Powell.* Agnes Ayres, George Irving, Anders Randolf, Hedda Hopper, Edward Earle, Taylor Holmes, Gertrude Short, Sidney Bracy.

The Awful Truth (Producers Distributing Corp.) D: *Paul Powell.* Agnes Ayres, Warner Baxter, Phillips Smalley, Raymond Lowney, Winifred Bryson, Carrie Clark Ward.

Morals for Men (Tiffany) D: *Bernard Hyman.* Conway Tearle, Agnes Ayres, Alyce Mills, Otto Matieson, Robert Ober, John Miljan, Mary Beth Milford, Eve Southern, Marjery O'Neill.

1926

The Son of the Sheik (United Artists) D: *George Fitzmaurice*. Rudolph Valentino, Vilma Banky, George Fawcett, Montague Love, Karl Dane, Bull Montana, B. Hyman, Agnes Ayres, Charles Requa, William Donovan, Erwin Connelly.

1927

Eve's Love Letters (2-reels) (Pathé) D: *Hal Yates and Fred Guiol*. Stan Laurel, Agnes Ayres, Forrest Stanley).

1928

Into the Night (Raleigh Pictures) D: *Duke Worne*. Agnes Ayres, Forrest Stanley, Robert Russell, Tom Lingham, Rhody Hathaway, Allan Sears, Corliss Palmer, Arthur Thalasso.

The Lady of Victories (short) (Technicolor Corporation) D: *Roy William Neill*. Agnes Ayres, George Irving, Otto Matieson.

1929

Broken Hearted (Tiffany) D: *Frank S. Mattison*. Agnes Ayres, Gareth Hughes, Eddie Brownell.

Bye, Bye, Buddy (Tiffany) D: *Frank S. Mattison*. Agnes Ayres, Robert "Buddy" Shaw, Fred Shanley, Ben Wilson, John Orlando, Dave Henderson, Hall Cline.

The Donovan Affair (Columbia) D: Frank Capra. Jack Holt, Dorothy Revier, William Collier Jr., Agnes Ayres, John Roche, Fred Kelsey, Hank Mann, Wheeler Oakman, Virginia Browne Faire, Alphonse Ethier, Edward Hearn, Ethel Wales, John Wallace.

1936

Small Town Girl aka *One Horse Town (M-G-M)* D: *William Wellman*. Janet Gaynor, Robert Taylor, Binnie Barnes, Andy Devine, Lewis Stone, Elizabeth Patterson, Frank Craven, James Stewart, Isabel Jewell, Charley Grapewin, Nella Walker, Robert Greig, Edgar Kennedy, Willie Fung, Harry Antrim, Agnes Ayres.

1937

Maid of Salem (Paramount) D: *Frank Lloyd.* Claudette Colbert, Fred MacMurray, Harvey Stephens, Gale Sondergaard, Louise Dresser, Benny Bartlett, Edward Ellis, Beulah Bondi, Bonita Granville, Virginia Weidler, Donald Meek, E.E. Clive, Halliwell Hobbes, Pedro de Cordoba, Madame Sul-Te-Wan, Lucy Beaumont, William Farnum, Ivan F. Simpson, Brandon Hurst, Sterling Holloway, Zeffie Tilbury, Babs Nelson, Mary Treen, J. Farrell MacDonald, Stanley Fields, Lionel Belmore, Kathryn Sheldon, Rosita Butler, Madge Collins, Amelia Falleur, Clarence Kolb, Russell Simpson, Colin Tapley, Tom Ricketts, Wally Albright, Ricca Allen, Agnes Ayres.

Midnight Taxi (20th Century-Fox) D: *Eugene Ford.* Brian Donlevy, Frances Drake, Alan Dinehart, Sig Ruman, Gilbert Roland, Harold Huber, Paul Stanton, Lon Chaney Jr., Russell Hicks, Regis Toomey, DeWitt Jennings, Agnes Ayres.

Souls at Sea (Paramount) D: *Henry Hathaway.* Gary Cooper, George Raft, Frances Dee, Henry Wilcoxon, Harry Carey, Olympe Bradna, Robert Cummings, Porter Hall, George Zucco, Virginia Weidler, Joseph Schildkraut, Gilbert Emery, Lucien Littlefield, Paul Fix, Tully Marshall, Monte Blue, Stanley Fields, Edward Van Sloan, Norman Ainsley, Stanley Andrews, Gertrude Astor, Agnes Ayres.

Morning Judge (RKO) D: *Leslie Goodwins.* Edgar Kennedy, Agnes Ayres, Billy Franey, George Irving, Harry Bowen, Bud Jamison.

OLIVE BORDEN

The sign over the door of the Sunshine Mission for Women and Children read, "There's Always Room for One More." Those words of welcome had offered hope for decades to scores of wayward women and children who had no other place to land.

Who would have guessed that the woman who stumbled drunk, broke, and desperate into the mission that day in 1944 was none other than Olive Borden, the raven-haired beauty of the silent screen? Just 20 years before, Hollywood called her the "Joy Girl" and advertised that she had the most perfect figure in Tinseltown. Her dazzling smile, flashed so effortlessly, gave everyone she met the idea she was having the time of her life.

Olive's rapid rise to fame came early in her life, her fame cresting in her early twenties. It was a heavy load for a young girl from Virginia and her influential mother, Sibbie, both of whom came from humble beginnings and had a proclivity for the bottle. Excessive spending and poor career decisions veered the youngster off course, and by the time movies learned to talk, she was on the skids.

With her looks intact, she stumbled through several quickies and made an unsuccessful bid for the New York stage. She tried marriage, but the union blew up in the headlines when her husband's *other* wife reemerged from the past. Dropping out of sight for the next decade, Olive married a blue-collar worker from Brooklyn, tried her hand at menial jobs, and used booze to dull the pain of her lost dreams.

With the mess Olive had made of her life since she left Hollywood, who could have looked at her the day she walked through the doors of the Sunshine Mission and thought "joy"? Sibbie, who herself had been rescued by the mission, was joyful and relieved to have her baby back with her.

The strict rules of the mission and Sibbie's dominating presence, however, often proved too much for the headstrong Olive. When she tired of scrubbing floors or washing laundry, she disappeared into the alleys of a seedy Hollywood. Sibbie rescued her time and again.

In June 1948, when it looked like she'd finally pulled herself together, Olive unraveled and fled from the safe confines of the Sunshine Mission and skidded down Skid Row once last time.

She was born Olive Marie Borden on July 14, 1906, in Richmond, Virginia.[1] Her father, Harry *(Henry)*, a distant relative of the Borden Milk family, died of typhoid fever when she was a year old.[2] Contrary to Olive's early publicity, the Bordens were not from a well to do family. Her father worked as a cook, and her mother, Cecilia *(Sibbie)* Shields Borden, after the death of her husband, struggled to keep a roof over their heads. In 1910, they were living with Sibbie's aunt. Sibbie worked as a sales clerk and hotel housekeeper.

Olive grew up a fan of the movies. As she blossomed into a teenager, she watched her cousins, Natalie Johnson and an older sister, make their way to New York and join the Ziegfeld Follies as the Joyce Sisters. In 1922, Natalie and her family moved to Los Angeles, where she danced in cafes, then broke into the movies.

Olive paid close attention. "I began to realize that somewhere in the direction of the setting sun, there lay a city where the marvels of fame, wealth, and success were obtainable if one could only find the key," she wrote in 1929.[3] "One day, I said to mother, 'Let's go to Hollywood. I'll be able to find work in the motion pictures and then we'll have a cunning little bungalow with loads of flowers and maybe a Ford.'"

Sibbie, with little to hold her in Virginia, agreed. Olive quit school *(she had completed two years of high school)* and Sibbie gave up her job as a hotel housekeeper. When the two hopefuls got to the West coast, they lived for a time with Sibbie's sister, Elizabeth Johnson, and her daughter, who, by now, had found work in the studios as Natalie Joyce. Olive climbed aboard streetcars and went from studio to studio seeking work as an actress. Natalie, who was also just starting out, could offer little help.[4]

Olive and Sibbie arrived in Los Angeles on a Tuesday, and by Thursday, Olive had a small role in an Al Christie comedy. Her instructions were to simply stand before the camera, look beautiful, and give her best imitation of the exotic actress Lila Lee.

The director was far from impressed with Olive's acting ability. "You'll never be an actress," he said. "Go back to school. Go anywhere. But go away."

Olive was deflated. "That night I went home to mother and wept my first tears of disappointment and discouragement," she later said.

She was back on the streets of Hollywood, making the rounds to the studios only to hear the same two words: "Nothing today."

With no work in sight, their bank account shriveled. Something had to develop fast or mother and daughter would have no choice but to return to Virginia. They opened a candy store to make ends meet. Despite their hard work, the store failed after six months.

Olive's luck began to turn in 1923 when she was given small roles in *Children of Jazz* and *Ponjola*. It was on the set of the latter that she was

Olive Borden, Hollywood's newest discovery, 1925.

given some wise advice from the cameraman. He suggested a new look for the 17-year-old: less makeup and more Olive.

She took his advice, and before the year was out, was working as a Mack Sennett Bathing Beauty. That exposure led to roles in two-reel comedies for producer Hal Roach.

All Hollywood is talking about this fairest of Eve's daughters!

Ever since Eve listened to the serpent, woman has worshipped the raiment that makes her fairest, and man has worshipped woman thus adorned. In the person of beautiful young

OLIVE BORDEN

millions of screen devotees will have found a new subject for their adoration. As revealed in the WILLIAM FOX Picture

FIG LEAVES

She has youth, radiant and unfettered, loveliness of a rare degree, a high quality of dramatic artistry—and oh, oh—how she can wear her clothes! A new screen "find" that the wise ones are all rejoicing over! In "Fig Leaves" this young actress is co-featured with one of your old favorites

GEORGE O'BRIEN

Well remembered and loved for his performance in "THE IRON HORSE" and other Fox pictures. Here George scores in a new type of role. "FIG LEAVES" is a gorgeously dressed photoplay, beautiful girls in lavish imported creations shown in full color, and a novel scene in the Garden of Eden. Directed by Howard Hawks, with Phyllis Haver, Andre de Beranger and other good supporting players.

Forthcoming FOX FILMS every one should see:
WHAT PRICE GLORY
THE MUSIC MASTER
7TH HEAVEN
all made from renowned stage successes
3 BAD MEN
staged by John Ford, who directed "The Iron Horse"
ONE INCREASING PURPOSE
from the best-selling book of the year by the author of "If Winter Comes"

Fox Film Corporation

Photoplay *magazine gave Olive high praise for her work in* Fig Leaves *(1926).*

Director Paul Bern, with his keen eye for beauty and talent, gave Olive small roles in *The Dressmaker from Paris* and *Grounds for Divorce*, both 1925 releases. When he learned that Olive was unable to afford the dress she was to wear as one of the 14 models in *The Dressmaker from Paris*, Bern, known for his generosity, bought one for her.[5]

Following a supporting role in *The Happy Warrior* and a leading role in *The Overland Limited*, Olive came to the attention of Fox Studios and Tom Mix. The famed cowboy used Olive as his leading lady in *The Yankee Señor* and *My Own Pal*, both 1925 releases.

Fox signed Olive to a long-term contract and selected her for the coveted of "Lee" in John Ford's classic Western, *3 Bad Men*, which starred George O'Brien. In October 1925, while on location in the Mojave Desert, Olive and two other actresses, Priscilla Bonner and Grace Gordon, contracted typhoid fever and returned to Hollywood for treatment.[6]

It was also during the filming of *3 Bad Men* that a hot romance developed between Olive and George O'Brien, already a star after his memorable performance in *The Iron Horse (1922)*. They became the talk of Tinseltown and one of Hollywood's most beautiful couples. Fox cashed in on the romance and starred the two skimpily-clad pair in *Fig Leaves (1926)*, a battle-of-the-sexes type of romantic comedy.

Photoplay gave Olive high praise for her work in *Fig Leaves*. "George O'Brien acts from the chest out. Miss Borden, however, runs away with the picture."[7]

Olive was given a further boost when she was named a 1925 Wampas *(Western Association of Motion Picture Advertisers)* Baby Star. She shared the honor with 12 other rising starlets, including her cousin, Natalie Joyce.

Within a short period of roughly six months, Olive graduated from playing vamps in two-reelers to leads in dramatic productions. Writer Virginia Morris interviewed the 20-year-old shortly after her success in *3 Bad Men*. Morris recorded her impressions. "Slightly over five feet, weighing but 105 pounds, her childish features and big brown eyes framed by black curls, she impresses one with the wistfulness of a Gish, the youthful spirit of a Pickford, plus a hoydenish individuality which is entirely all her own."[8]

Olive explained her screen transformation to Morris. "I feel a thousand times better equipped to handle really dramatic work now that I have had the benefit of this comedy experience," she said. "When I was getting my start, I thought it quite ridiculous when an extra would spoil her own chances by either declaring or thinking she wasn't right for a certain part, so, when the chance to play comedy vamps came to me, I took it gladly, trusting that clothes and cosmetics would make the woman.

"Now that I'm doing straight leads I am infinitely happier than in comedy work, though my experience there makes me feel secure in the thought that what talent I have is not single-tracked."[9]

Part of the reason Olive was "infinitely happier" playing leads at Fox must have been her sudden change in lifestyle. While under contract, her salary soon soared to $1,500 a week. She became one of Hollywood's best

Olive and her mother shortly after Olive's rise to fame

dressed, both in her private life and on the screen.

Olive developed a taste for the good life and went into debt to live in luxury. She is said to have been insulted when a salesperson in a boutique brought out a fur that cost less than $3,500. She had a maid who accompanied her to the set every morning and a chauffeur-driven French limousine on standby.

She bought a $65,000 mansion in Beverly Hills from actor Hobart Bosworth and surrounded herself with four servants who spared her the least exertion. The garage boasted a fleet of expensive cars, and her closet held the latest fashions.

"Almost any girl taken from obscurity and spotlighted, highly paid and catered to, would go haywire," Olive said at the time. "Precious few have escaped that stage of distorted viewpoint, unless they had very wise management."[10]

While she was decked out in furs at premiers and parties, at the studio, negligees seemed to be her primary attire. She later commented that a new one was created for every picture.

In *The Country Beyond*, Olive and her mother traveled on location to Canada's Jasper National Park. In the picture, Olive plays an orphan who first falls in love with a fugitive from justice *(Ralph Graves)*, then

Olive in one of her skimpiest negligees.

finds success on the stage. Her performance met with mediocre reviews. Said *Variety*, "Olive Borden is a graceful heroine, inclined to overdo the lovely child of nature in the wilderness screens, but coming into her own when the background of the Broadway musical stage is more to her liking."[11]

About the time Olive made The Monkey Talks *(1927)*.

As Olivette in *The Monkey Talks (1927)*, a drama focusing on the trials and tribulations of a trio in a small wagon circus, Olive plays a tightrope walker who is almost killed by an aggressive monkey.

In *The Joy Girl*, Olive traveled to Palm Beach, Florida, to appear as an impulsive flapper who dumps her chauffeur boyfriend for a millionaire playboy *(Neil Hamilton)*.

An advertisement for The Joy Girl *(1927)*.

As an artist's model in *The Secret Studio*, Olive draped herself in the latest negligees of the day. Little acting, only posing, was required of its star.

Variety took notice. "In all probability it *(The Secret Studio)* was written to order for Miss Borden's exquisite figure, which furnishes the principal kick of the footage when it is on display in scanty draperies."[12] After the release of *Pajamas*, another picture that showcase her figure and little else, *Variety* noted that if Fox cast its "s.a" *(sex appeal)* trio *(Olive, Madge Bellamy, and Dolores Del Rio)* in a film together, "something is liable to burn."[13]

Although she was now earning a weekly salary of $1,750, Olive began to tire of the shallow parts and skimpy underwear.

"I whined and pleaded for better roles for so long that when finally my temper flared, they were shocked and called me temperamental," Olive said at the time. "I was justified in kicking, but my manner at first was too subservient, then too demanding. Perhaps I wasn't tactful. When I saw the decrease in my popularity and read the criticisms, I begged them to feature me in good parts, instead of starring me as a dressed dummy. They claimed I was becoming ungovernable. Well, it was my career that was tilting lopsided."[14]

Olive Borden in Pajamas *(1927).*

Following *Come to My House (1927)*, for which she earned $2,000 a week, studio executives approached Olive about plans to reduce her salary. She refused initially to be involved; instead, she sent her lawyers to the negotiations and instructed them to hold firm against any pay cut.

As a star at Fox, Olive wore the finest furs.

One day, Olive found herself in the executive offices at her own defense. Rather than accept the new pay structure, she chose to end her employment with Fox.

"I wanted money, a lot of it," Olive said later. "Why? I don't know, except that earning it pleases the ego, spending it whets vanity. It adds to that absurd importance. With the inflated estimation of self, the more money you get the more you want, to increase prestige. And it is handy to purchase palaces and trinkets."[15]

When she walked out of the studio that day, Olive declared she was through with movies. Her first course of action was a change in lifestyle. She sold her mansion and a large portion of her furnishings. She cut her servants from her payroll and made repayment arrangements with her creditors. Finally, she moved to a small cottage at the beach.

In the middle of her professional problems, her relationship with George O'Brien unraveled. It was reported at the time that Olive was unhappy because O'Brien was taking a European vacation against her wishes.

"Dad's trip to Europe was not a vacation, only, but also a trip to meet F.W. Murnau in connection with the casting of *Sunrise*," Darcy O'Brien, George's son, recalled in 1994. "Dad was also taking his parents on their first trip to Europe, as my grandfather was ill with heart problems and

Olive and George O'Brien in happier times.

had retired recently as San Francisco Chief of Police."[16]

With Olive's mounting problems and the leeriness of O'Brien's family about their son's fiancée, the collapse of the Borden-O'Brien relationship seemed inevitable. "Olive had a very rather wild and profligate reputation," Darcy O'Brien said. "Grace DeCourcey, a stunt rider in my father's Westerns, and later his secretary, said that Olive was in debt to the stagehands, by which remark I gather that monetary indebtedness was meant."[17]

While Olive laid low at the beach during the spring of 1928, one of the most bizarre stories involving the actress surfaced in Texas. The headlines said it all: *Bank Teller Brother of Star, Killed,*[18] *Death Reveals Identity of a Noted Actress,*[19] *Auto Accident Fatal to City Bank Teller, Kin of Olive Borden.*[20]

The gist of the story went something like this: "The death here Sunday in an automobile accident of Joe Alton Tinkle, 24, revealed another Texas girl who has risen to fame in the movies unheralded in her native state. She is Olive Borden, sister of the dead man, whose real name is Sybil Tinkle. Miss Borden was notified of her brother's death but will not return to Texas for the funeral, relatives said."[21]

Certainly, it was not unusual for studio publicists to alter the ages of the stars, to change their names, or to invent glamorous backgrounds. The confusion, however, over Olive Borden and Sybil Tinkle being one and the same is one of Hollywood's most puzzling cases of mistaken identity.[22]

Even more bizarre was that the Tinkle family, still living in Texas in the 1990s, firmly believed that Olive Borden was their relative who left Texas in the early 1920s and became the screen beauty.[23] Actress Natalie Joyce, Olive's first cousin, was equally as stumped when asked about the Borden-Tinkle connection. "I've never heard of Tinkle," she said in 1991. "I've never heard anything but Borden."[24]

Whether Olive ever commented about the stories coming out of Texas is not known. If she knew about the mix-up, chances are she chose to remain silent. She was consumed at the time with her own problems.

While Olive licked her wounds along the Santa Monica shores, an agent was hard at work in Hollywood. Although Olive vowed she was finished with acting, she had to work and motion pictures had been all she'd known. The independent company, Tiffany-Stahl, came through with an offer: *The Albany Night Boat (1928)*. Then, she signed a deal to make pictures for Columbia.

With her career back in motion, Olive made two decisions: she moved to a small Hollywood apartment and she bobbed her famous locks to modernize her look.

"It's much nicer being in a little house," Olive confided to writer Helen Loring.[25] "Now I can sit in my bedroom and call to mother and she can hear me. It used to be that I had to write her a note."

As she gave her film career a second try, Olive was optimistic and humble. "I am sorry for having fought over salary," she said in retrospect. "That was unwise. It stamps you as a trouble maker. And none of us is worth, in comparison with other vocations we might follow, half of what we get. I regret being grandiloquent, and being sassy. And I am beaucoup glad that it is all over."[26]

With the coming of sound within earshot, Olive focused on securing parts that were right her. "I'm not that exotic, vampish type," she said. "I don't want to be a great dramatic actress. I'm not sophisticated. Why should I try to play sophisticated roles? I've two ambitions. On the screen

I want to be a good comedienne. And off the screen I want to be a real, honest-to-God woman!"[27]

For the next two years, she bounced back and forth between Columbia, FBO, and RKO. She had rare opportunity, however, to try her comedic skills. The low-budget programmers were, for the most part, romantic, light society, and crime dramas.

Olive and Morgan Farley in Half Marriage *(1929).*

"Not exactly sitting on top of the world," Olive noted, "but climbing up again. I'll hook onto each rung more carefully this time."[28] Sibbie Borden made sure of it. She kept an even closer watch on her daughter.

Famed cinematographer Joseph Walker filmed Olive in two of her Columbia efforts: *Virgin Lips (1928)* and *The Eternal Woman (1929)*. "Olive's mother, a large woman with dyed red hair and unmistaken ably

Olive Borden (R) with Kathlyn Williams, Arleen Manning, and Lois Wilson in Wedding Rings *(1929).*

Irish, trusted no one on the set; she watched us cagily and wouldn't allow her attractive daughter out of her sight."[29]

Mary Brian, who was enjoying a successful career at Paramount, recalled Olive's reluctance to mix with others on the set of *The Social Lion (1930)*. "Olive was a very attractive girl, but when her scenes were over, off she'd go, so I didn't see a lot of her.[30]

Although Olive expressed fondness for her role in *The Social Lion*, partly because she was able to display her comedic flair, the film turned out to be Olive's last film role of any merit. After the picture wrapped, she traveled to New York to try her luck on the stage.

In the fall of 1930, she appeared on the Loew's Circuit with Frieda Inescort in *The Devil is a Lady*. A critic called her voice charming and said she had acquired poise and polish; but, unfortunately, the play ended after seven weeks.

Olive's professional disappointments were lessened by a new lover. Olive met a stock broker who promised to turn her life around and give her financial security. Against her mother's advice, she eloped with Theodore Spector on March 28,1931.[31] They first tried to marry in Connecticut, however a state law required the couple wait five days between the issuance of a license and the marriage. They returned to New York, where they married in Harrison.[32]

The two settled in New York and Olive seemed on her way to fulfilling an earlier ambition, being that "real, honest-to-God woman" she'd talked about several years before.

Their union was rocky from the start, primarily, Olive later told, because of her theatrical work and ambitions. The couple separated in early 1932 and Olive returned to her mother.

"Ted wanted me to quit the stage, but I simply cannot do it," Olive said in April. "I've been in this profession quite a while, and I love it. He and I just could not agree on the subject, so we decided the only thing to do was to separate."[33]

The marital tangle jerked itself into a knot when one Pearl Haworth Spector, owner and operator of the Rouge Box Beauty Salon in Buffalo identified herself as Mrs. Theodore Spector.

Newspapers over the country provided the lurid details: *Bigamy Laid to Husband of Olive Borden*; *Spector's 'Other Wife' Says She's Still His*; *Jury to Probe Spector Marriage*. Olive, who tried to keep the marriage secret as long as she could, was addled.

"I never got such a surprise in my life," she said. "Of course, I knew Ted had been married before, but I naturally supposed there had been a divorce."[34]

The story remained in the headlines for much of 1932. In May, the bigamy case was thrown out of court by a grand jury when Pearl Spector failed to produce sufficient evidence that she was the legal Mrs. Spector.[35] In June, Pearl Spector sued her husband for divorce and had her day in court.

Pearl Spector told the court that she married "Teddy" Spector in 1919, but that he left her 18 months later, saying, "I've got plenty of brains and I'm not going to waste them fussing around here." A devastated Pearl remained silent for a dozen years while she plotted her revenge.

While meeting with Spector and his attorneys, Pearl later recounted how she asked her husband, "How is it that as brainy a man as you would marry a woman while still the husband of another?" He replied, "Well, I had to marry Miss Borden. She threatened to jump off a 10-story building if I didn't."

Pearl, when granted her divorce, said she was relieved to have the marriage debacle behind her. "He was a tall, good-looking brute, but I'm through with him."[36] She returned to the Rouge Box salon where she resumed her business of plucking eyebrows, giving facials, and making blondes out of brunettes.[37]

In August, Olive worked with Hal Skelly and other old-time vaudevillians in *Hotel Variety*, the first offering from Screencraft Productions.

Finally, in November 1932, Olive asked the court for an annulment. One newspaper account recorded Olive's court appearance this way: "The screen star's appearance — she is dark-haired, full-lipped and her svelte figure was clad in silk frock and cloak of mink — commanded the admiration of the veteran referee, who exclaimed, 'You are good looking indeed. You are one of the few actresses who appear to equal advantage on and off the screen.'"[38]

Olive Borden in court.

By the time her application for annulment was approved, Olive had sailed to England for a vacation. She planned to stay only a week, but actor-director Monty Banks talked her into playing the lead in *Leave It to Me (1933)*, produced by British International Pictures.

In May 1934, Olive traveled with director Marshall Neilan to St. Petersburg, Florida, to film *Chloe: Love is Calling*. The movie, produced on a shoe-string budget through Pinnacle Pictures, was Olive's final film.

She married John Moeller, a 26-year-old railroad technician, in November 1934 and went to live in his modest three-room apartment on Long Island. This time Olive was determined the press would not learn about her marriage. On the marriage license, she identified herself as Mary Borden and listed "none" as her occupation.[39]

Olive toured briefly in 1935 as the headliner in *Hollywood Revue*.[40] Then, she disappeared from sight. Over time, the Moeller marriage went on the rocks.

Using the name Olive Moeller, she worked as a nurse's aide, postal clerk, and mail carrier, but in December 1942, she joined the Women's Army Corps *(WACs)*.[41] She served as an Army chauffeur and drove an ambulance.

"I didn't have any children dependent on me," Olive told a reporter. "I wanted to help where I could do the most good. I figured the WACs would know where that was."

In December 1943, Jimmie Fidler reported that following her "Reno unhooking," Olive intended to return to Hollywood to see if "studios have a place for her."

When Olive finally returned to Hollywood in November 1944, she quickly dispelled rumors that she was seeking employment in the movies. Columnist Dorothy Manners wrote, "Olive Borden, glamour girl in the Clara Bow days, is back in Hollywood — a heroine. Olive was in the WACs and has received an Army citation for bravery in turning over an enemy ammunition truck. She's just been discharged from Walter Reed hospital with an honorable discharge — but says she isn't interested in a career anymore."

For a while, the Joy Girl made it on her own, going from job to job, but, as she put it, "something always went wrong."[42] Being back in a town where she had been a star 20 years before was too much for her fragile soul. She descended further into alcoholism and despair.

Broke and in ill health, Olive joined her mother at the Sunshine Mission for Women and Children. For two years she scrubbed floors, washed windows, and took care of abandoned babies.

"We called her Ollie," Essie Binkley West, founder of the mission, later said. "Everybody loved her. She was still a beautiful girl, with soft hands never made for the kind of work she insisted on doing. She'd do washings, change diapers for infants of all races, driving herself always to try and overcome what I know was only a sickness."[43]

Olive staged the mission's Christmas pageant in 1946 and spoke with pride of the part she played. "I have found the one thing Hollywood couldn't give me — happiness," she said. When questioned about her last film role, she smiled, but remained silent.

Does Olive wish she were back in pictures? the reporter asked Sibbie. "Yes, at times," admitted her mother. "She gets restless, of course. Sometimes, looking back, I think that I mothered her too much."[44]

Olive disappeared into the gritty streets of Los Angeles in June 1947. Sibbie searched frantically. She located Olive living in a cheap hotel on Main Street and begged her to return to the mission. Olive stayed put.

For the next two months, Sibbie checked on her and brought her small amounts of money for her basic needs.

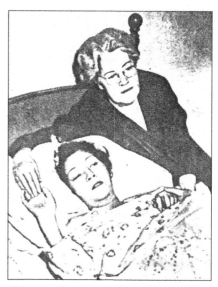

In late September, Sibbie found Olive, suffering from pneumonia, almost comatose in her hotel room. She brought Olive back to the mission where attempts were made to nurse her back to health. Even Olive decided to give life another try. "The whole world has fallen in on me," she said from her sickbed, "but the doctors will make me well again. What will I do then? Perhaps I can help my mother here where she's found her happiness."[45]

Olive, a few days before she died, and her mother, Sibbie.

The next morning, on October 1, 1947, Olive Borden, age 41, died in her mother's arms.[46] Two days later, a simple service was held at the mission's chapel. Director John Boland and actor Cornelius Keefe were the only representatives from the movie colony.

While George O'Brien, Olive's former co-star and fiancé, knew of her death, he chose not to attend. "I am sure *(fairly)* that Olive was his great love before my mother,"[47] Darcy O'Brien said. "My mother told me that when Olive died, she *(my mother)* urged George to go to the funeral, but he did not — I presume, knowing him, out of respect for my mother's feelings."[48]

Olive was buried in Glendale's Forest Lawn Cemetery. Her mother, Sibbie, continued working at the mission until 1956, when ill health forced her to move to a nursing home. She succumbed to a heart attack in 1959. She was buried beside her daughter.

Alan Williams, writing for *American Weekly* magazine, noted that Olive's death created "hardly a ripple in Hollywood's busy routine."

"Was not her death in such surroundings at the early age of 40 a logical climax to a steady descent from the heights to the depths? Was she not forgotten, unnoticed, a figure of the past without a future, a relic of the film world's transitory fame, an example of its fickle adulation? And who had time to mourn the past?"[49]

1. Delayed Certificate of Birth, Commonweath of Virginia, Department of Health, Division of Vital Records, #38227.

2. Burial records, Norfolk, Virginia. Courtesy of Michelle Vogel.

3. Borden, Olive, *How I Broke Into the Movies*, Yesteryear Press #1, 1930.

4. Natalie Joyce to Michael G.Ankerich, 1991.

5. Fleming, E.J., *Paul Bern: The Life and Famous Death of the MGM Director and Husband of Harlow*, McFarland & Company, 2009.

6. "Film Actresses Get Typhoid in Desert," 6 October 1925.

7. *Photoplay*, October 1926.

8. Morris, Virginia T., "Settling Down to the Serious Things in Life," unknown date and publication.

9. Ibid.

10. Genhart, Myrtle, "Olive Borden Repents Her Folly," *Picture Play*, March 1930.

11. *Variety*, 24 November 1926.

12. *Variety*, 15 June 1927.

13. *Variety*, 9 November 1927.

14. Genhart, Myrtle, "Olive Borden Repents Her Folly," *Picture Play*, March 1930.

15. Ibid.

16. Letter from Darcy O'Brien to Michael G. Ankerich, 6 April 1994.

17. Ibid.

18. *Houston Press*, 23 April 1928.

19. *Lufkin Daily*, 24 April 1928.

20. *Houston Post-Dispatch*, 23 April 1928.

21. *Lufkin Daily*, 24 April 1928.

22. Unfortunately, Sybil Tinkle is still used as Olive Borden's real name on most Internet sites and film reference books.

23. I explored the Sybil Tinkle mystery in an article I wrote for *Classic Images* magazine in November 1992: *Olive Borden: The Sybil Tinkle Connection*. In the text, I presented details from Borden's birth and death certificates, as well as her application for a Social Security number, all of which show she was clearly Olive Borden from Virginia. I noted the 1910 and 1920 U.S. Federal Censuses as showing Olive Borden living with her mother in Virginia and Sybil Tinkle with her family in Texas. In addition, the portraits the Tinkle family supplied of Sybil are definitely not Olive Borden. Tinkle's relatives, when contacted in the 1990s, maintained that after Sybil became Olive Borden of the screen, they never heard from her again. Several family members journeyed to Los Angeles in the 1930s after hearing that she had died, but they were unsuccessful in their attempts to locate her.

24. Natalie Joyce to Michael G. Ankerich, 1991.

25. Loring, Helen, "Olive in Quest of her Soul," *Photoplay*, December 1929.

26. Genhart, Myrtle, "Olive Borden Repents Her Folly," *Picture Play*, March 1930.

27. Loring, Helen, "Olive in Quest of her Soul," *Photoplay*, December 1929.

28. Genhart, Myrtle, "Olive Borden Repents Her Folly," *Picture Play*, March 1930.

29. Walker, Joseph, *The Light on her Face*, The ASC Press, 1984.

30. Mary Brian to Michael G. Ankerich, 1993.

31. New York Department of Health, Marriage License, 28 March 1931. Although she was living in New York City at the time, Olive listed her residence as Norfolk, Virginia, and "none" as her occupation. Copy of marriage license courtesy of Michelle Vogel.

32. "Confirms Wedding of Olive Borden: Harrison Town Clerk Says Film Actress and N.J. Broker Were Married March 28," unknown date or source.

33. "Husband Loses as Olive Borden Returns to Stage," unknown date and source.

34. "On Husband Shock to Miss Borden," unknown date and source.

35. "Spector Bigamy Case Thrown Out," 12 May 1932.

36. "Broker, 2 Beauties in Divorce Battle," known date or source.

37. Pearl Haworth died in 1977.

38. "Olive Borden Asks Court to Annul Bridal," 5 November 1932.

39. New York State Department of Health, Marriage License #25601, 2 November 1934. Copy of marriage license courtesy of Michelle Vogel.

40. "Comes Here in 'Hollywood Revue'", *The Sheboygan Press*, 6 February 1935.

41. U.S. World War II Army Enlistment Records.

42. Williams, Alan, "Olive Borden's Last Starring Role," *The American Weekly*, 15 February 1948.

43. "Olive Borden Mourned Along Skid Row; Filmland Forgets," 2 October 1947.

44. "Star of 30's Adopts Missionary Career," *Los Angeles Times*, 16 June 1946.

45. "Olive Borden Dies in Mission," 1 October 1947.

46. Olive Borden's death certificate lists cirrhosis of the liver as the cause of death. State of California, Department of Public Health, Certificate of Death, 2 October 1947.

47. Darcy O'Brien's mother was actress Marguerite Churchill, whom George O'Brien married in the early 1930s.

48. Letter from Darcy O'Brien to Michael G. Ankerich, 6 April 1994.

49. Williams, Alan, "Olive Borden's Last Starring Role," *American Weekly*, 15 February 1948.

FILMOGRAPHY

1924

Neck and Neck (short) (Jack White) D: *Fred Hibbard.* Lige Conley, Olive Borden, Cliff Bowes, Hank Mann.

Wide Open (short) (Jack White) D: *Fred Hibbard.* Lige Conley, Olive Borden, Otto Fries, Peggy O'Neil, George Ovey.

Air Pockets (Jack White) D: *Fred Hibbard.* Lige Conley, Earl Montgomery, Sunshine Hart, Olive Borden, Peggy O'Neil, Otto Fries.

Why Men Work (short) (Hal Roach) D: *Leo McCarey.* Charley Chase, Olive Borden, Billy Engle, William Gillespie, Katherine Grant, Earl Mohan.

Should Landlords Live? (Hal Roach) D: *Nicholas T. Barrows,* James D. Davis. Arthur Stone, Olive Borden, Helen Gilmore, Ena Gregory, Marie Mosquini, Robert Page, Martha Sleeper.

Too Many Mamas (short) (Hal Roach) D: *Leo McCarey.* Charley Chase, Martha Sleeper, Beth Darlington, Olive Borden, Noah Young, John T. Prince.

The Royal Razz (short) (Hal Roach) D: *Leo McCarey.* Charley Chase, Olive Borden, Katherine Grant, Jules Mendel, Robert Page, Martha Sleeper.

Just a Good Guy (short) (Hal Roach) D: *Hampton Del Ruth.* Arthur Stone, Olive Borden, Kewpie Morgan, Fay Wray, Noah Young, Katherine Grant.

1925

Should Husbands Be Watched? (short) (Hal Roach) D: *Leo McCarey.* Charley Chase, Katherine Grant, Olive Borden, Al Hallett,

Bad Boy (short) (Hal Roach) D: *Leo McCarey*. Martha Sleeper, Evelyn Burns, Hardee Kirkland, Noah Young, Olive Borden, Leo Willis.

Grounds for Divorce (Paramount) D: *Paul Bern*. Florence Vidor, Matt Moore, Harry Myers, Louise Fazenda, George Beranger, Gustav von Seyffertitz, Edna Mae Cooper, Olive Borden.

Good Morning, Nurse (short) (Mack Sennett) D: *Lloyd Bacon*. Ralph Graves, Olive Borden, Marvin Loback, William McCall, Eva Thatcher, Patrick Kelly, Irving Bacon, Eli Stanton, Natalie Kingston.

Tell It to a Policeman (short) (Hal Roach) D: *Fred Guiol*. Glenn Tryon, Olive Borden, James Finlayson, Jack Gavin, Blanche Mehaffey.

The Dressmaker from Paris (Paramount) D: *Paul Bern*. Leatrice Joy, Ernest Torrence, Allan Forrest, Mildred Harris, Lawrence Gray, Charles Crockett, Rosemary Cooper, Spec O'Donnell, Sally Rand, Olive Borden.

The Happy Warrior (Vitagraph) D: *J. Stuart Blackton*. Malcolm McGregor, Alice Calhoun, Mary Alden, Anders Randolf , Olive Borden, Gardner James, Otto Matieson, Wilfrid North, Eulalie Jensen, Andrée Tourneur, Jack Herrick, Philippe De Lacy, Robert Gordon, Leon Holmes.

The Overland Limited (Gotham) D: *Frank O'Neill*. Malcolm McGregor, Olive Borden, Alice Lake, Ethel Wales, Ralph Lewis, John Miljan, Roscoe Karns, Emmett King, Charles Hill Mailes, Charles West, Charles A. Post, Evelyn Jennings.

1926

The Country Beyond (Fox) D: *Irving Cummings*. Olive Borden, Ralph Graves, Gertrude Astor, J. Farrell MacDonald, Evelyn Selbie, Fred Kohler, Lawford Davidson, Alfred Fisher, Lottie Williams.

Fig Leaves (Fox) D: *Howard Hawks*. George O'Brien, Olive Borden, Phyllis Haver, George Beranger, William Austin, Heinie Conklin, Eulalie Jensen, Ralph Sipperly.

3 Bad Men (Fox) D: *John Ford*. George O'Brien, Olive Borden, Lou Tellegen, Tom Santschi, J. Farrell MacDonald, Frank Campeau, Priscilla Bonner, Otis Harlan, Phyllis Haver, Georgie Harris, Alec B. Francis, Jay Hunt.

The Yankee Señor (Fox) D: *Emmett J. Flynn.* Tom Mix, Olive Borden, Tom Kennedy, Francis McDonald, Margaret Livingston, Alec B. Francis, Kathryn Carver, Martha Mattox, Raymond Wells.

Yellow Fingers (Fox) D: *Emmett J. Flynn.* Olive Borden, Ralph Ince, Claire Adams, Edward Peil Sr., Otto Matieson, Nigel De Brulier, Armand Kaliz, Josephine Crowell, May Foster, John Wallace, Charles Newton.

My Own Pal (Fox) D: *John G. Blystone.* Tom Mix, Olive Borden, Tom Santschi, Virginia Marshall, Bardson Bard, William Colvin, Virginia Warwick, Jay Hunt, Hedda Nova, Tom McGuire, Helen Lynch, Jack Rollens.

1927

Come to My House (Fox) D: *Alfred E. Green.* Olive Borden, Antonio Moreno, Ben Bard, Cornelius Keefe, Doris Lloyd, Richard Maitland.

The Joy Girl (Fox) D: *Allan Dwan.* Olive Borden, Neil Hamilton, Marie Dressler, Mary Alden, William Norris, Helen Chandler, Jerry Miley, Frank Walsh, Clarence Elmer, Peggy Kelly, Jimmy Grainger Jr.

The Monkey Talks (Fox) D: *Raoul Walsh.* Olive Borden, Jacques Lerner, Don Alvarado, Malcolm Waite, Raymond Hitchcock, Ted McNamara, Jane Winton, August Tollaire.

Pajamas (Fox) D: *John G. Blystone.* Olive Borden, Lawrence Gray, Jack J. Clark, Jerry Miley.

Secret Studio (Fox) D: *Victor Schertzinger.* Olive Borden, John Holland, Noreen Phillips, Ben Bard, Kate Bruce, Joseph Cawthorn, Margaret Livingston, Walter McGrail, Lila Leslie, Ned Sparks.

1928

The Albany Night Boat (Tiffany-Stahl) D: *Alfred Raboch.* Olive Borden, Ralph Emerson, Duke Martin, Nellie Bryden, Helen Marlowe.

Gang War (FBO) D: *Bert Glennon.* Lorin Raker, Jack McKee, Mabel Albertson, David Hartman, Olive Borden, Jack Pickford, Eddie Gribbon, Walter Long, Frank Chew.

Sinners in Love (FBO) D: *George Melford.* Olive Borden, Huntley Gordon, Seena Owen, Ernest Hilliard, Daphne Pollard, Phillips Smalley, Henry Roquemore.

Stool Pigeon (Columbia) D: *Renaud Hoffman*. Olive Borden, Charles Delaney, Lucy Beaumont, Louis Natheaux, Ernie Adams, Al Hill, Robert Wilber, Clarence Burton.

Virgin Lips (Columbia) D: *Elmer Clifton*. Olive Borden, John Boles, Marshall Ruth, Alexander Gill, Richard Alexander, Erne Veo, Harry Semels, Arline Pretty, William H. Tooker.

1929

Dance Hall (RKO) D: *Melville Brown*. Olive Borden, Arthur Lake, Margaret Seddon, Ralph Emerson, Joseph Cawthorn, Helen Kaiser, Lee Moran, Tom O'Brien, Natalie Joyce.

The Eternal Woman (Columbia) D: *John McCarthy*. Olive Borden, Ralph Graves, Ruth Clifford, John Miljan, Nina Quartero, Josef Swickard, Julia Swayne Gordon.

Half Marriage (RKO) D: *William J. Cowen*. Olive Borden, Morgan Farley, Ken Murray, Ann Greenway, Anderson Lawler, Sally Blane, Hedda Hopper, Richard Tucker.

Love in the Desert (FBO) D: *George Melford*. Olive Borden, Hugh Trevor, Noah Beery, Frank Leigh, Pearl Varvalle, William H. Tooker, Ida Darling, Alan Roscoe, Hilliard Karr.

Wedding Rings (First National Pictures) D: *William Beaudine*. H.B. Warner, Lois Wilson, Olive Borden, Hallam Cooley, James Ford, Kathlyn Williams, Aileen Manning.

1930

Hello Sister (James Cruze Productions) D: *Walter Lang*. Olive Borden, Lloyd Hughes, George Fawcett, Bodil Rosing, Norman Peck, Howard C. Hickman, Raymond Keane, Wilfred Lucas, James T. Mack, Harry McDonald.

The Social Lion (Paramount) D: *Edward Sutherland*. Jack Oakie, Mary Brian, Richard 'Skeets' Gallagher, Olive Borden, Charles Sellon, Cyril Ring, E.H. Calvert, James Gibson, Henry Roquemore, William Bechtel, Richard Cummings, Jack Byron.

1932

The Divorce Racket (Paradise Pictures) D: *Audrey Scotto*. James Rennie, Olive Borden, Judith Wood, Wilfred Jessop, Harry Tyler, Adrian Rosley, Charles Eaton, Joseph Calleia, Walter Fenner, Harry Short.

1933

Hotel Variety (Screencraft Productions) D: *Raymond Cannon*. Hal Skelly, Olive Borden, Charlotte Walker, Sally Rand, Glorian Grey, Shannon Day, Martin Burton, Marshall Montgomery, Ned Norworth, Lilya Vallon, Herschel Mayall, Alan Brooks, Bernard Randall, Jackie Jordan.

Leave it to Me (British International Pictures) D: *Monty Banks*. Gene Gerrard, Olive Borden, Molly Lamont, George K. Gee, Gus McNaughton, Clive Currie, Toni Edgar-Bruce, Peter Godfrey, Syd Crossley, Melville Cooper, Wylie Watson, Monty Banks.

The Mild West (Vitagraph) D: *Joseph Henabery*. Janet Reade, Olive Borden, Paul Keast, Helene Denizon, Philip Ryder, The Vikings, Philip Loeb.

1934

Chloe, Love Is Calling You (Pinnacle Pictures) D: *Marshall Neilan*. Olive Borden, Reed Howes, Molly O'Day, Philip Ober, Georgette Harvey, Francis Joyner, Augustus Smith.

Grace Darmond, c. 1916.

GRACE DARMOND

It must have taken a special woman to come between newlyweds Rudolph Valentino and Jean Acker on their wedding night. She must have been a woman of incredible power to lure the one she loved from the honeymoon bed back into baby's arms. It would be quite an understatement to say that, indeed, Grace Darmond was no ordinary woman.

True, her film career was lackluster. She worked in films between 1915 and 1927, entering the business as a teenager in Chicago for the old Selig Company. At Vitagraph in the late 1910s, she became prominent, but, by the early 1920s, she was playing in serials and independent quickies.

No, her professional life is not what made Grace Darmond the fascinating woman she was. Her temperament, sometimes an asset, sometimes a deterrent, almost derailed her career before it started and frequently got her into trouble with the studio, in courts, and with lovers.

She was courageous, hard to intimidate, non-traditional, and non-conforming. In age where a desire for those of your own sex was generally kept from public view, Grace, a stunningly beautiful blonde, was not afraid to love the woman she wanted — and she wanted the woman she loved, even though her lover had just become Mrs. Rudolph Valentino.

Hours after saying "I do" to the Italian immigrant trying to make a name for himself in the movies, Jean Acker, herself a budding actress, realized her mistake. Before the union could be consummated, she fled from her unfortunate situation and into the arms of Grace Darmond, the mate she really wanted.

She was born Grace Marie Glionna to Vincent and Alice Sparks Glionna on October 7, 1898, in Toronto, Canada.[1] Her father, a violinist, was Italian, her mother, Canadian.

When Grace was a teenager, her father died, and she and her mother immigrated to the United States and settled in Chicago.[2] Although she was shy as a child, by the time she was a teenager, Grace had boosted her confidence and was appearing on the Chicago stage. She eventually took Grace Darmond as her professional name.

In the spring of 1914, Selig hired Grace for the comedy short *The Clock Went Wrong*, followed by the feature film *Your Girl and Mine*, a story about women's suffrage. The studio, impressed with her work, signed her to a contract.

Grace started her career on sound footing, playing leading roles in four 1915 releases for Selig: *A Texas Steer* (opposite Tyrone Power), *The Millionaire Baby*, *A House of a Thousand Candles*, and *A Black Sheep*.

Right after her initial success on the screen, Grace told writer Caroline Carr that she had worked several seasons with George M. Cohan, but that she liked working in films because the studio was in Chicago, where she lived.[3]

Carr noted that the actress before her was "MUCH prettier off the screen than on. She has light, wavy hair with a tinge of gold, and the complexion of peaches and cream that always goes with brown eyes and fair hair. She is also very modest."

Grace gave a rather odd response when Carr asked about her ambition. "I want to be fat more than anything else in the world," Grace said. "I eat anything fattening and try not to exercise too violently. I adore fat people. They look so comfortable and happy." Carr commented to her readers, "It is a queer world. Other film favorites are starving to get thin while this girl is eating to get fat."[4]

In early 1916, Selig, for reasons unknown, terminated Grace's contract. Based on correspondence from the Selig files in the special collections department of the Margaret Herrick Library, the studio also cautioned other companies for employing Grace.

H.M. Horkheimer, president of Balboa Feature Films, responding to a letter from Thomas Persons, head of Selig's West coast productions, assures Persons that "Miss Darmond has not called on us," that Balboa is "heartily in accord with your action in the matter, and in case anything comes up in regard to the matter, you have our cooperation and under no circumstances will we engage Miss Darmond in the event that she calls upon us."[5]

Grace was devastated. In a telegram to William N. Selig, studio head, Grace pled her case.

"I did not realize just how wrong you would think my conduct," she wrote. "I am very sorry. Won't you forgive me just this once and I promise to be a good, obedient little girl from now on. Stepdaddy isn't working and they need my help very badly. So, please let me stay."[6]

Whether the studio allowed her to return is not known, but Grace's filmography shows no 1916 Selig releases. As the year progressed, she became somewhat irritated with the studio on another front: publicity.

Grace, with nothing to lose at this point, composed a letter to William Lord Wright, a Selig executive in Chicago.

She writes in part:

"Of course I realize that it is within your power to withhold publicity from members of this company, but I have always supposed that you were too big and broadminded a man to let any personal feelings interfere with your business. I cannot help but feel that your personal attitude is very unjust, in as much that in the past you have without any solicitation on my part given me more than my share."

I am striving hard to make my work a success and, as you know, have always appreciated everything you have done for me."[7]

Despite Selig's apparent efforts to derail Grace's career, Pathé hired the struggling actress to star in her first serial, *The Shielding Shadow* (1916), a drama based on efforts to locate a cloak of invisibility.

In 1917, Vitagraph took a chance on Grace. She rose to prominence as Earle William's leading lady in seven feature films from 1917 to 1919.[8] Following her first film with Williams, *In the Balance* (1917), Grace starred with Harry T. Morey, in *The Other Man*, as a socialite who lives in the slums to fulfill the terms of a $10,000 wager that she can survive for a month without money.

Variety praised both the film and her performance. "*The Other Man* is one of the best that Vitagraph has released in some time. It has a corking story that starts with a bang and carries right up to the finish. Grace Darmond is the new leading ingénue at the Vitagraph plant and she is a corking looking blonde who will make a bit with the fans now that she is with a company making regular releases."[9]

Grace starred in the first Technicolor film, *The Gulf Between* (1918), as a young woman who was raised on board ship by a sea captain after she wanders away from her parents. She falls in love with a wealthy young man (Niles Welch), but his parents consider her beneath their standards and refuse to allow her into the family. It is only after she is revealed to be the long-lost daughter of their wealthy friends do they welcome her into the family.

In early 1919, Grace was cast with Wallace Reid in *The Valley of the Giants*, a film that marked the beginning of Reid's descent into drug addiction. The story deals with the struggle for land (named the Valley of the Giants) on which Reid's mother was buried. To complicate matters, Reid is in love with Grace, the niece of his rival (Ralph Lewis).

The cast and crew traveled by train to Arcata, a coastal town about 100 miles south of Oregon. Exteriors were shot in a local mining town high in the mountains.

A Grace Darmond profile portrait.

On the morning of March 2, 1919, the crew crammed into two railroad cars and set out for the day's shoot. While the train was crossing a trestle, it jerked loose from the tracks and plunged 15 feet into the creek below. Grace, like most others in the company, suffered only minor cuts and bruises, but Reid was seriously injured with a three-inch gash in his scalp.

With the group hundreds of miles from Hollywood, the studio couldn't afford to halt production while their star healed from his injuries. Studio boss Jesse L. Lasky ordered morphine to dull Reid's pain.[10] With the help of the powerful drug, Reid returned to work four or five days later. By the time the picture was finished, Reid was addicted.[11]

Again, Grace received high marks for her work in *The Valley of the Giants*. "In the acting line, Reid's own pleasant personality is charmingly supplemented by the blonde Grace Darmond who plays her love scenes charmingly," *Variety* noted.[12]

Perhaps her love scenes in *The Valley of the Giants* were not as convincing as those she would soon enjoy with actress Jean Acker, whom Grace met in mid-1919. Acker had arrived in Hollywood shortly before as the protégé and lover of Broadway giant Alla Nazimova. Grace fell hard for Acker and urged her to break from Nazimova and move in with her. Acker, feeling somewhat beholden to Nazimova, couldn't make up her mind to act on Grace's invitation. The lovers argued.

To clear her senses, Acker turned her attention to Rudolph Valentino, whom she'd met not long after arriving in Hollywood. The two became friends and enjoyed each other's company. After several nighttime horseback rides together, Acker agreed to marriage.

According to Emily W. Leider, in her biography of Rudolph Valentino, Acker saw in Valentino a possible "escape hatch, a way to extricate herself from both affairs and still have someone to lean on."[13]

Valentino and Acker were married at midnight on November 11, 1919, at the Hollywood home of Joseph Engel, Metro's treasurer. The newlyweds motored to the Hollywood Hotel, where Acker lived. They joined a dance in the lobby and twirled the night away. When the bride retired to her room, Valentino followed, only to find that a locked door separated the two lovebirds. No matter how hard he knocked, Jean had no intentions of letting a man into her bed that night. She realized too late that her decision to marry had been the worst mistake of her life.

When she was sure that Rudy had gone, Jean, like a frightened kitten hiding under the bed, fled her room and sought solace in the arms of her true love, Grace Darmond.

Rudy, unable to see his wife face to face, poured out his heart in a letter. "Since I can neither force my presence upon you, either at the hotel or at Grace's, where you spend most of your time, I guess I'd better give up," he wrote. He pleaded for her to "come to her senses" and give him the opportunity to "prove my sincere love and eternal devotion to you."

Grace Darmond (L) and Jean Acker (R) in a scene from See My Lawyer *(1921).*

During divorce testimony several years later, Rudy said his pleas to Jean became pointless. "I asked her to return to me and she replied: 'No, you go back like a good boy.' I could not see her alone. She was always accompanied by Mrs. Darmond (Grace's mother) or Miss Darmond."[14]

Jean couldn't be persuaded to change her mind. She left for Lone Pine in early 1920 to film *The Round-up*, a comedy-western, with Roscoe "Fatty" Arbuckle. According to testimony in the Valentino-Acker divorce case in late 1921, Acker insisted there were no accommodations at the Lone Pine Hotel for husbands and wives, only enough space for the cast and crew. Apparently, the unwritten rule didn't include lovers, as Acker made room for Grace in her hotel room.[15]

Back in Hollywood, according to later testimony, Rudy came looking for Jean at Grace's apartment, which was located on Franklin Avenue in a building owned by Grace's mother, Alice Johnson. Their encounter became known during the trial as "the bathroom incident."

"He called at the house, asked for his wife and when I told him she was upstairs," Alice Johnson testified, "he pushed me aside and went upstairs. He was very angry." Grace testified that she witnessed the scene, recalling that Jean, in middle of a bath, finally opened the bathroom door and confronted her husband. Mrs. Johnson continued, "I heard them quarreling and said it must stop. I saw her red and swollen face subsequently."[16]

Grace and Acker remained companions throughout the divorce trail and into the mid-1920s. They shared a small bungalow on Orange Avenue in Hollywood.[17] Grace secured Jean a supporting role in one of her 1921 films, aptly titled *See My Lawyer*, released about six months before the Valentino-Acker divorce trial.

With her successes at Vitagraph and her leading role at Paramount with Wallace Reid in *The Valley of the Giants*, success should have been in Grace's immediate future. She began the new decade with a winner: *Below the Surface*, the adventure story of naval officers stranded in a submarine at the bottom of the ocean and the workings of a shady promoter (George Webb) hoping to cash in on the event. Grace assists Webb in his scheme and is successful at "vamping" the son of the diver who is sent to rescue the crew.

Variety gave high marks to most of the cast, especially Grace and Hobart Bosworth, who played the diver. "With her pretty face and figure, it is no wonder the diver's son feel for her hard."[18]

Grace's work in *Below the Surface* was also important to her because of its director, Irvin Willat, who became a life-long friend.

While *Below the Surface* should have been a springboard for opportunities that might have mirrored her successes at Vitagraph, Grace got bogged down in two serials: *The Hawk's Trail*, memorable only because it was an early effort by director W.S. Van Dyke, and *A Dangerous Adventure*, a Warner Brothers series co-directed by Jack and Sam Warner.

Grace and Derelys Perdue starred in *A Dangerous Adventure* as two sisters wandering half lost across Africa looking for lost treasure. They were joined in their search by a menagerie of circus animals.

According to *Hollywood Be Thy Name: The Warner Brothers Story*, the serial was a disaster, as well as a failure at the box office. "The two heroines nearly tore each other's hair out with incessant fighting. When not acting as referee, Jack and Sam had to fend off attacks by an over-excited monkey and a foraging elephant."[19]

Pearl, the elephant, equally as temperamental as the film's stars, took her frustration out on Grace one afternoon by bucking her off her back and throwing her to the ground. Grace suffered numerous cuts and bruises, as well as torn ligaments in her left hip.[20]

Two years later, Warner Brothers edited the thirty reels down to seven and released *A Dangerous Adventure* as a feature film. It was moderately successful.

Grace appeared as the imperiled heroine in her fourth serial, *The Hope*

Grace Darmond, Lloyd Hughes, and Hobart Bosworth in Below the Surface *(1920).*

Diamond Mystery, an independent effort with 15 chapters. The 1921 series, which featured Boris Karloff and George Cheseboro, explored the curse of the Hope Diamond.

In *Handle With Care*, a romantic comedy, Grace enjoys the affections of five suitors. She picks one as her husband, but realizes her mistake when he fails to remember their anniversary. He agrees to give her a divorce if she can find a more suitable mate among her four ex-boyfriends.

Patsy Ruth Miller, remembered today as the damsel in distress in *The Hunchback of Notre Dame* (1922), remembered Grace as "a pleasant if not talented young lady."[21] One reviewer of *Handle With Care* noted Grace's "striking beauty."

In addition to her film work, Grace made a number of court appearances in the early 1920s. In 1921, she testified for Jean Acker in Acker's

Grace Darmond in The Hope Diamond Mystery *(1921).*

divorce from Valentino. In 1922, Grace was extricated from the courtroom when she shouted "Liar!" at the testimony of P.H. Daniels, whom Grace accused of inducing her to sign a $250 mortgage on her piano by telling her the document was a letter of recommendation. The man apparently borrowed $250 using the note, but failed to repay the loan. [22]

In January 1923, Grace testified that she unwittingly received and sold stolen property from her former chauffeur and friend, E.A. McNabb, who was on trial for robbery. According to her testimony, her friend once brought over a fur and beaded handbag and told her they belonged to an acquaintance who wanted to dispose of them. Grace sold the items to a neighbor. Jean Acker was called to testify in the case, but was in New York at the time of the trail.[23] The day before she was to testify, police guarded Grace and Jean's home, after authorities were notified of an attempt to intimidate and possibly kidnap Grace to prevent her testimony.[24]

It was during her entanglement in the McNabb robbery trial that Grace played a thief. In Universal's *The Midnight Guest* (1923), Grace breaks into the home of a wealthy man and is caught in the act of robbery. Instead of being turned over to the authorities, her victim focuses on turning her into a lady. Overnight, she becomes a refined woman. Her beauty stands out as she floats around the house in the most elegant fashions of the day.

Perhaps it was the stress of the trial hanging over her that affected her performance. Reviewers noted that Grace was not quite herself. *Harrison's Reports* thought Grace's acting was "marred greatly by her lack of grace, and by her stiffness as she moves about. She gives the impression of being too tightly laced — or something."[25]

Variety agreed. "Grace Darmond, who plays the lead, does a fashion parade all by herself, and that is about the best thing that she does do in the picture."[26]

By January 1925, Grace and Jean Acker were apparently no longer a couple. Grace, in an announcement that surprised the press, said she was engaged to Maurice "Lefty" Flynn, actor and former Yale University football star. No one was more surprised than Flynn himself by the announcement.

He vigorously denied the reports and declared that he "hardly knew Miss Darmond and certainly never asked her to marry." After his denial of their engagement, Grace said the affair was an "unfortunate incident which has shaken my faith in men terribly."[27]

Grace then jumped into a fast courtship with Harvey Leon Madison,[28] Notre Dame football hero. The two were married in April 1925, only four months after she named Maurice Flynn as her future husband.

"It was all sudden, our decision to get married, although I have known Harvey for some time," Grace told the press. "We first met five years ago, and even today, he can describe in faithful detail the dress, hat and shoes that I wore. That is unusual in a man."

Grace said she could continue her career in films "until I can't anymore — that is, until babies come. I am not emulating Gloria (Swanson),

Grace Darmond in the mid–1920s.

but I do want a home and children. I have retired time and time again but always that urge to get back in and conquer what I have set my mind upon has prevented me. Success is one thing, marriage is another, and they can be together — for the wife — if the husband is broadminded and considerate. Harvey is both. He is the only man I have ever loved."[29]

The high regards Grace held for her husband lasted almost four months. By her account, she was not able to "step" fast enough to suit her man.

Madison's 'stepping,' Grace said, was to and from Tijuana, Mexico, where he made earnest efforts to gain funds for the household. "Yes, he worked hard enough — at borrowing money to gamble on and at losing it," she testified. "He didn't drink. His great weakness was in drawing face cards at twenty-one or something like that. Anyway, he would borrow money from me and others, go to Tia Juana, and come home without any."[30]

Grace was skidding along in mostly independent films by the mid-1920s. Gone were the days when she was the star of her own pictures. When she worked for a major studio, her name was down in the cast and she was supporting other principals.

In 1928, after working for John Ince (brother of Thomas) in several independent films, Grace retired from the screen to marry Randolph N. Jennings, named in the press as a wealthy theater owner and miner operator from Mexico City and Beverly Hills. The two met in late 1927 when Jennings was visiting friends in Los Angeles.

After a wedding at Grace's home on Poinsettia Place in Hollywood, the couple settled in Jennings' home on North Beverly Drive in Beverly Hills. As a Beverly Hills housewife, the former actress shunned publicity.

The Jennings marriage fell apart in the early 1930s, but saying goodbye to each other was not so easy. Grace was granted an interlocutory decree in December 1933. Then, in March 1934, the couple reconciled. About a year later, they separated and were divorced in March 1935. She accused him of inflicting grievous physical and mental suffering and said that these acts constituted "extreme cruelty."

In May 1937, Grace hauled Jennings back to court. This time, she filed a petition to set aside the divorce decree she won in 1935 on the grounds that she was "not acting of her own accord." She filed a new suit asking for the assurance of $500 a month and the recovery of $163,000 in bonds, oil royalties, and real estate which she asserted had been conveyed to her as a gift.[31] She further claimed that she had abandoned her career for domesticity. Grace estimated her ex-husband's worth at $2 million.

In his answer to her suit, Jennings denied that Grace dropped her film career because of their marriage. Rather than persuading her to drop her work, he said he tried to help rejuvenate her career.

The couple settled out of court in September 1937. The terms were not disclosed.

Various sources suggest that Grace returned to the screen in an uncredited role in *Our Wife* (1941) as a "dress woman." Her participation in the film cannot be verified.

Grace retained her home on Poinsettia Place in Hollywood, where she lived into the 1950s. Eventually, she took an apartment at the San Ramon Hotel on Sunset Boulevard. Grace died there on October 7, 1963. She suffered from chronic nephritis and heart disease.[32]

In announcing her death to the press, director Irvin Willat, described in her obituary as "her longtime friend," said Grace had directed that her body be donated to the University of Southern California (USC).[33] According to her death certificate, the USC School of Dentistry took possession of her body.[34]

Because she gave few interviews while she was working or in later years, it's not easy to put together with words a portrait of the real Grace Darmond. We are left with only random pieces of the puzzle. In examining her professional life, it's obvious that she used her beauty, tenacity, and talent to carve out a career of almost 50 films that kept her working steadily for over 10 years.

As for her personal life, well, she will probably always be remembered in Hollywood trivia as the one who rescued Jean Acker, the woman she loved, from the Sheik's sheets.

1. 1898 is most often used as Grace's birth year. Her death certificate lists 1899 and the 1920 U.S. Federal census indicates 1896.

2. Alice Glionna later married Richard Johnson, a salesman of automobile tires.

3. Carr, Caroline, *Oakland Tribune*, 1915.

4. Ibid.

5. Correspondence from H.M. Horkheimer to Thomas A Persons, 9 February 1916, Special Collections, Margaret Herrick Library, Academy of Motion Picture Arts and Sciences.

6. Western Union Telegram from Grace Darmond to William N. Selig, 11 February 1916, Special Collections, Margaret Herrick Library, Academy of Motion Picture Arts and Sciences.

7. Correspondence from Grace Darmond to William Lord Wright, 14 December 1916, Special Collections, Margaret Herrick Library, Academy of Motion Picture Arts and Sciences.

8. Earle Williams, Vitagraph's leading man in the 1910s, was voted America's number one star in 1915.

9. *Variety*, 1 February 1918.

10. Film historian Anthony Slide, in his book, *Silent Players*, suggests that "at least one contemporary told me that Reid was supplied morphine by his leading lady, Grace Darmond, who was well known around Hollywood as a drug dealer." *Silent Players: A Biographical and Autobiographical Study of 100 Silent Film Actors and Actresses*, Kentucky Press, 2002.

11. Wallace Reid's addiction to both drugs and alcohol worsened, and in 1922, he was placed in a sanitarium, where he died in 1923 at age 32.

12. *Variety*, 5 September 1919.

13. Leider, Emily W., *Dark Lover: The Life and Death of Rudolph Valentino*, Farrar, Strauss and Giroux, 2003.

14. "Star Had Only Little Drinks," *Los Angeles Times*, 26 November 1921.

15. *"Wedded, Found Spouse Broke,"* *Los Angeles Times*, 24 November 1921.

16. Ibid.

17. Ellenberger, Allan R., "The Valentino Mystique: The Death and Afterlife of the Silent Film Idol," McFarland & Company, 2005.

18. *Variety*, 11 June 1920.

19. Warner Sperling, Cass, and Millner, Cork, with Warner, Jr., Jack, *Hollywood Be Thy Name: The Warner Brothers Story*, Prima Publishing, 1994.

20. "Film Elephant Bucks off Star," *Los Angeles Times*, 21 January 1922.

21. Miller, Patsy Ruth, *My Hollywood: When Both of us Were Young*, O'Raghailligh Ltd. Publishers, 1988.

22. "'Nobody Lied,' Revised", *Los Angeles Times*, 7 December 1922.

23. "Grace Darmond Witness," *Los Angeles Times*, 11 January 1923.

24. "Plot to Kidnap Film Star Feared," 10 January 1923.

25. *Harrison's Reports*, 17 March 1923.

26. *Variety*, 5 April 1923.

27. "Former Yale Star Denies Engagement," 23 January 1925.

28. He was also identified in the press as Henry J. Matson.

29. "Grace Darmond May Wed Today," *Los Angeles Times*, 2 April 1925.

30. "Court Cuts Marital Tie of Actress," 19 December 1926.

31. "Grace Darmond Sues Ex-Mate," 28 May 1937.

32. County of Los Angeles, Registrar/Recorder/County Clerk, Death Certificate, no. 20935, 11 October 1963.

33. "Silent Films' Grace Darmond Dies at 65," *Los Angeles Times*, 9 October 1963.

34. County of Los Angeles, Registrar/Recorder/County Clerk, Death Certificate, no. 20935, 11 October 1963.

FILMOGRAPHY

1914

The Clock Went Wrong (Selig) (short) Grace Darmond.

An Egyptian Princess (Selig) (short) Grace Darmond, Palmer Bowman, Vera Hamilton.

The Estrangement (Selig) (short) D: Oscar Eagle. Grace Darmond, Adrienne Kroell, Gayne Whitman.

Your Girl and Mine: a Woman Suffrage Play (Selig Polyscope) D: *Giles Warren*.

Olive Wyndham, Katherine Kaelred, Sydney Booth, John Charles, Clara Smith, Katherine Henry, Dr. Anna Howard Shaw, Grace Darmond, Helen Ware, Louis Mann.

1915

The Millionaire Baby (Selig Polyscope) D: *Lawrence Marston*. Grace Darmond, Harry Mestayer Mrs. A. C. Marston, John Charles, Frederick Hand, Charlotte Stevens, Charles Siddon, Robert Sherwood, Baby Erickson.

A Texas Steer (Selig Polyscope) D: *Giles Warren*. [Frederick] Tyrone Power, Grace Darmond, Francis Bayless, John Charles, Mrs. Tyrone Power, Walter Roberts, Frank Weed.

The House of a Thousand Candles (Selig Polyscope) D: *Thomas M. Heffron*. Harry Mestayer, Grace Darmond, John Charles, George Backus, Forrest Robinson, Edgar Nelson, Emma Glenwood, Gladys Samms, Mary Robson, Effingham Pinto.

A Black Sheep (Selig Polyscope) D: *Thomas M. Heffron*. Otis Harlan, Rita Gould, Grace Darmond, John Charles, James Bradbury, John D. Murphy, Fred Morley, Lou Kelso, Jack Rollins, Emma Glenwood, Virginia Ainsworth.

1916

The Shielding Shadow (serial, 15-chapters) (Pathé) D: *Louis J. Gasnier, Donald MacKenzie.* Grace Darmond, Léon Bary, Ralph Kellard, Madeleine Traverse.

The Black Orchid (short) (Selig Polyscope) D: *Thomas M. Heffron.* Kathlyn Williams, Wheeler Oakman, Edith Johnson, Earle Fox.

Temperance Town (short) (Selig Polyscope) D: *Thomas M. Heffron.* Otis Harlan, Grace Darmond, John Charles, James Bradbury Sr., Leslie King.

A Stranger in New York (short) (Selig Polyscope) D: *Thomas M. Heffron.* John Charles, Grace Darmond, Emma Glenwood, Otis Harlan, Charles Hoyt.

Badgered (short) (Selig Polyscope) D: *Thomas M. Heffron.* Harry Mestayer, Grace Darmond, Al W. Filson, Edith Johnson, James Bradbury Jr.

Wives of the Rich (short) (Selig Polyscope) D: *Thomas M. Heffron.* Harry Mestayer, Grace Darmond, Lafe McKee, Lillian Hayward, Emma Glenwood.

A Social Deception (short) (Selig Polyscope) D: *Thomas M. Heffron.* Eugenie Besserer, James Bradbury Sr., Grace Darmond, Al W. Filson, Harry Mestayer, Wheeler Oakman, Vivian Reed.

Her Dream of Life (short) (Selig Polyscope) D: *Frank Beal.* Grace Darmond, Harry Mestayer.

1917

In the Balance (Vitagraph) D: *Paul Scardon.* Earle Williams, Grace Darmond, Miriam Miles, Denton Vane, Robert Gaillard, Templar Saxe, Julia Swayne Gordon.

1918

The Other Man (Vitagraph) D: *Paul Scardon.* Harry T. Morey, Grace Darmond, Florence Deshon, Frank Norcross, Jessie Stevens, Stanley Walpole, Mrs. Chapin.

The Gulf Between (Wray Physioc) D: *Wray Physioc.* Grace Darmond, Niles Welch, Herbert Fortier, Charles C. Brandt, George De Carlton, Joseph Dailey, Caroline Harris, Virginia Lee, Violet Axzell, J. Noa, Louis Montjoy

The Crucible of Life (Author's Film Corp.) D: *Captain Harry Lambert.*
Grace Darmond, Jack Sherrill, Frank O'Connor, Winifred Harris,
Edwin Forsberg.

An American Live Wire (Vitagraph) D: *Thomas R. Mills.* Earle Williams,
Grace Darmond, Hal Clements, Miss Toner, Orral Humphrey,
Margaret Bennett, Malcolm Blevins.

The Seal of Silence (Vitagraph) D: *Thomas R. Mills.* Earle Williams,
Grace Darmond, Kathleen Kirkham, Martin Best, Kate Price, Colin
Kenny, Pat Moore.

The Girl in His House (Vitagraph) D: *Thomas R. Mills.* Earle Williams,
Grace Darmond, James Abrahams, Irene Rich, Margaret Allen, Harry
Lonsdale.

A Diplomatic Mission (Vitagraph) D: *Jack Conway.* Earle Williams,
Grace Darmond, Leslie Stuart, Kathleen Kirkham, Gordon Russell.

The Man Who Wouldn't Tell (Vitagraph) D: *James Young.* Earle Williams,
Grace Darmond, Charles Spere, Edward Cecil.

1919

The Highest Trump (Vitagraph) D: *James Young.* Earle Williams, Grace
Darmond, Robert Byrem, John Cossar, C. H. Geldart, Robert Bolder,
Miles McCarthy.

What Every Woman Wants (Jesse D. Hampton Productions) D: *Jesse
D. Hampton.* Wilfred Lucas, Grace Darmond, Forrest Stanley, Percy
Challenger, Bertram Grassby, Barbara Tennant, Claire Du Brey,
William De Vaull, Mary Warren, Charles French.

The Valley of the Giants (Famous Players–Lasky) D: *James Cruze.* Wallace
Reid, Grace Darmond, Will Brunton, Charles Ogle, Alice Taaffe,
Ralph Lewis, Kay Laurel, Hart Hoxie, Noah Beery, Guy Oliver, W.
H. Brown, Richard Cummings, Virginia Foltz, Ogden Crane, Lillian
Mason, Speed Hansen.

1920

Below the Surface (Thomas Ince Productions) D: *Irvin Willat.* Hobart
Bosworth, Grace Darmond, Lloyd Hughes, George Webb, Gladys
George, J. P. Lockney, Edith Yorke, George Clair.

The Invisible Divorce (Select Pictures) D: *Thomas R. Mills, Nat C. Deverich.* Walter McGrail, Leatrice Joy, Walter Miller, Grace Darmond, Tom Bates, J.P. Ryder, Pidgie Ryder.

So Long Letty (Robertson-Cole) D: *Al Christie.* T. Roy Barnes, Colleen Moore, Walter Hiers, Grace Darmond.

A Dangerous Adventure (15-chapter serial) (Warner Brothers) D: *S.L. Warner (Sam Warner), Jack Warner.* Grace Darmond, Philo McCullough, Jack Richardson, Robert Agnew, Derelys Perdue, Mabel Stark, Captain J.R. Riccarde.

The Hawk's Trail (15-chapter serial) (Burston Films Inc.) D: *W.S. Van Dyke.* King Baggot, Grace Darmond, Rhea Mitchell, Harry Lorraine, Fred Windermere, Stanton Heck, George Siegmann.

1921

See My Lawyer (Christie) D: *Al Christie.* T. Roy Barnes, Grace Darmond, Lloyd Whitlock, Jean Acker, Ogden Crane, Tom McGuire, J. P. Lockney, Lincoln Plumer, Bert Woodruff, Eugenie Ford.

The Beautiful Gambler (Universal) D: *William Worthington.* Grace Darmond, Jack Mower, Harry Van Meter, Charles Brinley, Herschel Mayall, Willis Marks.

White and Unmarried (Paramount) D: *Tom Forman.* Thomas Meighan, Jacqueline Logan, Grace Darmond, Walter Long, Lloyd Whitlock, Fred Vroom, Marian Skinner, Georgie Stone, Jack Herbert.

The Hope Diamond Mystery (15-chapter serial) (Kosmik Films) D: *Stuart Paton.* Harry Carter, Grace Darmond, George Chesebro, Boris Karloff, Carmen Phillips, Ethel Shannon.

1922

The Song of Life (Louis B. Mayer Productions) D: *John M. Stahl.* Edward Peil, George Woodthorpe, Gaston Glass, Grace Darmond.

Handle with Care (Rockett Film Corp.) D: *Philip E. Rosen.* Grace Darmond, Harry Myers, James Morrison, Landers Stevens, William Austin, William Courtleigh, Patsy Ruth Miller.

I Can Explain (Metro) D: *George D. Baker*. Gareth Hughes, Bartine Burkett, Grace Darmond, Herbert Hayes, Victor Potel, Nelson McDowell, Edwin Wallock, Albert Breig, Harry Lorraine, Tina Modotti, Sidney D'Albrook, Stanton Heck, William H. Brown.

A Dangerous Adventure (Warner Brothers) D: *Sam Warner, Jack Warner*. Philo McCullough, Grace Darmond, Derelys Perdue, Robert Agnew, Jack Richardson.

1923

Midnight Guest (Universal) D: *George Archainbaud*. Grace Darmond, Mahlon Hamilton, Clyde Fillmore, Pat Harmon, Mathilde Brundage.

Daytime Wives (R-C Pictures, Film Booking Offices of America) D: *Emile Chautard*. Derelys Perdue, Wyndham Standing, Grace Darmond, William Conklin, Edward Hearn, Katherine Lewis, Kenneth Gibson, Christina Mott, Jack Carlyle, Craig Biddle Jr.

Gold Madness (Principal Pictures) D: *Robert T. Thornby*. Guy Bates Post, Cleo Madison, Mitchell Lewis, Grace Darmond.

1924

Discontented Husbands (Columbia) D: *Edward J. Le Saint*. James Kirkwood, Cleo Madison, Grace Darmond, Carmelita Geraghty, Arthur Rankin, Vernon Steele, Baby Muriel McCormac.

Alimony (Robertston-Cole) D: *James W. Horne*. Grace Darmond, Warner Baxter, Ruby Miller, William A. Carroll, Jackie Saunders, Clyde Fillmore, Herschel Mayall, Alton Brown.

The Gaiety Girl (Universal) D: *King Baggot*. Mary Philbin, Joseph J. Dowling, William Haines, James O. Barrows, De Witt Jennings, Freeman Wood, Otto Hoffman, Grace Darmond, Thomas Ricketts, William Turner, Duke R. Lee, George B. Williams, Roy Laidlaw.

1925

Flattery (Chadwick) D: *Tom Forman*. John Bowers, Marguerite de la Motte, Alan Hale, Grace Darmond, Edwards Davis, Louis Morrison, Larry Steers.

The Great Jewel Robbery (Robertson-Cole) D: *John Ince*. Herbert Rawlinson, Grace Darmond, Frank Darmond, Carlton Griffin, Marcella Daly, Chester Conklin.

Where the Worst Begins (Truart) D: *John McDermott.* Ruth Roland, Alec B. Francis, Matt Moore, Grace Darmond, Roy Stewart, Derelys Perdue, Theodore Lorch, Ernie Adams, J.P. Lockney, Robert Burns.

1926

Her Big Adventure (Kerman Films) D: *John Ince.* Herbert Rawlinson, Grace Darmond, Vola Vale, Carlton Griffin, William Turner, Edward Gordon.

Midnight Thieves (Kerman Films) Herbert Rawlinson, Grace Darmond.

The Night Patrol (Richard Talmadge Productions) D: *Noel Mason Smith.* Richard Talmadge, Rose Blossom, Mary Carr, Gardner James, Josef Swickard, Grace Darmond, Victor Dillingham, Arthur Conrad.

Her Man o' War (Producers Distributing Corporation) D: *Frank Urson.* Jetta Goudal, William Boyd, Jimmie Adams, Grace Darmond, Kay Deslys, Frank Reicher, Michael Vavitch, Robert Edeson, Junior Coghlan.

Honesty–The Best Policy (Fox) D: *Chester Bennett.* Rockliffe Fellowes, Pauline Starke, Johnnie Walker, Grace Darmond, Mickey Bennett, Mack Swain, Albert Gran, Johnnie Walker, Dot Farley, Heinie Conklin.

The Marriage Clause (Universal) D: *Lois Weber.* Francis X. Bushman, Billie Dove, Warner Oland, Henri La Garde, Grace Darmond, Caroline Snowden, Oscar Smith, Andre Cheron, Robert Dudley, Charles Meakin.

1927

Wide Open (Sharlin Productions) D: *John Wesley Grey.* Dick Grace, Grace Darmond, Lionel Belmore, Ernest Hilliard.

The Hour of Reckoning (John E. Ince) D: *John E. Ince.* John E. Ince, Herbert Rawlinson, Grace Darmond, Harry von Meter, Virginia Castleman, John J. Darby, Edwin Middleton.

1928

Wages of Conscience (Superlative Pictures) D: *John Ince.* Herbert Rawlinson, Grace Darmond, John Ince, Henri La Garde, Margaret Campbell, Jasmine.

ELINOR FAIR

She had been desperate more times than she cared to remember in her 52 years. Those how-do-I-go-forward moments had come by way of failed marriages, career disappointments, poverty, mental distress, alcoholic delirium. Somehow, she was a survivor.

When it appeared she was at the end of her rope, she found another to grab on to. When it looked like a dead end ahead, the road suddenly curved in another direction and kept going. This time was different. Now, not only were her fame, money, and beauty long gone, her health was giving out after years of abuse and neglect. She knew the end was near.

In an act of desperation, but picked up the pointed object and prayed for relief from her misery. With pen in hand, she poured out her heart and soul.

"Dear Miss Hopper: I am Elinor Fair Martin, ex-wife of Bill Boyd — Hopalong Cassidy, and one time, made a picture with you, *Has the World Gone Mad*, at the old Tilford Studio in N.Y.C. I put this down so you can place me.

"Miss Hopper, I am dying of a very serious liver condition aggravated by years of struggle. I have worked when I shouldn't, couple jobs, anything to help my husband. Now, I can work no more. My energy is so depleted. I'm so tired and need help so badly — simple help."

Her cry for help continued on for four pages. Could dear Hedda simply run an item about her dire situation in a column so that perhaps her husband could get work and they would purchase medicine she needed to stay alive, another night's stay at the hotel they were living, or collect the luggage they had in storage at the Greyhound station?

Elinor Fair, whose film career spanned almost 20 years, was returning to Hollywood forgotten — for sure, but there was nowhere else to go and no one else to turn to.

"In coming here," she continued, "I hoped there might be someone who would remember me and give my husband some work, so I can get badly needed medical care and some clothes to clothe me and lift my damage morale."

Elinor Fair had been a beautiful brunette with dark brown hair and coal black eyes in her youth. She had been a popular silent film actress, equally versatile in her comedic and dramatic characterizations in almost 50 films. With mostly positive reviews, she landed a prominent role under the direction of Cecil B. DeMille and opposite husband William Boyd. Her popularity continued throughout the 1920s.

The movie couple divorced before the dawning of the new decade, and overnight, it looked like Elinor's life fell apart. Her career disintegrated into bit parts and she spiraled into a dark world haunted by mental illness and alcohol abuse.

After two more doomed marriages, she left Hollywood for Seattle, Washington, where she'd spent some of her youth. She married again, her fourth union, and then there was the onslaught of a terminal illness. As she had done so many years before, she put her hope in Hollywood and prayed that someone would remember her, just one more time.

She was born Eleanor Virginia Crowe on December 21, 1903, in Richmond, Virginia.[1] She was the only living child of Harry J. Crowe of Ohio and Helen S. Jones of Kansas.[2]

By 1910, the three were living in Seattle, Washington. Harry was the manager of a credit company. Helen was a housewife. For whatever reason, Harry seems to have disappeared from their lives shortly after 1910. He is not mentioned in early biographies or interviews the actress gave over the years. By all accounts, Helen was a restless wife and was eager to travel the country and world.

Elinor's early publicity states that she received her education in public and private schools in the United States and abroad.[3] One source states that, as a child, she wanted to be a violinist and traveled to Leipzig, Germany, to study music.[4] It's not clear whether little Eleanor studied music abroad, but immigration records suggest that she had traveled to Europe as a child.[5]

In a 1919 interview with *Motion Picture* magazine, Elinor described living and studying in Paris and developing a self reliance early in life. "I was but a child when over there, but I had always been accustomed to taking care of myself, for mother and I traveled extensively," she remembered. "Consequently, as mother was often not well and remained in bed until noontime, I had breakfast alone in the hotels. I used to order meals from the time I was three years old, long before I could read a menu."[6]

Elinor often recounted how she and her mother returned to the States at the outbreak of World War I in 1914.

Early biographies of the actress also suggest she had considerable stage experience before she broke into the movies. Her first stage appearance was as a dancer at the Alcazar Theater in Los Angeles.[7]

Elinor remembered her vagabond lifestyle, "I've traveled up and down the Pacific Coast twenty times, and if mother said, 'Come, Elinor; we're leaving town this afternoon for the coast' — that is, when we were in an Eastern city, it never bothered me any more than if she had told me to dress for a matinee. We are both rovers and accustomed to living in suit-cases."[8]

She made her film debut as Eleanor Crowe in *The End of the Trail* (1916), one of three Fox pictures she made in rapid succession with Gladys Brockwell.[9] In October 1916, it was announced that she had offers from several music houses to publish a nursery song she composed.[10]

By the time she appeared with Clara Kimball Young in *The Road Through the Dark* (1918), she had changed her name to Eleanor Fair. Her role as Marie-Louise, a casualty of war, was her first role of significance. William Fox saw her performance, was impressed by the 16-year-old beauty with the olive complexion and dark features, and signed her to a five-year contract.

She spent most of 1919 at Fox playing opposite Albert (Al) Ray in a string of light comedies. Critics were reserved in their reviews. In *Love is Love, Variety* noted that "Mr. Ray looks too weak-chinned for a hero type and Miss Fair just looks sympathetically pretty. There is no pep, vigor or sprightliness in their actions."[11]

In *Words and Music by —Xxx*, the two portray youngsters trying to establish themselves in the big city. In *Be a Little Sport*, Ray and Elinor rush to get married so he can collect $100,000 his uncle has promised him. "Miss Fair is fine foil for Mr. Ray. She is vivacious, of pleasing screen appearance, and acts well."[12]

In *The Lost Princess*, the comedic duo plays newspaper reporters. Ray is hired, thanks to the literary efforts of Elinor, who writes a story about a princess and gives him the byline. She falls asleep and dreams that she is the princess he is writing about. She isn't, but he asks her to marry him by the last reel. *Variety* called the story far-fetched and that "while the inserts (titles) are consistently funny, Ray or Fair are not."[13]

Also, in 1919, Elinor was cast as a crippled teenager who is healed by a faith healer in *The Miracle Man*, starring Lon Chaney. The story deals with four crooks, one of whom is Chaney, who try to take financial advantage of a blind faith healer (Thomas Meighan).

With nine pictures to her credit in 1919, Elinor was busier than ever. She took time mid-year to discuss her career with *Motion Picture* magazine reporter Doris Delvigne. While she insisted she was content in Hollywood, especially after having signed a long-term contact with Fox,

Elinor Fair, on the cusp of fame (c. 1920).

she did admit her long-term ambitions were become a scenarist or to return to Italy to continue her vocal studies.

"I honestly don't know which 1 love best, music or writing," she said from her dressing room. "I believe that both, together with acting, are mediums for emotional expression. The creative instinct must have some outlet, and whether I will eventually succeed best as actress, singer, or writer — I'm sure I don't know.

"Mother says I will be happiest as a singer and, of course, I can't let my voice go to waste and must study for its development. I feel that writing will become my greatest hobby, and meantime acting is not only an obsession with me, but the means of earning money enough to enable me to follow out my hobbies. I'm a lucky girl, don't you think?"[14]

Lucky, perhaps, but as the new decade unfolded, she left Fox and began working for other studios. She would not work again for Fox until 1925.

In the meantime, Elinor became romantically linked with Lew Cody, her leading man in *Occasionally Yours* and *Wait for Me* in 1920.

Mary Pickford hired Elinor to appear with her in *Through the Back Door* (1921) as a rather unsavory character who, as a weekend party guest, plans to fleece her stepfather. Adolphe Menjou appeared as Elinor's father.

Variety called Elinor's performance "unusual." "She does not try to play the cutie, but looks good just the same and gets over the right notion of a designing young woman."[15]

She also garnered positive reviews from her performance as Marsinah in *Kismet* (1920). "Elinor Fair and Rosemary Theby contrasted youth and jealous disappointment with admirable command," noted *Variety*.[16]

After her work in *Through the Back Door*, Elinor took a five-month hiatus from her film career. The break, from mid-March 1921 into the fall, didn't help the momentum of her career. When she returned, she worked in only three 1922 releases, all for independent studios. In March 1922, she put an end to the rumors that she and Lew Cody were engaged to be married. "I haven't seen him in over a year," she told the press.

In 1923, Elinor was back in independents for such production companies as Equity, Robertson-Cole, and American Releasing Company. In *The Mysterious Witness*, she joins forces with an accused ranch hand to solve the murder of her father. *Harrison's Reports* noted, "By far the best acting is done by Elinor Fair."[17]

She turned out an "especially noteworthy" performance in *Has the World Gone Mad?* (1923).[18] Hedda Hopper portrayed a middle-aged housewife who jumps from the Victorian Era into the Roaring Twenties with complete abandon. She leaves her husband and conducts an illicit affair with the father of her son's girlfriend (Elinor).

The Western Association of Motion Picture Advertisers (Wampas) named Elinor one of their Wampas Baby Stars of 1924.[19] Publicity at the time credited her performance in *Through the Back Door* (three years earlier) as a pivotal factor in her Wampas nomination.

Elinor Fair in a 1924 portrait.

Being a Wampas Baby in 1924 didn't seem to have an immediate impact on Elinor's career. She was credited with only one feature film that year.

In 1925, after almost 10 years of ups and downs in a rather stagnant run in Hollywood, her career gained momentum when she was cast opposite popular Western star Buck Jones in *Gold and the Girl* and *Timber Wolf*. W.S. (Woody) Van Dyke, director of *Timber Wolf*, praised Elinor, referring to her as a "fine trooper."

The turning point in Elinor's Hollywood adventure came when she was selected by Cecil B. DeMille in late 1925 to play Princess Vera in *The Volga Boatman* (1926). In his biography of the famed director, Charles Higham wrote that Jetta Goudal, who was under contract to DeMille at the time, was his first choice for the role, but that she "felt the part was too slapstick" for her. DeMille released her from that obligation. "He

William Boyd and Elinor Fair in The Volga Boatman (1926).

signed Elinor Fair who resembled her."[20]

Publicity at the time indicated that DeMille had noticed and admired Elinor's work in her two films with Buck Jones. He credited her "beauty, ability, and youth" in selecting her for the role.[21]

The Volga Boatman, a small scale epic about the Russian Revolution was the first of DeMille's independently produced films of the 1920s. William "Bill" Boyd was cast as one of the leaders of the revolution movement against the Russian aristocracy. Elinor Fair, as Princess Vera, is engaged to Prince Dimitri (Victor Varconi), an arrogant, snobbish aristocrat who looks upon the common people as mere animals. When the revolution takes hold, Feodor (Boyd) becomes a high ranking Red Army officer. He is ordered to execute Princess Vera, but is so intrigued by her bravery in facing execution that he spares her life, risking his own life and sacrificing his high standing.

Bill Boyd, it turns out, was equally enamored of his leading lady. It was during the scene in which he faced a firing squad that he proposed marriage. While the cameras cranked, she told him she would be honored to be the next Mrs. William Boyd. As soon as the picture wrapped in January 1927, the two eloped to Santa Ana. It was her first marriage, his third.

Variety praised both DeMille and Boyd for their work on the picture, but expressed disappointment in Elinor's performance. "This picture from an artistic and box office standpoint looks to be about as good as anything that Cecil B. DeMille has ever done. William Boyd walks away with all the honors in the title role. Some fault is to be found with his leading lady who seemed rather stiff and failed to rise to the heights of her role."[22]

Elinor not only got a husband out of *The Volga Boatman*, but also a Pathé contract. It should have been the start of great things for this actress who had put in almost a decade of hard work in the movie studios.

The film, as it turned out, was the climax of her career. The downhill slide was soon to follow.

To capitalize on their success as both a movie and real-life couple, Pathé teamed them in two 1927 films: *Jim the Conqueror* and *The Yankee Clipper*.

The Yankee Clipper told of the rivalry for the world tea trade between England and America during the mid-1800s. To settle the score, a race was held from China to Boston Harbor. The loser was required to relinquish both the tea trade and their ship to the winner. William Boyd appeared as the captain of "The Yankee Clipper," and Elinor as Lady Jocelyn, a member of the British aristocracy who is stranded on the ship by accident, along with her fiancé (John Miljan).

Frank "Junior" Coghlan, who played Mickey, a tobacco-chewing stowaway, remembered spending six months at sea on a real clipper. They came into port only twice to collect provisions. Bill Boyd, he said, treated him like the son he never had, said Coghlan, "and I was also very fond of Elinor Fair."[23]

Coghlan appeared again with Elinor in *Let 'er Go Gallegher* (1928), as a street urchin who, after witnessing a murder, relates the details to his buddy, a newspaper reporter (Harrison Ford), who gains journalistic fame and almost loses his girl (Elinor) in the process.

The New York Times had little praise for Elinor's work. "Elinor Fair, who has little to do, at times looks strangely like Gertrude Lawrence."[24]

Elinor's career came to an abrupt halt after *Let 'er Go Gallegher*. It was generally thought that she, intent on making her marriage a success, was retiring from the screen. In a 1928 joint interview with *Los Angeles Times*, Elinor told writer Alma Whitaker that Boyd was "of good character."

After Elinor left the room, Boyd confided that he "loved his wife better than ever."[25]

While visiting Boyd on the set of *The Flying Fool* (1929), Elinor agreed to take a part in *Sin Town*, a film being shot on an adjacent soundstage. The role turned out to be little more than a walk-on. At the time, it didn't seem to matter to Mrs. Boyd.

Elinor Fair and Junior Coghlan in Let 'er Go Gallegher *(1928)*.
COURTESY OF FRANK "JUNIOR" COGHLAN

Their friends in the movie colony were stunned when the couple separated in October 1929. "We just couldn't agree," Elinor told the press.[26] Boyd blamed their separation on a number of disagreements. "We are still friendly. Divorce has not been mentioned nor can I say whether there is a possibly of a reconciliation."[27]

Grace Bradley, whom William Boyd married in 1937, expressed her own ideas about the Boyd-Fair break-up in her 2008 book, *Hopalong Cassidy: An American Legend.*

"Bill said she (Elinor) had mental problems, and I later learned she had a reputation for being promiscuous," she wrote.[28]

After her split from Boyd, Elinor dropped out of sight for several years. She underwent intestinal surgery in early 1932. Later that year, on December 27, Elinor, in a bizarre twist of events, eloped by plane to Yuma, Arizona, with movie stunt pilot Thomas W. Daniels. Her fiancé, actor Frank Clark, was stunned and apparently not informed of her plans.

"Miss Fair and I were to have been married," said Clark, "and I still think Miss Fair merely made a little mistake. I know why she did it. I hold

Elinor Fair's relationship with movie stunt pilot Thomas W. Daniels kept her name in the headlines for over two years.

her in the highest esteem and believe this will be corrected."[29]

No sooner had they said, "I do," did Elinor reply, "I shouldn't have." Daniels called Elinor his five-hour wife. The estranged newlyweds returned to Los Angeles by plane six hours later.

To add to the debacle, when Daniels touched down, he was met at the hanger by authorities who arrested him for the check he wrote to secure the plane. The check, for $97.50, bounced all the way to Yuma and back. Daniels reclaimed his diamond ring from Elinor and presented it to the owner of the airplane.

The next day, with a clearer mind and under a physician's care, Elinor explained the wedding as "just a big mistake" and that her actions were meant to spite Clark.

"I was blue after having quarreled with Frank Clark, my sweetheart," Elinor told the press. "And I thought I'd show him how smart I was. It was just a big mistake."[30]

"Frank and I have made up and he has forgiven me and we are engaged again," Elinor announced to the press. Clark agreed and added that he was concerned about his future wife's behavior and health.[31]

An annulment of the Fair-Daniels union was granted in mid-January 1933.

Elinor seemed to pull herself together enough to appear in several 1932 films: *45 Caliber Echo* and *The Night Rider*. She had extra roles in *Midnight Club* (1933) and *The Scarlett Empress* (1934).

In July 1934, Elinor and Thomas Daniels eloped to Las Vegas and walked the aisle of matrimony a second time. This union lasted into 1935, when Elinor filed for divorce. She charged that he "nagged her, criticized her, and called her unseemly names."[32]

"We were not happy," she explained to the judge in June. "He would absent himself for several days at a time and refuse to explain where he had been."[33]

After her second divorce, Elinor's emotional health spiraled. She lived with her mother in a tiny apartment. With no steady income, they dreaded going to the mailbox to face another bill. They cringed at seeing the landlord walking their way.

The two were given an eviction notice in October 1935. Elinor, as she circled the drain, turned to her former husbands, William Boyd and Thomas Daniels, for help. The two men came to their rescue. Daniels told the press that he financially helped his former wife from time to time, but "I didn't know it had gotten as bad as this."[34]

The Motion Picture Relief Fund also stepped in to rescue the troubled actress and her mother.

"Everything is gone — money, furs, jewelry, cars," Helen Crowe lamented. "I don't know what we're going to do when another rent day comes around. If Elinor could just get her health back, I just know she could go into pictures again. But her nerves won't stand it."[35]

On a cool morning, just before dawn, in December 1936, a police patrol came upon an auburn-haired woman wandering on La Miranda Street in Hollywood. She was dazed and confused and dressed in shabby clothes. She couldn't remember her name, where she lived, or how she got there.

Police officers took her to the emergency room at Hollywood Receiving Hospital, where a doctor diagnosed her ailment as an acute nervous condition. They identified the woman as Elinor Fair.

When asked where she lived, Elinor replied, "It doesn't matter anyway; the rent will be up at noon."[36]

Around 9:30 that morning, she regained her senses and asked to use the telephone. When police and nurses were out of the room, Elinor fled into the new day.[37]

Motion Picture Relief Fund officials again stepped in and rescued her. She was eventually placed in a private home. "We think she's worth saving," officials said.[38]

In 1938, Elinor and other silent film players, joined a petition for a law, Career Insurance or Mandatory Film Savings, that would compel actors and actresses to save at least 10 percent of their income for use in the years when they were no longer in demand. Unfortunately, the petition was nothing more than a shameful publicity stunt to exploit fallen stars in order promote a new movie.[39]

Elinor dropped out of sight until the early 1940s, when it was revealed she had married Jack White, actor and strongman, on August 13, 1941, in Las Vegas.[40] The marriage ended like all her others. White filed for divorce charging that Elinor was continuously drunk. In early 1944, the marriage was annulled.

A broken Elinor Fair at Hollywood Receiving Hospital

From there, Elinor descended into an alcoholic stupor and emotional haze. Life's highway led her to Seattle, where she sought help from those she had known in her youth. She remarried. The two scraped out a living, a pitiful existence for a former beauty and star.

By 1956, Elinor Fair Martin was stricken with a life-threatening liver condition brought on by years of alcoholism. It had been hard enough for the Martins to make ends meet and pay for life's basic necessities in their ordinary day-to-day world. Now, with her health failing, Elinor had no insurance and no way to pay for health care.

Desperate, the two boarded a Greyhound bus and headed south for Los Angeles. Exhausted from the long trip, the 52-year-old former actress appealed once again to the Motion Picture Relief Fund for help. The agency sent them to the Royal Palms Hotel on Westlake Avenue and paid for two night's stay.

It was then that Elinor reached out to gossip queen Hedda Hopper for help. "The MPR (Motion Picture Relief Fund) can really do nothing for me, as I have lost my motion picture rating, having been away 13 years," Elinor wrote. "They, in the past, have been very kind."

She continued,

> "I trust I trust you don't consider this an imposition, but when you're told by the Seattle County doctors that you are dying you'll try anything to help yourself. I need potent vitamin A, certain strict diet I can't get here, and we are utterly without funds.
>
> "If my husband could get some, even temporary work, so we could get a tiny apartment and I could live an ordered life, he could pay for medicine, food, rent, etc.
>
> "You can see that I am in a desperate 'spot' not mentioning the fact that each night, I don't sleep or have medical care. I am just that close to my end.
>
> "I've always felt you, of the newspaper women, were understanding, so I appeal to you, if only for advice."[41]

It is not known how or if Hopper responded to Elinor's plea for help. From all indications, help from Hollywood either didn't come at all or not in time to keep the Martins in town. The former actress had returned to Hollywood in hopes that someone would remember her and lend another helping hand in her desperate plight for survival.

To be remembered, was it too much to ask? Elinor Fair returned to Seattle knowing the answer to her question.

In April 1957, Elinor entered the King County Hospital in Seattle. She slipped into the hepatic coma and died there on April 26, 1957. Chronic alcoholism and cirrhosis, not surprisingly, were listed as the causes of death.[42]

Her death went unnoticed by those who *once* remembered her as a dark-haired beauty of the silent screen.

A single-line death notice in the *Seattle Times* said it simply, *"Martin, Elinor V, — 53, 1521 Eighth Av., April 26."*[43]

This time, what looked like a dead end ahead *was* a dead end, the end of the line.

Her final goodbye, her funeral notice, like her death announcement, was also brief: *"Martin, Elinor, Services 10 a.m. Wednesday at Home Undertaking Co. AMPLE PARKING."* [44]

Her final dangerous curve ended in a parking lot at the Home Undertaking Company, where, in their funeral notice, they boasted of having ample parking for mourners. Sad, but true, a few parking spaces would have sufficed.

1. Although she often used 1904 as her year of birth, her death certificate, the 1910 U.S. Federal Census, and a 1912 immigration record indicates 1903 as Elinor's year of birth.

2. Harry and Helen Crowe had another child who died in infancy.

3. Fox, Charles Donald and Silver, Milton L., *Who's Who on the Screen*, 1920.

4. Fox, Charles Donald, *Famous Film Folk*, 1925

5. Mother Helen and her daughter were passengers on the Adriatic that sailed from Liverpool, England, on April 18, 1912.

6. Delvigne, Doris, "All is Fair — When Elinor's Around," *Motion Picture*, June 1919.

7. Fox, Charles Donald, *Famous Film Folk*, 1925

8. Delvigne, Doris, "All is Fair — When Elinor's Around," *Motion Picture*, June 1919.

9. *The Fires of Conscience* and *The Price of her Soul* were her other two films with Gladys Brockwell in 1916 and 1917.

10. *Democrat-Tribune*, Jefferson City, Missouri, 13 October 1916.

11. *Variety*, 15 August 1919.

12. *Variety*, 4 July 1919.

13. *Variety*, 31 October 1919.

14. Delvigne, Doris, "All is Fair — When Elinor's Around," *Motion Picture*, June 1919.

15. *Variety*, 20 May 1921.

16 *Variety*, 20 October 1920

17. *Harrison's Reports*, 23 June 1923.

18. *Harrison's Reports*, 5 May 1923.

19. Other Wampas babies for 1924 were Clara Bow, Carmelita Geraghty, Gloria Grey, Ruth Hiatt, Julanne Johnston, Hazel Keener, Dorothy Mackaill, Blanche Mehaffey, Margaret Morris, Marian (Marion) Nixon, and Alberta Vaughn.

20. Higham, Charles, *Cecil B. DeMille*, Scribners, 1973.

21. *Zanesville Signal*, Zanesville, Ohio, 29 November 1925.

22 *Variety*, 21 April 1926

23. Frank "Junior" Coghlan interview with Michael G. Ankerich, 1990.

24. *The New York Times*, 16 January 1928.

25. Whitaker, Alma, "Boyd is Incurable Film Fan," *Los Angeles Times*, 13 November 1927.

26. "Volga Boatman, Princess Drift Apart on Life's Cruel Stream," 8 October 1929.

27 "Film Hair Kinda Yoko Ichmann," *Los Angeles Times*, 9 October 1929

28. Boyd, Grace Bradley, and Cochran, Michael, *Hopalong Cassidy: An American Legend*, Gemstone Publishing, 2008.

29. "Actress Got Wrong Man," 28 December 1932.

30. "'A Big Mistake,' Says Actress After Wedding," 29 December 1932.

31. "Elinor Fair's Marriage was Spite Affair," 28 December 1932.

32. "Divorce Asked by Elinor Fair," *Los Angeles Times*, 12 March 1935.

33. "Couple Twice Married Separated by Divorce," *Los Angeles Times*, 13 June 1935.

34. "Mother Laments, 'Everything is Gone,' Does Not Know What to Do," 22 October 1936.

35. Ibid.

36. "Ex-Film Beauty is Found Dazed on Hollywood Street," 16 December 1936.

37. "Elinor Fair Flees Hospital After Police Give her Aid," *Los Angeles Times*, 15 December 1936.

38. Harrison, Paul, "Hollywood," 23 January 1937.

39. www.dorothysebastian.com/efair.html.

40. *The Daily Messenger*, Canandaigua, New York, 8 November 1941.

41. Letter from Elinor Fair Martin to Hedda Hopper, 1 September 1956, Hedda Hopper Collection, Academy of Motion Picture Arts and Sciences Library, Los Angeles, California.

42. County of King, Washington State Department of Health, Certificate of Death, no. 2241, 30 April 1957.

43. *Seattle Times*, 1 May 1957.

44. *Seattle Post-Intelligencer*, 30 April 1957.

FILMOGRAPHY

1916

The Fires of Conscience (Fox) D: *Oscar Apfel.* William Farnum, Gladys Brockwell, Nell Shipman, Henry A. Barrows, Henry Hebert, William Burress, Elinor Fair, Willard Louis, Fred Huntley.

The End of the Trail (Fox) (as Eleanor Crowe) D: *Oscar Apfel.* Henry A. Barrows, Gladys Brockwell, William Burress, Ogden Crane, Harry De Vere, Elinor Fair, William Farnum, Henry Hebert, Hermina Louis, Willard Louis, Slim Whitaker.

1917

The Price of Her Soul (Fox) D: *Oscar Apfel.* Gladys Brockwell, Jack Standing, Monroe Salisbury, Brooklyn Keller, Elinor Fair, Jack Abbott, Willard Louis.

1918

The Turn of a Card (Paralta Plays Inc.) D: *Oscar Apfel.* J. Warren Kerrigan, Lois Wilson, Eugene Pallette, William Conklin, David Hartford, Frank Clark, Clifford Alexander, Elinor Fair, Roy Laidlaw, Albert R. Cody, Wallace Worsley, Eleanor Cruze.

The Reckoning Day (Triangle) D: *Roy Clements.* Belle Bennett, Jack Richardson, J. Barney Sherry, Tom Buckingham, Elinor Fair, Louise Lester, Lee Phelps, Lucille Desmond, Sidney De Gray, Joseph Bennett.

The Road Through the Dark (Clara Kimball Young Film Corporation) D: *Edmund Mortimer.* Clara Kimball Young, Jack Holt, Henry Woodward, Elinor Fair, Bobby Connelly, John Steppling, Lillian Leighton, Edward Kimball, Elmo Lincoln, Eugenie Besserer.

1919

The End of the Game (Jesse D. Hampton Productions) D: *Jesse D. Hampton.* J. Warren Kerrigan, Lois Wilson, Gayne Whitman, Jack Richardson, George Field, Milton Ross, Walter Perry, Elinor Fair, Bert Appling, Joseph Franz.

Be a Little Sport (Fox) D: *Scott Dunlap.* Albert Ray, Elinor Fair, Lule Warrenton, George Hernandez, Leota Lorraine, Eugene Pallette.

Love Is Love (Fox) D: *Scott Dunlap.* Albert Ray, Elinor Fair, William Ryno, Hayward Mack, Harry Dunkinson, John Cossar.

The Lost Princess (Fox) D: *Scott Dunlap.* Albert Ray, Elinor Fair, George Hernandez, Maggie Halloway Fisher, Edward Cecil, Burt Wesner, H. C. Simmons, Fred Bond.

Married in Haste (Fox) D: *Arthur Rosson.* Albert Ray, Elinor Fair, Robert Klein, Don Bailey, B. M. Turner, Thomas Jefferson, William Carroll, William Elmer.

Vagabond Luck (Fox) D: *Scott Dunlap.* Albert Ray, Elinor Fair, Jack Rollens, John Cossar, William Ryno, George Millum, Al Fremont, Lloyd Bacon, Johnny Ries.

Tin Pan Alley (Fox) D: *Frank Beal.* Albert Ray, Elinor Fair, George Hernandez, Louis Natho, Kate Price, Ardito Mellonino, Frank Weed, Thomas H. Persee.

Words and Music by -Xxx (Fox) D: *Scott Dunlap.* Albert Ray, Elinor Fair, Robert Bolder, Eugene Pallette, Edwin Booth Tilton.

The Miracle Man (Famous Players–Lasky) D: *George Loane Tucker.* Thomas Meighan, Betty Compson, Lon Chaney, J. M. Dumont, W. Lawson Butt, Elinor Fair, F. A. Turner, Lucille Hutton, Joseph J. Dowling, Frankie Lee.

1920

Broadway and Home (Selznick Pictures) D: *Alan Crosland.* Eugene O'Brien, Elinor Fair, Warren Cook, Frank Losee, Ellen Cassidy, Edward Kepler.

Occasionally Yours *(Robertson-Cole Distributing Corp.)* D: *James W. Horne.* Lew Cody, Betty Blythe, J. Barney Sherry, Elinor Fair, Yvonne Gardelle, Cleo Ridgely, Lillian Rambeau, Lloyd Hamilton, Gertrude Astor.

The Girl in Number 29 (Universal) D: *John Ford.* Frank Mayo, Elinor Fair, Claire Anderson, Robert Bolder, Ruth Royce, Ray Ripley, Bull Montana, Arthur Hoyt, Harry Hilliard.

Kismet (Waldorf Photoplays) D: *Louis J. Gasnier.* Otis Skinner, Rosemary Theby, Elinor Fair, Marguerite Comont, Nicholas Dunaew, Herschel Mayall, Fred Lancaster, Léon Bary, Sidney Smith, Hamilton Revelle, Tom Kennedy, Sam Kaufman, Emmett King, Fanny Ferrari, Emily Seville.

1921

Through the Back Door (Mary Pickford Company) D: *Jack E. Green,* Jack Pickford. Mary Pickford, Gertrude Astor, Wilfred Lucas, Helen Raymond, C. Norman Hammond, Elinor Fair, Adolphe Menjou, Peaches Jackson, Doreen Turner, John Harron, George Dromgold, Jeanne Carpenter, Kate Price.

Cold Steel (Robertson-Cole) D: *Sherwood MacDonald.* J.P. McGowan, Kathleen Clifford, Stanhope Wheatcroft, Arthur Millett, Charles Inslee, Milton Brown, Nigel De Brulier, George Clair, Andrew Waldron, Elinor Fair, V.L. Barnes.

1922

The Ableminded Lady (Pacific Film Corp.) D: *Ollie Sellers.* Henry B. Walthall, Elinor Fair, Helen Raymond.

Big Stakes (Metropolitan Pictures) D: *Clifford S. Elfelt.* J.B. Warner, Elinor Fair, Les Bates, Willie May Carson, H.S. Karr, Robert Grey.

White Hands (Graf Productions) D: *Lambert Hillyer.* Hobart Bosworth, Robert McKim, Freeman Wood, Al Kaufman, Muriel Frances Dana, Elinor Fair, George O'Brien.

1923

Driven (Universal) D: *Charles J. Brabin.* Emily Fitzroy, Burr McIntosh, Charles Emmett Mack, George Bancroft, Fred Koser, Ernest Chandler, Leslie Stowe, Elinor Fair.

The Eagle's Feather (Metro) D: *Edward Sloman.* Mary Alden, James Kirkwood, Lester Cuneo, Elinor Fair, George Siegmann, Crauford Kent, John Elliott, Charles McHugh, William Orlamond, Jim Wang.

Has the World Gone Mad (Equity Pictures) D: *J. Searle Dawley*. Robert Edeson, Hedda Hopper, Vincent Coleman, Mary Alden, Charles Richman, Elinor Fair, Lyda Lola.

The Mysterious Witness (Robertston-Cole Pictures) D: *Seymour Zeliff.* Robert Gordon, Elinor Fair, Nanine Wright, Jack Connolly, J. Wharton James.

One Million in Jewels (American Releasing Corp.) D: *William B. Brush.* Helen Holmes, J.P. McGowan, Elinor Fair, Nellie Parker, Charles Craig, Leslie Casey, Herbert Pattee .

1924

The Law Forbids (Universal) D: *Jesse Robbins*. Baby Peggy, Robert Ellis, Elinor Fair, Winifred Bryson, James Corrigan, Anna Hernandez, Joseph Dowling, Ned Sharks, Eva Thatcher, Victor Potel, Hayden Stevenson.

1925

Gold and the Girl (Fox) D: Edmund Mortimer. Buck Jones, Elinor Fair, Bruce Gordon, Claude Peyton, Lucien Littlefield, Alphonz Ethier.

Timber Wolf (Fox) D: William S. Van Dyke. Buck Jones, Elinor Fair, David Dyas, Sam Allen, William Walling, Jack Craig, Robert Mack.

Trapped (Denver Dixon Productions) Carl Miller, Elinor Fair.

The Wife Who Wasn't Wanted (Warner Brothers) D: *James Flood*. Irene Rich, Huntley Gordon, John Harron, Gayne Whitman, June Marlowe, Don Alvarado, Edward Piel, George Kuwa, Jimmie Quinn, Wilfred Lucas.

Flyin' Thru (Al Wilson Pictures) D: *Bruce Mitchell*. Al Wilson, Elinor Fair, George French, James McElhern, Clarence Burton, Fontaine La Rue, Garry O'Dell.

1926

Bachelor Brides (Producers Distributing Corp.) D: *William K. Howard.* Rod La Rocque, Eulalie Jensen, Elinor Fair, George Nichols, Julia Faye, Lucien Littlefield, Sally Rand, Eddie Gribbon, Paul Nicholson.

The Volga Boatman (Producers Distributing Corp.) D: *Cecil B. DeMille.* William Boyd, Elinor Fair, Robert Edeson, Victor Varconi, Julia Faye, Theodore Kosloff, Arthur Rankin.

1927

Jim the Conqueror (Producers Distributing Corp.) D: *George B. Seitz.*
William Boyd, Elinor Fair, Walter Long, Tully Marshall, Tom Santschi,
Marcelle Corday.

My Friend from India (Pathé) D: *E. Mason Hopper.* Franklin Pangborn,
Elinor Fair, Ben Hendricks, Jr., Ethel Wales, Jeanette Loff, Tom
Ricketts, Louis Natheaux, Tom Dugan, George Ovey, Edgar Norton.

The Yankee Clipper (Producers Distributing Corp.) D: *Rupert Julian.*
William Boyd, Elinor Fair, Junior Coghlan, John Miljan, Walter Long,
Louis Payne, Burr McIntosh, George Ovey, Zack Williams, William
Blaisdell, Clarence Burton, Stanton Heck, Julia Faye, Harry Holden, W.
Sousania, James Wong.

1928

Let 'Er Go Gallegher (Pathé) D: *Elmer Clifton.* Junior Coghlan, Harrison
Ford, Elinor Fair, Wade Boteler, E.H. Calvert, Ivan Lebedeff.

1929

Sin Town (Pathé) D: *J. Gordon Cooper.* Elinor Fair, Ivan Lebedeff, Hugh
Allan, Jack Oakie, Robert Perry.

1932

45 Calibre Echo (Robert J. Horner Productions) D: *Bruce M. Mitchell.* Jack
Perrin, Ben Corbett, Elinor Fair, Olin Francis, Richard Cramer, George
Chesebro, Jimmy Aubrey, C.V. Bussey, Ruth Renick.

The Night Rider (Supreme Pictures) D: *Fred Newmeyer.* Harry Carey,
Elinor Fair, George 'Gabby' Hayes, Julian Rivero, J. Carlton Wetherby,
Nadja, Tom London, Walter Shumway, Bob Kortman, Cliff Lyons.

1933

Midnight Club (Paramount) D: *Alexander Hall, George Somnes.* Clive
Brook, George Raft, Helen Vinson, Alison Skipworth, Guy Standing,
Alan Mowbray, Ferdinand Gottschalk, Ethel Griffies, Forrester Harvey,
Billy Bevan, Richard Carlyle, Rita Carlyle, Charles Coleman, Jean
De Briac, Elinor Fair, Julanne Johnston, Mary MacLaren, Elinor Fair,
Charles McNaughton, Dennis O'Keefe, Jeffrey Sayre, Teru Shimada,
Leo White.

1934

The Scarlet Empress (Paramount) D: *Josef von Sternberg*. Marlene Dietrich, John Lodge, Sam Jaffe, Louise Dresser, C. Aubrey Smith, Gavin Gordon, Olive Tell, Ruthelma Stevens, Davison Clark, Erville Alderson, Philip Sleeman, Marie Wells, Hans Heinrich von Twardowski, Gerald Fielding, Maria Riva, Eric Alden, Richard Alexander, Nadine Beresford, Thomas C. Blythe, Hal Boyer, James Burke, Jane Darwell, Clyde David, John Davidson, George Davis, Anna Duncan, Elinor Fair, May Foster, Julanne Johnston, James A. Marcus, Petra McAllister, Eunice Murdock Moore, Patricia Patrick, Warner Richmond, Blanche Rose, Barbara Sabichi, Katherine Sabichi, Dina Smirnova, Agnes Steele, Minnie Steele, Elaine St. Maur, Belle Stoddard, Akim Tamiroff, Kent Taylor, Jameson Thomas, Edward Van Sloan, Bruce Warren, Leo White, Harry Woods.

Broadway Bill (Columbia) D: *Frank Capra*. Warner Baxter, Myrna Loy, Walter Connolly, Helen Vinson, Douglass Dumbrille, Raymond Walburn, Lynne Overman, Clarence Muse, Margaret Hamilton, Frankie Darro, George Cooper, George Meeker, Jason Robards Sr., Ed Tucker, Elinor Fair *(uncredited)*.

Whom the Gods Destroy (Columbia) D: *Walter Lang*. Walter Connolly, Robert Young, Doris Kenyon, Scotty Beckett, Rollo Lloyd, Hobart Bosworth, Gilbert Emery, Akim Tamiroff, Henry Kolker, Macon Jones, Maidel Turner, George Humbert, Hugh Huntley, Yale Puppeteers, Ruth Clifford, Elinor Fair *(uncredited)*.

JUANITA HANSEN

"This is one hell of a way to spend a Christmas Eve," the crazed woman barked from behind bars.

The papers on Christmas Day described her as a "middle-aged woman, her gaunt, thin face streaked with tears and her frizzled blonde hair fading to a dirty gray," who "sat in a city jail last night and sobbed to whoever would listen."[1]

The authorities, she wailed, had it all wrong. First, the morphine and syringe found in her purse were for a friend she was trying to wean off the drug. Second, her name was Dorothy Craig, not Juanita Hansen.

The sad truth, however, is that the woman rattling the bars *was* Juanita Hansen, the former Sennett Bathing Beauty and serial queen.

It is believed that from the time she was a teenager, Juanita had skirted along a dangerous curve that took the form of drug addiction. She'd been pronounced cured several times, only to fall back into dope's evil clutches.

In the early 1920s, her arrest on drug charges derailed her film career, during which it was estimated she'd earned and lost over $1,000,000. She wrote a series of newspapers articles documenting her descent into addiction and embarked on a crusade to warn the public of the devastating effects of drugs.

Later in the decade, in a hotel room in New York, Juanita suffered a setback when a malfunctioning shower head sprayed scalding water in her face. Drugs helped her through the pain, but, again, she became addicted and struggled through a long rehabilitation. Her crusade continued and now, Christmas Eve 1936, she sat in jail accused of something she'd preached against for almost two decades.

A female jailer begged Juanita to calm down. She stepped back from the bars, sat down on the cot and continued pleading. "I was to play in a Christmas play this evening," she explained. "Last night, there was a dress rehearsal and tonight, the play. Why can they do this? I haven't done anything wrong. I've got to get out of jail. By God, I can't spend Christmas in jail!"[2]

But, here she was, in a Los Angeles jail with a long night ahead of her. While she waited on freedom and Santa Claus, Juanita Hansen had plenty of time to ponder how far down she'd fallen in life.

She was born Juanita Hanson on March 3, 1895, in Des Moines, Iowa, to Henry and Sophia Pederson Hanson. Her father was born in Wisconsin; her mother, in Iowa. Both parents came from Danish lineage.

In 1903, when Juanita was eight, the three Hansons moved to Los Angeles, where Henry opened a real estate office. Juanita attended and graduated from Los Angeles High School.

She made her film debut at age 19 in *The Patchwork Girl of Oz (1914)*, a film based on L. Frank Baum's book. Although she played the small role of a bell ringer, in the next "Oz" film, *The Magic Cloak,* she was elevated to a supporting role.

Although urged by producers to change her name for the screen, Juanita more or less kept her real name. Early in her career, she used Wahnetta Hanson. Finally, she replaced the "o" in Hanson with "e."

"The name Hansen never seemed to belong to the Juanita," the ever-outspoken actress told Louella Parsons in 1920, "but I refused to change it to Imogene Winthrop or Gladys Dewdrop, because I wanted to keep my own identity and I had the peculiar feeling the loss of my name meant a metamorphoses of my personality — and that's one thing I prefer to keep always."[3]

Juanita had the great fortune to work with some of the industry's most skilled directors early in her career: Allan Dwan, Christy Cabanne, and Lois Weber. Her popularity with movie-going audiences increased considerably, however, when she was cast as the lead with Tom Chatterton in *The Secret of the Submarine (1915)*, a 15-chapter serial, a story of political intrigue leading up to World War I about attempts to keep a submarine from falling into enemy hands.

Newspapers told stories about Juanita becoming the "leading feminine daredevil of the screen," and of having to be rescued from quicksand and a water-logged submarine just before death consumed her.[4]

By 1916, she was recognizable to movie fans and established in her profession. Only several years before spiraling into narcotics addiction that would eventually ruin her career and beauty, Juanita freely offered advice to young hopefuls. "If you have been joy riding and imbibing tea freely the night before, when you report for work, your eyes will probably be bloodshot," she warned. "If you have eaten too much rich food, your face may have a pimple or two. This will completely spoil the effect of your close-ups."[5]

She encouraged those wanting careers in Hollywood to stick close to their mothers, as she had done. "Girls who live with their mothers usually succeed faster than those who live by themselves or with other girls. The mother watches a daughter's health, sees that she has good nutritious food, that her wardrobe is well taken care of, and that she does not go to too many parties. I attribute a large part of my success to my mother,

Juanita Hansen (R) and Gloria Swanson, Mack Sennett leading ladies.

with whom I am still living. We share an apartment, and no girl could ask for a better chum."[6]

In 1916, partially for her comedic talent and certainly because of her beauty, Juanita was selected was one of Mack Sennett's Bathing Beauties. In a string of two-reel comedies for Sennett's Keystone Comedies unit, she appeared alongside other bathing beauties, such as Gloria Swanson,

Juanita Hansen posing at the beach (ca. 1920).

Phyllis Haver, and Mary Thurman, who became Juanita's closest Hollywood friend. Juanita also worked with the best of Sennett's comedians: Ben Turpin, Chester Conklin, Bobby Vernon, Bobby Dunn, and others.

At an annual beauty contest in Venice Beach in June 1917, Mack Sennett's girls took top honors. Juanita, winner of the second prize, wore "a dazzling costume of gold cloth and gold lace, finished off with a green flop hat and shoes and hosiery to match."[7] Mary Thurman placed first, and Marie Prevost and Maude Wayne came in third.

Juanita stayed with Sennett through 1916 and into the fall of 1917. Although she made at least seven films with Sennett, she later downplayed the importance of her Keystone run.

"I never could understand why people continually refer to me as a Keystone girl," she told Louella Parsons. "I served only a very brief period throwing pies. I did not like comedy, and slapstick comedy I loathed. I hated it so much I left the Keystone company with only $200 to my name and no job in sight."[8]

She had always been grateful to Mack Sennett for giving her a chance, and fearing that he would try to talk her out of leaving the company, she waited until he left town to make her "getaway." "Mr. Sennett had always been so kind to be, but I knew pie-throwing was not my forte."[9]

Juanita joined Universal, where she starred in several minor features in 1918 and completed an 18-chapter serial, *The Brass Bullet*, as an imperiled heiress with a fortune in gold. Her star continued to rise and Universal took advantage of her good looks and versatility.

It was while under contract to Universal that Juanita first experimented with drugs. "It was at a party to which I had been invited in Hollywood, and felt quite flattered to be present, inasmuch as there were seven or eight of our prominent artists there when I was initiated into the 'fraternity,' as it is called in the West."[10]

A guest handed Juanita heroin and instructed her to place some of the white powder on the edge of a nail file. "I did as I was told, but instead of inhaling, I exhaled and blew the powder all over the room, which, of course, caused a great deal of mirth," she later recounted. "With the second attempt, I succeeded in inhaling a small amount of this powder. The effect was very pleasant."[11]

She attended these parties periodically and continued using the drug recreationally, but went on about her work at Universal without any thought of addiction.

In October 1918, Juanita battled a serious case of influenza. Several months later, in January 1919, she was stricken with sleeping sickness, an aftereffect of the flu, which incapacitated her for almost three months. During this time, she contracted with Selig Polyscope to star in her third serial, *The Lost City (1920)*. The studio wasn't prepared to start immediate production and Juanita was in no condition to work. The lag time gave her an opportunity to recuperate, and the studio had no problems paying her salary while she rested.

When she was better, her manager informed her she had been loaned to Fox Studios to star with Tom Mix in *Rough-Riding Romance*. For three weeks, Juanita struggled through the strenuous shoot. Then, before her scenes were complete, she was called to begin work on *The Lost City*. An exhausted Juanita realized she would be working night and day at two studios.

"I did not dream," she wrote, "that I would be kept working 16 to 18 hours a day for three weeks. After one week of this strain of double work, I fainted while doing my work on the serial. It made me realize that I had overtaxed my strength." [12]

It was at this point that Juanita said made her first drug purchase. A sniff of heroin was all she needed to get through the demanding stunts required of her in *The Lost City*, which she filmed during the day. With the help of the white powder, Juanita was able to get through *Rough-Riding Romance* and focus on the serial.

Before she had time to stop and think what was happening to her, Juanita was hooked. "No one had told me, or warned me, of the habit, but merely against taking an overdose," she said. "It never occurred to me to stop taking it when it made me feel so much better. I have often wondered if it was weakness or cowardice, whether a sin or virtue to want to work, work, work. That is all I wanted to do. There was not thought of pleasure." [13]

In October, while in the middle of filming *The Lost City*, Juanita got an offer to travel East to star with Warner Oland in another serial, *The Phantom Foe*. She vowed to beat her drug addiction before her new assignment, which was to begin filming in New York in January. With a schedule that kept her working night and day and a mad rush to finish *The Lost City* by the end of the year, Juanita found she had no time to commit herself to treatment.

Shooting on *The Lost City* wrapped on Christmas Eve, and by 8 p.m. that night, a beleaguered Juanita was on a train bound for New York.

The Lost City boosted Juanita's popularity to new heights and positioned her to replace Pearl White and Ruth Roland as the industry's leading serial queen. Early publicity suggested the cast and crew journeyed to the jungles of Africa to live and work among natives and wild animals. In truth, the action was filmed in Hollywood at the Selig Studio with animals from the Selig Zoo.

The action centers on Juanita, as Princess Lola *(Juanita)*, from the South African province of Wanda. She has been kidnapped and is held prisoner in the jungle, given the choice of either marrying her kidnapper

A wired Juanita Hansen.

or becoming a slave. She endures a number of dangerous stunts for the enjoyment of her fans, including being trapped in a pit of lions and leopards. Her hero *(George Chesebro)* rescues her from a pit by helping Juanita board the aircraft while the plane is still flying.

While the serial was successful in its day, modern reviewers of *The Lost City* criticize the quality of the production and the "wired" appearance of Juanita. Perhaps she was already showing the effects of drug abuse.

"While the film is a bit on the campy side, with some especially ludicrous sounding titles and over-exaggerated expressions on Hansen's part," wrote reviewer Robert K. Klepper, "it is an enjoyable film and a good opportunity to see Hansen in her glory days."[14]

Robert Howard Reid, reviewing for the Internet Movie Database, called the film "a primitive production. True, a fair bit of money has been spent on sets and extras — $1 million, according to movie publicity *(we don't believe it!)* — but the script is as childish as they come and the acting, with the one exception of Hector Dion's smilingly courteous villain, incredibly hammy. The worst offender is undoubtedly Juanita Hansen whose frizzy hairstyle and eye-popping dramatics have to be seen to be believed."[15]

Later that year, Selig consolidated the 15 chapters of *The Lost City* into a 50-minute feature film and released it as *The Jungle Princess (1920)*.

Juanita complained that "my life seemed always to be lived in a hurry, rushing — rushing from the studio to home, rushing back to the studio and rushing from one end of the country to another."[16]

Her pace only accelerated when her train pulled into a frigid New York City in late December. Only two days after she arrived, Juanita was at work with Warner Oland on *The Phantom Foe (1920)*, which was created for her by the same team that elevated Pearl White to fame: producer/writer/director George B. Seitz, writer/director Bertram Millhouser, and writer Frank Leon Smith.

Already a dope addict, Juanita had to quickly seek a source to feed her drug habit. An acquaintance of Juanita's told her that there was only one way to really take narcotics, and that was intravenously. The narcotic the acquaintance had in mind was morphine. In no time, Juanita was injecting morphine for her kicks.

"Soon a languid feeling overcame me and I felt like only being quiet," she wrote. "The effect was indeed wonderful. I had found a new toy."[17]

Never satisfied and needing more and more to maintain her ability to work at the studio, Juanita was introduced to cocaine. During the day, she took cocaine to keep her up, and in the evening, she injected morphine to bring her down so she could rest. She was veering perilously out of control.

Not only was her habit wrecking her health, it was also draining her bank account. "One hundred and fifty dollars a week alone for cocaine! One hundred and twenty-five dollars an ounce for morphine! When narcotics are needed and while under the influence, one never regrets

Juanita Hansen in a scene from The Phantom Foe *(1920) with Warner Oland (R), Joe Cuny, Wallace McCutcheon, Tom Goodwin, and William N. Bailey.*

the price paid," Juanita wrote. "In one frenzied year in New York, I spent $65,000 and ran $10,000 in debit in addiction."[18]

An overdose in the summer of 1920 brought her addiction to light. Her doctor confronted her with the reality that she would not live out the month if she didn't get herself under control. Her weight dropped to 105 pounds. Her appearance was shocking to those around her.

Then, in August, she was named a co-respondent in the divorce suit between Evelyn Nesbit and Jack Clifford, her dancing partner. Juanita flatly denied the charges against her.[19]

The day she finished work on *The Phantom Foe*, in December 1920, Juanita boarded a train for upstate New York, where a room at a sanitarium waited, the place where she could confront *her* phantom foe.

After three weeks of treatment, she left the sanitarium free of narcotics, but the urge was as strong as ever. She returned to New York City, where she made plans to go home to California. As she faced the long trip home, she told herself there was only one way she could make the trip: cocaine and heroin.

Back in Hollywood, at her mother's plea, Juanita sought the help of a Christian Science practitioner, who worked with her day and night for

Juanita Hansen (ca. 1920).

more than three months. She fought, and found hard. After an extended rest in a "science home" on the outskirts of Los Angeles, Juanita was thought to be cured.

News of her condition leaked out in April, when *Variety* reported that Juanita had been confined to a sanitarium for two weeks and would not be in "condition to commence picture work for over a month." They listed her illness as a nervous breakdown.[20]

While she struggled with her addiction, Juanita's fifth serial, *The Yellow Arm*, in which she was reunited with Warner Oland, was released.

An opportunity to bring her talent to the stage came her way in the fall of 1921. She spent the next three months before footlights: a matinee every afternoon and two shows in the evening. Her life sped up. In addition to entertaining, there were interviews, personal appearances, and publicity. Little time was left for Juanita and the preservation of her will.

When she got to Winnipeg, Juanita sought release and found a dealer who sold her a bag of cocaine. In every town and city from Winnipeg to San Diego, she found an easy fix. She was soon drowning in her familiar quagmire. After three months and 25 towns, Juanita arrived back in Hollywood just days before Christmas 1921.

A few days of rest and she was off to San Francisco to work on a film. Juanita spent a good portion of 1922 in the San Francisco area. Later in the year, she entered an Oakland treatment facility operated by Dr. John Scott Barker. Again, it was said that she left the facility cured of her disease, seven months drug free.

In January 1923, state and federal authorities raided the Barker sanitarium in Oakland and seized records pertaining to the treatment of patients and the handling of narcotics. Among the many files taken, the ones for Juanita and Wallace Reid[21] were of particular interest to authorities. The raid hit front pages of newspapers everywhere.

Overnight, Juanita's battle with narcotics was public knowledge. Mother Sophia explained her desperate plight. "I did not know exactly what caused my daughter to begin the use of stimulants, but overwork was getting to her — her nerves were going to pieces and everything in general was affecting her health," she told reporters. "She was ill and thin and worn to pieces, and weighed less than 100 pounds. When she came back from Oakland, she was just healthy and fine looking as she had been, and she weighed about 145 pounds."[22]

After her name was linked to the Barker sanitarium, Juanita dropped out of sight. Authorities were interested in questioning her about a drug ring which smuggled large quantities of narcotics into Hollywood and Los Angeles use by members of the movie colony. Juanita, however, was no longer in Hollywood. They tracked the actress to New York City, where they found and arrested her in a West 81st Street apartment. They alleged that she was in possession of a "box containing cocaine and a hypodermic needle."[23]

Juanita, who first said her name was Jane Hansen and denied she was the actress of serial fame, protested her arrest, saying the authorities had operated without a search warrant and that she was set up. Further, their actions, she said, would "ruin my career."[24] She was released the next morning.

At a hearing five days later, Juanita, dressed in black and hiding behind a veil, waited three hours before her case was called. She sat quietly with her head bowed and appeared to gawkers to be dozing.

Detective Patrick Cotter, the arresting officer, testified that he broke into the apartment and found Juanita with cocaine and a syringe. "She had the needle in her right hand and when I came in she grabbed for the box of cocaine with her left, to destroy it," he told the court.[25]

He asked what she intended to do with the needle. He quoted Juanita as saying, "My God, give me a chance. Do you know what this means to my career? Haven't you anyone to love. I'm supporting my family."

In court, Juanita admitted that she was once an addict who had been cured the year before. "I am trying to live right and why don't the police leave me alone? If I were doing dope now, I could not have stayed in a cell fourteen hours when I was arrested without asking for a stimulant. At the time I was arrested, I was lighting incense."[26]

The judge, having pity on Juanita and believing that perhaps she was indeed cured, dismissed the charges and released her. As she was leaving the court, Juanita passed the arresting officer in the corridor. She glared at him and proclaimed, "You are a liar — one of the worst liars."[27]

Wallace Reid lost his battle with drugs soon after Juanita's exposure as a dope addict. By her own account, Juanita was cruising toward a similar fate and would have met the same dead end had she not gotten help when she did. Coming out as a drug addict *(and by mid-1923, a former drug addict)* put an end to her career in films. Then, there were more bad headlines. In April, she declared bankruptcy, declaring she had $1,157 in liabilities and no assets.[28]

Rather than retreating into the shadows with the unfortunate circumstances in her life, the former serial queen used her celebrity and personal story to embark on a crusade to save women from the clutches of dope.

In the spring of 1923, she penned an account of her struggle with drug addiction, becoming the first celebrity to come clean about coming clean. The chronicle ran in newspapers around the country.[29] In the final chapter, she blasted police detectives over how they handled her recent arrest. She called for reforms in police departments.

"My arrest nearly broke my heart," she wrote. "It almost crushed everything I believed was good. Would it not have been a little more human, a little more Samaritan-like, to have come to me, and quietly asked: 'I am not quite sure, Miss Hansen. I have read of your cure. But I want to make sure. Will you come to my office for an examination before the medical board?' Had I been approached this way, I would gladly have gone to the Commissioner's office. My examination would have proved that I was cured. No publicity. No experience with cells and detectives. I might have been spared all this."[30]

Being rehabilitated and committed to telling others about the evils associated with drug addiction posed an uncertain future for Juanita. With her fortune gone and her career behind her, the question remained: Could she stay clean?

In the final words of her chronicle, Juanita wondered the same about herself. "Today I am pronounced cured — one of the few known to medical science. But only my death, at the will of God, will prove it so."[31] "My death certificate will show that I was cured of the drug habit."[32]

With her story in print, Juanita hit the vaudeville circuit, traveling from town to town speaking in theaters, before Rotary and Kiwanis clubs, to newspapers and radio listeners, to anyone who would listen, about her experiences with drugs.

In March 1924, Juanita was called as star witness for the defense in the federal case against Dr. John Scott Barker, the man she claimed was instrumental in her cure.[33]

In addition to speaking out against drugs, Juanita was in much demand as a judge for beauty contests. In the summer and fall of 1925, she appeared at contests from Ohio to Pennsylvania to New York. In Uniontown, Pennsylvania, she was the sole judge of a male beauty revue.

"Who knows but that we may find a future Valentino among youth of Fayette and adjoining counties," Juanita told the local press. "I am looking for a real Sheik to play with me this fall in what promises to be the greatest serial ever produced by Warner Brothers."[34]

Juanita and her closest friend, actress Mary Thurman, traveled to New York for a vacation in December 1925. While there, Mary contracted pneumonia and remained in serious condition for days. On Christmas

Day, she succumbed to her illness. A devastated Juanita accompanied Mary's body back to Utah for the funeral and burial.

In May 1928, Juanita appeared on Broadway in *The High Hatters*, a play set in the dressing room of a vaudeville theater and a sanitarium for psycho neurotics. The production closed after 12 performances.

Juanita was seriously injured in June 1928 when she was scalded in the bathroom of her suite at the Hotel Lincoln in New York. Her physician

A down-and-out Juanita Hansen.

told reporters that "Miss Hansen had turned on the hot water faucet full force, mistaking it for cold, and the boiling water took her off her balance and made her fall to the floor." She remained in serious condition for two weeks, after which she was declared to the "out of danger."[35]

She filed suit against Hotel Lincoln in April 1929 alleging that she was so badly burned, she lost the use of her left shoulder and arm. Her original request for $100,000 was later amended to $250,000.

At the trial that November, Juanita told the jury she had been scalded about the head and body when she stepped into the shower and set the indicator midway between hot and cold. Her lawyer said her injuries, which were periodically painful and marred her appearance, were of a nature to "permanently affect her earning power on the stage."[36]

The defense brought forth a surprise witness who testified that Juanita had been under the influence of a narcotic when she entered the bath and had improperly manipulated the shower faucets.

The jury deliberated only two hours before awarding Juanita $167,500. The verdict was appealed and stayed in the headlines for several years. In 1930, the Supreme Court of New York set aside the verdict. "The amount of the verdict is grossly excessive and undoubtedly reflects the jury sympathy for the injured plaintiff, a comely woman, rather than the jury's unbiased judgment on the facts," New York Supreme Court Justice George H. Taylor Jr. wrote.[37]

In his editorial, writer Ted Cook suggested that Juanita should "sex appeal" the case to a higher court. "Why not order retrial, with a stipulation that the plaintiff wear long skirts?"[38]

In November 1931, the Court of Appeals in Winchester County, New York, affirmed Juanita's $100,000. With interest, her final award totaled $109,269.[39]

Right after Christmas in 1931, Juanita, once again a wealthy woman, boarded the Panama Pacific liner and sailed to California, arriving in San Francisco. With her troubles behind her, she announced she would try for a comeback in the movies.[40] Her resurgence amounted to a small role in a Monogram picture, *Sensation Seekers (1933)*.

The money Juanita was awarded in 1931 evaporated almost as fast as her hopes for a comeback. In September 1933, she filed suit against Clarence M. Leavy, her financial advisor, for the recovery of $5,000 cash and $20,000 in Liberty bounds she had entrusted to his care the year before.

"The $25,000 was practically all the money I had in the world," she told reporters. "I gave it to Leavy with the understanding that he was to buy for me the very best of gilt-edged securities so that I might have a small income for life. When I later asked for its return, he told me he didn't owe me anything — that he had bought stocks with the money and it was all 'washed up.'"[41]

Juanita made the rounds of studios again in mid-1935 hoping for work in films. Reminiscent of the scene from *Sunset Boulevard* in which Gloria Swanson returns to the Paramount lot to speak with director Cecil B. DeMille, Juanita went to the Warner Brothers set where former Mack Sennett actors *(Chester Conklin, Ben Turpin, Marie Prevost, and others)* were gathered to film a comedy short, *Keystone Hotel (1935).*

Director Ralph Staub walked up and took her hand. "Juanita," he said. Then, one by one the old-timers gathered around the former Sennett Bathing Beauty and serial queen. When enough chatter had ensued, Staub called, "On the set! Miss Hansen, you sit there."[42]

For a short time, Juanita scratched out a scanty existence *($94 a month)* in Federal Theater Project *(FTP)* work, a New Deal project to fund theatre in the U.S. during the Great Depression and to provide employment for out-of-work artists, writers, and directors.

On Christmas Eve, the night she was to appear in an FTP Christmas play, Juanita, living in a cheap rooming house in Los Angeles, was arrested for possession of morphine and hauled to jail. "It's a lie — a frame-up," she cried. "I haven't taken dope since 1928 — for eight years. I can't understand why they have done this."

Juanita insisted she was taking the morphine and hypodermic needle to an addicted friend who, in the process of being cured, was working through withdrawals. Juanita rattled the bars, begging the authorities to phone a physician who would verify her story. "By God, I can't spend Christmas in jail."[43] Friends from the theater project collected her $1,000 bail and Juanita was released.

Juanita appealed to the mercy of the court, explaining that she had made it her life's work to help addicts cure themselves. Her physician corroborated her unlikely story. The judge cleared her of all charges.[44]

Juanita renewed her cause to preach against the devastating effects of drug addiction. She put together a lecture, *Red Grows the Poppy*, and toured the country talking about her own experiences and crusading against drug trafficking. Juanita preached, "This vile curse is no respecter of persons. None of you is immune. Protect your loved ones before they are tempted. Make your warnings against the dope evil so strong and so persistent your children will believe you."[45]

In 1938, Juanita wrote *The Conspiracy of Silence*, a book in which she pleaded for drug addicts to be institutionalized in medical facilities, not correctional facilities. She planned to use any funds she raised from her tour and book to open a sanitarium, similar to the controversial one in Oakland that had been part of her cure in the early 1920s.[46]

She continued her crusade into the early 1940s. She found, however, that at the outset of World War II, groups were interested in hearing about the conflict between nations and where the war was headed. They

Juanita Hansen spoke often about the damaging effects of drugs.

lost interest in hearing about one former actresses' struggle with dope.

Juanita became increasingly dependent on the kindness of friends. By 1941, she was living in a modest hotel in Chicago. Her only companion was a pet bulldog, Tiny Alexander, but she was forced to give him to a friend when she could no longer afford his care.

Overwhelmed by her worsening circumstances, Juanita swallowed a handful of sedatives in June 1941. She woke up in a charity hospital and told police she had "nothing to live for."[47]

"I gathered many friends during my January days of luxury," she said. "They've been grand to me. I've been living off their gratitude for some time. I just couldn't go on being a parasite."[48]

Juanita recovered and continued working at whatever job she could secure. In March 1942, Juanita was hired as a banquet planner for The Lockwood, a Chicago nightclub. She was in charge of making arrangements for all weddings, anniversaries, and other parties.[49]

She eventually returned to California and was hired by Southern Pacific Railroad as a telegraph clerk. In 1950, she was working in Los Angeles and living in a $12-a-week room in a downtown hotel.

Juanita Hansen worked as a telegraph clerk later in life.

On the occasion of her 55th birthday, which she celebrated with her mother and other friends, Juanita told the press she had finally found peace in her life. "Fifteen years ago," she smiled at reporters, "I took my last treatment for the horrible curse of drug addiction. It was then that I won the greatest victory of my life."[50]

Of the past, Juanita harbored no regrets. "The millions slipped through my fingers easily enough, and vanished — but not the memories. I have those — and my health. And I'm happy."[51]

In retirement, Juanita lived at 858 Hilldale Avenue in West Hollywood. It was there that her maid, Pearl Edwards, found her dead on September 26, 1961. Edwards told authorities that Juanita suffered from a heart ailment.[52] She was interred at Holy Cross Cemetery.

Juanita, who never married, left $500 in personal belongings to lifelong friends Harold Hull and Pearl Edwards.[53]

Juanita Hansen could be considered the ultimate survivor. She might have easily suffered the same sad fates as Wallace Reid, Alma Rubens, or Marie Prevost, but she fought hard against a disease that snapped at her heels for much of her life and never gave up her courageous crusade to warn others of the destruction of drug addiction.

Her life-long struggle against narcotics, her many attempts at comebacks, her struggle through poverty, and the eventual peace she found late in life are admirable, indeed, but what a hell of a way to live a life!

1. "Queen of Silents Sobs Denial of L.A. Dope Charge," *The Fresno Bee*, Fresno, California, 25 December 1936.

2. Ibid.

3. *New York Telegraph*, by Louella Parsons, 2 May 1920.

4. "NewsNotes — Movieland," by Daisy Dean, 1916.

5. "Succeeding in the Movies," by Juanita Hansen, 1916.

6. *New York Telegraph*, by Louella Parsons, 2 May 1920.

7. "Keystone Beauties Victors in Great Beauty Parade in Venice," *Mack Sennett Weekly*, 25 June 1917.

8. *New York Telegraph*, by Louella Parsons, 2 May 1920.

9. Ibid.

10. Hansen, Juanita, *New York American*, 1923.

11. Hansen, Juanita, *New York American*, 1923.

12. Ibid.

13. Ibid.

14. Klepper, Robert K., *Silent Films, 1877-1996, A Critical Guide to 646 Movies*, McFarland and Company, 2000.

15. Reid, Robert Howard, Internet Movie Database *(imdb.com)*, 25 January 2008.

16. Hansen, Juanita, *New York American*, 1923.

17. Hansen, Juanita, *New York American*, 1923.

18. Ibid.

19. "Denies Evelyn Nesbit's Charges," *The New York Times*, 19 August 1920.

20. *Variety*, 22 April 1921.

21. On January 18, 1923, Wallace Reid lost his battle with drugs, just days after the Barker sanitarium was raided.

22. "Narcotics Crew Seizes Papers: Officers Raid Sanitarium Where Actress and Reid Were Treated," *The Ogden Standard Examiner*, Ogden City, Utah, 3 January 1923.

23. "Movie Actress Held Narcotics," *Evening State Journal and Lincoln Daily News*, 11 January 1923.

24. "Arrest Noted Film Actress as Hop User: Juanita Hansen Occupies Jail Cell for Time, Claims Frame-Up," *The Davenport Democrat and Leader*, Davenport, Iowa, 12 January 1923.

25. "Movie Star is Released," *Evening State Journal and Lincoln Daily News*, 17 January 1923.

26. "Juanita Hansen Not Drug Addict," *The Hamilton Daily News*, Hamilton, Ohio, 19 January 1923.

27. "Movie Star is Released," *Evening State Journal and Lincoln Daily News*, 17 January 1923.

28 "Ex-Film Actress Bankrupt," *The New York Times*, 21 April 1923.

29. Juanita's own story can be read in its entirety by accessing Taylorology at www.taylorology.com.

30. Hansen, Juanita, *New York American*, 1923.

31. Hansen, Juanita, *New York American*, 1923.

32. "Former Drug-Using Star Tells How She Was Cured," *Ogden Standard-Examiner*, Ogden, Utah, 16 November 1923.

33. Barker was convicted and sentenced to five years in prison *("Court OK's Barker Dope Conviction," Oakland Tribune, 15 June 1925.)*

34. "Male Beauty Contest Saturday Decided by Miss Hansen Alone," *Daily News Standard*, Uniontown, Pennsylvania, 8 May 1925.

35. "Scalded Actress Better," *The New York Times*, 9 July 1928.

36. "$167,500 Verdict for Burns in Bath," *The New York Times*, 17 November 1929.

37. "Court Sets Aside Actress' Award," *San Antonio Express*, San Antonio, Texas, 15 March 1930.

38. "Cook-Coos," by Ted Clark, *Ogden Standard-Examiner*, Ogden, New York, 11 April 1930.

39. "Wins Bath Scalding Case: Juanita Hansen has $100,000 Verdict Against Hotel Affirmed," *The New York Times*, 18 November 1931.

40. "Juanita Hansen Rich, Seeks Job," *Oakland Tribune*, 29 December 1931.

41. "Juanita Hansen Sues S.F. Man," The Modesto Bee and News-Herald, Modesto, CA, 12 September 1933.

42. "Juanita Hansen in Films, Returns to Movie Comedy: She's Fat, but Trying," 23 May 1935.

43 "Queen of Silents Sobs Denial of L.A. Dope Charge," *The Fresno Bee*, Fresno, CA, 25 December 1936.

44. "Juanita Hansen is Cleared by Doctor," *The Fresno Bee*, Fresno, CA, 8 January 1937.

45. Publicity for Juanita's lecture, *Herald*, Washington D.C., 1937.

46. "Movie Thriller Heroine Now Preaches Evils of Dope," *San Antonio Light*, San Antonio, Texas, 13 June 1937.

47. Larsen, Carl, "Juanita Hansen, Star of Long Ago, Attempts Suicide," *Oakland Tribune*, Oakland, CA, 22 June 1941.

48. Ibid.

49. "Screen Star at Night Club for Banquet Planning," *Southeast Economist*, Chicago, Illinois, 5 March 1942.

50. "Millions Gone, Actress Happy," *Los Angeles Examiner*, 12 March 1950.

51. Ibid.

52. Juanita's death certificate mentions coronary occlusion, arteriosclerosis, and hypertension as the causes of death. California Death Certificate Extract, Certificate #17475, Los Angeles County District: 7097.

53. "Ex-Actress' Will in Probate," *Hollywood Citizen*, 11 September 1961

FILMOGRAPHY

1914

The Patchwork Girl of Oz (The Oz Film Manufacturing Company)
D: *J. Farrell MacDonald*. Violet MacMillan, Frank Moore, Raymond
Russell, Leontine Dranet, Bobbie Gould, Marie Wayne, Richard
Rosson, Frank Bristol, Fred Woodward, Todd Wright, Bert Glennon,
Hal Roach, Andy Anderson, Jessie May Walsh, William Cook, Ben
Deeley, Lon Musgrave, Pierre Couderc, Jacqueline Lovell, Charles
Ruggles, Juanita Hansen, Blanch Lang, Harold Lloyd, Vivian Reed,
Queenie Rosson.

The Magic Cloak (The Oz Film Manufacturing Company) D: *J. Farrell
MacDonald*. Mildred Harris, Violet MacMillan, Fred Woodward,
Vivian Reed, Pierre Couderc, Juanita Hansen, Jacqueline Lovell, Frank
Moore, Bernadine Zuber.

1915

The Love Route (Famous Players Film Company) D: *Allan Dwan*. Harold
Lockwood, Winifred Kingston, Donald Crisp, Jack Pickford, Dick La
Reno, Juanita Hansen, Marshall Neilan.

The Absentee (Majestic Motion Picture Company) D: *Christy Cabanne*.
Robert Edeson, Allan Sears, Arthur Paget, George Beranger, Augustus
Carney, Charles Lee, Elmo Lincoln, Olga Grey, Loretta Blake, Juanita
Hansen *(as Wahnetta Hanson)*, Mildred Harris.

Betty in Search of a Thrill (Hobart Bosworth Productions) D: *Lois Weber*,
Phillips Smalley. Elsie Janis, Owen Moore, Juanita Hansen, Herbert
Standing, Vera Lewis, Harry Ham, Roberta Hickman.

The Secret of the Submarine (15-chapter serial) (American Film Manufacturing Company) D: *George L. Sargent.* Juanita Hansen, Tom Chatterton, Hylda Hollis, Lamar Johnstone, George Clancey, William Tedmarsh, Harry Edmondson, George Webb, Hugh Bennett, Joseph Beaudry, Perry Banks, Leona Hutton, George Gebhardt.

The Failure (Reliance Film Company) D: *Christy Cabanne.* John Emerson, Juanita Hansen *(Wahneta Hanson)*, Allan Sears, Olga Grey, Augustus Carney.

The Root of All Evil (Majestic Motion Picture Company) D: *Spottiswoode Aitken.* Juanita Hansen, Jennie Lee, Elmo Lincoln.

Martyrs of the Alamo (Fine Arts Film Company) D: *Christy Cabanne.* Sam De Grasse, Allan Sears, Walter Long, Alfred Paget, Fred Burns, John T. Dillon, Douglas Fairbanks, Juanita Hansen, Ora Carew, Tom Wilson, Augustus Carney.

1916

Black Eyes and Blue (short) (Keystone) D: *Robert P. Kerr.* Juanita Hansen, Martha Trick, Billy Armstrong, Arthur Allardt, Dorothy Hagan, Jack Henderson.

His Pride and Shame (short) (Keystone) D: *Charley Chase, Ford Sterling.* Juanita Hansen, Bobby Vernon, Bobby Dunn, Guy Woodward, James Donnelly, Robert Eddy, Frank Hayes, James Rowe.

The Finishing Touch (short) [Independent Moving Pictures Co. of America *(IMP)*] D: *George Cochrane.* Juanita Hansen, Rex De Rosselli, Marjorie Ellison, Buddy McQuoid.

The Mediator (Fox) D: *Otis Turner.* George Walsh, Juanita Hansen, James A. Marcus, Lee Willard, Pearl Elmore, Sedley Brown.

1917

A Noble Fraud (short) (Triangle) D: *Harry Williams.* Juanita Hansen, Lew Cody, Laura La Varnie, Billy Armstrong, Dale Fuller.

Glory (M.L.B. Film Company) D: *Francis J. Grandon, Burton L. King.* Max Dill, Clarence Kolb, Juanita Hansen, May Cloy, Wellington A. Playter, Allan Forrest, William Lampe, Doris Baker, Frank Mayo.

When Hearts Collide (short) (Triangle) Billy Armstrong, Hallam Cooley, Juanita Hansen, Dale C. Renton, Joe Murphy.

A Royal Rogue (short) (Keystone) D: *Ferris Hartman, Robert P. Kerr.* Billy Armstrong, Raymond Griffith, Juanita Hansen, Hallam Cooley, Jack Henderson, Martha Trick, Raymond Russell.

Cactus Nell (short) (Keystone) D: *Fred Hibbard.* Ben Turpin, Chester Conklin, Wallace Beery, Juanita Hansen, Claire Anderson, James Donnelly, Cliff Bowes, Billy Jacobs, Joey Jacobs, Bob Kortman, Polly Moran, Wayland Trask, Mai Wells.

Dangers of a Bride (short) (Keystone) D: *Clarence G. Badger, Ferris Hartman.* Gloria Swanson, Bobby Vernon, Agnes Vernon, Fritz Schade, Juanita Hansen, Jay Dwiggins, Robert Milliken, Al McKinnon, Martha Trick, F.B. Cooper, Baby Spofford.

A Clever Dummy (short) (Keystone) D: *Ferris Hartman, Robert P. Kerr.* Ben Turpin, Chester Conklin, Wallace Beery, Juanita Hansen, Claire Anderson, James Donnelly, James Delano, Marvel Rea.

Whose Baby? (short) (Keystone) D: *Clarence G. Badger.* Bobby Vernon, Gloria Swanson, Jay Dwiggins, Martha Trick, Robert Milliken, Fritz Schade, Juanita Hansen, Sylvia Ashton, Helen Bray, Florence Clark, Phyllis Haver, William Irving, Edgar Kennedy, Myrtle Lind, Roxana McGowan, Virginia Nightingale, Marvel Rea, Earle Rodney, Vera Steadman, Ethel Teare, Edith Valk, Guy Woodward.

His Busy Day (short) (Triangle) Nick Cogley, Raymond Griffith, Juanita Hansen.

1918

Broadway Love (Universal) D: *Ida Mae Park.* Dorothy Phillips, Juanita Hansen, William Stowell, Harry von Meter, Lon Chaney, Gladys Tennyson, Eve Southern.

Fast Company (Universal) D: *Lynn Reynolds.* Franklyn Farnum, Katherine Griffith, Lon Chaney, Fred Montague, Juanita Hansen, Edward Cecil.

The Risky Road (Universal) D: *Ida Mae Park.* Dorothy Phillips, William Stowell, Juanita Hansen, Claire Du Brey, George Chesebro, Edward Cecil, Joseph W. Girard, Sally Starr.

The Mating of Marcella (Thomas H. Ince Corporation) D: *Roy William Neill.* Dorothy Dalton, Thurston Hall, Juanita Hansen, William Conklin, Donald MacDonald, Milton Ross, Spottiswoode Aitken, Buster Irving.

The Brass Bullet (18-chapter serial) (Universal) D: *Ben F. Wilson.* Juanita Hansen, Jack Mulhall, Charles Hill Mailes, Joseph W. Girard, Harry Dunkinson, Helen Wright, Ashton Dearholt, Charles Force, Hallam Cooley *(Chapter titles: A Flying Start; The Muffled Man; The Mysterious Murder; Smoked Out; The Mock Bride; A Dangerous Honeymoon; Pleasure Island; The Magnetic Bug; The Room of Flame; A New Peril; Evil Waters; Caught by Wireless; $500 Reward; On Trial for His Life; In the Shadow; The Noose; The Avenger; The Amazing Confession).*

The Rough Lover (Universal) D: *Joseph De Grasse.* Franklyn Farnum, Juanita Hansen, Catherine Henry, Martha Mattox, Fred Montague.

The Sea Flower (Universal) D: *Colin Campbell.* Juanita Hansen, Gayne Whitman, Fred Huntley, Eugenie Besserer, Fred Starr, George C. Pearce, Alfred Allen.

1919

Breezy Jim (David Horsley Productions) D: *Lorimer Johnston.* Crane Wilbur, Juanita Hansen.

Yankee Doodle in Berlin (Mack Sennett Comedies) D: *Richard Jones.* Bothwell Browne, Ford Sterling, Malcolm St. Clair, Bert Roach, Ben Turpin, Charles Murray, Marie Prevost, Eva Thatcher, Joseph Belmont, Chester Conklin, Phyllis Haver, Juanita Hansen, Jane Allen, Heinie Conklin, Bobby Dunn, James Finlayson, Eddie Foy, Harry Gribbon, Laurel Lee Hamilton, Harriet Hammond, Frank Hayes, Fanny Kelly, Edgar Kennedy, Tom Kennedy, Myrtle Lind, Marvel Rea, Wayland Trask.

A Midnight Romance (Anita Stewart Productions) D: *Lois Weber.* Anita Stewart, Jack Holt, Edwin B. Tilton, Elinor Hancock, Helen Yoder, Juanita Hansen, Montague Dumond.

The Poppy Girl's Husband (William S. Hart Productions) D: *Lambert Hillyer, William S. Hart.* William S. Hart, Juanita Hansen, Walter Long, Fred Starr, David Kirby, George Stone, Leo Pierson.

Devil McCare (David Horsley Productions) D: *Lorimer Johnston*. Crane Wilbur, Juanita Hansen, Ethel Stewart, Kate Schiller, Carl von Schiller, A. Newman, Frederick Vroom.

Taking Things Easy (short) (Universal) D: *Harry Edwards*. Eddie Lyons, Lee Moran, Juanita Hansen, Harry Nolan, Fred Gamble.

Rough-Riding Romance (Fox) D: *Arthur Rosson*. Tom Mix, Juanita Hansen, Pat Chrisman, Spottiswoode Aitken, Jack Nelson, Sid Jordan, Frankie Lee.

Lombardi, Ltd. (Screen Classics Inc.) D: *Jack Conway*. Bert Lytell, Alice Lake, Vera Lewis, Juanita Hansen, George A. McDaniel, Joseph Kilgour, Thomas Jefferson, Thea Talbot, Ann May, John Steppling, Jean Acker, Virginia Caldwell, Golda Madden, Patricia Hannan.

1920

The Lost City (15-chapter serial) (Selig Polyscope) D: *E.A. Martin*. Juanita Hansen, George Chesebro, Frank Clark, Hector Dion, Irene Wallace, Al Ferguson, Marjorie Lake, Jack Abraham *(Chapter titles: The Lost Princess; The City of Hanging Gourds; The Flaming Tower; Jungle Death; The Puma's Victim; The Man-Eater's Prey; The Bride of Death; Tragedy in the Sky; In the Palace of Black Walls; The Tug of War; In the Lion's Jaw; The Jungle Fire; In the Cave of Eternal Fire; Eagle's Nest; The Lost City).*

The Phantom Foe (15-chapter serial) (George B. Seitz Productions) D: *Bertram Millhouser*. Warner Oland, Juanita Hansen, Wallace McCutcheon Jr., William Bailey, Nina Cassavant, Tom Goodwin, Harry Semels, Joe Cuny, Al Franklin Thomas. *(Chapter titles: Doom; Disappearance of Janet Dale; Trail of the Wolf; The Open Window; The Tower Room; The Crystal Ball; Gun Fire; The Man Trap; The Mystic Summons; The Foe Unmasked; Through Prison Walls; Behind the Veil; Attack at the Inn; Confession; and Retribution).*

The Jungle Princess (Selig Polyscope) D: *E.A. Martin*. Juanita Hansen, George Chesebro, Frank Clark, Hector Dion, Al Ferguson.

1921

The Red Snow. Juanita Hansen.

The Yellow Arm (15-chapter serial) (George B. Seitz Productions) D: *Bertram Millhouser.* Juanita Hansen, Warner Oland, Marguerite Courtot, Stephen Carr, William Bailey, Tom Keith, Al Franklin Thomas. *(Chapter titles: House of Alarms; Vengeance of the East; A Strange Disappearance; At Bay; Danger Ahead; A Nest of Knaves; Into the Dead of Night; Smuggled Aboard; Kingdom of Deceit; The Water Peril; Pawns of Power; Price of a Throne; Behind the Curtain; The False Goddess; The Miracle).*

1922

The Eternal Flame (Norma Talmadge Film Corporation) D: *Frank Lloyd.* Norma Talmadge, Adolphe Menjou, Wedgwood Nowell, Conway Tearle, Rosemary Theby, Kate Lester, Tom Ricketts, Otis Harlan, Irving Cummings, Juanita Hansen.

The Broadway Madonna (Quality Film Productions) D: *Harry Revier.* Dorothy Revier, Jack Connolly, Harry von Meter, Eugene Burr, Juanita Hansen, Lee Willard, Lydia Knott.

Girl from the West (Sam Warner Productions) D: *Wallace MacDonald.* Jack Richardson, Juanita Hansen, Edward Sutherland.

1933

Sensation Hunters (Monogram) D: *Charles Vidor.* Arline Judge, Preston Foster, Marion Burns, Kenneth MacKenna, Juanita Hansen, Creighton Hale, Cyril Chadwick, Nella Walker, Harold Minjir, Finis Barton, Zoila Conan, Sam Flint, Walter Brennan.

WANDA HAWLEY

Timing, for Wanda Hawley, was everything. It had been her whole life, positioning herself where she needed to be when it mattered and making connections and acquaintances when they were expected.

She'd been at the right place at the right time when director Cecil B. DeMille discovered her in the music world and steered her on the road to fame. Her timing was perfect when she became a star for Realart Pictures and progressed to Paramount, where she played opposite such matinee idols as Rudolph Valentino and Wallace Reid.

Now, in mid-January 1923, while she considered timing everything, it seemed to no longer be on her side. Her life was in chaos and she had to get out of town, out of the country — fast! Her recent headlines hinted of her predicament.

"Blackmail Plot Kept Secret."
"News to Me, Says Wanda on Divorce."
"Wanda, Peeved at Dumbbell Role, is Anxious to Sail."

The papers, however, told only half the story. Life had begun to unravel for Wanda Hawley. She had recently terminated her contact with Paramount — no more playing dumbbells for her — and she was separated from her husband of seven years, who was threatening to expose a "story that would astound the cinema fans of the world."

Get out of the country while there was still time and where she'd be safe from authorities, she surmised. Perhaps she'd make a name for herself in a couple of pictures abroad to show everyone in Hollywood that she could do better than what was being thrown her way.

Wanda applied for a passport, giving her name as Selma Hawley, her occupation as housewife, and pleasure as the reason for traveling overseas. When questioned by suspicious immigration authorities, she denied she was Wanda Hawley of the screen, but after she submitted a photo of her famous face, she had no choice but to admit her true identity.

Ten days later, as the S.S. Celtic pulled from port, the 28-year-old movie star finally believed she was putting her sorted past behind her, or at least, on hold.

The blonde beauty turned her attention to matters at hand and focused on the future, the here and now. She stepped forward and into the arms of her handsome business manager and future husband.

Perfect timing, again, Wanda!

When Wanda gave her name as Selma on her passport application, it was not a name she pulled from the air or the phonebook. Selma was the name of an older sister[1], one of six children born to German immigrants, Robert (a blacksmith) and Martha Stein Pittack.

Wanda Pittack was born July 30, 1895, in Scranton, Pennsylvania.[2] While Wanda was still a child, the family relocated to Bremerton, Washington.

At least two of the Pittack children showed early talent for music. Wanda's older brother, Harold, later moved to Australia where his family formed an orchestra. Wanda showed great promise in singing and playing piano. Although she was an "ardent" movie fan as a teenager, becoming an opera soprano was her earliest ambition.

"I was always a picture fan," Wanda told *Pantomime* magazine in 1921. "It was my favorite form of diversion, and I saw every good picture I could find time for. You see, my secret ambition was to sing roles in grand opera, and I knew I must learn everything I could about acting. Norma Talmadge was my favorite actress at the time and I fairly drank in her emotional work. But, I just couldn't see myself on the 'silent' stage or screen."[3]

As a teenager, Wanda often played the pipe organ for church and accompanied voice students at recitals. She also developed a fine singing voice and was recruited to sing in the Sunday morning church services on a "prison ship in the harbor." "I have never had a more appreciative audience than I found there."[4]

Early in life, Wanda developed two qualities that never failed to enhance her performance in her movies: her sense of humor and fun-loving spirit. "I was anything but serious as a child. For one thing, I was sent home more often than anyone else in my class for giggling. I think 'funny bones' stuck out all over me and any chance word or action was likely to touch one and set me off. I guess I was what the teachers call, 'irrepressible.'"[5]

Wanda graduated from Union High School in Bremerton when she was 16. At the University of Washington, she specialized in music and supplemented her income by instructing other students.

Her first professional engagement was with the Chautauqua organi-
zation "in and not very far from Seattle, as, at my tender age of 17, my
parents did not care to have me get far from home."[6] On recommendation from several members of the Ladies Musical Club of Seattle, Wanda
applied and was accepted to the Master School of Music in Brooklyn,
New York.

Wanda Hawley, not long after she arrived in Hollywood.

"I felt that my misty dreams were beginning to take form and substance. I was the happiest girl West!"[7]

In the summer of 1915, a voice culture student studying with Wanda introduced her to her brother, Allen Burton Hawley, an employee at the New York Telephone Company. A romance blossomed between the two, and a year later, on September 16, 1916, at a ceremony in New York City, she became Wanda Hawley.

According to Wanda's niece, it while playing at a piano concert that Wanda was introduced to the director, Cecil B. DeMille, who encouraged her to bring her beauty and talent to the movie screen. Wanda's family also believes that Wanda became one of DeMille's mistresses.

In early 1917, Wanda, using the name Wanda Petit, joined Fox Studios with a one-year contract and made a successful film debut with Stuart Holmes in *The Derelict* (1917). In quick succession at Fox, she made *The Broadway Sport*, *This is the Life*, and *The Heart of a Lion*. Wanda made a big splash in *The Derelict*.

"Other than Mr. Holmes," *Variety* reported, "there is but one person in the picture who stands out and it is Wanda Petit, who did not appear until long toward the end. But when she does show, she simply walks away with the only big punch. She is a find if there ever was one and whoever dug her up deserves a lot of credit."[8]

In the summer of 1917, Wanda received an offer to make pictures in Hollywood. Allen Hawley agreed to accompany his wife to California. He quit his job to focus on her career. Shortly after they arrived in Hollywood, Hawley was drafted into the Army. While away serving his country, Wanda's star continued to rise.

Douglas Fairbanks hired Wanda for the female lead in *Mr. Fix-it* (1918). With employment came the request that she drop Petit as her professional name.[9] She became Wanda Hawley both personally and professionally.

In the picture, Fairbanks plays an American college student studying in England. His roommate wants to escape an arranged marriage, so Fairbanks agrees to impersonate his friend and marry Wanda.

With *Mr. Fix-it* and the support of Cecil B. DeMille, Wanda began her long association with Paramount. The famed director used Wanda in the first two offerings of his sophisticated romantic comedy series: *Old Wives for New* and *We Can't Have Everything*. In the latter, Elliott Dexter has grown tired of his wife. DeMille uses the sexy and perky Wanda to portray Sophy before marriage and the frumpy Sylvia Ashton as Sophy after years of marriage.

DeMille grabbed Wanda, whose career suddenly took off — she made nine films in 1919 and 10 in 1920, for a prominent role in *For Better, For Worse*, a story of romantic twists against a backdrop of World War I. Again, Wanda received positive reviews.

Wanda supported early heartthrob Wallace Reid in *You're Fired, The Lottery Man*, and *Double Speed*, in which *Variety* referred to Wanda as

Gloria Swanson, Wanda Hawley, Elliott Dexter, and Raymond Hatton in For Better, For Worse *(1919).*

"extremely easy to look at upon. Miss Hawley shares the honors with Reid and the latter does not seem in the least reluctant to go 50-50 with his good looking leading lady."[10]

Her success continued as a Southern belle in *The Secret Service*, an adaptation of William Gillette's successful play about the Civil War and the love of a Northern spy (Robert Warwick) in Virginia for his Southern sweetheart (Wanda). Their love endures through his capture, the fall of Richmond, and Reconstruction. "Miss Hawley makes a very pretty Southern girl of the period," *Variety* reported. "She acts intelligently and she never fails to score in a part which suits her down to the ground."[11]

In 1920, Wanda joined Realart Pictures, a subsidiary of Paramount formed to showcase the studio's most promising players.[12] She came roaring into the Roaring Twenties. In her first assignment, *Miss Hobbs* (1920), Wanda was cast as a feminist who hates men and breaks up the romances of two girls friends in order to convert them to her own ideas.

"In a way, I think Miss Hobbs will be a wholesome warning to girls who are inclined to fads and things that detract their attention from really worthwhile things of life," Wanda said of her role. "Miss Hobbs is laughable because she is abnormal. Normality is what makes and keeps friends. Miss Hobbs has her own narrow ideas and tries to make everyone else conform to them. The truly broadminded person will make generous expressions to the feelings and opinions of others."

Wanda Hawley on the cover of Motion Picture Classic *magazine (ca. 1920).*

After only a few years on the screen, and with almost 30 movies to her credit, *The New York Times* offered an assessment of Wanda's acting style. "Invariably, Miss Hawley has been such a heroine as to make whatever her hero might do for her seem reasonable, or, at least, justifiable. She would probably be classed as an ingénue, but that only shows how inadequate in description are simply classifications, for while she is usually 'artless, ingenuous and innocent,' as ingénues are supposed to be, she is also intelligent, genuine and substantial, which ingénues seldom are. She smiles, but does not simper. She doesn't become silly trying to be cute, and she succeeds in being pleasant without appearing unnatural."[13]

While Wanda positioned herself for fame, her husband, Allen, now a dealer of automobile tires, was content to follow his own track. Wanda's brother, Robert Pittack, to whom she'd always been close, moved to Los Angeles and lived with the Hawleys in their apartment on St. Francis

Court in Hollywood.[14] Wanda, now with some clout behind her name, secured her brother a job in the studios.[15] He also served as her chauffeur and bodyguard.

During her first year with Realart, the studio invested heavily into their star by assigning some of industry's most skilled directors to bring out her best work. James Cruze directed her in *Food for Scandal* and Donald Crisp guided her through *The Six Best Cellars*, *Miss Hobbs*, and *Held by the Enemy*. She received exceptional training under Sam Wood, a director known for polishing the dullest material, in *Double Speed*, *Her Beloved Villain*, *Her First Elopement*, and *The Snob*.

In *Her Beloved Villain*, a light comedy based on the French farce *La Veglione*, Wood pulled out exceptional performances from both his leads, Wanda and Harrison Ford.

Variety noted that *Her Beloved Villain* was received with "well deserved laughter and was punctuated now and then with even uproarious outbursts. Miss Hawley does some excellent characterization in impersonating a tipsy girl with alternate sober moments."[16] Wanda's work on *The Snob* (1921) garnered less praise from the critics. "The elimination of a few hundred feet of needless bromide subtitles and extended close-ups of the star would have made this Realart comedy-drama one of real merit."[17]

In the domestic comedy *The House That Jazz Built* (1921), Wanda was willing to endure three hours in the make-up room each morning in preparation for her role as a housewife whose weight doubles. "I play a young wife who grows lazy and heavy through breakfasts in bed and too much candy," Wanda said. It was a part that "gives full swing to her interpretive powers."

Wanda scored a big hit when Cecil B. DeMille cast her in a leading role in *The Affairs of Anatol* (1921), a film that allowed her to standout from other female stars at Paramount: Gloria Swanson, Bebe Daniels, and Agnes Ayres.[18] In the picture, Wallace Reid and Gloria Swanson are newlyweds. One evening at a nightclub, they bump into Emilie (Wanda), a school chum of Anatol's, who is a paid companion to a much older man (Theodore Roberts). Anatol decides to rescue her from her profession. He sets her up in an apartment. To show her gratitude, she sets about to steal him from his wife. After he refuses her advances, she returns to her old life, leaving Anatol to proclaim to his wife, "If you ever see me trying to rescue any woman again — for heaven's sake, rescue me!"

"Wanda Hawley is fascinating," raved *The New York Times*. "Gloria Swanson is decorative and Bebe Daniels does one of the best mock vampire acts."[19]

Tim Lussier, in a modern review, called Wanda's performance "excellent" and noted that she is given more screen time and a bigger role than either Agnes Ayres or Bebe Daniels. "She is provided ample opportunity for a range of emotions — disappointment when Anatol tells her to throw her jewels away, devilishness when she figures out how to trick Anatol and keep her jewels, coquettishness in her scenes with the aging wolf Burton,

Wanda Hawley and Wallace Reid in The Affairs of Anatol *(1921).*

and seductiveness in trying to win the noble Anatol."[20]

George Melford, fresh from directorial success in *The Sheik* (1921), assembled another spectacular cast, including Wanda, Milton Sills, Jacqueline Logan, and Louise Dresser, for *Burning Sands* (1922), a desert romance between an English beauty (Wanda) and a philosopher (Milton Sills).

About 350 cast and crew members lived for several weeks in a Coptic mission in Oxnard, California, and filmed scenes on a set that represented an Arab encampment in the Libyan Desert.

In the picture, which *Photoplay* called *The Sheik's Little Sister*, Wanda throws caution to the wind and goes into the desert to pursue the man she adores. Amid the burning sands, she struggles to keep her man, confronts her rival (Jacqueline Logan), and fights off the unwanted advances of an English official all while the camp is under siege.

Perhaps she was exhausted from her grueling schedule over the past several years, but Wanda was not her best in *Burning Sands*. Critics were quick to assess her performance. *Variety* weighed in that Jacqueline Logan "overshadowed" Wanda's role and "takes away the acting honors. In the billing, Miss Hawley has the preference, a place that on the strength of the work done, should have gone to Miss Logan."[21] A review from

An ad for Burning Sands *(1922).*

a Grand Rapids, Michigan, paper referred to Logan as a "much better actress" than Wanda.

Mae Tinee, writer for *The Chicago Tribune*, offered an explanation for Wanda's weak performance in *Burning Sands*. "Wanda Hawley is splendid when it comes to straight comedy or when she depicts the tempestuous emotions of inexperienced youth," Tinee wrote. "But, she has not the poise nor the bearing for her role in *Burning Sands*. As the governor's daughter, she reminds one of a maid who has carefully observed her mistress's manners and is fairly apt at imitation."[22]

The Young Rajah (1922), another disappointing venture for Wanda, was released soon after *Burning Sands*. The picture, in which Wanda played Rudolph Valentino's love interest, was generally panned by the critics. "The surviving pallid love scenes between Rudy's character, Amos

Judd, and his New England sweetheart, Molly Cabot (played by Wanda Hawley), have the blandness of some of Valentino's pre-Julio love scenes, minus their spark of comedy," Emily W. Leider, Valentino's biographer, wrote of the film.[23]

Beginning in mid-1922, a series of rather bizarre events seemed to parallel the unraveling of Wanda's career. First, in July, Wanda surprised

Rudolph Valentino and Wanda Hawley in The Young Rajah *(1922).*

a burglar when she returned from an outing. When she marched upstairs with a gun in hand expecting to confront the intruder, she discovered her valuables strewn about the room. The thief had escaped.[24]

In August, the *Los Angeles Times* reported that Wanda and "federal officers" attempted to catch a blackmailer when the mystery person came to collect $2,000 that had earlier been demanded of the actress. Wanda neglected to tell the local police that she had received a letter demanding money. She was told to leave the cash on a certain fire plug in Long Beach. Wanda and the "government men" waited into the wee hours of the morning, but the blackmailer never showed up to collect the money.[25]

Shortly before Christmas, Wanda was questioned about reports that her husband was about to file for divorce in Buffalo, New York. Reporters located Wanda at her residence at Sycamore Apartments. "It's all news to me," was her curt reply. "I have nothing further to say."[26]

On January 12, 1923, Wanda and Jay Stewart Wilkinson, her business manager, hastily applied for passports, giving their traveling date as January 27. Wanda provided officials at least four false statements. First, she used the name Selma Hawley, which, according to the 1900 and 1910 U.S. Federal censuses, had been the name of her older sister. Second, she gave her occupation as being "at home." Third, she indicated her husband, Allen B. Hawley, was living in "parts unknown." Finally, she told officials that she intended to travel around the world for pleasure, including such countries as England, France, Italy, Spain, Egypt, Germany, Monaco, Switzerland, Japan, India, and China.[27]

With the application, Wanda presented a passport photograph that only elicited questions from the passport agent. "Aren't you Wanda Hawley of the screen?" the passport official asked noting the resemblance of "Selma" to "Wanda." Wanda denied she was the screen actress and said she had no knowledge of her. The next day, however, after some

Wanda Hawley's 1923 passport photograph, signed Selma Hawley.

investigation, Wanda had no choice but to admit her true identity.

When her plot to leave the country incognito was exposed in the press, Wanda came forth with the news that she had terminated her contract with Paramount.

"I asked to have my contact cancelled because I got tired of being cast as a dumbbell," Wanda said. "After four years of starring, I found myself being placed in all star casts, featuring the director. I was given smiling parts where all I did was to wear fine clothes and do no real acting. I couldn't stand it, so I asked for the cancellation. We quit as friends, but I will never again sign a contract without specifying that I am not to be cast in dumbbell parts."[28]

The press could only imagine what was behind Wanda's strange behavior and why she needed to quickly leave the country. The Associated Press reported that Wanda was getting "herself out of the United States a few jumps ahead of a threatened narcotics expose".

Whatever the reason, the mystery tarnished Wanda's reputation in the public's discriminating eyes. "No more sweet motion picture magazine interviews with Wanda Hawley, where the beautiful blond star is pictured with her apron on making a salad of her own invention and telling how she loves her husband and her kitchen even more than making pictures for Paramount, which she surely adores." The story mentioned Wanda's passport ordeal and her intentions of traveling abroad with Wilkinson. "With her was a young man who seemed to be acting as a sort of male chaperon. Possibly they are planning to star Miss Hawley abroad."[29]

For Wanda, January 27 couldn't have come fast enough. The truth was, Wanda had plenty of plans in the works. Getting out of town was only part of it.

She and her "chaperon" sailed for London on the S.S. Celtic. There, on February 8, Wanda, as she was preparing for a comeback in motion pictures, filed for divorce from Allen B. Hawley.

In her complaint, Wanda noted her husband's "failure to provide, brutality, refusal to work, and dissipation of large sums of money I gave him." She also intimated that other women were involved and that he frequently entertained men and women when she was away on location. "Being Wanda Hawley's husband seemed to be the only occupation he was engaged in," she asserted. In addition, her mate routinely treated her with contempt. He often called her a "brainless fool" and on numerous occasions, swore and cursed at her in the presence of others.[30]

With Wanda being thousands of miles from home, she was unavailable for further comment. Her husband, however, had plenty to say. "A story that will astound the cinema fans of America will be unfolded if I decide to start a countersuit for divorce," Allen Hawley told the *Los Angeles Times*. "I was certainly surprised she has the nerve to start anything. None of our friends would have been surprised had I started a suit against her but her action is a great piece of effrontery."[31]

Allen Hawley told the press that he left his wife in October 1922 after a dramatic scene in which Wanda had admitted that her love for him had "grown cold." He denied the charges Wanda brought against him and insisted he was not a deadbeat.[32]

"Shortly after our arrival in Hollywood, I was drafted for the Army and served 10 or 11 months," he replied. "Upon my return to civil life, I started a garage in Hollywood and also entered the real estate business. I continued both these business up to the time of my departure from Hollywood last fall (October 1922) and with every motion-picture magazine in the country carrying pictures of my garage in Hollywood, Wanda's charges of nonsupport and my asserted failure to work seem rather absurd."[33]

Two days after she filed for divorce, Wanda and J. Stewart Wilkinson left London for Marseilles, France, where they boarded a ship for Cairo. London's Gaumont Studios had cast Wanda in *Fires of Fate*, a picture to be made on location in Egypt. In the picture, which was shot around Cairo and the Valley of the Kings, Wanda is taken by an Arab prince (Pedro de Cordoba). She is rescued by Nigel Barrie, a British military officer who has been told he has only one year to live.

Wanda filmed her second Gaumont film, *The Lights o' London*, in England. Then, on July 7, Wanda, registered as Selma W. Hawley, and traveling companion Wilkinson, sailed home from Liverpool.

Back in Hollywood, Wanda avoided discussion of her marital drama. Instead, she issued a "final *coup de grace* to the Sahara sheik as the lover par excellence."

"The average American girl," said Wanda, "Wouldn't recognize the desert lord if she saw one. And, after she recognized him, she'd probably take the first boat back to her main street. I couldn't have imagined one of them attempting to carry me off. That would lose him all caste with his folk, for to the Bedouin, it is an abomination to marry outside of his faith."[34]

Wanda admitted to only one proposal of marriage, that from Prince Sacchuini, "a man of 80, who wanted to add me to his harem. He made love to me in French and handed me roses with the most courtly gesture. But much as I wanted to be thrilled by the compliment, I had to decline with thanks."[35]

In late October 1923, Wanda was granted an uncontested divorce decree when her husband failed to show up in court. On the arm of her brother and bodyguard, Robert "Robbie" Pittack, and two other female friends, Wanda was escorted into the courtroom, where she told of her marital distress.

"He never gave me a cent toward my support in his life," she lamented. "Instead, I supported him all that time."[36]

Judge Summerhold asked about his treatment of her. "Well, not very well," she replied. "I can't ever remember that he was ever kind to me. He called me a brainless fool and a dumbbell." The witnesses she brought with her corroborated her assertions. "It embarrassed her terribly," one witness testified. "But Wanda was so sweet about it and tried to cover up her embarrassment with a smile."[37]

The actress was granted her divorce on the grants of cruelty, and, according to the *Los Angeles Times*, Wanda, dressed in a black robe to resemble a widow's garment, "tripped out of the courtroom."[38]

After her departure from Paramount, the circumstances surrounding her trip to Europe, and the publicity associated with her divorce, Wanda's career sank to new lows. She had only four releases in 1924. The next year, she made nine films, most of those for such independent companies as Encore, PDC, Aywon, Chadwick, and Arrow.

In July 1925, Wanda and Jay Stewart Wilkinson finally got around to officially announcing their impending wedding. "Our engagement is a real love match and we are going to be very happy," Wanda gushed to reporters. "The romance started three years ago while we were riding camels in the shadow of the Sphinx during the filming of a picture in Egypt."[39]

The next month, in the company of a handful of friends, Wanda and Jay exchanged vows at the Congregational Church in Hollywood. Lottie Pickford, sister of Mary, served as maid of honor; Producer Arthur Beck, husband of actress Leah Baird, gave the bride away; and actors Alan Forrest (husband of Lottie Pickford) and George Whiting were the head ushers. Grace Kingsley described Wanda as looking like a "Greek goddess. She was so pale and still. Her pink chiffon dress over silk, with the winged chiffon picture hat, were exquisite."[40]

By the time Wanda walked the aisle and became Mrs. Wilkinson, her personal life seemed healthy; her career, however, was on life support. She struggled for a comeback to reclaim the star position she had enjoyed — or not enjoyed, it seemed — at Paramount. Under the guidance of her husband, Wanda worked hard in 1926, making nine films, most of which were ground out by independent, low-budget studios.

In *A Desperate Moment*, a quickie made for Banner Productions, Wanda is a stowaway on a ship and is marooned on a cannibal island with Theodore von Eltz. *Variety*, in its review, seemed to sympathize with Wanda's downward career spiral. "How in the name of heaven, anything else, will the independents ever continue to establish themselves if they make a picture like this, for any reason? Any audience will either yawn over or kid it — none can like it — there's nothing to like in it. Everything about the film is silly, from its story in the first place to the direction, with naught between some fair acting, with Wanda Hawley in on that.

"Is this a return for Miss Hawley or a comeback? She's playing a daughter here, and fairly looks it, doing quite well otherwise, but Miss Hawley is too experienced a trouper not to have sensed that this one wasn't right."[41]

Wanda is a circus equestrienne in *Hearts and Spangles* (1926), a Gotham Pictures production. A wealthy college boy (Robert Gordon) falls for Wanda, and despite warnings he will lose his inheritance, he forgoes his fortune and joins the circus to be near his love. "Wanda Hawley is the bareback rider," noted *Variety*, "but all Wanda did on the horse was to sit quietly while it walked slowly. Wanda's years are taking their toll."[42]

By the end of 1926, Wanda's reputation in Hollywood had obviously skidded into the gulley of has-beens. Two films for Pathé in early 1927, and it was over. She wouldn't appear on screen again until 1931.

Reviewers, her fans, all of Hollywood, really, wanted to know why the career of one of the brightest actresses in the early part of the decade could have derailed as it did. Wanda's niece, who asked that her name not be used, offered her assessment of Wanda's plight.

"Wanda had a drinking problem," she said. "That's the reason she left the movies. She drank and smoked, and with her gravelly voice, she could have never made it in talkies."

She drifted for several years, then, in 1929, Hunter Keasey, writer and director, hired Wanda to appear in his play, *Illegitimate*. On the night of April 24, Keasey was forced to stop the show and bring down the curtain at the Egan Theater when his star, apparently intoxicated, could no longer continue her performance. Keasey filed suit against Wanda for $50,000, alleging breach of contract. Mickey Powell, a friend of Wanda's, was named as co-defendant. He was charged with "providing and serving" her alcohol between acts.[43]

In 1930, writer Dorothy Herzog reported that Wanda was traveling to South America on a personal appearance tour. "Silent pictures are still popular in that part of the world," continued Herzog. "Likewise, Wanda's pictures, odd though they may be."[44]

Wanda surfaced again in mid-1931 when she toured the West promoting the Studio Face Lift beauty gimmick. It was touted as the facelift without a knife. In department stores from Fresno to Oakland, from Ogden to Salt Lake City, Wanda and six beauticians from "beauty shops in Hollywood" demonstrated the beauty product and told how ordinary women could look like movie stars in their own humdrum towns.

Wanda's appearance in Ogden, Utah, made big news. "Miss Hawley herself appears Friday and Saturday on the first floor of Wright's at 2 o'clock and 4 o'clock each day to tell you interesting, up-to-the minute gossip of Hollywood and of her friends among the stars.[45]"

With that bit of obvious humiliation out of the way, Wanda disappeared from public life. Her name surfaced briefly in 1933 when her husband sued her for divorce suit on the grounds of "willful absence."[46]

What became of Wanda Hawley? Did she, as it has been rumored, make ends meet by becoming a San Francisco call girl? Film historian Anthony Slide printed the assertion in his book, *Silent Portraits*.[47] The

Wanda Hawley in an ad for the Studio Face Lift beauty product.

information, he said, came on good authority from an acquaintance who knew Wanda in those days. Her family could only speculate.

"I heard that, too," Wanda's niece said. "I don't know for sure. I never heard it talked about around the family. However, I've been around the movie business all my life, so I wouldn't doubt that it was true."[48]

In the early 1940s, it was reported that Wanda Hawley had been found living in retirement as Mrs. Charles Fulcher on a farm in Camden, New Jersey.[49] The next year, the press reported that Wanda Hawley (Mrs. Fulcher) had died of pneumonia in Utica, New York.[50] In a case of mistaken identity, it was revealed the next day that Mrs. Charles Fulcher was actually silent screen actress Ormi Hawley, not Wanda.[51]

In truth, Wanda Hawley was very much alive and living with her third husband, insurance salesman Jack Richey, in Twin Falls, Idaho. The quiet life in Idaho might have been a bit too tranquil for the former silent film star. Her niece recalls Wanda frequently sending the family newspaper clippings from Idaho with headlines similar to *The Famous Movie Star Living in Our Town.* "She was the type who was always trying to generate publicity for herself."[52]

Wanda's niece grew up knowing that her aunt had once been a famous movie actress in the silent film days. "When she would return to California for visits, she would stay with us and I would have to give up my room for her."

Later in life, Wanda returned to California a widow and lived in an apartment on Oakhurst Drive in Beverly Hills. She worked for the Republican Party at the group's Beverly Hills headquarters.

Wanda's niece last saw her aunt at a birthday party for her daughter in 1961.

On March 18, 1963, Wanda passed away at home from heart disease at age 67. She was cremated and inurned at Hollywood Memorial Park Cemetery. Her death went unnoticed in the papers.

Wanda Hawley at a family gathering in the early 1960s.

When pressed to describe what Wanda was like in later years, Wanda's family remembers her flair for the dramatic, her need for attention, and her desire to always be *on*, the center of attention. Her niece said, "I remember she would always brag that she was one of the big 10, was a great, big, beauty doll, and had once sat on the lap of King Fuad (Egypt).

Did Wanda retain in older age the beautiful of her youth? "I wouldn't say that," her niece replied. "To be honest about it, I thought Wanda was a pain in the neck. You see, she was always acting. When she would arrive or leave our house, she'd wave very dramatically as if she was leaving for a premiere or going on a long voyage."[53]

Or, could Wanda have simply been waving to the parade gone by?

1. A bit of a mystery surrounds Wanda's use of the name Selma over the years. The 1900 U.S. Federal Census shows Wanda and her four siblings living with their parents, Robert and Martha Pittack. The statistics show that Martha was the mother of five children (including Wanda and Selma) and that all five are living. The 1910 U.S. Federal Census shows another son, Arthur, born to the family in 1905. The Pittack household now contained four children. One was married and lived nearby. Selma was shown in the household; Wanda was not. For Martha, their mother, the statistics show that, of the six children born to her, only five are living. All are accounted for, with the exception of Wanda. An interview with a member of Wanda's family failed to shed light on which sibling died.

2. The birth year is consistent with the 1900 U.S. Federal Census and her death certificate, County of Los Angeles, Registrar/Recorder/County Clerk, Death Certificate, no. 5316. Wanda typically used 1897 as her year of birth.

3. Hawley, Wanda, "The Story of My Life," *Pantomime*, 29 October 1921.

4. Ibid.

5. Ibid.

6. Hawley, Wanda, "The Story of My Life," *Pantomime*, 29 October 1921.

7. Ibid.

8. *Variety*, 27 April 1917.

9. *"Wanda Changes Name,"* March 1918.

10. *Variety*, 6 February 1920.

11. *Variety*, 27 June 1919.

12. Bebe Daniels, Alice Brady, Mary Miles Minter, May McAvoy, Constance Binney, and Julia Faye were other actresses who joined Realart.

13. "In the Film Firmament," *The New York Times*, 21 March 1920.

14. 1920 U.S. Federal Census.

15. Robert Pittack later became a successful cameraman at Paramount.

16. *Variety*, 10 December 1920.

17. *Variety*, 25 February 1921.

18. *The Affairs of Anatol* also provides film buffs the best opportunity to see Wanda Hawley at her best.

19. *The New York Times*, 21 September 1921.

20. Tim Lussier, *Silents are Golden* (http://www.silentsaregolden.com/featurefolder3/aacommentary.html).

21. *Variety*, 8 September 1922.

22. Tinee, Mae, *The Chicago Tribune*, 22 October 1922.

23. Leider, Emily W., *Dark Lover: The Life and Death of Rudolph Valentino*, Farrar, Straus and Giroux, 2003.

24. "Woman With Pistol Afraid of Thieves? Never! Says Wanda," July 1922.

25. "Blackmail Plot Kept as Secret, *Los Angeles Times*, 17 August 1922.

26. "News to me, Says Wanda on Divorce," *Los Angeles Times*, 20 December 1922.

27. United States of America, Department of State, passport applications for Selma Hawley and J. Stewart Wilkinson, issued 19 January 1923.

28. Wanda, Peeved at Dumbbell Role, is Anxious to Sail, 18 January 1923.

29. *The Lincoln State Journal*, 21 January 1923.

30. "Film Vampire Asks Divorce," *Los Angeles Times*, 9 February 1923.

31. "Wanda's Mate is Incensed," *Los Angeles Times*, 10 February 1923.

32. Ibid.

33. Ibid.

34. Jungmeyer, Jack, "*Real Sheiks Seldom Found Under 50*," 28 October 1923.

35. Ibid.

36 "Decree to Wanda Hawley," *Los Angeles Times*, 31 October 1923.

37. "Decree to Wanda Hawley," *Los Angeles Times*, 31 October 1923.

38. Allen Burton Hawley, according to the *Los Angeles Times*, died at age 30, on 12 September 1925. He had been ill for several months.

39. "Ince Star will Wed Again," *Los Angeles Times*, 22 July 1925.

40 Kingsley, Grace, "Stella Thrills Over Mabel Normand Party and Hawley Wedding," Los Angeles Times, 16 August 1925.

41. *Variety*, 27 January 1925.

42. *Variety*, 14 July 1926.

43. "Actress is Sued on Drunk Charge," 29 May 1929.

44. *The Sheboygan Press*, Sheboygan, Wisconsin, 6 May 1930.

45. "Wanda Hawley Here in Person," *The Ogden Standard-Examiner*, 6 August 1931.

46. "Movie Actress Divorced," *The Times Recorder*, Zanesville, Ohio, 10 June 1933.

47. Slide, Anothony, *Silent Portraits: Stars of the Silent Screen in Historic Photographs*, The Vestal Press, 1999.

48. Interview with Michael G. Ankerich, 2009.

49. "Female Star of Old Silent Movies Enjoys Farm Life," *The Lowell Sun*, 17 April 1941.

50. 'Wanda Hawley Dies in Utica," 4 June 1941.

51. "Identity of Former Film Star Confused," 5 June 1941.

52. Interview with Michael G. Ankerich, 2009.

53. Ibid.

FILMOGRAPHY

1917

The Derelict (Fox) D: *Carl Harbaugh.* Stuart Holmes, Mary Martin, Vinnie Burns, Carl Eckstrom, Dan Mason, Wanda Hawley *(Petit)*, Olive Trevor.

The Broadway Sport (Fox) D: *Carl Harbaugh.* Stuart Holmes, Wanda Hawley *(Petit)*, Dan Mason, Mabel Rutter, William B. Green, J. Sullivan, Mario Majeroni, Jay Wilson.

This is the Life (Fox) D: *Raoul Walsh.* George Walsh, Wanda Hawley *(Petit)*, James A. Marcus, Ralph Lewis, Jack McDonald, William Ryno, Hector Sarno.

The Heart of a Lion (Fox) D: *Frank Lloyd.* William Farnum, Mary Martin, William Courtleigh Jr., Wanda Hawley *(Petit)*, Walter Law, Marc Robbins, Rita Bori.

1918

Cupid's Roundup (Fox) D: *Edward J. LeSaint.* Tom Mix, Wanda Hawley *(Petit)*, Edwin B. Tilton, Roy Watson, Verna Mersereau, Alfred Paget, Frederick R. Clark, Eugenie Forde.

Cheating the Public (Fox) D: *Richard Stanton.* Enid Markey, Ralph Lewis, Bertram Grassby, Tom Wilson, Edward Peil, Charles Edler, Wanda Petit, Carrie Clark Ward, Fanny Midgley, Frankie Lee, Barbara Conley, Baby Cohen, James Titus, Henry Peal, Joseph Hartley, James Morgan, Arthur Glynn, James McNeil, Arthur Shilling, Count von Hardenburg, Miles McCormack, Beverly Griffith.

Mr. Fix-It (Famous Players-Lasky, Artcarft) D: *Allan Dwan.* Douglas Fairbanks, Wanda Hawley, Marjorie Daw, Frank Campeau, Katherine MacDonald, Leslie Stuart, Ida Waterman, Alice H. Smith, Mrs. H.R. Hancock, Mr. Russell, Fred Goodwins, Margaret Landis, Pauline Curley, Jack Pickford.

We Can't Have Everything (Artcraft) D: *Cecil B. DeMille.* Kathlyn Williams, Elliott Dexter, Wanda Hawley, Sylvia Breamer, Thurston Hall, Raymond Hatton, Tully Marshall, Theodore Roberts, James Neill, Ernest Joy, William Elmer, Charles Ogle, Sylvia Ashton.

Old Wives for New (Artcraft) D: *Douglas Fairbanks.* Elliott Dexter, Florence Vidor, Sylvia Ashton, Wanda Hawley, Theodore Roberts, Helen Jerome Eddy, Marcia Manon, Julia Faye, J. Parks Jones, Edna Mae Cooper, Gustav von Seyffertitz, Tully Marshall, Lillian Leighton, Mayme Kelso, Alice Terry.

A Pair of Silk Stockings (Select Pictures) D: *Walter Edwards.* Constance Talmadge, Harrison Ford, Wanda Hawley, Vera Doria, Florence Carpenter, Thomas Persse, Louis Willoughby, Helen Haskell, Larry Steers, Robert Gordon, Sylvia Ashton.

The Border Wireless (Famous Players-Lasky) D: *William S. Hart.* William S. Hart, Wanda Hawley, Charles Arling, James Mason, E. von Ritzen, Berthold Sprotte, Marcia Manon.

The Gypsy Trail (Paramount) D: *Walter Edwards.* Bryant Washburn, Wanda Hawley, Casson Ferguson, C. H. Geldart, Georgie Stone, Edythe Chapman.

The Way of a Man with a Maid (Famous Players-Lasky) D: *Donald Crisp.* Bryant Washburn, Wanda Hawley, Fred Goodwins, Clarence Geldart, Jay Dwiggins, Bessie Eyton, William Elmer, James Neill.

1919

The Poor Boob (Famous Players-Lasky, Paramount) D: *Donald Crisp.* Bryant Washburn, Wanda Hawley, Dick Rosson, Theodore Roberts, Raymond Hatton, Jay Dwiggins, Charles Ogle, Jane Wolff, Mary Thurman, Guy Oliver, Clarence Geldart.

Virtuous Sinners (States Rights) D: *Emmett J. Flynn.* Norman Kerry, Wanda Hawley, Harry Holden, David Kirby, Bert Woodruff, Eunice Woodruff.

Greased Lightning (Famous Players-Lasky, Paramount) D: *Jerome Storm.* Charles Ray, Wanda Hawley, Robert McKim, Willis Marks, Bert Woodruff, John P. Lockney, Otto Hoffman.

For Better, for Worse (Famous Players–Lasky, Artcraft) D: *Cecil B. DeMille.* Elliott Dexter, Tom Forman, Gloria Swanson, Sylvia Ashton, Raymond Hatton, Theodore Roberts, Wanda Hawley, Winter Hall, Jack Holt, Fred Huntley.

Peg O' My Heart (Famous Players–Lasky, Paramount) D: *William C. DeMille.* Wanda Hawley, Barbara Castleton, Mayme Kelso, James Neill, Casson Ferguson.

You're Fired (Famous Players–Lasky, Paramount) D: *James Cruze.* Wallace Reid, Wanda Hawley, Henry Woodward, Theodore Roberts, Lillian Mason, Herbert Pryor, Raymond Hatton, William Lesta.

Secret Service (Famous Players–Lasky, Artcraft) D: *Hugh Ford.* Robert Warwick, Wanda Hawley, Theodore Roberts, Edythe Chapman, Raymond Hatton, Casson Ferguson, Robert Cain, Irving Cummings, Guy Oliver, Lillian Leighton, Stanley Wheatcroft, Norman Selby, Shirley Mason.

Told in the Hills (Famous Players–Lasky, Artcraft) D: *George Melford.* Robert Warwick, Ann Little, Tom Forman, Wanda Hawley, Charles Ogle, Monte Blue, Margaret Loomis, Eileen Percy, Hart Hoxie, Jack Herbert, Guy Oliver.

The Lottery Man (Famous Players–Lasky, Artcraft) D: *James Cruze.* Wallace Reid, Harrison Ford, Wanda Hawley, Fannie Midgely, Sylvia Ashton, Carolyn Rankin, Wilton Taylor, Clarence Geldart, Marcia Manon, Winifred Greenwood, Fred Huntley.

Everywoman (Famous Players–Lasky, Artcraft) D: *George H. Melford.* Theodore Roberts, Violet Heming, Clara Horton, Wanda Hawley, Margaret Loomis, Mildred Reardon, Edythe Chapman, Bebe Daniels, Monte Blue, Irving Cummings, James Neill, Raymond Hatton, Lucien Littlefield, Noah Beery, Jay Dwiggins, Tully Marshall.

1920

The Tree of Knowledge (Famous Players–Lasky, Artcraft) D: *William C. DeMille.* Theodore Kosloff, Yvonne Gardelle, Robert Warwick, Kathlyn Williams, Wanda Hawley, Tom Forman, Winter Hall, Irving Cummings, Loyola O'Connor, Clarence Geldart, William Brown.

179

The Six Best Cellars (Famous Players-Lasky, Artcraft) D: *Donald Crisp.* Bryant Washburn, Wanda Hawley, Clarence Burton, Elsa Lorimer, Josephine Crowell, Fred Vroom, Jane Wolfe, Richard Wayne, Julia Faye, Howard Gaye, Zelma Maja, Parker MacConnell, Ruth Ashby, William Boyd.

Double Speed (Famous Players-Lasky, Artcraft) D: *Sam Wood.* Wallace Reid, Wanda Hawley, Tully Marshall, Theodore Roberts, Lucien Littlefield, Guy Oliver, Maxine Elliott Hicks.

Mrs. Temple's Telegram (Famous Players-Lasky, Artcraft) D: *Bryant Washburn.* Wanda Hawley, Carmen Phillips, Walter Hiers, Sylvia Ashton, Leo White, Anne Schaefer, Edward Jobson.

Miss Hobbs (Realart Pictures) D: *Donald Crisp.* Wanda Hawley, Harrison Ford, Helen Jerome Eddy, Walter Hiers, Julianne Johnston, Emily Chichester, Frances Raymond, Jack Mulhall.

Food for Scandal (Realart Pictures) D: *James Cruze.* Wanda Hawley, Harrison Ford, Ethel Grey Terry, Margaret McWade, Minnie Provost, Juan de la Cruz, Sidney Bracey, Lester Cuneo.

Her Beloved Villain (Realart Pictures) D: *Sam Wood.* Wanda Hawley, Ramsey Wallace, F. Templar Powell, Tully Marshall, Lillian Leighton, Gertrude Claire, Robert Bolder, Margaret McWade, Harrison Ford, Irma Coonly, Jay Peters.

Held by the Enemy (Famous Players-Lasky, Paramount) D: *Donald Crisp.* Agnes Ayres, Wanda Hawley, Josephine Crowell, Lillian Leighton, Lewis Stone, Jack Holt, Robert Cain, Walter Hiers, Robert Brower, Clarence H. Geldart.

Her First Elopement (Realart Pictures) D: *Sam Wood.* Wanda Hawley, Jerome Patrick, Nell Craig, Lucien Littlefield, Jay Eaton, Helen Dunbar, Herbert Standing, Edwin Stevens, Margaret Morris, Ann Hastings, John MacKinnon.

1921

The Snob (Realart Pictures) D: *Sam Wood.* Wanda Hawley, Edwin Stevens, Walter Hiers, Sylvia Ashton, William E. Lawrence, Julia Faye, Richard Wayne.

The Outside Woman (Realart Pictures) Wanda Hawley, Clyde Fillmore, Sidney Bracey, Rosita Marstini, Misao Seki, Thena Jasper, Mary Winston, Jacob Abrams.

The House That Jazz Built (Realart Pictures) D: *Penrhyn Stanlaws.* Wanda Hawley, Forrest Stanley, Gladys George, Helen Lynch, Clarence Geldert, Helen Dunbar, Robert Bolder.

A Kiss in Time (Realart Pictures) D: *Thomas N. Heffron.* Wanda Hawley, T. Roy Barnes, Bertram Johns, Walter Hiers, Margaret Loomis.

Her Sturdy Oak (Realart Pictures) D: *Thomas N. Heffron.* Wanda Hawley, Walter Hiers, Sylvia Ashton, Mayme Kelso, Leo White, Frederick Stanton.

The Affairs of Anatol (Paramount) D: *Cecil B. DeMille.* Wallace Reid, Gloria Swanson, Elliott Dexter, Bebe Daniels, Monte Blue, Wanda Hawley, Theodore Roberts, Agnes Ayres, Theodore Kosloff, Polly Moran, Raymond Hatton, Julia Faye, Charles Ogle, Winter Hall.

Her Face Value (Paramount) D: *Thomas N. Heffron.* Wanda Hawley, Lincoln Plummer, Dick Rosson, T. Roy Barnes, Winifred Bryson, Donald MacDonald, Harvey Clark, George Periolat, Eugene Burr, Ah Wing.

The Love Charm (Realart Pictures) D: *Thomas N. Heffron.* Wanda Hawley, Mae Busch, Sylvia Ashton, Warner Baxter, Carrie Clark Ward, Molly McGowan.

1922

Too Much Wife (Realart Pictures) D: *Thomas N. Heffron.* Wanda Hawley, T. Roy Barnes, Arthur Hoyt, Lillian Langdon, Leigh Wyant, Willard Louis, Bertram Johns, John Fix.

Bobbed Hair (Realart Pictures) D: *Thomas N. Heffron.* Wanda Hawley, William Boyd, Adele Farrington, Leigh Wyant, Jane Starr, Margaret Vilmore, William P. Carleton, Ethel Wales, Junior Coghlan, Robert Kelly.

The Truthful Liar (Realart Pictures) D: *Thomas N. Heffron.* Wanda Hawley, Edward Hearn, Charles Stevenson, Casson Ferguson, Lloyd Whitlock, George Siegmann, E.A. Warren, Charles K. French.

The Woman Who Walked Alone (Paramount) D: *George Melford.* Dorothy Dalton, Milton Sills, E.J. Radcliffe, Wanda Hawley, Frederick Vroom, Maym Kelso, John Davidson, Harris Gordon, Charles Ogle, Mable Van Buren, Maurice B. Flynn, Cecil Holland, John MacKinnon.

Burning Sands (Paramount) D: *George Melford.* Wanda Hawley, Milton Sills, Louise Dresser, Jacqueline Logan, Robert Cain, Fenwick Oliver, Winter Hall, Harris Gordon, Albert Roscoe, Cecil Holland, Joe Ray.

The Young Rajah (Paramount) D: *Philip Rosen.* Rudolph Valentino, Wanda Hawley, Pat Moore, Charles Ogle, Fanny Midgley, Robert Ober, Jack Giddings, Edward Jobson, Josef Swickard, Bertram Grassby, J. Farrell MacDonald, George Periolat, George Field, Maude Wayne, William Boyd, Joseph Harrington, Spottiswoode Aitken.

1923

Thirty Days (Paramount) D: *James Cruze.* Wallace Reid, Wanda Hawley, Charles Ogle, Cyril Chadwick, Herschel Mayall, Helen Dunbar, Carmen Phillips, Kalla Pasha, Robert Brower.

Nobody's Money (Paramount) D: *Wallace Worsley.* Jack Holt, Wanda Hawley, Harry Depp, Robert Schable, Walter McGrail, Josephine Crowell, Julia Faye, Charles Clary, Aileen Manning, James Neill.

Brass Commandments (Fox) D: *Lynn F. Reynolds.* William Farnum, Wanda Hawley, Tom Santschi, Claire Adams, Charles Le Moyne, Joe Rickson, Lon Poff, Al Fremont, Joseph Gordon, Cap Anderson.

Masters of Men (Vitagraph) D: *David Smith.* Earle Williams, Alice Calhoun, Cullen Landis, Wanda Hawley, Dick Sutherland, Charles Mason, Bert Apling, Jack Curtis, Martin Turner.

Mary of the Movies (Columbia) D: *John McDermott.* Marion Mack, Florence Lee, Mary Kane, Harry Cornelli, John Geough, Raymond Cannon, Rosemary Cooper, Creighton Hale, Francis McDonald, Henry Burrows, John McDermott, Jack Perrin, Ray Harford, Barbara La Marr, Douglas MacLean, Bryant Washburn, Johnnie Walker, J. Warren Kerrigan, Herbert Rawlinson, Alec Francis, Richard Travers, David Butler, Louise Fazenda, Anita Stewart, Estelle Taylor, Rosemary Theby, Bessie Love, Marjorie Daw, Tom Moore, Elliott Dexter, ZaSu Pitts, Carmel Myers, Rex Ingram, Maurice Tourneur, Edward J. Le Saint, Wanda Hawley.

The Man from Brodney's (Vitagraph) D: *David Smith.* J. Warren Kerrigan, Alice Calhoun, Wanda Hawley, Miss Du Pont, Pat O'Malley, Kathleen Key, Bertram Grassby.

1924

The Desert Sheik (Truart Film Corp.) D: *Tom Terriss.* Wanda Hawley, Nigel Barrie, Pedro De Cordoba, Edith Craig, Arthur Cullen, Stewart Rome, Douglas Munro, Percy Standing, Cyril Smith, Hamed El Gabrey.

Bread (Metro-Goldwyn Pictures) D: *Victor Schertzinger.* Mae Busch, Robert Frazer, Pat O,Malley, Wanda Hawley, Eugenie Besserer, Hobart Bosworth, Myrtle Stedman, Ward Crane.

Reckless Romance (Producers Distributing Corp) D: *Scott Sidney.* T. Roy Barnes, Harry Myers, Wanda Hawley, Sylvia Breamer, Tully Marshall, Jack Duffy, Lincoln Plumer, Morgan Wallace, George French.

The Man Who Played Square (Fox) D: *Al Santell.* Buck Jones, Ben Hendricks Jr., David Kirby, Hank Mann, Howard Foster, William Scott, Wanda Hawley.

1925

Barriers Burned Away (Encore Pictures) D: *W.S. Van Dyke.* Mabel Ballin, Eric Mayne, Frank Mayo, Wanda Hawley, Wally Van, Arline Pretty, Harry T. Morey, James Mason, J.P. Lockney, Mrs. Charles Craig, William V. Mong, Pat Harmon, Frankie Mann.

Let Women Alone (Producers Distributing Corp) D: *Paul Powell.* Pat O'Malley, Wanda Hawley, Wallace Beery, Ethel Wales, J. Farrell MacDonald, Harris Gordon, Betty Jane Snowdon, Lee Willard, Marjorie Morton.

Smouldering Fires (Universal) D: *Clarence Brown.* Pauline Frederick, Laura La Plante, Malcolm McGregor, Tully Marshall, Wanda Hawley, Helen Lynch, George Cooper, Bert Roach, Billy Gould, Rolfe Sedan, Jack McDonald, William Orlamond.

Who Cares (Columbia) D: *Douglas Doty.* C: Dorothy Devore, William Haines, Lloyd Whitlock, Beverly Bayne, Wanda Hawley, Vola Vale, Charlie Murray, Vera Lewis, Ralph Lewis, William Austin, Carrie Clark Ward.

Stop Flirting (Producers Distributing Corp) D: *Scott Sidney*. John
T. Murray, Wanda Hawley, Hallam Cooley, Ethel Shannon, Vera
Steadman, Jimmie Adams, Jack Duffy, Jimmy Harrison, David James.

Graustark (First National) D: *Dimitri Buchowetzki*. Norma Talmadge,
Eugene O'Brien, Marc MacDermott, Roy D'Arcy, Albert Gran, Lillian
Lawrence, Michael Vavitch, Frank Currier, Winter Hall, Wanda
Hawley.

Flying Fool (Aywon Film Corp) D: *Frank S. Mattison*. Gaston Glass,
Dick Grace, Wanda Hawley, Mary Land, Dorothy Vernon, Dick
Sutherland, Eddie Harris, Milburn Morante.

American Pluck (Chadwick Pictures) D: *Richard Stanton*. George Walsh,
Wanda Hawley, Sidney De Grey, Frank Leigh, Tom Wilson, Leo
White, Dan Mason.

The Unnamed Woman (Arrow Pictures) D: *Harry O. Hoyt*. Katherine
MacDonald, Herbert Rawlinson, Wanda Hawley, Leah Baird, John
Miljan, Mike Donlin, Grace Gordon, J. Emmett Beck.

1926

A Desperate Moment (Banner Productions) D: *Jack Dawn*. Wanda
Hawley, Theodore von Eltz, Sheldon Lewis, Leo White, Dan Mason,
James Neill, Bill Franey.

Midnight Limited (Rayart Pictures) D: *Oscar Apfel*. Gaston Glass,
Wanda Hawley, Sam Allen, William Humphrey, Mathilda Brundage,
Richard Holt, L.J. O'Connor, Eric Mayne, Fred Holmes, Hayford
Hobbs.

The Combat (Universal) D: *Lynn Reynolds*. House Peters, Wanda Hawley,
Walter McGrail, C.E. Anderson, Charles Mailes, Steve Clemento,
Howard Truesdale.

The Last Alarm (Rayart Pictures) D: *Oscar Apfel*. Rex Lease, Wanda
Hawley, Maurice Costello, Florence Turner, Theodore von Eltz, Hazel
Howell, Jimmy Aubrey.

Hearts and Spangles (Gotham Productions) D: *Frank O'Connor*. Wanda
Hawley, Robert Gordon, Barbara Tennant, Eric Mayne, Frankie
Darrow, Larry Steers, J.P. Lockney, Charles Force.

Men of the Night (Sterling Pictures) D: *Albert Rogell.* Herbert Rawlinson, Garethh Hughes, Wanda Hawley, Lucy Beaumont, Jay Hunt, Mathilda Brundage.

The Midnight Message (Goodwill Pictures) D: *Paul Hurst.* Wanda Hawley, Mary Carr, John Fox Jr., Stuart Holmes, Creighton Hale, Mathilda Brundage, Otis Harlan, Earl Metcalf, Karl Silvera, Wilson Benge.

The Smoke Eaters (Rayart Pictures) Cullen Landis, Wanda Hawley, Edward Cecil, Aryel Darma, Broderick O'Farrell, Mae Prestelle, Harold Austin, Baby Moncur.

Whom Shall I Marry (Aywon Film Corp) Wanda Hawley, Elmo Lincoln, Mary Carr.

1927

Eyes of the Totem (Pathé) D: *W.S. Van Dyke.* Wanda Hawley, Tom Santschi, Anne Cornwall, Gareth Hughes, Bert Woodruff, Monte Wax, Violet Palmer, Mary Louise Jones, Dorothy Llewellyn, Nell Barry Taylor.

Pirates of the Sky (Pathé) D: *Charles Andrews.* Charles Hutchison, Wanda Hawley, Crauford Kent, Jimmy Aubrey, Ben Walker.

1931

Trails of the Golden West (States Rights) D: *Leander De Cordova.* Buffalo Bill Jr., Wanda Hawley, Tom London, George Reed, Horace Carpenter, William Bertram, William McCormick, Chief White Eagle.

The Pueblo Terror (States Rights) D: *Alvin J. Neitz.* Buffalo Bill Jr., Jack Harvey, Wanda Hawley, James P. Spencer, Aline Goodwin, Art Mix, Yakima Canutt, Horace Carpenter, Al Ferguson, Hank Bell, Robert Walker.

Gratefully
Natalie Joyce

NATALIE JOYCE

"Oh, my God, you're kidding!" was Natalie Joyce's response when her husband told the phone was for her and that the caller wanted to talk about silent films. The year was 1991, and Natalie was almost 90, blind, and in poor health.

As it turned out, Natalie was more than willing to answer a few questions about her cousin Olive Borden, a hard luck girl included in this book, but when it came to discussing her own career, she quickly put on the brakes.

A follow-up letter to her was answered by her son who said his mother politely declined to discuss her work in silent films and that "she did not give a reason."

Cousins Olive Borden and Natalie Johnson — their mothers were sisters — were always being compared. They were born in Virginia and both given the middle name Marie. Olive was raised an only child by her mother after her father died when Olive was an infant. Natalie had seven siblings.

Natalie got to Hollywood first, in the early 1920s. Olive and her mother came several years later with all hopes resting on her for the two's future. 1925 was a pivotal year for both dark-haired, exquisite beauties. They signed a contact with Fox Studios and were Wampas Baby Stars for their star potential.

Olive quickly overshadowed Natalie in popularity and became the star of the family. After several years of blazing across the Hollywood sky, however, Olive, the Joy Girl of the silent screen, crashed and burned, professionally, financially, and personally. She ended up skidding down a one-way street into skid row.

Natalie was more measured in her quest to become somebody in films. She was not willing to do anything for a successful stint in Hollywood. Having ended her career as she began, in comedy shorts, Natalie bowed out while she still had her sanity. She got the hell out of Hollywood.

Natalie offered two explanations why her career never really took off. First, she took seriously a response made by director Howard Hawks when she asked his opinion about her future in the movies.

Second, Natalie told a friend at the time that her career was hampered by her avoidance of the proverbial casting couch. She believed her refusal to put out directly impacted her weak cinema output. Sure, she was chased around the desk, but unlike other gals, she kept moving!

She was born Natalie Marie Johnson on November 6, 1902, in Virginia. She was one of eight children (six girls and two boys) born to Henry Frank[1] and Elizabeth Shields Johnson. Natalie was third in line.

The Johnsons moved to Pittsburgh when Natalie was still a child. It was there that her and her sisters recognized and cultivated their theatrical talent. By the time she was 18, Natalie was intent on pursuing a career on the stage.

By 1920, Natalie and her oldest sister had made their way to New York and were soon dancing in the Ziegfeld Follies. In 1922, Natalie and her family moved to Los Angeles. Natalie had little trouble getting work as a dancer in cafes and hotels around Hollywood.

It was while Natalie was twirling on her feet one evening that comedy pioneer Al Christie noticed the dark-haired beauty and went backstage to meet her. The "you should be in pictures" talk ensued and before she knew it, Natalie had signed a contract with Christie Comedies. She traded the footlights for the Klieg lights.

The news of her contract hit the papers. "Natalie Johnson, formerly of the Ziegfeld Follies, is new in the movies with Christie Comedies. While Christie has contributed a number of his comedy girls to New York shows, this is the first instance in which he has received one back."[2] "She is a petite little maid and promises to brighten up many a two-reeler in the future."[3]

She was billed as Natalie Johnson for the first year or so in such comedies as *Mile-a-Minute Mary*, *Be Yourself*, *Take Your Choice*, *Savage Love*, and *Why Hurry?* She later adopted Natalie Joyce as her professional name.

The studio quickly capitalized on Natalie's beauty and curvy figure. They dressed her in the finest gowns and cast her often as the vamp out to pull the man into her web.

After Natalie established herself in the movies, her aunt and cousin, Sibbie and Olive Borden, packed up their lives and moved from Virginia to Hollywood in hopes of getting Olive into the action. Natalie said the two relatives lived with her and her mother when they first arrived in town.

While it would seem feasible that Natalie would use her contacts in the industry to secure Olive work in the movies, Natalie insisted in an interview that she had no part in helping her cousin. Olive's ambition and Sibbie's guidance and oversight were all they needed.

Natalie and Olive were named Wampas Baby Stars in 1925 for their potential star power, along with Dorothy Revier, June Marlowe, Betty Arlen, Madeline Hurlock, Violet Avon, Anne Cornwall, Ena Gregory, Joan Meredith, Evelyn Pierce, and Duane Thompson. Roy Liebman, author of *The*

Natalie Joyce in a scene from The Daffy Dill *(1926).*

Wampas Baby Stars, noted that 1925 was another year of mixed results for the chosen starlets. "Some remained in obscurity while a few, including June Marlowe, Dorothy Revier, and Olive Borden, found minor stardom."[4]

Being named a Wampas Baby had no immediate impact on Natalie's career. She continued working in two-reelers through 1925 and most of 1926.

In early 1927, she left Christie Comedies and signed a contract with Fox Studios. She was cast first with cowboy Buck Jones in *Whispering Sage* (1927). Natalie, as Mercedes, is among a group of Basque settlers who have located in the Nevada desert. They are terrorized by a greedy landowner whose intent is to drive them from the area.

Variety singled out Natalie for her performance. "In Natalie Joyce, lead-

Natalie Joyce (fifth from the left) and her cousin, Olive Borden (fourth from the left), among other Wampas Baby Stars of 1925]

ing woman, who seems to be a newcomer, the cast has a strong set. She is thoroughly in the picture for the Spanish type and plays with a good deal of restrained force and reserve. With this role as a sample, she looks like a possibility for more ambitious parts calling for the flashing, dark-eyed brunet type."[5]

Natalie followed *Whispering Sage* with another success, *The Circus Ace*, with Tom Mix, the king of the silent cowboys. In the picture, Mix, a sharpshooter and roping specialist, joins a traveling circus and falls for Natalie, the beautiful trapeze artist. It was perhaps Natalie's finest performance on film.

"It's a evenly balanced picture, and has a new leading woman or at least one who sounds new, Natalie Joyce, a girl who can do something else besides wearing make-up, may be adding an extra charm," noted *Variety*. "Miss Joyce is an athlete or gymnast. Despite any doubling or camera faking, the girl handles herself like an aerialist. And, Miss Joyce can smile without her mouth looking like a purple chasm."[6]

Natalie reunited with Mix in *Daredevil's Reward*, one of Mix's greatest successes. In this Western, Mix portrays a daredevil ranger on the trail

A glamorous Natalie Joyce.

of a gang of outlaws. Along the way, he falls for Natalie, the niece of the gang leader (William Welch). The film climaxes when Mix saves Natalie from a runaway car.

In *A Girl in Every Port* (1928), the action focuses on the rivalry of two sailors, Victor McLaglen and Robert Armstrong, for the women they have stashed away in ports around the world. Natalie portrays one of the

Tom Mix and Natalie Joyce in The Circus Ace *(1927)*

girls in Panama. Most of the attention from the public and critics went to Louise Brooks as Marie, the girl in France.

The film did nothing for Natalie's career, primarily because, as *Variety* stated, it "has a dozen ingénues and no heroine."[7] Natalie left Fox after *A Girl in Every Port* and worked in comedy shorts for Sennett and independent features for the rest of her career.

She was leading lady to Tom Tyler in two independent Westerns: *Law of the Plains* and *The Man from Nevada*. In her final features, other newcomers, such as Alice White, Alice Day, Sally Eilers, and Myrna Loy were the female leads.

Olive and Natalie appeared in *Dance Hall*, their first and only film together. Olive, in the leading role, comes to a nightclub where Natalie, in a bit role, served as hostess.

In May 1929, Natalie and actress Mildred Harris were question by authorities looking into the death of their friend, dancer Delphine Walsh, who succumbed following an illegal abortion. Natalie told investigators she had not seen Walsh in over a year.[8]

After her appearance in *Police Court*, an independent film featuring other silent film actors on the decline (King Baggot, Henry B. Walthall, and Aileen Pringle), Natalie abruptly retired from the screen.

She confessed in a conversation with silent film historian Roi Uselton that her quick departure from Hollywood centered on the realization that she had reached the limits of her success in the movie profession. She recalled a conversation with Howard Hawks, who directed her in *A Girl in Every Port*, in which she asked him for an honest assessment of her chances for success in the movies.

"Get married," was Hawks' short, but honest, answer. Rather than being offended by the comment, she took his words to heart.

In the early 1930s, with her film career behind her, Natalie married William Morris Pryce. The two moved to Hawaii, where Natalie embarked on a new profession. She and a sister opened a beauty salon. The Pryces had a son, Michael.

When her career was over and she'd left Hollywood, Natalie said she lost touch with Olive and never again heard from her cousin. In later years, the Pryces moved to Rancho Bernardo, California, where she died on November 9, 1992, three days after her 90th birthday. Her husband died four months later.

Natalie, in a later interview, concluded that she made the right decision to leave Hollywood when she did. First, she took serious Howard Hawks' advice to quit while she was ahead.

Alice Jordan, wife of Syd Jordan, a friend of Tom Mix who worked with him in many of his films, also recalled a conversation she had with Natalie way back in the 1920s.

"I'll never get anywhere in this business," Natalie told Jordan. "I won't put out!"[9]

1. The 1910 U.S. Federal Census lists Henry's occupation as a wallpaper hanger; the 1920 census indicates he was the owner of a retail market.

2. *Times*, Hammond, Indiana, 24 October 1922.

3. "Screen Comedies Lure Follies Girls: Petite Natalie Johnson Joins Christie Studios," *Capital Times*, Madison, Wisconsin, 2 September 1922.

4. Liebman, Roy, *The Wampas Baby Stars: A Biographical Dictionary, 1922-1934*, McFarland & Company, Inc., 2000.

5. *Variety*, 6 April 1927.

6. *Variety*, 6 July 1927.

7. *Variety*, 22 February 1928.

8. "Movie Actresses Fail to Help Solve Mystery," *San Antonio Light*, San Antonio, Texas, 10 May 1929.

9. Birchard, Robert S., *King Cowboy: Tom Mix and the Movies*, Riverwood Press, 1993.

FILMOGRAPHY

1922

Mile-a-Minute Mary (short) (Christie) D: *Harold Beaudine.* Dorothy Devore, Henry Murdock, Isabel Bryant, Ward Caulfield, Harry Edwards, George B. French, Natalie Joyce *(as Natalie Johnson)*, Helen Thomas.

1923

Be Yourself (short) (Christie) D: *Al Christie.* Neal Burns, Ward Caulfield, George B. French, Natalie Joyce *(as Natalie Johnson)*, Babe London, Charlotte Merriam, Henry Murdock, Lincoln Plumer.

Take Your Choice (short) (Christie) D: *Scott Sidney.* Bobby Vernon, Charlotte Stevens, Harry Dunkinson, Ward Caulfield, William Irving, Duane Thompson, Natalie Joyce *(as Natalie Johnson)*, Gladys Baxter, Margaret Cloud.

Roll Along (short) (Christie) D: *Scott Sidney.* Jimmie Adams, Natalie Joyce, William Irving, Babe London, Don Bailey, Ward Caulfield.

Fool Proof (short) (Christie) D: *Harold Beaudine.* Neal Burns, Rosa Gore, Natalie Joyce, Lincoln Plumer, Vera Steadman.

1924

Dandy Lions (short) (Christie) D: *Archie Mayo.* Neal Burns, Natalie Joyce, Lila Leslie, Jay Belasco.

Tootsie Wootsie (short) (Christie) D: *Archie Mayo.* Neal Burns, Jay Belasco, Natalie Joyce, Earle Rodney, Vera Steadman, Bobby Vernon.

Savage Love (short) (Christie) D: *Scott Sidney.* Jimmie Adams, Vera Steadman, Earle Rodney, James Harrison, Lila Leslie, Harry Dunkinson, Natalie Joyce *(as Natalie Johnson)*, Jack Duffy.

Why Hurry? *(short) (Christie)* D: *Harold Beaudine.* Jimmie Adams, Kathleen Myers, Baby Bunting, Eddie Baker, Natalie Joyce *(as Natalie Johnson)*, Ward Caulfield.

Easy Pickin's (short) (Christie) D: *Harold Beaudine.* Neal Burns, Eddie Baker, Ward Caulfield, Natalie Joyce *(as Natalie Johnson)*, Molly Malone, Victor Rodman.

1925

Call a Cop (short) (Christie) D: *Walter Graham.* William Blaisdell, Neal Burns, William Irving, Natalie Joyce.

1926

Fresh Faces (short) (Christie) D: *Harold Beaudine.* Walter Hiers, Duane Thompson, Yola d'Avril, Natalie Joyce, William Blaisdell, Eddie Baker.

The Daffy Dill (short) (Christie) D: *William Watson.* Neal Burns, Edna Marion, Natalie Joyce, William Irving.

Wife Shy (short) (Christie) D: *William Watson.* Bobby Vernon, Frances Lee, Natalie Joyce, William Irving, James Harrison.

A Briny Boob (short) (Christie) D: *William Watson.* Billy Dooley, Natalie Joyce.

1927

Break Away (short) (Christie) D: *Harold Beaudine.* Jimmie Adams, Natalie Joyce, Neal Burns, Jack Duffy, Eddie Baker, William Irving, Gale Henry.

Whispering Sage (Fox) D: *Scott R. Dunlap.* Buck Jones, Natalie Joyce, Emile Chautard, Carl Miller, Albert J. Smith, Joseph W. Girard, William Steele, Ellen Winston, Hazel Keener, Enrique Acosta, Joe Rickson.

A Spanish Omelet (Fox) (short) D: *Ray Flynn.* Natalie Joyce.

The Circus Ace (Fox) D: *Benjamin Stoloff.* Tom Mix, Natalie Joyce, Jack Baston, Duke R. Lee, James Bradbury Sr. , Stanley Blystone, Dudley Smith, Buster Gardner.

1928

Daredevil's Reward (Fox) D: *Eugene Forde.* Tom Mix, Natalie Joyce , Lawford Davidson, Billy Bletcher, Harry Cording, William Welsh.

A Girl in Every Port (Fox) D: *Howard Hawks.* Robert Armstrong, Louise Brooks, Natalie Joyce, Maria Casajuana, Leila Hyams, Elena Jurado, Natalie Kingston, Caryl Lincoln, Dorothy Mathews, Francis McDonald, Phalba Morgan, Sally Rand, Eileen Sedgwick, Felix Valle.

Caught in the Kitchen (Mack Sennett) (short) D: *Phil Whitman.* Billy Bevan, Natalie Joyce, Irving Bacon, Alice Ward, Barbara Pierce.

Through the Breakers (Gotham) D: *Joseph C. Boyle.* Billy Bevan, Natalie Joyce, Irving Bacon, Alice Ward, Barbara Pierce.

Hubby's Weekend Trip (Sennett) (short) D: *Harry Edwards.* Billy Bevan, Dot Farley, Vernon Dent, Carmelita Geraghty, Alma Bennett, Carole Lombard, Anita Barnes, Lucille Miller, Kathryn Stanley, Leota Winters, Betty Amann, Natalie Joyce.

Naughty Baby (First National) D: *Mervyn LeRoy.* Alice White, Jack Mulhall, Thelma Todd, Doris Dawson, James Ford, Natalie Joyce, Frances Hamilton, Fred Kelsey, Rose Dione, Fanny Midgley, Larry Banthim, George E. Stone, Benny Rubin, Andy Devine.

His New Steno (Sennett) (short) D: *Phil Whitman.* Billy Bevan, Irving Bacon, Natalie Joyce, Alice Ward.

Hubby's Latest Alibi (Sennett) (short) D: *Phil Whitman.* Billy Bevan, Natalie Joyce, Alice Ward, Otto Fries, Virginia Vance.

1929

Pink Pajamas (Sennett) (short) D: *Phil Whitman.* Billy Bevan, Vernon Dent, Elinor Field, Madeline Hurlock, Natalie Joyce, Alice Ward.

Laughing at Death [Film Booking Offices of America (FBO)] D: *Wallace Fox.* Bob Steele, Natalie Joyce, Captain Vic, Kai Schmidt, Ethan Laidlaw, Armand Triller, Hector Sarno, Golden Wadhams.

Motoring Mamas (Sennett) (short) D: *Phil Whitman.* Billy Bevan, Glen Cavender, Vernon Dent, Billy Gilbert, Natalie Joyce, Alice Ward.

Pals of the Prairie [Film Booking Offices of America (FBO)] D: *Louis King*. Buzz Barton, Frank Rice, Thomas G. Lingham, Duncan Renaldo, Milburn Morante, Natalie Joyce, Bill Patton.

Law of the Plains (J.P. McGowan Productions) D: *J.P. McGowan*. Tom Tyler, Natalie Joyce, Al Ferguson, J.P. McGowan.

The Man from Nevada (J.P. McGowan Productions) D: *J.P. McGowan*. Tom Tyler, Natalie Joyce, Al Ferguson, Alfred Hewston, Kip Cooper, Godfrey Craig, Frank Hall Crane, William L. Nolte.

Sailor's Holiday (Pathé) D: *Fred C. Newmeyer*. Alan Hale, Sally Eilers, George Cooper, Paul Hurst, Mary Carr, Charles Clary, Jack Richardson, Natalie Joyce, Philip Sleeman.

Times Square (Gotham) D: *Joseph C. Boyle*. Alice Day, Arthur Lubin, Emile Chautard, Ann Brody, John Miljan, Arthur Housman, Josef Swickard, Natalie Joyce, Eddie Kane, Nat Ross.

The Fatal Forcep (Christie) (short) D: *William Watson*. Ford Sterling, Bert Roach, Will King, Natalie Joyce.

Weak But Willing (Sennett) (short) D: *William Watson*. Billy Bevan, Dot Farley, Otto Fries, Natalie Joyce, Will King, Jean Harlow.

Camera Shy (Educational Films Corporation of America) D: *Gilbert Pratt*. Lloyd Hamilton, Ruth Hiatt, Harry Woods, William T. Hayes, Natalie Joyce, Charles King.

1930

The Bearded Lady (Christie) (short) D: *William Watson*. Louise Fazenda, George E. Stone, Charley Grapewin, Frank Rice, Monte Montague, Natalie Joyce, Carol Wines, Rosemary La Planche.

Cock o' the Walk (James Cruze Productions) D: *Walter Lang*, Roy William Neill. Joseph Schildkraut, Myrna Loy, Philip Sleeman, Edward Peil Sr., John Beck, Olive Tell, Wilfred Lucas, Frank Jonasson, Sally Long, Natalie Joyce.

Midnight Daddies (Sennett) (short) D: *Mack Sennett*. Andy Clyde, Harry Gribbon, Rosemary Theby, Addie McPhail, Alma Bennett, Jack Cooper, Kathrin Clare Ward, Vernon Dent, Natalie Joyce.

Police Court *(I.E. Chadwick Productions)* D: *Louis King*. Henry B. Walthall, Leon Janney, Lionel Belmore, King Baggot, Al St. John, Edmund Breese, Aileen Pringle, Walter James, Al Bridge, Bud Osborne, Paul Panzer, Natalie Joyce, Jack Richardson, Fred 'Snowflake' Toones.

Lest you forget
Barbara La Marr

BARBARA LA MARR

Eighteen-year-old Reatha Dale Watson stood before the chief juvenile officer and waited anxiously for his declaration.

"We're sending you back home to your parents," he told her. Her offense? It was decided she was too beautiful to be alone in Los Angeles. "There are no charges against Miss Watson unless it be that she is dangerously beautiful."[1]

Reatha, with already one marriage behind her, returned to her parents, but vowed she would be back. Less than 10 years later, Reatha, now the famous Barbara La Marr, had vamped her way to the top echelon of Hollywood and through the endless nightlife and into the beds of countless suitors.

The moniker given to her by her juvenile officer in 1914, "Too Beautiful Girl," was a permanent part of her legend.

In the early 1920s, Barbara was living life in the fast lane that seemed to follow one dangerous curve after another. A writer for *Photoplay* likened Barbara to one of Edna St. Vincent Millay's famous poems:

"My candle burns at both ends;
It may not last the night;
But ah, my foes, and oh, my friends —
It gives a lovely light." [2]

For awhile, her candle burned bright, brighter than the Klieg lights that illuminated her "too beautiful" face, yet her world remained in darkness.

Barbara had tossed aside husbands and lovers, seemly never able to find the love she was craving. "I take my lovers, like roses, by the dozen," she was fond of saying.

Like the vamp she played on the screen, Barbara haunted the nightspots, her diet of booze and drugs kept her going to twilight. She had little time for rest. "I cheat nature," she would boast. "I never sleep more than two hours a day. I have better things to do."

Then, as her candle was burning low and her body and soul were wearing out, she discovered a bright light growing inside her body, a son that would ultimately illuminate her world.

Little Marvin gave her the unconditional love she was never able to find in five husbands and a string of lovers. Their life together spanned only five years, until her body, ravaged from dieting and addictions and neglect, gave out.

While she was lighting up the Jazz Age and life was good, Barbara penned a poem about moths and flames:

Moths? — I hate them.
You ask me "Why?"
Because to me they seem
Like the souls of foolish women
Who have passed on.
Poor illusioned, fluttering things
That find, now as always,
Irresistible the warmth of the
Flame —
Taking no heed of the warning
That merely singed their wings,
They flutter nearer, nearer —
Till wholly consumed
To filmy ashes of golden dust.
Foolish — fluttering — pitiful things —

And, in time, when the girl who was too beautiful finally gave out, she found her wings and joined the flutter.

Barbara La Marr was born Reatha Dale Watson on July 28, 1896[3] in Yakima, Washington, to William Wright and Rose Watson.[4] Barbara had two step siblings, Henry and Violet, from Rose's previous marriage, and a brother, William Watson Jr., born in 1886.[5]

Reatha grew up in the Pacific Northwest, where, early on, she developed a talent for acting and dancing. She made her professional debut in a stock company production of *Uncle Tom's Cabin* in 1904.

As she grew up, Reatha became a successful child actress and dancer. Her dark, exotic looks evolved along with her talent. From all accounts, Reatha Watson was already a stunning beauty when she entered her teenage years.

From Washington, the Watsons moved first to Fresno, California,[6] then to Burbank.

Reatha's long string of recorded escapades made printer's ink first in 1913 when her half-sister Violet and her companion, C.C. Boxley, were accused of kidnapping the 16-year-old. In the bizarre incident, Reatha told authorities she was taking a long ride with her sister and companion when, after they had driven through the San Fernando Valley and to Santa Barbara, she realized they intended to take her to San Francisco. Fearing bodily harm, she told authorities she offered no resistance and made no attempt to escape.[7]

Meanwhile, her concerned parents in Burbank alerted authorities, who issued warrants for the arrest of the alleged kidnappers. Violet and Boxley gave Reatha the money to return to Los Angeles and urged her to report to authorities a story that would protect them from any charges. The pair continued north.[8]

Back in Los Angeles, Reatha quickly become a fixture in the cafes, cabarets, and roadhouses. She started dancing professionally and was soon hoofing the nights away. She also began doing extra work in the movies. Her parents, concerned about the nightlife temptations that awaited their daughter, moved the family to El Centro, California, near the Mexican border.

For young Reatha, however, temptation was just around the corner. While visiting friends in nearby Yuma, Arizona, she met one Jack Lytell, a rancher, who fell madly for the stunning beauty. Perhaps to get away permanently from her parents, she agreed to marriage. The two reportedly lived happily for two months, but Mrs. Lytell soon became bored with the wide open spaces.

After several months in the desert, 16-year-old Reatha told friends she was returning to Los Angeles a widow; Jack Lytell, she said, had died of pneumonia. A queen of the night, Reatha's grief played out on the dance floor and in the arms of lounge lizards who comforted her.

Somewhere along the way, she caught the attention of juvenile authorities who declared she could no longer remain alone in Los Angeles. The reason? She was pronounced "too beautiful."

"There is no charge against Miss Watson unless it be that she is dangerously beautiful," the chief juvenile officer declared. "She is such an attractive girl that men follow her about. We found her at the Rockwood Apartments. We investigated and found that everything was satisfactory. There is, however, a constant danger hanging over girls who are alone in a city."[9]

What to do with the young beauty? Through information Reatha provided police, officials contacted her parents in El Centro, who asked that Reatha be returned home.

"Seizing this opportunity we told her she could choose between returning voluntarily to her parents and thus keep away from the white lights of the city, and being a ward of the juvenile court," the officer said. "She decided to return to her parents. We believe that despite the oddity of threatening to arrest a girl because she is beautiful, we are taking the right steps. We would rather find her guilty of being beautiful than anything else."[10]

Her stay in El Centro was brief, however. In June 1914, Reatha married Lawrence Converse.[11] They honeymooned in San Francisco. Back in Los Angeles, Amelia Converse told authorities she was the real Mrs. Converse and that her husband was mentally unbalanced after injuries he suffered while in prison in Mexico. San Francisco authorities began searching incoming trains in hopes of grabbing Converse on bigamy charges.[12]

When Converse surrendered to authorities, he said he did not remember marrying Reatha. "When I awoke this morning, I was lying under an orange tree beside the road. I had no recollection of how I came to be sleeping there or how I had come into possession of the suit case on which my head was pillowed. I was still more mystified when I opened the case and found it filled with cold cream and theatrical makeup and dainty pieces of women's wearing apparel. I was thunderstruck when my mother told me I was wanted on a charge of bigamy. I remember nothing about such a wedding. I know that I have been drinking heavily, and if I really did what I am charged with doing, I believe I must also have been drugged."[13]

Reatha told a different tale. "Lawrence was both sane and sober when I married him," she maintained. "If he had not been, the minister would not have married us."

Converse's problem of two wives was settled several weeks later when he collapsed and died of a cerebral hemorrhage.[14]

Several days later, Reatha, who had been appearing in small movie roles for some time, was officially barred from the studios. Studio heads were concerned about her exploits playing out in headlines.

One studio manager explained. "We don't want public characters or limelight beauties in our pictures; it may be a fine thing for stage folks, but it is ruinous for men and women who pose for the movies. It's hard enough to get things by the boards of censorship as it is. There are more morality demands in picture dramas which are seen by young children than is required from stage people."[15]

Reatha understood her dilemma. "The managers say perhaps when people have forgotten that my beauty made Lawrence Converse forget that he was married and caused him to lead me to the altar despite the fact that he had a wife and three children, and also when the public has ceased to think about some other matters which have caused my name to be printed in the papers, then I can get back to work — and not before."[16]

A few lurid headlines and queasy studio chiefs, however, couldn't saddle Reatha for long. She was soon back to work. It was while filming a two-reel Western that Reatha became Barbara La Marr.

"The lead, a Miss Marr, fell off her horse," Barbara's son explained in an interview for this book. "Someone asked my mother, 'Can you ride a horse?' 'Oh, sure,' she answered. When she finished the scene, they pegged her 'La Marr'".[17]

In 1915, after she concluded that perhaps the headlines had impaired her film possibilities, Barbara went north to San Francisco, where she formed a dancing partnership with Robert Carville. They soon became the most popular pair of dancers at Old Faithful Inn, Kisich's Saddle Rock, and other supper clubs.

Friends expected them to marry; however, Barbara had her sights on Phil Ainsworth, a popular musical comedy actor and ballroom dancer she met in San Francisco. Barbara eventually replaced Carville with Ainsworth as her dance partner. The two were married within a month. Their bliss, if there was such a thing, was short lived.

Two days after the wedding, Ainsworth was arrested on charges of selling an automobile that didn't belong to him or his wife; the automobile in question belonged to Robert Carville. Barbara had told Ainsworth she owed a car that was stored in an Oakland garage. They retrieved the car and were soon enjoying their honeymoon. Several days later and hard-up for cash, Ainsworth sold the automobile for $300. [18]

In a retaliatory move, Carville ordered Ainsworth's arrest. It was suspected that seeking revenge on the man who had robbed him of his dancing partner was more important than Carville's lost car. Testimony in the case revealed that Barbara had been in love with Carville, but he had rejected her advances, believing they would be more successful on the dance floor than the bed. The court, confused over the twists and turns of the case, eventually dropped the charges against Ainsworth.[19]

In June 1918, Ainsworth initiated divorce proceedings against Barbara, naming Robert Carville as correspondent. Several days later, a rumor circulated that Barbara had died from injuries she suffered to her back. She was found alive and working in a hotel grill in Salt Lake City. Those involved believed Barbara started the rumor in hopes that Ainsworth's suit against her would be dropped. The proceedings continued.[20]

Freed from Ainsworth, Barbara joined a vaudeville tour that took her across the country. Nicholas Bernard Deely, an actor in the group, fell hard for the young beauty. Deely, who was 18 years her senior, proposed almost immediately. Barbara explained that her divorce from Ainsworth was not final. He suggested Barbara get a divorce on her own account. The pair stopped in Chicago long enough for her to obtain the divorce.

In September 1918, Barbara became Mrs. Ben Deely. Despite their differences in age, the two were quite compatible. They shared an interest in literature, art, and writing. They were also heavy drinkers. The pair lived at the Hotel Pontiac in Manhattan, where Barbara spent considerable time writing stories she hoped to adapt for the movies.

Sometime in late 1919, the Deelys packed up and moved to Los Angeles, where Barbara tested the waters for interest in her screenplays. She found immediate success. At Fox, she wrote the scripts for *The Mother of His Children*, *Rose of Nome*, *The Little Grey Mouse*, *The Land of Jazz*, and *Flame of Youth*, all 1920 productions. While Barbara worked behind the scenes, Deely broke into the movies with supporting parts in *Flames of the Flesh* (1919) and *Molly O* (1921).

It came as little surprise to anyone when trouble erupted in the Deely household. When the two separated, Deely said that being married to the "too beautiful" girl had been "too strenuous."[21] In his complaint, Deely maintained that Barbara "brought her parents to live them and connived with them to have a girl make love to him; smoked incessantly; had uncontrollable fits of temper; threatened to kill him or have someone else do it; concealed from him the facts about her previous marriages; had him falsely arrested for stealing an automobile."[22]

Barbara aired her own complaints. She charged that Deely "persecuted, annoyed and shamed her; called her indecent and opprobrious names; threatened to kill her; kissed another young woman good night; and squandered the money she earned."[23]

Their marriage, Deely concluded, had a "good start, but the finish was bum."[24]

Strangely enough, with as many complaints as the two had against each other, they put aside their differences and reconciled

In mid 1920, Louis B. Mayer lured Barbara into accepting a small role in *Harriet and the Piper*, a starring vehicle for Anita Stewart.

It was Mary Pickford who soon told Barbara she was too beautiful to be working behind the camera. Her face was one of the movies.

Douglas Fairbanks cast Barbara in the role of a vamp in *The Nut* (1921), which starred her friend Marguerite de la Motte. After appearing in a John Ford western, *Desperate Trails*, Fairbanks gave her the plum role of Milady de Winter in *The Three Musketeers* (1921), a box office sensation.

During the production, the Deelys separated. He returned to New York and the vaudeville stage. Though still married, Barbara went around town as if she had no attachments. She carried on with John Gilbert during the production of *The Three Musketeers* and while the two worked together on *Arabian Love* (1922).

It was while hanging out at Gilbert's Tower Road (Beverly Hills) home that she met the man who many believe was the love of her life: Paul Bern. They were a couple from the fall of 1921 through most of 1922, but remained friends for the rest of her life.

Barbara's career was set in stone when director Rex Ingram hired her and newcomer Ramon Samaniegos (Ramon Novarro) to support his wife, Alice Terry, in the epic *The Prisoner of Zenda* (1922). The film became a commercial success.

"At first I was almost a little jealous of Barbara La Marr," Alice Terry said many years later, "but after working with her and getting to know her while on *The Prisoner of Zenda*, I became quite fond of her. She was as lovely in her personality as she was in her ravishing looks."[25]

It was during the production of *The Prisoner of Zenda*, in late December 1921, that Barbara discovered she was pregnant. Rex Ingram reunited the successful Novarro — La Marr team in *Trifling Women* (1922). Barbara was soon featured on the covers of movie magazines around the world. Her salary soared to a reported $6,500 a week and she was rated one of the screen's most popular stars.

Adela Rogers St. Johns, who had known Barbara as Reatha Watson for almost 10 years, introduced her friend to readers of *Photoplay* in June 1922.

"Barbara La Marr's face at fifteen, when I first knew her, was the kind that could no more go peacefully through a world of men than a cobble-stone could pass through a plateglass window without busting things up," St. John's wrote. Barbara's overcoming the struggles of her youth to discover fame and fortune on her own in Hollywood, was, for St. Johns, a triumph for all women.[26]

"I am willing to salute the unconquerable soul of a girl who can beat her own destiny and with her bare hands climb back up the cliff over which life has thrown her. As women, we ought to be very proud of Barbara La Marr."[27]

What the readers of *Photoplay* and the movie-going public didn't know was that, on July 23, 1922, Barbara La Marr quietly gave birth to a son, Marvin Carville La Marr.[28]

With her career in full swing and a nightlife that kept her busy into the wee hours, one wonders how motherhood fit into Barbara's plans. She could have chosen to abort the fetus or give the child up for adoption.

Barbara La Marr and Ramon Novarro in Trifling Women *(1922).*

She chose to keep her son.[29]

In an interview for this book, her son, Marvin, later renamed Don Gallery, offered a theory about her acceptance of motherhood.

"Barbara finally found out she couldn't find a man she could love," he said. "She thought, 'I can love Marvin and he will love me unconditionally,' and that's something she didn't get from the men she married. The men she married were screwy. But this time, she would raise me and I would love her no matter what."[30]

Barbara sent little Marvin to live with family friends until she could put together a plan to orchestrate an adoption. In the meantime, she focused on work.

She appeared with Lon Chaney, Blanche Sweet, and Louise Fazenda in *Quincy Adams Sawyer*, a rural comedy about a crooked lawyer

(Chaney) who comes to town to settle her father's estate. She made *The Hero* and *Poor Men's Wives* simultaneously, one during the day, the other at night.

Variety gave Barbara high marks for her work in *The Hero*. "She was everything that anyone could have wanted on the screen and off of it, for that matter, and she managed to put over some very emotional stuff without overacting it."[31]

In *Poor Men's Wives*, which was shot at night following her work on *The Hero*, Barbara traded her fine gowns for gingham in her highly-praised portrayal as the wife of a struggling taxi driver (David Butler).

"Barbara La Marr was a lovely girl," David Butler later recalled. "I had a Buick automobile and she didn't have a car so I used to drive her home every night." Paul Bern, still very much part of Barbara's life, would show up. "The bell

Barbara and son.

would ring, and he'd be there with his bunch of roses, and I'd go out the back way."[32]

It was also during the production of *Poor Men's Wives* that Barbara met and became close friends with actress ZaSu Pitts.

Movie-going audiences took another look at Barbara La Marr after her performance in *Poor Men's Wives*. They saw not only an exotic vamp dressed in the finest velvet and brocade, but also an actress who could handle non-glamorous roles with equal ease and a talented writer who could bring her own stories to the screen.

For sure, fans knew about her tumultuous past and her multiple trips to the altar. They wanted to know who she was, what she thought, the real Barbara La Marr behind the lurid headlines. They wanted to peer beneath her mysterious allure. Barbara made herself assessable.

Los Angeles Times writer William Foster Elliott, after lunching with Barbara at a Hollywood Boulevard restaurant, concluded that she was the most "natural person imaginable. The impression that I came away with me was not one of a strange exotic, a woman with a past, a vamp with a string of scalps at her belt. She is remarkably straight forward and man to man in her attitude."[33]

"I enjoy every bit of life. I want to get all I can out of every minute of it," she confided to Elliott. "There are two things I can't endure: stupidity and insincerity." She then turned the conversation to her profession and her ambitions. "I am sick of men who say the expected thing at the 'right time' and of pictures that end with the assumption that someone lives happily ever after. Routine compliments are the stupidest things in the world. If people do live happily ever after, they should be shown doing it, so that others will know how it's done. Because I have these complexes, my ambition is awfully simple and awfully difficult. I want to play a woman for once as a woman really feels and acts — not as, according to the conventions, she is supposed to act."[34]

To Willis Goldbeck, writer for *Motion Picture*, Barbara said simply, "When I am happy I am like a cat, sleek and purring, quite useless. It is when I am unhappy, with an ache perhaps in my heart, that I do my finest work."[35]

Barbara's road through fame — and life — took an unfortunate turn during the filming of *Souls for Sale* (1923), a story of behind-the-scenes Hollywood in which Barbara played a famous movie vamp. It was during a dance scene that Barbara sprained her ankle. To keep the picture on schedule and their vamp on her feet, producers asked studio doctors to administer morphine and cocaine. By the end of the picture, Barbara, with her proclivity for addiction, was hooked.

Mixed with her heavy drinking, obsession over dieting, and her enjoyment of the nightlife, drug addiction proved destructive to the "too beautiful" actress.

When her child was roughly six months old, Barbara hatched a plan to "adopt" her own son. In February 1923, the *San Antonio Evening News* reported that Barbara had appeared in Dallas at the Southwest Auto Show and Food and Home Exposition and would be coming to San Antonio for personal appearances at the local theatres.[36] What the public didn't know was that Barbara, along with her best friend, Virginia Carville, and her manager, A. L. Sawyer, had planned the adoption around her trip to Texas.

In an interview for this book, Barbara's son explained his adoption. "There was a druggist with the last name of Marvin who owned a lot of drugstores in Dallas. He arranged for Barbara to use a local orphanage (Hope Cottage) in Dallas for the adoption. That's how I got my first name, Marvin."[37] The last name used for the adoption was Carville, the last name of her friend, Virginia Carville.[38] Barbara's son was adopted from the Hope Cottage orphanage as Marvin Carville.

Several days later, Barbara wove a story of pure fabrication for reporters about how she selected little Marvin from 60 other orphans.

"He smiled and gurgled, and I smiled — and that was all," she gushed. "I didn't have any idea of adopting a baby when I went there, but something about him just made me pick him up — and then I couldn't bear to go away without him, so that very afternoon I cut through all the red tape and adopted him."[39]

While she was at it, Barbara gave reporters two other erroneous pieces of information: she was once a foster child herself and she had lost a child two years before. "I was a foster child myself so I know what it means to feel that there is no one in all the world that belongs to you."[40]

Back in Hollywood, Barbara wrote an article for *Photoplay* in which she explained her reasoning behind adopting a child. "I adopted a baby because I wanted something to love. And the only thing I've found in this world that is at all satisfactory to love is a baby. I took this little trusting man-child that nobody wanted out of a foundling home because my heart was empty and my soul needed an altar upon which to sacrifice." [41]

Barbara La Marr, at the height of her fame.

She also took the opportunity to disarm those who thought that because of her questionable past, she should have avoided bringing a tot into her world. "You can't put a fence around mother love and say — this kind of woman shall have it, and this shan't. No. I've seen it in the gutter and I've seen it in palaces. I've seen it shining in the eyes of some worn, flat-chested spinster. I've seen it still glorified in the eyes of women who had sold or sacrificed or been robbed of every other glory. I'm not silly enough to pretend I'm an ingénue. It isn't my line — on or off the screen. I don't want to be an ingénue. I just want to be a woman. I'm not an angel — I'm just a plain ordinary human being."[42]

In the article, Barbara also harkened to the day when her party would be over. "I've had wisdom thrust upon me until it isn't hard for me to look ahead to a loveless, lonely old age. When what they are pleased to call my beauty is faded. When they've forgotten the tinkle of this thing called fame and my name is wiped from the slate of the world's favor. When money will only buy you hats you can't wear and food you can't eat. Then — then you want somebody to love you."

With these comments, Barbara may have understood that old age was fast approaching, even prematurely.

Back in Hollywood, Barbara and John Gilbert reignited their affair during their second picture together, *St. Elmo* (1923). Actress Leatrice Joy, who was married to Gilbert at the time, recounted a phone conversation she had with Barbara in the wee hours of the morning. "That night the phone rang at about two in the morning. I answered it and it was Barbara La Marr. She said, "Oh, Leatrice darling, may I speak to Jack, please?' I said, 'Of course, dear," and then threw the phone under the bed and went back to sleep."[43]

Fred Niblo, who directed Barbara's breakthrough picture, *The Three Musketeers*, guided her performance in *Strangers of the Night* (1923), in which the vamp (Barbara) brings romance and adventure to a husband (Matt Moore) who has fallen into a marriage rut.

It was during the filming of *Strangers in the Night* that Barbara almost tripped on her own marital entanglements. She had been dating actor Virgil "Jack" Daugherty[44] off and on for over a year. Like most other men she met, he pleaded for her hand in marriage. She told him that someday she would walk down the aisle with him, but remained vague about her intentions.

When their relationship became serious in the spring of 1923, Barbara had to get rid of one husband before acquiring another. True, she had previously filed for divorce from Ben Deely, but quickly withdrew the suit. They decided to live apart.

Barbara had concerns on two fronts. First, she was concerned that if she died unexpectedly, Deely, according to California law, would be entitled to half of her estate. She voiced her intent to provide as much as possible for the raising of little Marvin. Second, it was brought to light that the hasty divorce she obtained in Illinois in 1918 from Phil Ainsworth was illegal;[45] therefore, when she married Deely, she was perhaps guilty of bigamy and of fraudulently attempting to obtain a divorce (from Ainsworth).[46]

A Cook county (Illinois) judge signed a court order annulling the Deely La Marr marriage and cleared the two of any fraud based on a statue of limitations.

The judge issued the following statement: "Inasmuch as Miss La Marr was divorced from Ainsworth by virtue of Ainsworth's own complaint and the decree granted him, and inasmuch as the Chicago judge annulled her marriage to Deely, Miss La Marr is free to marry whomever she pleases, or provide for 9-months-old Marvin in any way she pleases, without fearing an encroachment on her bankroll or persecution for perpetrating a fraud. Not only this, but she's comfortably rid of two husbands."[47] Ben Deely, however, eventually filed suit against Barbara for statutory adultery, claiming she was living with Daugherty without having been legal separated from him.[48]

Barbara returned to work on *Strangers of the Night,* but when shooting shut down for the weekend, Barbara and Jack Daugherty, along with her parents, drove to Ventura, where, at the parsonage of the First Congregational Church, the silent siren became Mrs. Daugherty. Paul Bern, her old paramour and friend, served as best man.[49] The wedding party returned to Los Angeles. The Daughertys journeyed on to Santa Barbara.

"I made up my mind to marry Jack some day," Barbara admitted to reporters, "but at noon today I had no more idea of marrying him than — well — than of marrying — you. Then — well — I just decided."[50]

Bright and early Monday morning, Barbara returned to the studio to continue work on *Strangers of the Night* and Daugherty showed up for work at Universal, where he was starring in two-reel Westerns.

Several days after her wedding, Barbara was pulled into the divorce case of Oscar Maryatt, a cameraman, and his wife, Mildred. Introduced into court were letters written by Oscar to his wife claiming that Barbara was infatuated with him and that, "I love Barbara more than I do you." Oscar later admitted that he had composed the letters as a way to make his wife jealous and that his accusations about the actress were false.

Barbara and her husband issued a joint statement claiming some unknown person was attempting to tarnish her reputation and damage her film career. Barbara added, "I have some right to happiness and these continuous slanders are making a nightmare of my life."[51]

With the Maryatt divorce scandal looming, Barbara and Daugherty sailed for Europe on June 6, 1923. They honeymooned in Paris before Barbara reported for work on her next picture, *The Eternal City,* which was shot in Rome. Little Marvin stayed with family and friends.

The Eternal City, one of the first films to be shot abroad, had as its backdrop the Coliseum, the Forum, the Roman Baths, and the Appian Way as its backdrops. Premier Benito Mussolini, infatuated with the too beautiful Barbara, placed the army at the command of the film's producer. Mussolini himself even played a cameo on the balcony of the palace.

While Barbara was abroad, the *Los Angeles Times* reported that she had adopted another child, "a real son of this Latin country with big brown eyes and curly hair."[52]

"Barbara apparently became acquainted with the child but never brought him home," her son said. "I went to Italy once to check, but the war (World War II) had destroyed the records."[53]

The Eternal City, especially Barbara, scored a hit with the critics. "Barbara La Marr is a vision of loveliness in her role of Donna Roma in *The Eternal City*. She is one of the most beautiful women of the cinema and let her but once flicker across the screen, and it becomes instantly vital with beauty and glamour."[54] "This is undoubtedly one of the most beautiful pictures ever filmed. It is also one of the most interesting, and one no lover of the best in pictures can afford to miss. Barbara La Marr as Roma has the best role of her career and does by far her finest acting. She is very beautiful as always and plays with a skill and spirit that she never before has equaled."[55]

When Barbara sailed into the port of New York on August 17, 1923, she returned to her country a major star. She was in town long enough to sign a contract with Associated Pictures and prepare for her upcoming production, *Thy Name is Woman* (1924). When the Santa Fe pulled into the Los Angeles station, a delegation that consisted of her old friend Ramon Novarro, scenarist Bess Meredyth, studio executives, her father, and little Marvin greeted her. She pushed aside many well wishers and bouquets of flowers to get to her son.[56]

Filming soon began on *Thy Name is Woman* under the direction of Fred Niblo. Barbara plays the unhappy wife of an old smuggler (William V. Mong) who falls in love with an officer (Novarro) in the Spanish Army.

Barbara and Novarro had been close friends for several years. He reached out to help her overcome her growing addictions to alcohol and drugs. One day, after the shooting of *Thy Name is Woman* was complete, Barbara told the Latin lover he would have a shining career on the screen.

"But," he said, "your career will be as great as mine."

"Oh no," she replied prophetically, "In two years I will be forgotten."[57]

Movie critic Lamar Lane, writing in *Photoplay*, called *Thy Name is Woman*, "the most human and absorbing photoplay of a twelve month period. No more fascinating figure has ever been viewed on the screen than that presented by Barbara La Marr as the wife of the old smuggler.

She is a revelation of beauty and artistry, and she does it all without the aid of fine feathers."[58]

Harrison's Reports termed Barbara's performance, "as good a piece of acting as she has ever done."[59] *The New York Times* noted that Barbara was "efficient in many of her scenes, but occasionally has a spell of panting which does not look natural."[60]

Barbara La Marr and Ramon Novarro in Thy Name is Woman *(1924).*
COURTESY OF ALLAN ELLENBERGER

In her next film, *The Shooting of Dan McGrew* (1924), Barbara was cast as a showgirl who leaves her husband (Percy Marmont) and two-year-old son for another man (Lew Cody) who promises to help her find success on the New York stage. Eventually, "the lady known as Lou," ends up in an Alaskan dancehall, a mistress of the man who took her to New York. Her husband locates her after years of searching, shoots the man who broke up his home, and reunites his family.

The *New York Herald* put it simply, "We have never seen Barbara La Marr act better or look so well. She seems to be getting more soulfully beautiful as time goes on." While *Harrison's Reports* reported there was a "chockfull of action" from beginning to end, they warned audiences that "Barbara La Marr's obvious parading of her physical charms might prove not only distasteful but disgusting to the family circle."[61]

According to her son, Barbara, herself, was ashamed of the picture and her role as a prostitute. "She refused to see the film and never wanted me to see it," he said.[62]

After seeing *The Shooting of Dan McGrew*, Myrtle Gebhart, writing for the *Los Angeles Times*, put into words Barbara's emerging screen persona. "She lacks the brash crudeness of a Naldi, the mystery of the vamp Theda Bara made famous. Coupled with her perfection of body, her beauty of face, she has that quality of gracile mentality, expressing feminine psychology, which somehow gives subtlety, meaning, to every gesture. What other sirens say in capitals, she says with greater affect in italics. What they shriek, she whispers, more tantalizing by far to sophistication."[63]

Barbara left Metro after *The Shooting of Dan McGrew* and signed a lucrative deal with First National, the home studio of Colleen Moore, Norma Talmadge, and Corinne Griffith.

As 1924 got underway, the future had never looked brighter for Barbara. By all accounts her home life was stable for the first time in her adult life and her career was at its zenith. Yet, 1924 would be the year that Barbara La Marr, her personal life and health, began to unravel.

While she continued to make successful pictures, the effects of increased alcohol and drug abuse began to show on her face and figure. Her marriage collapsed, and she spent most of 1924 embroiled in a lawsuit that threatened to expose her reckless sex life. Lurid headlines that unfolded throughout the year kept her pictures under the constant threat of being banned.

In November 1923, while Barbara was hard at work on *The Shooting of Dan McGrew*, attorney Herman L. Roth was charged with extorting $400 from the actress. In return for this amount, a portion of the $20,000 he demanded, Roth agreed not to file an amended complaint that would have added 37 correspondents to the original divorce action filed against Barbara by Bernard Deely.[64] Roth also threatened to expose a romantic relationship between Barbara and her manager, Arthur Sawyer, and to publish a story accusing her of renting a Hollywood hideaway for her numerous trysts.[65]

Barbara La Marr and her dangerous curves.

Barbara, in answering the Deely suit, denied that the two were ever legally married or that she had ever associated with men other than her husband.[66]

In February 1924, as the Roth trial got underway, Barbara, the star witness, began work on *The White Moth* (1924). Based on one of Barbara's poems, *The White Moth*, under the direction of Maurice Tourneur, is a tale about a sophisticated man-of-the-world (Conway Tearle) who tries to save his younger brother (Ben Lyon) from the snares of a Parisian dancer (Barbara).

It didn't take long for Lyon to fall for the screen vamp. "I fell in love — perhaps not seriously, but certainly with a more serious and ardent regard than I had had for any other screen personality," Lyon wrote in his autobiography. "There was only one difficulty — Barbara was not in love with me, and the more the gossip-writers and movie-columnists linked our names the more Barbara denied it both to the press and to me."[67]

Harrison's Reports called the film a "sex drama," adding, "the introduction of such coarseness into a picture adds nothing to it and takes away much."[68] *Variety* was equally critical. "Barbara La Marr, the great undressed, would be accurate billing for Barb, the vamp, in this picture. Maurice Tourneur has gone just about as far as the law will allow in undraping the physical allurement of Barbara, but by the same token he has not made her display any great histrionic ability."[69]

In mid-February, Barbara took the stand to testify against the attorney charged with attempted extortion. When she was questioned about her marriages, the actress "broke into sobs and fell across the witness stand. It was believed she had fainted, but she quickly regained her composure."[70]

Barbara was asked to identify the divorce complaint, which claimed she had "intimate" relations with seven men, including actor Roscoe "Fatty" Arbuckle. "I'm afraid I can't," she said, weeping. "My eyes are too full of tears."[71]

Roth was found guilty of extortion and sentenced from one to five years at San Quentin.[72]

Though relieved to have the suit behind her, the ordeal pushed the already fragile Barbara closer to the edge. Without much of a break following her work on *The White Moth*, Barbara began *Sandra* (1924), a romance story about a troubled woman who cheats on her husband in search of a more exciting life. She eventually realizes her mistakes and plans to commit suicide. She goes to a church to pray and, by chance, meets her husband (Bert Lytell), who embraces her and takes her home.

Barbara had been lucky that years of drug and alcohol abuse had little effect on her exquisite beauty. She also battled weight gain, but was able to lose the pounds through extreme dieting[73] and cocaine use. With *Sandra*, however, the cameras could no longer conceal the fact that Barbara was slowing killing herself.

Actress Ethlyne Clair, an extra in *Sandra*, remembered going out to sea on a yacht with the crew and painfully observing an intoxicated Barbara struggle to get through her scenes.[74]

In April 1924, Barbara led a delegation on a cross country tour to promote tourism in Southern California. Alma Whitaker, writing in the *Los Angeles Times*, was astonished that chambers of commerce around the area selected the screen siren for the honor.

"Wasn't she rather a peculiarly notorious little girl in this city before she became worth $15,000 a year? Weren't the recent revelations about her five marriages, brought out in a recent court trial, a bit staggering, even in these days? Wasn't she rather quaintly vague about these various hasty and embarrassing adventures?"[75]

"Actually, this is peculiarly tactless affront to the women of Southern California. If the men want to be represented by Barbara La Marr I am sure the women don't."[76]

Seven days later, the women's council in Sacramento adopted a resolution urging movie houses in the city to ban Barbara's films. Her appearance on movie screens, they added, "will have a demoralizing effect upon the young people who go to the movies for amusement." The council based their action on an alleged statement Barbara made in which she declared that "a woman must be immoral in order to be a movie vamp."[77]

Barbara garnered additional unwanted publicity when she was linked to Miguel Escoto, a self-described Spanish count trying to make a name for himself in the movies as Mario Escobar. A bizarre tale emerged when a prisoner in the Los Angeles county jail told authorities he witnessed a fight Escoto had over the actress. The scuffle, he maintained, ended in his death. The prisoner gave specifics about the location of the body.

Police began a search for the struggling actor along the coast near San Juan Capistrano. Meanwhile, Barbara publicly denied knowing the man. Police soon located Escoto, who told authorities he met Barbara on a boat from San Francisco to Los Angeles and that since making her acquaintance, he had been subjected to two mysterious beatings.[78]

Who could have been surprised that, by the fall of 1924, the La Marr-Daugherty marriage was on the rocks? In short, Daugherty blamed Barbara's stardom for the breakup, claiming, "I couldn't stand being 'Mr.

Barbara La Marr.'"[79] In an essay he wrote for *Photoplay*, Daugherty said if his wife hadn't become a screen idol, "we would have been a thoroughly happy and devoted married couple."

Instead, Barbara, as a screen goddess, was surrounded by hangers-on who rarely told her the truth about her increasingly perilous lifestyle," Daugherty maintained. "Now I think Barbara is wonderful and glori-

Barbara and Ben Finney in The Heart of a Siren.

ous, too," he wrote. "But I know she isn't perfect. I had to sit by and hear them flatter and stretch the truth every minute of the day. And in order to counteract that, in order to help her keep her head and her feet firmly planted in reality, I often had to remind her of her failings or to argue against these people. And that isn't a happy situation for a man who loves a woman. He doesn't want to appear to his loved one as a policeman always warning her against dangers."[80]

Barbara, exhausted from constant scandal, traveled east with little Marvin to film her next picture, *The Heart of a Siren*. What started as a sexual fling with Ben Finney, who played her romantic interest in the film, soon turned into serious romance. Daugherty, who had just returned to Los Angeles from seeing Barbara in New York, was alerted to his wife's indiscretions.

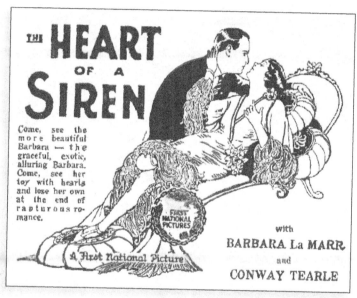

Advertisment for The Heart of a Siren *(1925).*

"We are just three close friends and are often seen around New York together," he told reporters. "I don't care who goes around with Miss La Marr, as I am very fond of her and would do anything in the world for her. Just because we couldn't get along is no reason she should not be happy. Just as soon as some legal red tape is out of the way, a divorce suit will be started."[81]

When filming of *The Heart of a Siren* wrapped, Barbara remained in New York and went right to work on *The White Monkey* (1925), another tale of infidelity in which a wife (Barbara) falls in love with her husband's best friend.

Neither picture scored with moviegoers or critics. In *The Heart of a Siren*, "Barbara La Marr again proves that she cannot act; her facial contortions when she tries to act are nothing short of ludicrous," *Harrison's Reports* concluded.[82] *Variety* termed the film, "nothing less than a ridiculous picture."[83]

The New York Times likened *The White Monkey* to "warm champagne" or a "rose without perfume."[84]

With her work complete in New York, First National ordered their star to return to Hollywood and begin work on *The Girl from Montmartre* (1926).

It became obvious to those around her that something was terribly

A seriously ill Barbara La Marr and Lewis Stone in The Girl from Montmartre *(1926).*

wrong with the screen siren. Her weight had plummeted to a little over 100 pounds. It was first written off in the press as a throat infection complicated by intestinal disorders.[85]

Barbara pressed on, and when she was well enough to begin work on *The Girl from Montmartre*, sat down with Barbara Miller from the *Los Angeles Times* to talk about the poor performance of her previous three films and her belief that her new film would be her comeback. She insisted she was through with portraying sirens on the big screen.

"If my next picture is no good," she said emphatically, "I will simply be kicked off the screen. And it would be so much nicer to retire gracefully."[86]

Her strength was slow to return, however. Barbara was able to work only three or four hours a day. She arrived on the set with the support of a cane and her nurse.

In October, Barbara collapsed while filming a scene and had to be carried from the set. Her physicians ordered her to temporarily retire from the screen until she regained her strength.[87] Following several weeks of rest, the ailing Barbara returned to the studio. "Tell everybody I am getting along fine," she shouted as she drove through the studio gates.[88]

Advertisement for Barbara La Marr's last picture,
The Girl from Montmartre.

Despite her best effects, the ailing actress was unable to finish the picture. Actress Lolita Lee, said to look more like Barbara than Barbara herself, was hired to complete the film.[89]

Meanwhile, Barbara left her beloved Whitley Heights home in the Hollywood Hills and went into seclusion at her Altadena home. There, she battled for her life, seeing no one but her father and mother. Little Marvin was taken under the temporary care of Barbara's close friend, actress ZaSu Pitts.

By November, rumors that the screen siren was dying began appearing in the press. While Barbara fought for life, writer Daisy Dean all but wrote her obituary. "Barbara is making a brave stand against the Reaper. Doctors say that the end is near. Her voice is gone, her body wasted to 80 pounds. Miss La Marr fights on; but a hopeless fight, the physicians declare."[90]

"Personally," declared Cal York in *Photoplay*, "I think Bobby's fight in the mountains is a fight for life, and she needs the earnest prayers and sympathy of everyone of us who have loved her on the screen in the past if we are ever to see her there in the future."[91]

The *Los Angeles Times* ran a photo of an emaciated Barbara La Marr lying in her sickbed. "Hello, everybody! I'm getting better. I'll be all right

Barbara La Marr and her father.

pretty soon. It gets awfully tiresome sometimes," she whispered, "but I'll be all right."[92]

In late November, Barbara seemed to rally. Her father reported that she was up to 112 pounds. "The quiet of her home here, the excellent care of her physicians and nurses and her courage have overcome nearly all traces of her disease," he said.[93] Friends from the studio were allowed brief visits.

On one of her good afternoons, Barbara summoned actress ZaSu Pitts to her bedside with a plea. "If I don't make it," Barbara asked Pitts, "would you raise my little boy?" Pitts agreed. Barbara, according to her son, gave Pitts $100,000 for his care.[94]

After showing significant signs of improvement, Barbara suffered a relapse in late January 1926 and slipped into a coma. She died at 4 p.m. on January 30. The press initially gave "broken nerves" and "complications" as the cause of death.[95]

Barbara's father made plans to cremate his daughter's remains. Paul Bern, according to Barbara's son, protested and issued explicit written orders: "Too Beautiful to Cremate."[96]

For four days, an estimated 40,000 grief-stricken fans filed by her bier as she lay in state at the Walter C. Blue Funeral Home on Washington Street.[97] Her Christian Science funeral was private, attended only by her

An estimated 40,000 grief-stricken fans filed by the screen siren's bier.
COURTESY OF E.J. FLEMING

family and closest friends. Claire Windsor, Ramon Novarro, Ruth Roland, and Katherine Clifford were spotted among the mourners.[98]

The funeral cortege to Barbara's final resting place at Hollywood Cemetery (now Hollywood Forever) stopped traffic for an estimated 15 minutes.[99]

True to her word, ZaSu Pitts and her husband, Tom Gallery, adopted little Marvin, giving him the name Don Gallery. As far as he knew, he never had further contact with Barbara's parents.[100]

While Gallery grew up with the full knowledge that Barbara La Marr was his birth mother, "ZaSu never called me her adopted son. I was always part of the family," he said. "She was also truthful about my mother's addictions, but only later on, as I got older."[101]

Gallery inherited his good looks, but little else, from his mother. "ZaSu and Barbara were opposites of one another. When I was growing up, ZaSu didn't allow liquor in the house. I never drank, smoked, or swore, so those traits I didn't pick up from Barbara."[102]

Speaking of her legendary looks, was she really the "too beautiful girl?" Her friend, writer Adela Rogers St. John, thought so. In a tribute to her

Barbara La Marr's final resting place at the Hollywood Forever Cemetery.

friend several months after her death, St. John wrote that Barbara's beauty "carried her to the very pinnacle. But sometimes, knowing her as I did, I think it gave her none of the things her heart really longed for, and that the saddest thing about Barbara La Marr was not her death but her swift, hot, violent life, that preyed vampire-like upon her beauty and allowed so much of her genius and womanliness to waste."[103]

"That fatal beauty! Helen's laid mighty Troy in ashes and Cleopatra's cost Mark Antony the world. But Barbara destroyed only herself."

1. "Beauty Too Dangerous, Girl Ordered From City," 25 January 1914.

2 York, Cal, "Can Barbara Come Back?" *Photoplay,* January 1926.

3. The 1900 U.S. Federal Census gives July 1896 as her month and year of birth.

4. Although early publicity suggests that Barbara was born in Virginia and adopted by a couple in Washington, Barbara's son, Don Gallery, in a March 2009 interview for this book, said she was born in Washington and was not adopted.

5. William Watson Jr. eventually took the stage name Billy Devore when he became a vaudeville comedian.

6. The 1910 U.S. Federal Census lists the family living in Fresno. William is registered as a laborer.

7. "Two Are Accused of Kidnapping Girl," *Oakland Times*, 5 January 1913.

8. Ibid.

9. "Beauty Too Dangerous, Girl Ordered From City," *Oakland Tribune*, 25 January 1914.

10. Ibid.

11. Lawrence Converse became a subject of international dispute during the Mexican Revolution in 1911 when he was arrested and imprisoned in Mexico for spying.

12. "One Wife Too Many," *Oakland Tribune*, 4 June 1914.

13. "Barbara La Marr and the Pace That Killed," *Oakland Tribune*, 11 April 1926.

14. "Man Who Wedded 'Too Beautiful Girl' Dead, 29 June 1914.

15. "Managers Place Ban on Beautiful Actress," *Oakland Tribune*, 5 July 1914.

16. Ibid.

17. Don Gallery to Michael G. Ankerich, March 2009.

18. "Barbara La Marr and the Pace That Killed," *Oakland Tribune*, 11 April 1926.

19. Carville, whose real name was Robert Hobday, went on to join the Army; Ainsworth was later arrested for passing bad checks and served time in California State Prison. He is listed in the U.S. Federal Census as a cook in the facility's mess hall.

20. "Watson Girl is Alive, Declares Commissioner," *Oakland Tribune*, 1 June 1917.

21. "'Too Beautiful,' Wife Says; She Seeks Divorce," *Oakland Tribune*, 8 June 1920.

22. "Barbara La Marr and the Pace That Killed," *Oakland Tribune*, 11 April 1926.

23. Ibid.

24. "'Too Beautiful,' Wife Says; She Seeks Divorce," *Oakland Tribune*, 8 June 1920.

25. Alice Terry to Jimmy Bangley, "The Legendary Barbara La Marr," *Classic Images*, February 1999.

26. St. Johns, Adela Rogers, "The Girl Who Was Too Beautiful," *Photoplay*, June 1922.

27. Ibid.

28. Barbara sometimes referred to her son as Ivan or Ivon. He is referred to as "Ivon" on a passenger manifest in 1925.

29. Barbara never revealed which lover was her son's father. Her son grew up believing that producer Paul Bern was his dad. "I would guess that Paul Bern was my father," Don Gallery told this writer in a 2009 interview. "He came over about every Sunday and we'd spend the day together. I'd wonder why this man was coming to see me."

30. Don Gallery to Michael G. Ankerich, March 2009.

31. *Variety*, March 8, 1923.

32. Atkins, Irene Kahn, *David Butler*, Scarecrow Press, 1993.

33. Elliott, William Foster, "Not Like the Fan Stories," *Los Angeles Times*, 17 September 1922.

34. Elliott, William Foster, "Not Like the Fan Stories," *Los Angeles Times*, 17 September 1922.

35. Goldbeck, Willis, "The Black Orchid," *Motion Picture*, November 1922.

36. "Screen Beauty to Visit City," *San Antonio Evening News*, 17 February 1923.

37. Don Gallery to Michael G. Ankerich, March 2009.

38. Barbara, according to Gallery, often passed Virginia Carville off as her sister. Carville later married Jules Roth, a one-time operator of the Hollywood Memorial Cemetery.

39. "Smile Wins Home for Boy," *Los Angeles Times*, 2 March 1923.

40. Ibid.

41. La Marr, Barbara, "Why I Adopted a Baby," *Photoplay*, May 1923.

42. La Marr, Barbara, "Why I Adopted a Baby," *Photoplay*, May 1923.

43. Fountain, Leatrice Gilbert, *Dark Star: The Untold Story of the Meteoric Rise and Fall of the Legendary John Gilbert*, St. Martin's Press, 1985.

44. Virgil Daugherty (1897-1938) had been a clerk in a stock yard before wandering out to the West Coast and breaking into the movies.

45. Illinois law at the time required those seeking divorce in the state to establish residency in the state for a sufficient time length. Barbara did not live in Illinois, she, caught up in the "marrying mood," was merely passing through on a vaudeville tour.

46. "Film Beauty Free Again," *Los Angeles Times*, 1 May 1923.

47. Ibid.

48. Deely's battle with Barbara continued until his death in September 1924.

49. "Barbara La Marr Weds," *Los Angeles Times*, 6 May 1923.

50. "Film Newlyweds Must Be at Studio Today," *Los Angeles Times*, 7 May 1923.

51. "Screen Beauty Troubled Again, *Los Angeles Times*, 9 May 1923.

52. "By Official Sanction," *Los Angeles Times*, 10 February 1923.

53. Don Gallery to Michael Ankerich, March 2009.

54. *Movie Weekly*, December 1923.

55. *Photoplay* magazine.

56. "Screen Actress Returns as Star," *Los Angeles Times*, 29 September 1923.

57. Ellenberger, Allan R., *Ramon Novarro*, McFarland, 1999.

58. *Photoplay*, January 1924.

59. *Harrison's Reports*, 1 March 1924.

60. *The New York Times*, 4 March 1924.

61. *Harrison's Reports*, 5 April 1924.

62. Don Gallery to Michael G. Ankerich, March 2009.

63. Gebhart, Myrtle, "Film is Frank Appeal to Eye," *Los Angeles Times*, 10 February 1924.

64. "Roth Gives Bail in Actress Suit," *Los Angeles Times*, 17 November 1923.

65. "H.L. Roth is Indicted by Grand Jury," *Los Angeles Times*, 21 November 1923.

66. "Miss La Marr Files Answer," *Los Angeles Times*, 27 November 1923.

67. Lyon, Ben, *Life With the Lyons* (co-written with Bebe Daniels), Odhams Press Limited, 1953.

68. *Harrison's Reports*, 14 June 1924.

69. *Variety*, 18 June 1924.

70. "Weeps as She Tells of Her Marriages," 13 February 1924.

71. Ibid.

72. "Roth is Given Prison Term," *Los Angeles Times*, 1 March 1924.

73. It was rumored that one of her diets consisted of ingesting oxygenated tape worms.

74. Ethlyne Clair to Michael G. Ankerich, March 1991.

75. Whitwaker, Alma, "Commerce and the Angels," *Los Angeles Times*, 10 April 1924.

76. Ibid.

77. "Barbara La Marr is Put Under Ban," *Oakland Tribune*, 17 April 1924.

78. "'Slain' Film Actor Count Found Alive," *Oakland Tribune*, 18 June 1924.

79. Dougherty, Jack, "Why I Quit Being Mr. Barbara La Marr," *Photoplay*, October 1924.

80. Ibid.

81. "'Three Close Friends,' Says La Marr's Husband of Triangle," *Oakland Tribune*, 15 November 1924.

82. *Harrison's Reports*, 21 March 1925.

83. *Variety*, 8 April 1925.

84. *The New York Times*, 9 June 1925.

85. "Illness of Film Vamp is Serious," *Los Angeles Times*, 13 August 1925.

86. Miller, Barbara, "La Marr Faces Last Chance," *Los Angeles Times*, 13 September 1925.

87. "Barbara La Marr Collapses at Work," 6 October 1925.

88. "Miss La Marr Resumes Work in Film Studio," October 1925.

89. "Doubles for Star Who Was Too Beautiful to Live," *The Sheboygan Press*, Sheboygan, Wisconsin, 18 February 1926.

90. Dean, Daisy, "Death Poised to Write Finis to Colorful Career of Girl Who Was 'Too Beautiful,'" *The Lincoln Star*, Lincoln, Nebraska, 18 November 1925.

91. York, Cal, "Can Barbara Come Back?," *Photoplay*, January 1926.

92. "Star Battles for Health," *Los Angeles Times*, 10 November 1925.

93. "Actress Ill for Months Recovering," 21 November 1925.

94. Don Gallery to Michael G. Ankerich, March 2009. "But, of course, ZaSu spent a lot more than $100,000 sending me to college and boarding school," he added.

95. Her death certificate lists pulmonary tuberculosis as the cause of death.

96. Don Gallery to Michael G. Ankerich, March 2009.

97. "Barbara to Be Laid to Rest Today," *Los Angeles Times*, 5 February 1926.

98. Bert Lytell, Tom Gallery, Henry Hathaway, Henry Victor (actor), Alfred E. Green (film director), and R.D. Knickerbocker (her attorney) were her pallbearers.

99 "Women Riot at Star's Funeral," *Los Angeles Times*, 6 February 1926.

100. Don Gallery to Michael G. Ankerich, March 2009.

101. Ibid.

102. Ibid.

103. Rogers St. John, Adela, "Hail and Farewell," *Photoplay*, April 1926.

FILMOGRAPHY

1920

The Mother of his Children (writer only).

Rose of Nome (writer only).

The Little Grey Mouse (writer only).

Flame of Youth (writer only).

The Land of Jazz (writer only).

Harriet and the Piper (Louis B. Mayer Productions) D: *Bertram Bracken.* Anita Stewart, Ward Crane, Charles Richman, Myrtle Stedman, Margaret Landis, Byron Munson, Loyola O'Connor, Irving Cummings, Barbara La Marr Deely.

1921

The Nut (Douglas Fairbanks Pictures Corporation) D: *Theodore Reed.* Douglas Fairbanks, Marguerite De La Motte, William Lowery, Gerald Pring, Morris Hughes, Barbara La Marr.

Desperate Trails (Universal) D: *John Ford.* Harry Carey, Irene Rich, Georgie Stone, Helen Field, Edward Coxen, Barbara La Marr, George Siegmann, Charles E. Insley.

The Three Musketeers (Douglas Fairbanks Pictures Corporation) D: *Fred Niblo.* Douglas Fairbanks, Leon Barry, George Siegmann, Eugene Pallette, Boyd Irwin, Thomas Holding, Sidney Franklin, Charles Stevens, Nigel De Brulier, Willis Robards, Lon Poff, Mary MacLaren, Marguerite De La Motte, Barbara La Marr, Walt Whitman, Adolphe Menjou, Charles Belcher.

Cinderella of the Hills (Fox) D: *Howard M. Mitchell.* Barbara Bedford, Barbara Bedford, Carl Miller, Cecil Van Auker, Wilson Hummel, Tom McGuire, Barbara La Marr Deely.

1922

Arabian Love (Fox) D: *Jerome Storm*. John Gilbert, Barbara Bedford, Barbara La Marr, Herschel Mayall, Robert Kortman, William H. Orlamond.

The Prisoner of Zenda (Metro) D: *Rex Ingram*. Lewis Stone, Alice Terry, Robert Edeson, Stuart Holmes, Ramon Samaniegos *(Ramon Novarro)*, Barbara La Marr, Malcolm McGregor, Edward Connelly, Lois Lee.

Domestic Relations (Preferred Pictures) D: *Chet Withey*. Katherine MacDonald, William P. Carleton, Frank Leigh, Barbara La Marr, Gordon Mullen, George Fisher, Lloyd Whitlock.

Trifling Women (Metro) D: *Rex Ingram*. Barbara La Marr, Ramon Novarro, Pomeroy Cannon, Edward Connelly , Lewis Stone, Hughie Mack, Gene Pouyet, John George, Jess Weldon , B. Hyman, Joe Martin.

Quincy Adams Sawyer (Paramount) D: *Clarence Badger*. John Bowers, Blanche Sweet, Lon Chaney, Barbara La Marr, Elmo Lincoln, Louise Fazenda, Joseph Dowling, Claire McDowell, Edward Connelly, June Elvidge, Victor Potel, Gale Henry, Hank Mann, Kate Lester, Billy Franey, Taylor Graves, Harry Depp, Andrew Arbuckle.

1923

The Hero (Preferred) D: *Louis J. Gasnier*. Gaston Glass, Barbara La Marr, John Sainpolis, Martha Mattox, Frankie Lee, David Butler, Doris Pawn, Ethel Shannon, Cameo *(dog)*.

Poor Men's Wives (Preferred) D: *Louis J. Gasnier*. Barbara La Marr, David Butler, Betty Francisco, Richard Tucker, ZaSu Pitts, Muriel McCormac, Mickey McBan.

Brass Bottle (First National) D: *Maurice Tourneur*. Harry Myers, Ernest Torrence, Tully Marshall, Clarissa Selwyn, Ford Sterling, Aggie Herring, Charlotte Merriam, Edward Jobson, Barbara La Marr, Otis Harlan, Hazel Keener, Julanne Johnston.

Souls for Sale (Goldwyn) D: *Rupert Hughes.* Eleanor Boardman, Mae Busch, Barbara La Marr, Richard Dix, Lew Cody, Arthur Hoyt, David Imboden, Roy Atwell, William Orlamond, Forrest Robinson, Edith Yorke, Dale Fuller, Snitz Edwards, Jack Richardson, Aileen Pringle, Eve Southern, May Milloy, Sylvia Ashton, Margaret Bourne, Fred Kelsey, Jed Prouty, Yale Boss, William Haines, George Morgan, Auld Thomas, Leo Willis, Walter Perry, Sam Damen, R. H. Johnson, Rush Hughes, L. J. O'Connor, Charles Murphy, Hugo Ballin, Mabel Ballin, T. Roy Barnes, Barbara Bedford, Hobart Bosworth, Charles Chaplin, Chester Conklin, William H. Crane, Elliott Dexter, Robert Edeson, Claude Gillingwater, Dagmar Godowsky, Raymond Griffith, Elaine Hammerstein, Jean Haskell, Alice Lake, Bessie Love, June Mathis, Patsy Ruth Miller, Marshall Neilan, Fred Niblo, Anna Q. Nilsson, ZaSu Pitts, John Sainpolis, Milton Sills, Anita Stewart, Erich von Stroheim, Blanche Sweet, Florence Vidor, King Vidor, Johnny Walker, George Walsh, Kathlyn Williams, Claire Windsor.

Strangers of the Night (Metro) D: *Fred Niblo.* Matt Moore, Enid Bennett, Barbara La Marr, Robert McKim, Mathilde Brundage, Emily Fitzroy, Otto Hoffman, Thomas Ricketts.

St. Elmo (Fox) D: *Jerome Storm.* John Gilbert, Barbara La Marr, Bessie Love, Warner Baxter, Nigel de Brulier, Lydia Knott.

The Eternal Struggle (First National) D: *Reginald Barker.* Renée Adorée, Earle Williams, Barbara La Marr, Pat O'Malley, Wallace Beery, Josef Swickard, Pat Harmon, Anders Randolf, Edward J. Brady, Robert Anderson, George Kuwa.

The Eternal City (First National) D: *George Fitzmaurice.* Barbara La Marr, Lionel Barrymore, Bert Lytell, Richard Bennett, Montagu Love.

Mary of the Movies (Columbia) D: *John McDermott.* Marion Mack , Florence Lee, Mary Kane, Harry Cornelli, John Geough, Raymond Cannon, Rosemary Cooper, Creighton Hale, Francis McDonald, Henry Burrows, John McDermott, Jack Perrin, Ray Harford, Barbara La Marr, Douglas MacLean, Bryant Washburn, Johnnie Walker, J. Warren Kerrigan, Herbert Rawlinson, Alec Francis, Richard Travers, David Butler, Louise Fazenda, Anita Stewart, Estelle Taylor, Rosemary Theby, Bessie Love, Marjorie Daw, Tom Moore, Elliott Dexter, ZaSu Pitts, Carmel Myers, Rex Ingram, Maurice Tourneur, Edward J. Le Saint, Wanda Hawley.

1924

Thy Name Is Woman (Metro) D: *Fred Niblo*. Ramon Novarro , Barbara La Marr, William V. Mong, Wallace MacDonald, Robert Edeson, Edith Roberts, Claire McDowell.

The Shooting of Dan McGrew (Metro) D: *Clarence Badger*. Barbara La Marr, Lew Cody, Mae Busch, Percy Marmont, Max Ascher, Fred Warren, George Siegmann, Nelson McDowell, Bert Sprotte, Ina Anson, Philippe De Lacy, Harry Lorraine, Eagle Eye, Milla Davenport, William Eugene.

The White Moth (First National) D: *Maurice Tourneur*. Barbara La Marr, Conway Tearle, Charles De Roche, Ben Lyon, Edna Murphy, Josie Sedgwick, Kathleen Kirkham, William Orlamond.

My Husband's Wives (writer only).

Sandra (First National) D: *Arthur H. Sawyer*. Barbara La Marr, Bert Lytell, Leila Hyams, Augustin Sweeney, Maude Hill, Edgar Nelson, Leon Gordon, Leslie Austin, Lillian Ten Eyck, Morgan Wallace, Arthur Edmund Carewe, Helen Gardner, Alice Weaver, Ethlyne Clair.

1925

The Heart of a Siren (First National) D: *Phil Rosen*. Barbara La Marr , Conway Tearle, Harry Morey, Paul Doucet, Ben Finney, Florence Auer, Ida Darling, William Ricciardi, Clifton Webb, Florence Billings, Mike Rayle, Katherine Sullivan.

The White Monkey (First National) D: *Phil Rosen*. Barbara La Marr, Thomas Holding, Henry Victor, George F. Marion, Colin Campbell, Charles Mack, Flora Le Breton, Tammany Young.

1926

The Girl from Montmartre (First National) D: *Alfred E. Green*. Barbara La Marr, Lewis Stone, Robert Ellis, William Eugene, E. H. Calvert, Mario Carillo, Mathilde Comont, Edward Piel, Nicholas De Ruiz, Bobby Mack

MARTHA MANSFIELD

Working in motion pictures when the industry was in its infancy could be risky business, even hazardous to one's health. At times, it was downright deadly. It was especially unpredictable when the group traveled hundreds, or even thousands of miles into such remote locations as the desert, into rugged lands and along rivers, into the wilds of Africa.

Pauline Curley was shooting some scenes along the Columbia River in Oregon when the cable connected to her boat snapped and hurled her into the treacherous water. She tore her nails to the bloody quick as she clung for life on rocks while waiting for help to arrive.[1]

Serial queen Pearl White was often hung up and strung up, but insisted on doing most of her own stunts. Grace Darmond was once thrown 40 feet into the air by a temperamental elephant. Edwina Booth contracted malaria and dysentery in Africa, almost fractured her skull in a fall, and suffered sunstroke from the intense heat.

Matinee idol Wallace Reid, while filming *Valley of the Giants* with Grace Darmond, suffered a severe head injury in a train accident. He was treated with morphine to ease the pain and to get him through the picture. His subsequent addiction to the painkiller led to his death several years later.

Then, there is the tragic story of Martha Mansfield, the Ziegfeld Follies beauty who entered pictures in the late 1900s and began her ascent to fame after playing opposite John Barrymore in *Dr. Jekyll and Mr. Hyde* (1920). Her climb to popularity was slow, but steady.

Her youth and beauty were used to full advantage in numerous roles as the other woman or the worldly vamp on the make for unsuspecting prey.

When she was cast in *The Warrens of Virginia* in 1923, it looked like Martha Mansfield had finally reached a new realm of fame. The role of Agatha Warren, a wholesome Southern Belle in love with a Union lieutenant at the end of the Civil War, was expected to make her a star—finally!

The cast and crew were spending part of November working in Texas. The day before, they'd filmed battle scenes. The next day, Thanksgiving

Day, was devoted to some final scenes of Martha and her leading man, Wilfred Lytell.

They had shot some interiors, after which, a break was called to prepare for exterior shots. Dressed in a huge hoop skirt of the Confederate period, Martha used the break to rest in the back seat of her limousine. The sparks from a discarded match ignited the lace and frills of her costume and flames engulfed the petrified actress before anyone could rescue her.

Within seconds, the stunningly-beautiful Martha Mansfield, on the cusp of stardom at age 24, was gone with the wind.

Martha Mansfield came into the world as Martha S. Ehrlich on July 14, 1899, in New York City.[2] Her parents were Maurice J. Ehrlich, originally from Pennsylvania, and Harriett Gibson, who emigrated to the United States from Ireland in 1885. The Ehrlichs had another child, a daughter, Edith, born around 1905.[3]

From a very early age, Martha had her sights on becoming a stage actress. While visiting her grandmother, Mrs. D.H. Gibson, one summer in Mansfield, Ohio, Martha and her friends staged a presentation of *Romeo and Juliet*. Martha played Romeo in the production.[4]

"When I was 14 years old," Martha said in 1920, "I made up my mind that I should become an actress, and therefore, immediately went to see Mr. [William] Brady, who was at the time casting for *Little Women*. He poked fun at me because I was so young and earnest and finally told me that I would receive notice at the end of the week if he wanted me." Brady, whose daughter, Alice, was the star of the show, cast Martha in a small role as a boy.[5]

In addition to stage work, Martha also found work as a model for artists and photographers. She became a favorite of photographer Alfred Cheney Johnston, who described Martha as "an exquisite pastel — fragile flower." Martha, however, soon grew bored just sitting around and looking pretty.

"I tired of this within a year's time," she said. "It was so inactive and did not call for the use of one's facilities. I wanted to be more than a mere doll."[6]

In 1913, at the age of 14, she danced in the chorus of the musical *Hop o' My Thumb* and appeared in a Winter Garden revue. She worked in such shows as *The Century Girl* (1916) and *On With the Dance* (1917).

When an actress friend of hers, Hazel Dawn, was unable to take a part in Max Linder's films, she recommended Martha for the job. Martha, who had taken the name Martha Early, signed a contract with Essanay for three films with the French comedian who was making his debut in the

United States. She was offered a year's contract, but would only agree to six months at $250 a week.[7]

Martha became friendly with the eccentric and ailing actor, but American audiences didn't care for his work. He soon returned to France. Martha returned happily to the stage.

Florenz Ziegfeld glorified Martha in the *Ziegfeld Follies of 1918*, the year she made her first feature film, *Broadway Bill*, as the love interest of Harold Lockwood, who portrays a Manhattan playboy. *Variety* was far from impressed with her work. "Miss Mansfield had little to do except to pose in some wasted scenes with her New York chaser. When in close-ups with Bill (Lockwood), her hardest work seemed to be an effort to maintain the position until the camera clicked off."[8]

For awhile, Martha staggered back and forth from the Klieg lights of the studio to the footlights of the New Amsterdam Theater. She told *Photoplay* that, after her evening appearance in the Follies, she would snatch a bit of sleep, eat a bite of breakfast before arriving at the studio by nine. Then, she'd return to the theater in the evening. "Wake up, Martha!" they'd say to her. "Come to."[9]

Martha Mansfield draped in fur.

"Well," said Martha, "when I'd get down to the studio, only half-awake and dead tired, I'd feel like reviving the old joke of the beautiful chorus girls who are the toast of the town at night, but 'you should see us in the morning!'"[10]

After making an announcement in early 1919 that she was abandoning the stage and would concentrate her energies on her moving pictures, Martha supported Eugene O'Brien in *The Perfect Lover*, the first of four films she made with the handsome star at Selznick Pictures.[11]

Martha had one more fling with the stage in the *Ziegfeld Midnight Frolic*, which opened in October 1919. Then, late in the year, she left the stage production after John Barrymore chose her to play his fiancée in *Dr. Jekyll and Mr. Hyde* (1920). It was a breakthrough role for the 20-year-old.

In an interview with *Photoplay*, Martha admitted to being an "easy-go-lucky" sort of person and was "really scared to death" to appear with

Martha Mansfield and John Barrymore in Dr. Jekyll and Mr. Hyde *(1920).*

the great Barrymore on the screen. When production was underway, she found the actor formidable only in his Mr. Hyde make-up.[12]

Martha's role as Dr. Jekyll's meek and mild fiancée stands in sharp contrast to the exotic cabaret singer, played by the equally exotic Nita Naldi. Modern reviewers make reference to Martha's theatrical abilities. "The contrasting Martha Mansfield, as good girl Millicent Carew, is the standard ingénue but she, too, is allowed a couple of nice moments in what essentially is a Barrymore *tour de force*."[13] "Mansfield is appealing not only for her beauty, but for her very competent, underplayed performance."[14]

While Martha's appearance in *Dr. Jekyll and Mr. Hyde* boosted her popularity and set her own a course for a successful film career, most movie fans knew very little about her private life. Her entry in the 1920 *Who's Who on the Screen* refers to her as "one of the screen's most charming actresses" and informs fans that she is "five feet four inches high, weighs a hundred and twenty-two pounds and has blonde hair and gray eyes."[15]

Studio publicity was mum about Martha Mansfield's apparent marriage, which must have taken place in the late 1910s. At least two sources allude to the fact that Martha had a husband. In the 1920 U.S. Federal Census, Martha's marital status is listed as married.[16] Also, a 1919 news item from her mother's hometown paper, *The Mansfield News*, told of Martha arriving in Mansfield for a two week visit with her grandmother and sister, Edith. "She and her husband," the article continued, "have been spending several weeks at their summer home, Twin Lakes, Wisconsin, while later she will go to New York."[17]

After appearing in another Famous Players-Lasky feature, *Civilian Clothes* (1920) with Thomas Meighan, Martha signed an exclusive contract with Lewis J. Selznick to make films for Selznick Pictures. While Selznick was apparently taken by his young discovery, *Photoplay* magazine was skeptical. They wrote of her performance in *Civilian Clothes*, "Martha Mansfield is pretty but fearfully inadequate dramatically."[18]

One news account mentioned Martha as succeeding the late actress Olive Thomas in the "Selznick screen constellation."[19]

Martha was reunited with Eugene O'Brien in three films: *The Last Chance*, *Gilded Lies* (1921), and *The Last Door*. In *Gilded Lies*, at the strong urging of her ambitious aunt, Martha marries into society after her fiancé (O'Brien) is reported lost in an expedition to the North Pole.

In *The Last Door*, Martha is hired by a party guest of Somerset Carroll (O'Brien) to show up at the party and claim she is being pursued by police. The mystery — and comedy — unfolds when it turns out that Carroll himself is an imposter and is really a master thief who has kidnapped the real Carroll and hidden him in the house.

After working at her home studio in *The Man of Stone* (1921), in which she dumps her fiancé for someone with more money, Selznick lost interest in promoting Martha's career. Instead, he began loaning her to such minor and obscure studios as Arrow, Lee-Bradford, and Hodkinson.

In 1921, shortly after Martha temporarily left the screen to tour in vaudeville, she was romantically linked to the recently-divorced Crane Wilbur, known primarily at the time as the male lead opposite Pearl White in *The Perils of Pauline*. The two appeared on the San Francisco stage in the fall of 1921.

The *Oakland Tribune* suspected that the increased cost of glycerine tears had driven Martha from Eugene O'Brien, her movie love, into vaudeville and into the arms of a real-life amour (Crane Wilbur).

"As a Selznick leading woman she glycerined seven dress coats for Eugene O'Brien and then declared a movie vacation. Now, she weeps on Crane Wilbur's shirt front twice a day and has no glycerine bills to pay."[20]

When asked about their impending nuptials, Wilbur emphatically denied the rumor. "I haven't lost hope," Wilbur continued. "If I can find a real pal, a girl who understands and has a mind, partner, a girl who loves a home, I'd rush her to death."[21]

Selznick used her in only two films in 1922, again for minor, independent companies Pyramid and Dependable. Martha spent most of the year on the vaudeville stage. "The stage is best college of acting in the world," she told reporters," and I am always seeking to improve myself. So few realize how hard it is to act for the movies. On the speaking stage, verbal action so to speak, actuates physical action, which renders one's acting more spontaneous and natural."[22]

Appearing in Cleveland, Ohio, in February, Martha weighed in on the sensational murder of director William Desmond Taylor just days before in Hollywood. She said the murderer was a dope fiend for whom Taylor failed to find work in the movies. "Find the man who has been hounding Taylor for a job for the past few weeks and you'll have his slayer," she said. Mary Miles Minter "is just a baby. Her mother never left her long enough for her to get into any mischief. Mabel Normand is a happy go-lucky and carefree girl. Whenever I saw her, she seemed to be caring nothing about anything in particular. I do not think she is at all affectionate."[23]

Martha's talent was wasted in eight films in 1923, most of which were supporting roles in independent productions. She often played flashy vamps, her roles superficial and undefined.

In *Fog Bound*, a Paramount story about the pursuit of a murderer in the Florida swamps, Martha took the acting honors from the star, Dorothy Dalton. *Variety* reported, "Miss Dalton is an actress of great appeal, both for her beauty and from her acting sense, but she requires special surroundings. Here she is a plain country girl, and the flashy passages go to Martha Mansfield. Miss Mansfield's role is an unsympathetic one,

A profile of Martha Mansfield, ca. 1920.

but it is one that compels attention, and this rather takes away from the star."[24]

Finally, in 1923, Martha was released from her obligations to Selznick and signed a long-term contract with Fox. It looked as though her career was back on track after years of lackluster roles with Selznick productions.

Fox used her in a small role in *The Silent Command*, a story of the United States Navy, revolving around naval captains, warships, and an enemy effort to blow up the Panama Canal. Moviegoers were promised "a real hero, a vamp, and a flock of thrills." They weren't disappointed.

Variety praised Martha's handling of her role, but felt she was not often presented in the best lighting. "Miss Mansfield as the vamp handles herself well, but needs lighting before the camera. In her natural stuff she is fine, but there are times when the cameraman let the shadows creep in, and that injured her chances, especially so because it was in the scenes she was to do her heavy vamping stuff."[25]

By the time *The Leavenworth Case* was in theaters in November 1923, Martha was hard at work on *The Warrens of Virginia*, thought to be her breakthrough film. After years of mediocre success, industry insiders predicted this Fox production was the one film destined to boost Martha Mansfield into the next level of stardom.

Fox selected Martha to play a young woman of the Confederacy who is in love with and engaged to a lieutenant in the Union army.

After some work at the Fox studios in Hollywood, the cast and crew traveled to San Antonio, Texas, in mid-November 1923 to complete location scenes. They awoke early Thanksgiving morning to shoot the final interior and exterior scene.

In the dining room of the Saint Anthony Hotel, the cast and crew gathered for breakfast. Martha exuded excitement over having a new radio in her room and promised to entertain them that evening with a radio party.

"Why, it's simply wonderful!" she told the group. "Last night, I heard Chicago and Cincinnati, and tonight I'm sure I'll be able to get Philadelphia and New York. Do you know, it seemed almost as good as seeing mother to think that probably she was listening in on just the same things I was."[26]

After breakfast, the group traveled about three miles to the end of Brackenridge Park, where some shacks were serving as servant's quarters for the film's plantation. Martha waited in her nearby limousine until she was needed on the set.

The camera operators shot several exterior scenes. The director then called a 30-minute break so that sets used for the final interior shots could be assembled. Martha returned to her car.

Ten minutes later, the park's serene surroundings were shattered by a woman's piercing screams. Those gathered nearby looked in the direction of the commotion to see the ill-fated actress, engulfed in flames, running from her limousine.

Her leading man, Wilfred Lytell, was the first to reach Martha. He threw his coat over her and, with the help of others, extinguished the flames.

Those who accompanied Martha on the short ride to the hospital remembered how brave the young woman was. She said she was not in serious pain.

"Are you sure my face is not harmed?" she cried. "Won't my cheeks and neck be scarred forever?"

The hospital physicians found her in serious condition, but thought at first that her injuries were not life threatening. Her condition worsened throughout the night. The next morning, just before noon, Martha Mansfield, only 24 years old, succumbed to her injuries.

Her death certificate indicated she died from "burns of all extremities, general toxemia and suppression of urine."[27]

The film crew was shocked and devastated at the loss of life before their eyes, not to mention overcome by their helplessness as Martha's Civil War costume became her death shroud.

The general theory behind Martha's death is that a lighted match thrown to the ground ignited her dress. The question was never answered whether it was a fellow crew member or Martha who struck the match.

Passersby at the time of the accident reported seeing the flash of a match through the window of Martha's car. It was theorized that Martha, after a morning of work, was soothing her nerves. Her mother discredited that theory by insisted Martha rarely smoked and had a general distaste for cigarettes.

"Martha often told me," Harriett Ehrlich said, "that smoking made her very uncomfortable, and that she really didn't care for it. In fact, she seldom used cigarettes except when they were called for in a picture, and even then they made her feel ill.

"I can never believe that she lighted a cigarette if she was, as they tell me, sitting quite alone in her car. If it was a match or a cigarette that set my poor darling's dress on fire, it was not of her own lighting. Of that I am positive."[28]

It didn't take long for conspiracy theorists to raise their suspicions about her death. Was Martha Mansfield a victim of murder? "What man or woman would have tortured a girl like this in order to kill her or ruin her beauty forever? Only a maniac, police think, and they can find no evidence that any such person was in or near Brackenridge Park that morning."[29]

Some even wondered whether Martha took her own life. That theory was quickly suppressed. "Few girls at twenty-three are as sane, as sensible, as thoroughly happy and contended as was Martha Mansfield. Her buoyant spirits and complete satisfaction with life and the success it was bringing her were as notable as her good looks and her talent for acting."[30]

Actor Phillip Shorey accompanied Martha's body to New York. Former chorus girl and life-long friend Florence Leeds, who captured lurid headlines in the early 1920s as a correspondent in the James A. Stillman divorce case, came out of hiding to assist with funeral arrangements. She provided a medal of the Virgin Mary for Martha's burial attire.[31]

Much of Broadway was stricken with grief. An estimated 5,000 mourners waited two hours to pass by the "silver plush coffin holding the little silken-clad body."[32]

Follies girls Betty Hale, Diana Allen, and Lillian McKenzie passed by the casket, as did Frances Grant, who played Martha's maid in *The Warrens of Virginia*. "That sweet child," Grant cried. "She was too young to die."[33]

John Barrymore, Gloria Swanson, Betty Compson, and Anita Stewart were among the mourners at her funeral, which was held at a chapel in Campbell's Funeral Home. Samuel Goldwyn, David Selznick, Edmund Goulding, and others served as pallbearers.[34]

Flo Leeds came after the service to say goodbye to her childhood friend. "She hurried over to the coffin, leaned above her dead friend for a second and then vanished into the passing crowd."[35]

Martha Mansfield was buried at Woodlawn Cemetery in Bronx, New York.

Sadly, Martha's role in *The Warrens of Virginia* was edited to a minimum. What could have been a tribute to the rising star turned out to be a fleeting bit. Rosemary Hill was promoted as the supporting actress.[36]

When the picture was released in October 1924, *Variety* noted that because of Martha's death while making the picture, no actresses were listed in the "title leader."

"Only the men are mentioned, and of the lot there is but one who stands out, the hero played by Wilfred Lytell opposite Miss Mansfield in the role of Lieutenant Burton. There is an effort to make the picture stand on the fact that it features the characters of General U.S. Grant and General Robert E. Lee in the advertising, but in reality, they are decidedly subsidiary characters to the hero and heroine (Martha), who carry the real story."[37]

Variety opined that had Martha lived, "she gave promise in this picture of being a screen actress of some ability, a good ingénue lead for program productions."

It was too early to tell whether Martha, as was predicted, would have risen in the ranks while under contract to Fox or whether she would have continued to find herself in thankless roles, routine programmers.

The really sad and unfortunate fact is, Martha never got a chance to find out! While in the middle of living her dream, she awoke to the reality of life's sometimes cruel twist of fate.

1. Pauline Curley interview with Michael G. Ankerich, March 1993.

2. Date of birth verified by the New York City Births registry (1891-1902), certificate #31888. Also, contrary to a number of biographies, Martha was not born in Mansfield, Ohio. Her maternal grandmother lived in Mansfield.

3. 1910 U.S. Federal Census.

4. *The Mansfield News*, 5 August 1911.

5   Golden, Eve, *Golden Images: 41 Essays on Silent Film Stars*, McFarland and Company, 2001.

6. Ibid.

7   " Pretty Good Business for 17-year-old Girl," *The Mansfield News*, 15 January 1917.

8. *Variety*, 15 February 1919.

9. Evans, Delight, "Making Over Martha," *Photoplay*, July 1920.

10. Ibid.

11. "Martha Mansfield Turns to the Films," *The Mansfield News*, 31 May 1919.

12. Evans, Delight, "Making Over Martha," *Photoplay*, July 1920.

13. Wollstein, Hans J., *All Movie Guide*.

14. Klepper, Robert K., *Silent Films, 1877-1996: A Critical Guide to 646 Movies*, McFarland and Company, 1999.

15. Fox, Charles Donald, and Silver Milton L., *Who's Who on the Screen*, Ross Publishing, Inc., 1920

16. Also of interest, the 1920 U.S. Federal Census lists Martha living alone with her mother. Her sister Edith was apparently living with her grandmother in Ohio. Martha's mother, Harriett, is listed as a widow.

17. "Martha Mansfield is Guest in the City," *The Mansfield News*, Mansfield, Ohio, 3 September 1919.

18. *Photoplay*, November 1920.

19. Olive Thomas, who was once a Ziegfeld Follies girl, died in Paris, France, on 10 September 1920. Refer to *Olive Thomas: The Life and Death of a Silent Film Beauty*, by Michelle Vogel, McFarland and Company, 2007.

20. "Martha Leaves Screen," *Oakland Tribune*, 14 August 1921.

21. "Does Fireside Lure Her?" *Oakland Tribune*, 19 August 1921.

22. *San Antonio Press*, 4 June 1922.

23. *Cleveland Press*, 9 February 1922.

24. *Variety*, 30 May 1923.

25. *Variety*, 6 September 1923.

26. "Mystery of What Burned Martha Mansfield to Death," *The Ogden Standard-Examiner*, 30 December 1923.

27. Texas Board of Health, Bureau of Vital Statistics, Standard Certificate of Death, #31506.

28. "Mystery of What Burned Martha Mansfield to Death," *The Ogden Standard-Examiner*, 30 December 1923.

29. Ibid.

30. Ibid.

31. "Flo Leeds, Designer, Mourns Martha Mansfield, Life Chum," The Mansfield News, Mansfield, Ohio, 6 December 1923.

32. "Stars of Stage and Screen Mourn Over Bier of Martha Mansfield," *The Mansfield News*, Mansfield, Ohio, 7 December 1923

33. Ibid.

34. Ibid.

35. Ibid.

36. *Variety*, 8 October 1923.

37. Ibid.

FILMOGRAPHY

1917

Max Comes Across (short) (Essanay) D: *Max Linder*. Max Linder, Martha Mansfield, Ernest Maupain.

Max Wants a Divorce (short) (Essanay) D: *Max Linder*. Max Linder, Martha Mansfield, Helen Ferguson, Francine Larrimore, Ernest Maupain.

Max in a Taxi (short) (Essanay) D: *Max Linder*. Max Linder, Martha Mansfield, Helen Ferguson, Francine Larrimore, Ernest Maupain.

1918

Broadway Bill (Metro) D: *Fred J. Balshofer* , Harold Lockwood, Martha Mansfield, Cornish Beck, Stanton Heck, Raymond C. Hadley, Bert Starkey, W. W. Black, Tom Blake, William Clifford, Art Ortego.

The Spoiled Girl (short) (Thomas Edison Inc.) D: *Jack Eaton.* James Montgomery Flagg, Martha Mansfield.

1919

The Hand Invisible (World Film Corp.) D: *Harry O Hoyt*. Montagu Love, Virginia Hammond, William Sorrelle, Marguerite Gale, Martha Mansfield, Kate Lester, George Le Guere, Muriel Ostriche.

The Perfect Lover (Selznick) D: *Ralph Ince*. Eugene O'Brien, Lucille Lee Stewart , Marguerite Courtot, Mary Boland, Martha Mansfield, Tom McRayne.

Should a Husband Forgive? (Fox) D: *R.A. Walsh* Miriam Cooper, Mrs. James K. Hackett, Eric Mayne, Vincent Coleman, Lyster Chambers, Percy Standing, Charles Craig, Martha Mansfield, James Marcus, Johnny Ries, Tom Burke.

1920

Dr. Jekyll and Mr. Hyde (Famous Players-Lasky) D: *John S. Robertson.*
John Barrymore, Martha Mansfield, Brandon Hurst, Charles Lane, J.
Malcolm Dunn, Cecil Clovelly, Nita Naldi, George S. Stevens, Louis
Wolheim.

Mothers of Men (Edward José Productions for Film Specials, Inc.)
D: *Edward José.* Claire Whitney, Lumsden Hare, Martha Mansfield,
Miss E. Roma, Cesare Gravina, Arthur Donaldson, William Gaton,
Zeffie Tilbury, Gaston Glass, Pierre Collosse, Julia Hurley.

Civilian Clothes (Famous Players-Lasky) D: *Hugh Ford.* Thomas
Meighan, Martha Mansfield, Maude Turner Gordon, Alfred Hickman,
Frank Losee, Marie Shotwell, Warren Cook, Albert Gran, Isabelle
Garrison, Halbert Brown, Kathryn Hildreth.

The Wonderful Chance (Selznick) D: *George Archainbaud.* Eugene O'Brien,
Tom Blake, Rudolph Valentino, Joe Flanagan, Warren Cook, Martha
Mansfield.

Women Men Love (Bradley Film Corp.) D: *Samuel R. Bradley.* William
Desmond, Marguerite Marsh, Martha Mansfield, Baby Doris Noldie,
Evan Burroughs Fontaine, Denton Vane, Josephine Dempsey, Alice
Fleming.

1921

Gilded Lies (Selznick) D: *William P.S. Earle.* Eugene O'Brien, Martha
Mansfield, Frank Whitson, George Stewart, Arthur Donaldson.

His Brother's Keeper (American Cinema Corp.) D: *Wilfrid North.* Albert
L. Barrett, Martha Mansfield, Rogers Lytton, Frazer Coulter, Gretchen
Hartman, Gladden James, Anne Drew.

The Last Door (Selznick) D: *William P.S. Earle.* Eugene O'Brien, Charles
Craig, Nita Naldi, Helen Pillsbury, Martha Mansfield, Katherine Perry
Warren Cook.

The Man of Stone (Selznick) D: *George Archainbaud.* Conway Tearle,
Betty Howe, Martha Mansfield, Colin Campbell, Warren Cook,
Charles D. Brown.

1922

Till We Meet Again (Dependable Pictures) D: *William Christy Cabanne.* Julia Swayne Gordon, J. Barney Sherry, Mae Marsh, Martha Mansfield, Norman Kerry, Walter Miller, Tammany Young, Danny Hayes, Dick Lee, Cyril Chadwick.

Queen of the Moulin Rouge (Pyramid Pictures) D: *Ray C. Smallwood.* Martha Mansfield, Joseph Striker, Henry Harmon, Fred T. Jones, Jane Thomas, Tom Blake, Mario Carillo.

1923

The Woman in Chains (Amalgamated Producing Corp.) D: *William P. Burt.* E.K. Lincoln, William H. Tooker, Mrs. Rudolph Valentino, Martha Mansfield, Joseph Striker, Coit Albertson.

The Little Red Schoolhouse (Arrow Film Corp.) D: *John G. Adolfi.* Martha Mansfield, Harlan Knight, Sheldon Lewis, E.K. Lincoln, Edmund Breese, Florida Kingsley, Paul Everton.

Youthful Cheaters (W.W. Hodkinson Corp.) D: *Frank Tuttle.* William Calhoun, Glenn Hunter, Martha Mansfield, Marie Burke, Nona Marden, Dwight Wiman.

Fog Bound (Famous Players–Lasky) D: *Irvin Willat.* Dorothy Dalton, Dave Powell, Martha Mansfield, Maurice Costello, Jack Richardson, Ella Miller, Willard Cooley, William David, Warren Cook.

The Silent Command (Fox) D: *J. Gordon Edwards.* Edmund Lowe, Bela Lugosi, Carl Harbaugh, Martin Faust, Gordon McEdward, Byron Douglas, Theodore Babcock, George Lessey, Warren Cook, Henry Armetta, Rogers Keene, J.W. Jenkins, Alma Tell, Martha Mansfield, Florence Martin, Betty Jewel, Kate Blancke, Elizabeth Foley.

Is Money Everything? (D.M. Film Corp.) D: *Glen Lyons.* Norman Kerry, Miriam Cooper, Andrew Hicks, John Sylvester, Martha Mansfield, William Bailey, Lawrence Brooke.

Potash and Perlmutter (Goldwyn) D: *Clarence Badger.* Alexander Carr, Barney Bernard, Vera Gordon, Martha Mansfield, Ben Lyon, Edward Durand, Hope Sutherland, De Sacia Mooers, Jerry Devine, Lee Kohlmar, Leo Donnelly, Tiller Girls.

The Leavenworth Case (Vitagraph) D: *Charles Gilbyn*. Seena Owen, Martha Mansfield, Wilfred Lytell, Bradley Barker, Paul Doucet, William Walcott, Frances Miller Grant, Fred Miller.

1924

The Warrens of Virginia (Fox) D: *Elmer Clifton*. George Backus, Rosemary Hill, Martha Mansfield, Robert Andrews, Wilfred Lytell, Harlan Knight, James Turfler, Helen Ray Kyle, Lieutenant Wilbur J. Fox, J. Barney Sherry, Frank Andrews.

MARY NOLAN

The bottled blonde sitting on the edge of the bed across the room from her was deflated, defeated, and depressed. The ever observant Grace Hall, who had written about film stars for years, knew she had this one pegged. Not only was the sobbing woman famous, she was infamous; not only was she glorious, she was notorious; not only was she beautiful, she was damned.

Depending on the year and the scandal of the time, the woman was either Mary Robertson, Imogene "Bubbles" Wilson, or Mary Nolan. For over a decade, her life had gone something like this: a new scandal, a new identity, a new name.

The year was 1931, and the thin, pale woman was Mary Nolan, film actress. Her translucent skin did little to conceal her sad, sick soul beneath. Gladys Hall summed up her appearance this way: "So fragile she looked untouchable. Her gray eyes were wet with slow and completely unheeded tears. She cried as one cries who is used to crying and doesn't even notice it anymore."

She weathered a miserable childhood, eventually finding fame as a Ziegfeld Follies girl while still a teenager. Imogene Wilson fell in love with a married man, a famous comedian of the stage, who ended up physically and emotionally abusing her. The screaming headlines detailing her suit against her lover sent her in shame to Europe, where she started over, this time as Mary Robertson, a star of German films. She mounted debt, lots of it, and was all too happy to be rescued by an American film producer who brought her to the States and changed her name to Mary Nolan.

Despite the leeriness of the Hays Office, Mary became a popular leading lady with American audiences in the last years of the silent era. Her reputation, however, loomed over her like a waiting noose. There were more abusive affairs, additional debt that was never paid, and addiction to drugs and alcohol.

Ruined in Hollywood, Mary hit the road, singing and dancing in cheap theaters and roadhouses in New York and across the country.

She vowed never to give in to the one prediction many foes made for her — suicide. Yet, that seems to be how her sad life ended in 1948 at the age of 42.

Gladys Hall, unlike other writers who'd burned her in the past, was there that afternoon not to rip Mary to shreds, but to come to her defense and offer hope against the odds that Mary would find her way out of the darkness.

"What chance have they, really?" Hall concluded. "These beautiful things enlisted on a frail craft without a pilot. How dare we condemn them, born with the face of angels and delivered into the hands of devils."

It seemed Mary Imogene Robertson was born into a life from hell. She came from a poor Kentucky family, the youngest of five children born on December 18, 1902,[1] to Africanus Gabriel and Viola Pitman Robertson. When she was three, her mother died at age 46, leaving her father, a sickly farmhand and carpenter, in charge of five children, three of which were under 10.

At some point, Africanus could no longer look after young Mary. She lived for a time with a foster family in Kentucky, but ended up in a Catholic orphanage in St. Joseph, Missouri, separated from her family. It was there she was given her nickname — "Bubbles."

The other Robertson children stayed with their father, who managed to scrap out a living, until he died of heart disease in January 1911.[2]

In June 1912, the nuns received word that Mary was to return temporarily to Kentucky. Her oldest sister, Myrtle, and the child she had given birth to in January, were near death. Myrtle McDaniels died from tetanus on June 2;[3] her six-month old son died two weeks later.[4]

Mary spent some time with an elderly grandmother in Kentucky who was not able to look after her. She later returned to the orphanage, where she lived until she was 13.[5] She then made her way to New York City to be near her sister, Mabel, who was now an actress and the wife of actor Charles Rondeau.[6] It was Mabel who introduced Mary to the stage.

Not long after her arrival in New York, Mary met Arthur William Brown, a magazine illustrator, who took special interest in the teenager during her first months in New York. Brown took her home to meet his wife, who bought Mary new clothes. Soon, Mary was posing for Brown and living at the Artists and Models Club.

"Things had happened to me so rapidly in this new world that I wasn't shocked when Mr. Brown had me to take off some of my clothes," Mary later recounted. "I stood before him, partly draped, without shame. His manner put me at ease. His interest was in his art, not in my body."[7]

Mary soon became one of the top artist's model in the day, posing for such illustrators as James Montgomery Flagg, Norman Rockwell, and Charles Dana Gibson.

In August 1922, while still posing for artists, Mary made her stage debut in the musical comedy *Daffy Dill,* which ran for two months at the Apollo Theater. She then appeared for five months in the chorus of another musical, *Lady Butterfly.*

It was while appearing in *Daffy Dill* that Mary met Frank Tinney, the 44-year-old star of the show. One evening after the show, Mary found herself on the curb in a thunderstorm trying to hail a cab. The taxi that stopped for her was carrying Tinney. He offered to take her home. She invited him to her apartment and Tinney stayed the night with the teenager.

Mary fell for Tinney, and fell hard! For the first time in her life, she felt special. Finally, someone cared for her. Someone loved her. Then, Mary learned there was a Mrs. Tinney. She exploded and demanded an explanation.

"Sure," Tinney responded, "I have a wife and a mortgage and an appendix, but why should I bring those things up to spoil a pleasant evening? I believe a man should keep his troubles to himself."

It was too late to change course; Mary was hooked. So was Tinney. They maintained their apartment and kept their relationship secret. Their life together became tumultuous and explosive.

"It was the perfect love match," DeWitt Bodeen wrote of the pair. "He was a sadist with a violent temper; she was a masochist, who kept taunting him to beat her some more. Which he always did."[8]

In the meantime, Mary, now Imogene "Bubbles" Wilson, joined the *Ziegfeld Follies.* She first appeared in the 1923 edition with Eddie Cantor, Fanny Brice, and Ann Pennington.

It was during her run in the 1924 edition of the *Follies* that all hell broke loose. In May, following a usual row between the two, Mary attempted suicide. Several days later, she invited Mark Hellinger, a reporter from *New York Daily News,* to her apartment. She wanted him to have the story firsthand.

Following rehearsal that evening, Mary was home waiting for the reporter when Tinney showed up and went into another room for a nap. Around 9:30 p.m., the reporter arrived and Tinney was stirred from his sleep. Convinced that Mary was fooling around on him, Tinney went into action.

Mary recalled the incident in court. "Mr. Tinney walked out of the room in my blue silk kimono and with the maid's earrings on. He used vile language — I don't want to repeat it. 'Who is that?' asked Tinney. 'A reporter,' I explained. Tinney said, 'I don't believe you.'"⁹

The reporter left and Tinney went to work on her. "When the reporter closed the door and went out Tinney kicked me on the right instep," Mary testified. "He was wearing walking shoes. I said, 'Don't kick me that way.' He went into the kitchen. When I followed him, he hit me in the head

Mary appeared in the Ziegfeld Follies as Imogene "Bubbles" Wilson

with his fist. I fell to the floor. He dragged me into the sitting room, sat on me, and beat me between the shoulders until I had a hemorrhage of the nose and mouth. He was calling me names. He pulled my hair and then threw me on a chair. He threw an ash receiver at me. I flung up my arm to protect my face and got it on the arm."[10]

The next day, Tinney was arrested for assaulting the young chorus girl. The abuser took the charge lightly, claiming Mary would never go through with her suit. Edna Davenport Tinney, his wife, said, "Why this is just a foolish little girl that has believed everything Frank told her. She has my sympathy and I am very sorry for her."[11]

The next morning, Mary arrived in court supported on either side by her sister, Mabel, and her maid. She stated her intentions of proceeding with the case. She filed a $100,000 civil suit against her accuser. On her way out of the courtroom, Mary collapsed and "hung limp in the arms of her attendants. It was necessary for her to rest on one of the rear benches. She remained there until the crowd had left the courtroom. Then, she was supported to the head of the stairs and a reporter carried her down."[12]

A week later, Mary took the stand against Tinney. She told of routine beatings and several suicide attempts because, "I wanted to die. I was tired of being beaten by Frank Tinney." Her maid, Carrie Sneed, corroborated her story, remembering that Mary had once told her, "Carrie, don't let him kill me."[13]

Tinney's attorney asked that the case be dismissed, insisting that the whole debacle was a publicity gimmick. Magistrate Max Levine denied the motion. In his remarks, Levine explained that, while the acting profession is a "great and honorable one, the troubles between actors and chorus girls and the stories of so-called love nests are all too frequently set forth in the public press. If we had fewer young women who love unwisely, we would have less notoriety. But, above all else, if we had fewer men in high position on the stage who offer temptation to the young and struggling girls at the bottom of the ladder, we would have a cleaner profession."[14]

Later in the month, the case went before a grand jury, which, in the end, refused to indict Tinney on the evidence Mary gave. "Things looked pretty dark for me," Tinney told reporters later. "That's the first time I ever made good without raising a laugh." He repeated his contention that the whole affair had been a publicity stunt. "If a woman beats a man, that isn't news. If a man beats a woman, that's news. I also know why they call actors and actresses hams: she's been cured now."[15]

Perhaps Mary was cured of her ill feelings for her lover. In a bizarre twist of events, Mary reconciled with Tinney, who had made immediate plans to sail to England to fulfill a vaudeville engagement. Before he could depart, Edna Tinney filed for separation, charging her husband with desertion.

Reporters hounded Mrs. Tinney for any shred of news to keep the scandal in the headlines. "I don't want to answer any questions about any other lady or ladies that may be in Frank's life," she said. "I don't want to be coupled with these various individuals in any way, shape or form. I'm plugging in my own way without any aid or enthusiasm from skyrocketing persons who need a brass band and a three-ring circus to keep them happy." Speaking of herself, she said, "You can use a postage stamp only once and I guess that about describes me."[16]

To avoid the press, Tinney boarded the Columbus liner in the early morning hours of August 5. Mary was at his heels. The lovers disappeared into his cabin. When the whistle blew, signaling departure, it took the combined persuasion of Tinney and the crew to persuade a sobbing Mary to cross the gangplank.

When news of Mary's dramatic farewell scene made the papers, a disappointed Florenz Ziegfeld issued his own farewell. "I dismissed Miss Wilson from the cast of the Follies this afternoon because she promised me that she would not have anything further to do with Frank Tinney," Ziegfeld said. "She broke her promise and I discharged her on account of the notoriety and also to prevent a possible disruption of the morale of my cast."[17]

Mary seemed unfazed by Ziegfeld's action against her. When she met with reporter Mark Hellinger several weeks later, Frank Tinney was her only concern. Was she happy? Hellinger asked.

"Happy? And why shouldn't I be? I have something that nobody else in the world has stronger than I. I have love. Frank Tinney is the only thing in my life. You know it. Everybody knows it. So why should I beat around the bush?"[18]

Hellinger asked whether Tinney was a "poor lot on whom to lavish your devotion."

"Don't preach to me about Frank Tinney," she screamed. "Every man in this world is rotten — and Frank is no worse than anyone else. Is he the only married man who has had an affair? Just because I am Imogene Wilson and he is Frank Tinney people point at us and whisper. Whisper, I should have said, broadcast! Wherever I go, I feel accusing eyes upon me."[19]

Perhaps Europe was the only place where accusing eyes would not linger on the former Follies girl. In early September, Mary applied for a passport, stating she would be traveling to the British Isles, France,

Germany, Italy, and Austria, the locations Frank Tinney noted on his application.[20]

On September 20, 1924, Mary sailed for Europe. She spoke with reporters before boarding. "I certainly am not going to dodge Frank if we happen to meet in Europe," she said. "I am very unhappy and I want to go away. I may stay away forever. From now on, I will lead a quiet life."[21]

Mary's first stop on her new adventure was London, where she foolishly reconciled with Tinney. By December, Tinney's drinking and physical abuse had worsened, and Mary, through black eyes, saw in him a pathetic soul. She was looking for a way out, and found the avenue to freedom when she received an offer to make films in Germany.

Billed as Imogene Robertson, Mary made her film debut for UFA (Universum Film AG) in *Die Feuertänzerin*. Her work was received enthusiastically, so much so, that UFA offered her a contract. Her salary reached the equivalent of $1,500 a week. She was making good feature films in the golden age of German cinema. She earned respect for her talent, and the public seemed to be forgetting her sordid past.

One who hadn't forgotten her past was actress Gertrude McCoy, an American film star whose career began around 1910. Now married to British actor Duncan McRae, McCoy was making films in Europe. She worked with Mary in *Verborgene Gluten* (1925). Years after her retirement from films, she returned to her home state of Georgia and settled in Atlanta. She became acquainted with silent film historian Roi Uselton, who routinely questioned her about her film work and various co-workers, including Mary Nolan.

At the mention of her name, McCoy bristled. "How dare you mention that woman's name to me," she snapped. "I'll have you know that she is the reason I once switched hotels in Germany. She had the audacity to come down the grand staircase in a dress that was slit all the way down the middle. Disgusting!"

Mary, looking quite spectacular in her revealing gowns, worked steadily in German films during 1924 and 1925. She routinely received offers from Hollywood producers to return to her homeland. While she wanted to eventually reclaim some respectability and offer something worthwhile in Hollywood pictures, Mary took few offers seriously. When producer Joseph Schenck came calling, Mary couldn't turn away. She signed a contact with United Artists and, in January 1927, sailed for New York.

Part of the reason Mary wanted a fresh start in her own country was to escape mounting debt. She was unable to pay the $20,000 for gowns and other finery she couldn't resist adding to her closet. While in Berlin, she had also undergone an operation, which she said, resulted from injuries she suffered at the hands of her former lover. During her last months in Germany, Mary was assisted by a nurse, who many claimed was hired only to ward off bill collectors.[22]

When her return to the States to make films in Hollywood made headlines, Mary's hopes of starting over were dashed. Women's groups protested and Hollywood watchdog Will B. Hays had grave reservations about her working in the motion picture industry.

In Hollywood, Mary rented a house on Beachwood Drive high in the Hollywood Hills and waited several months before finally being called to the studio. She was told the perfect vehicle for her couldn't be found. Would she consent to having her contract canceled and returning to Germany? Mary explained that didn't want their money, that if she didn't make pictures there, she would try other studios.

United Artists consented, but expressed concern that her name, Imogene Wilson, was too long for marquees. Would she consider changing her professional name to Mary Nolan? She agreed.

"Of course, they were trying to tell me in a polite way that Imogene Wilson and everything associated with that name would be booed from the screen all over the land. They had given me a new identity, a fresh start, in an effort to bury my past," Mary wrote later.[23]

She was given a small role in *Topsy and Eva* (1927), which starred the Duncan Sisters, Rosetta and Vivian. She was then cast as Nils Asther's girlfriend in *Sorrel and Son* (1927). The cast, which also included H.B. Warner, Anna Q. Nilsson, Carmel Myers, Lionel Belmore, Alice Joyce, and Louis Wolheim, sailed to England in July 1927 for production.

Back in Hollywood in mid-August, Mary signed a starring contract with Universal. Also, as she was just getting settled in the movie capital, she jumped into another disastrous affair, this time with M-G-M executive Eddie Mannix, whom she met one evening at the Cocoanut Grove. His marriage didn't stop either from falling hard for the other.

"He was a man's man," Mary later wrote, "masculine in every sense of the word. That's the only kind that ever has appealed to me. I've had no time for sissy, slick-haired Romeos."[24]

Mary tried hard to focus on her first Universal outing, *Good Morning, Judge* (1928), in which she played a wealthy social worker who runs a haven for reformed criminals. *Variety* concluded that "the former Imogene Wilson should get applause for her work. It is not only sincere and convincing, but registers her as possessing the camera and lighting appreciation of an old-timer."[25]

She was equally praised for her next picture, *Foreign Legion* (1928). "Mary Nolan plays a selfish, gold-digging blonde, and she does it very well. She is the type of impersonal, characterless beauty, and with a narrow range of characterization should prosper on the screen. Here she was distinctly an asset on merit and without reference to her publicity possibilities."[26]

An autographed portrait of Mary Nolan.

On loan to M-G-M in mid-1928, Mary was cast as Maizie in *West of Zanzibar* (1929). In the picture, Flint (Lon Chaney), a former vaudeville performer, is paralyzed after a confrontation with his former friend, Crane (Lionel Barrymore), who also took his fiancée from him. Time passes, the fiancée is dead, and Chaney is now an ivory merchant bent on revenge against Crane and his daughter (Maizie). Flint arranges for Maizie to

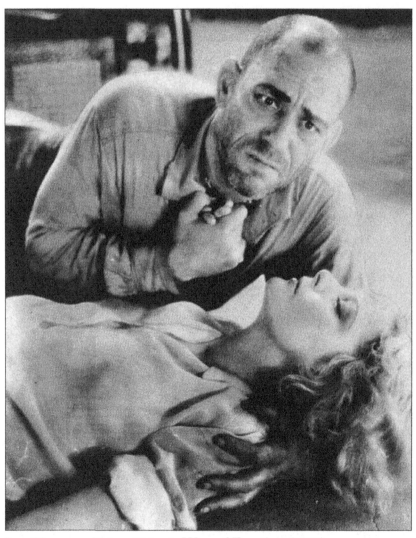

Lon Chaney and Mary Nolan in West of Zanzibar *(1929).*

become a prostitute and eventually plots for her to be sacrificed in an African ritual. In the final reel, he learns that he is Maizie's father (Maizie was conceived before his fiancée ran away) and manages to stop to sacrifice.

West of Zanzibar was an overwhelming success with the public and provided Mary her finest opportunity in Hollywood. Bret Wood, in writing about the film for *Filmfax* magazine, said Mary was "ideally cast."

John Gilbert and Mary Nolan in Desert Nights *(1930).*

Wood wrote, "She was able to radiate the deep sensuality of an experienced woman while managing to evoke sympathy for the innocent's girl plight."[27] Another critic noted, "There is a tragedy in Miss Nolan's eyes that seems more heartbreaking than the histrionics of two dozen far more experienced actresses." *Motion Picture* magazine said the real reason to see the picture is "the blonde and beautiful Mary Nolan, who looks very fair indeed against the mud and slime of Zanzibar."[28]

Mary's career was further boosted when she played opposite John Gilbert in his final silent film, *Desert Nights* (1930). "Miss Nolan does better work than usual in this picture," *Variety* concluded. "She is a good teammate for Gilbert."[29]

Eddie Mannix, like Frank Tinney, was an abuser who became fond of using his mistress as a punching bag. One incident sent Mary seriously injured to the Los Angeles hospital where she underwent a series of operations. Recovery, this time, was painful, requiring the use of a wheelchair — and drugs. It was because of her injuries suffered at the hands of her abuser that she became addicted to narcotics.

Sliding into drug addiction and another ill-fated relationship took the momentum from Mary's film career. She put in lackluster performances in her Universal work. Ironically, in *Shanghai Lady* (1929), she played a

William Janney and Mary Nolan, already showing signs of drug addiction, in Young Desire (1930) COURTESY OF WILLIAM JANNEY

prostitute who spends several months in an opium den before deciding to reform. In *Undertow*, she is the restless and bored wife of a lighthouse keeper (Johnny Mack Brown).

Playing a dancer in a carnival sideshow in *Young Desire* (1930), Mary falls for a young and innocent socialite (William Janney). Knowing she's wrong for the lad and that the relationship is doomed, she jumps to her death.

Mary Nolan and William Janney clowning around on the set of Young Desire. COURTESY OF WILLIAM JANNEY

Young and rather innocent in real life, William Janney was perfect for the lead in *Young Desire*. Although he'd spent years working in the theater, he had never encountered a woman quite like Mary Nolan.

"The picture was a mess because of Mary Nolan," Janney told this author in 1991. "She took dope and practically everything else. She was supposed to have had all these things (diseases) and it scared me to death when she would stick her tongue down my throat during our love scenes and rub herself all over me. I would go to the dressing room and gargle with Listerine because I was terrified she was going to give me something."[30]

By the time she worked with William Janney, Mary was a drug addict. "A nurse was with me constantly. I had been given hypodermics to ease my excruciating pain. The nurse always was at hand to give me a relieving shot when the torture became unbearable after I finished a scene."[31]

Her death scene at the end of *Young Desire* was especially torturous. "I was supposed to commit suicide by jumping from a high platform. My double had performed the more dangerous episodes, but I had to do this one, a close-up, myself.

"I leaped off. The hidden net was only a few feet below me, but that short fall wrenched my injuries and almost killed me. I was in a state of collapse when I was taken down. Again my nurse was waiting with a hypo that brought relief. I thought nothing of it. I didn't know that I had been given up as incurable by the doctors, that they were pampering my wishes to continue my screen work. I felt I had to carry on while my talents were in demand."[32]

In July 1930, Mary became the subject of a narcotics investigation when two nurses signed affidavits that they had recently cared for the actress and that she was constantly under the influence of illegal drugs. One nurse swore that Mary's arms were "full of needle punctures from hypodermic needles."[33]

In the middle of the investigation, severe sunburn sent Mary to St. Vincent's Hospital, thereby allowing her to temporarily evaded narcotics agents who had warrants to search her home. One of the investigators went to the hospital to examine Mary.

"I failed to find a single mark of a needle," the investigator told reporters. "I am firmly convinced that Miss Nolan is not an addict."[34]

Mary summed up the investigation as an attempt to derail her career and further damage her reputation in Hollywood.[35]

Her temperament did little to restore Mary's standing in Hollywood. At Universal, she went to battle with the Laemmles, studio heads, over her latest picture, *What Men Want* (1930). She blew up at director Ernst Laemmle, complaining she'd been left out of close-ups in which others in the cast were included. One morning, she showed up for work to find herself barred from the set. She complained of unfair treatment by her director to production chief Carl Laemmle Jr.

"That's ridiculous," Laemmle said. "It's merely a matter of too much

Mary Nolan and Edward G. Robinson in Outside the Law *(1930).*

temperament. We have taken only 30 scenes in nine days of the picture." Mary was fired from the picture and replaced with Pauline Starke.

Mary was enraged. "I'll never set foot on the lot again, even if I have to sacrifice my career in pictures by doing it. My reputation as an actress has been injured by their actions." She prepared to file suit.

Carl Laemmle stood firm. "Her charges are ridiculous. We had lived up to every clause in Miss Nolan's contract. By the terms of her contract with us, we reserve the right to remove her from a cast at any time we see fit to do so."

The matter was settled in January 1931 when Universal bought up the remaining time on Mary's contract.

Cal York, writing for *Photoplay*, wrote, "That Nolan girl has torn Universal limb to limb. She has passed fighting talk to everyone from Carl Laemmle down to the boy who waters the elephants. She has demanded, raged, stormed, and caused more trouble than a hundred ordinary actresses."[36]

There was nothing left for her but forgettable roles in various fly-by-night studios. Her life continued skid out of control.

In February 1931, she was sought by police after a rug became missing from a house she had leased from director Lambert Hillyer. The rug

Mary Nolan and her husband, Wallace T. Macrery.

showed up at the office of a physician, who said Mary had given it to him as partial payment for a medical bill.[37]

Although she had recently stated she had no interest in matrimony until her career was finished, Mary wed millionaire broker Wallace T. Macrery in March 1931. She told the press she was soon starting a picture about racketeering, after which she and her husband would go on a vaudeville tour.[38]

A week before their marriage, Macrery lost over $3 million in a downward turn of the stock market. In the meantime, she and Macrery opened a dress shop in Beverly Hills with the $9,000 he had left of his fortune.

More troubles were ahead for the couple when Mary filed for bankruptcy in August. She listed her assets as $3,000 and her liabilities as almost $93,000.[39] Later that month, while standing on a street corner in

Beverly Hills, two police officers tapped her on the shoulder and took her to court, alleging she failed to pay wages to five employees, including her cook, chauffeur, nurse, maid, and a musician. She was released after posting bail.[40]

Several months later, employees of the dress shop she owned with her husband filed wage claims with the state labor commission. She was ordered, but failed to appear, in municipal court. Warrants were issued for her arrest.[41] A second bench warrant was issued in December when she again failed to make a court appearance.[42]

In March 1932, Mary and her husband were convicted of 17 labor law violations. She was ordered to pay the $1,300 claim and was sentenced to 30 days in jail.[43] Mary Nolan fan clubs around the country signed petitions to free the actress.

Mary was determined to start afresh. She went to New York, where in June, she announced she was divorcing Wallace Macrery.

"Yes, I am going to divorce Wallace. He is the nicest man I know and I am terribly fond of him, but we are a drawback to each other," she told the *Los Angeles Times*. "It's just another lot of trouble. We were married in New York a week after he lost his whole fortune in one afternoon on the Stock Exchange. Like children, we thought money didn't matter and married anyway. We went to Hollywood, but Hollywood did not want me to be married. Everything I do is wrong, even when it is the right thing."[44]

In Hollywood, she made her final film, *File 113*, for Allied Pictures in 1933. She then settled in New York.

A five-state, all points bulletin was issued for Mary in November 1934. Police were interested in questioning her about a $2,000 bankroll that impresario Louis Kessman reported missing. Kessman told authorities that he had been looking for theatrical talent when he saw Mary singing in Green Gables Tavern in Hazelton, Pennsylvania. He asked for an introduction and offered to drive her to Hotel Altamont, where she was staying.

He took her home at 4 a.m. After she got out and he was driving home, Kessman noticed his $2,000 bankroll was missing. He had no luck in contacting her. Mary was arrested the next night and spent the evening behind bars. A hearing was underway the next morning in New York when a telegram reached the court saying the charges had been withdrawn.[45]

In 1935, she filed a $500,000 suit against her old lover, Eddie Mannix, now vice-president and general manager of M-G-M, claiming he physically assaulted her and used his influence to prevent her from finding work.[46] Later that year, she was off to London, where she performed a vaudeville singing act at the Piccadilly theatre.

Back in the States, Mary could find little work other than singing in cheap roadhouses and nightclubs. She was hired for the Queen's Terrace cabaret in Lancaster, Ohio, in March 1936. One of her standards was "Out in the Cold Again."

Mary Nolan on the downside of fame.

"I don't like nightclubs, but I have to live," she said at the time. "I'm not a singer, but I have to make a living."[47]

Through the cigarette smoke of her dim-lit world, she could only see a few feet in front of her, but she kept a clear vision in her mind of the stages of Broadway and the movie studios of Hollywood, which she believed were still in her future.

It was in a New York nightclub that William Janney, with whom she had appeared in *Young Desire* only a few years before, was reacquainted with his former leading lady.

"I was walking down Broadway when I found this saloon where Mary was working," he remembered. "From the stage she announced, 'Ladies and gentlemen, this is my leading man.' I felt really bad because she was drinking. I asked her how she was.

She said, "Oh, everything's fine with me."[48] He knew she was far from well.

In May 1937, Mary's past caught up with her again when she was arrested for failure to pay a $400 debt from five years before. She was released when a representative from a collection agency agreed to give her more time to pay the debt. From jail, she was taken to the psychiatric ward at Bellevue Hospital, where she was described as "worn and pale."[49]

Only days following her release, she talked about her arrest and her need for work. "The shock of my recent arrest and brief imprisonment for an old debt put me under a severe nervous strain," she said. "I am gaining strength daily, and am sure that in the near future, I shall be a strong healthy woman."

Of her career, she said frankly, "I'll do anything to earn an honest living, although I still believe that it is in Hollywood that I belong."[50]

Recovery was slow in coming. Later that year, she underwent medical and psychiatric treatment at Brunswick Home in Amityville, New York. In October, she was rushed to Bellevue Hospital after overdosing on a sedative.[51]

After spending a year in a New York sanitarium, a fragile Mary returned to Hollywood, where she moved in with her sister, Mabel, and claimed she would make the rounds of the studios in hopes of work.

"I am a competent actress, and there should be a place for me here," she said. "I want to go back to work."[52]

By now, however, her looks were gone and there was no work for her in films. She changed her name to Mary Wilson and made ends meet by managing a bungalow court. She was content to keep a low profile.

She sold her story to *The American Weekly* in 1941, and that fall, details of her torrid past ran in newspapers for several months. This sparked conversation about writing her memoirs and turning her life into a story for the big screen.

In the spring of 1948, Mary was taken to Cedars of Lebanon Hospital and treated for malnutrition. Her weight had dropped to just 80 pounds. Doctors also treated her for a gall bladder ailment.

She moved into a room in a bungalow court at 1504 S. Mansfield Avenue. Her only possession was a massive antique piano that once belonged to Rudolph Valentino. It practically filled the room.

"I think she worshipped Rudy's memory," her sister, Mabel, said later. "She clung personally to this piano and always kept Rudy's picture on the music rack. I think it reminded her of her own greatness and helped her profoundly in her discouragement."

In the fall of 1948, Mary, believing the end was near, contacted writer Jack Preston and asked him to work with her on her autobiography. "I am going to die," she told him. The two worked on the project for over two months.[53]

Around midnight on Saturday, October 30, Edward Gallagher, a neighbor in the court, returned home at 1504 S. Mansfield Avenue to find Mary ill. He summoned Mary's sister, who called her doctor, Leo

Gelfand. He treated her around 1 a.m. At about 4 a.m., Gallagher awoke to find Mary unconscious on the floor. He put her to bed in another room. At 8 p.m., he called Dr. Gelfand because he suspected Mary was dead. Dr. Gelfand arrived and confirmed Gallagher's suspicion. Mary Nolan died in the wee hours of Sunday, October 31, 1948. She was only 46 years old.

An original advertisement for her story in The American Weekly.

Investigators initially had trouble determining the cause of death. A note tied around an empty pill bottle on her dresser hinted at suicide.[54] An autopsy revealed she died of barbiturate poisoning due to an ingestion of Seconal. Her death certificate indicates an accidental death or suicide.[55]

And, what of the piece of paper attached to the empty bottle of pills? It contained the words to *A Child's Prayer*, a poem by William Hawley Smith.

When it gets dark, the birds and flowers,
Shut up their eyes and say goodnight;
And God, Who loves them, counts the hours
And keeps them safe till it gets light!
Dear Father! Count the hours to-night,
When I'm asleep and cannot see;
And, in the morning, may the light
Shine for the birds, the flowers, and me!

Scrawled on the back in Mary's handwriting were the words, "If this were only true."[56]

1   There is some speculation about Mary's year of birth. She gave 1902 as her year of birth on her U.S. Passport application in 1924. Also, in a 1924 court hearing, she gave an age that correlated to a 1902 year of birth. Her death certificate states 1905, the date most often used.

2   Certificate of Death 898, Commonweath of Kentucky, 23 January 1911.

3   Certificate of Death 15017, Commonweath of Kentucky, 6 June 1912.

4   Certificate of Death 15152, Commonwealth of Kentucky, 13 July 1912.

5   Nolan, Mary, "Confessions of a Follies Beauty," *The American Weekly*, 1941.

6   The 1920 U.S. Federal Census shows Charles and Mabel Rondeau living with their two children in Brooklyn in 1920.

7   Nolan, Mary, "Confessions of a Follies Beauty," *The American Weekly*, 1941.

8   Bodeen, DeWitt, "The Hard Luck Girl," *Films in Review*, May 1980.

9   "Tinney's Accuser on Witness Stand," *The New York Times*, 7 June 1924.

10   Ibid.

11   "Tinney in Court; Girl Ill at Home," *The New York Times*, 30 May 1924.

12   "Chorus Girl to Accuse Tinney," *The New York Times*, 1 June 1924.

13   "Tinney's Accuser on Witness Stand," *The New York Times*, 7 June 1924.

14   "Tinney's Accuser on Witness Stand," *The New York Times*, 7 June 1924.

15   "Grand Jury Lets Frank Tinney Off," *The New York Times*, 28 June 1924.

16   "Tinney, Sued, Sails; Follies Drops Girl," *The New York Times*, 6 August 1924.

17   Ibid.

18   "Imogene, Drooping Flower, In Upper West Side Flat Awaits Call of Her Frank," *The Bridgeport Telegram*, Bridgeport, Connecticut, 20 August 1924.

19   Ibid.

20   U.S. Passport application, Mary Robertson, 8 September 1924.

21   "Imogene Wilson Left U.S. Today," *Lebanon Daily News,* Lebanon, Pennsylvania, 20 September 1924.

22   "Imogene Wilson Quits Berlin for America," *The New York Times,* 19 January 1927.

23   Nolan, Mary, "Confessions of a Follies Beauty," *The American Weekly,* 1941.

24   Ibid.

25   *Variety,* 27 June 1928.

26   *Variety,* 27 June 1928.

27   Wood, Bret. "West of Zanzibar: A Hybrid of Melodramatic Horror," *Filmfax.*

28   *Motion Picture,* January 1929.

29   Variety, 8 May 1929.

30   Interview with Michael G. Ankerich, October 1991, Atlanta.

31   Nolan, Mary, "Confessions of a Follies Beauty," *The American Weekly,* 1941.

32   Ibid.

33   "Star's 'Nerves' Halt Warrant," 31 July 1930.

34   "Sunburn on Record," unknown date and publication.

35   "Imogene Wilson Sees Plot on Reputation," *The New York Times,* 31 July 1930.

36   *Photoplay,* June 1930.

37   "Mary Nolan, Former Imogene Wilson, Sought by L.A. Police," 17 February 1931.

38   "Follies Girl Weds Broker," 28 March 1931.

39   "Mary Nolan in Bankruptcy," 1 August 1931.

40   "Mary Nolan in Row Over Pay," 20 August 1931.

41   "Warrants Out for Mary Nolan, Actress," 28 November 1931.

42   "Mary Nolan Again Keeps Court Waiting," 8 December 1931.

43   "Mary Nolan Faces Jail," *The New York Times,* 10 March 1932.

44   "Mary Nolan Wants Divorce," *Los Angeles Times,* 17 July 1932.

45   "Mary Nolan Freed, Charge Quashed," *San Antonio Express,* 7 November 1934.

46   "Mary Nolan, Screen Star, Plaintiff in Half Million Dollar Damage Suit," *The Muscatine Journal and News-Tribune,* Muscatine, Iowa, 9 July 1935.

47   *Daily Globe,* Ironwood, Michigan, 11 March 1936.

48   William Janney interview with Michael G. Ankerich, October 1991.

49   "Mary Nolan is Released," *The New York Times,* 6 May 1937.

50   "Mary Nolan Tells of Loves," *Los Angeles Herald,* 11 May 1937.

51   "Mary Nolan Ill of Poisoning," *The New York Times,* 19 October 1937.

52   "Mary Nolan Returns to Seek Work as Actress," 10 September 1938.

53   Preston, Jack, "Mary's Writer Tells of Work," November 1948.

54   "Mystery Clouds Death of Ex-Film Star Mary Nolan," *Los Angeles Examiner,* 1 November 1948.

55   State of California, Certification of Vital Record, 1 December 1948.

56   "Ex-Actress Leaves Poem."

FILMOGRAPHY

1925

As Imogene Robertson:

Verborgene Gluten *[Münchner Lichtspielkunst AG (Emelka)]* D: *Einar Bruun*. Alfons Fryland, Mary Nolan, Lisa Deihle.

Wenn die Liebe nicht wär! *(Phoebus-Film AG)* D: *Richard Dinesen*. Fritz Alberti, Harry Halm, Antonie Jaeckel, Jenny Jugo, Frieda Lehndorf, Mary Nolan, Karl Platen, Hans Adalbert Schlettow, Daisy Torrens, Elsa Wagner.

Das Parfüm der Mrs. Worrington [Münchner Lichtspielkunst AG *(Emelka)*] D: *Franz Seitz*. Ernst Reicher, Mary Nolan, Maria Mindzenty, John Mylong, Otto Wernicke, Karl Falkenberg, Ferdinand Martini, Claire Kronburger, Manfred Koempel-Pilot.

Die Feuertänzerin *(Phoebus-Film AG)* D: *Richard Dinesen*. Mary Nolan, Alfred Abel, Ruth Weyher, Trude Berliner, Carl Auen,.

Die Unberührte Frau *(Greenbaum-Film)* D: *Constantin J. David*. Mary Nolan, Hans Junkermann, Constantin J. David.

1926

Fünf-Uhr-Tee in der Ackerstraße *(Domo-Film GmbH)* D: *Paul L. Stein*. Reinhold Schünzel, Mary Nolan, Maria Kamradek, Fritz Kampers, Heinrich Schroth, Angelo Ferrari, Frigga Braut.

Unser täglich Brot *(Greenbaum-Film)* D: *Constantin J. David*. Fritz Kampers, Mary Nolan, Dina Gralla, Elza Temary, Harry Nestor, Leona Bergere, Paul Rehkopf.

Die Elf schillschen Offiziere [Internationale Film AG *(IFA)*] D: *Rudolf Meinhart.* Rudolf Meinert , Gustav Adolf Semler, Grete Reinwald, Leopold von Ledebur, Mary Nolan, Ernst Rückert, Werner Pittschau, Fritz Greiner, Albert Steinrück, Charles Willy Kayser, Camilla von Hollay, Henri Peters-Arnolds, John Mylong, Else Reval, Aruth Wartan,.

Wien, wie es weint und lacht (Aafa-Film AG) D: *Rudolf Walther-Fein.* Fritz Greiner, John Mylong, Mady Christians, Frida Richard, Hans Brausewetter, Erich Kaiser-Titz, Mary Nolan, Hermann Picha, Werner Pittschau, Julius Falkenstein, Paul Biensfeldt, Max Menden, Wilhelm Diegelmann.

Das Süße Mädel (Noa-Film GmbH) D: *Manfred Noa.* Mary Nolan, Paul Heidemann, Nils Asther, Mary Parker, Eugen Burg, Hanni Reinwald, Loo Hardy, Ernst Pröckl, Karl Platen, Henry Bender, Sophie Pagay, Bobbie Bender, Alex Angelo, Ernst Morgan, Geza L. Weiss.

Die Welt will belogen sein (Nero-Film AG) D: *Peter Paul Felner.* Harry Liedtke, Georg Alexander, Mady Christians, Walter Rilla, Paul Biensfeldt, Mary Nolan, Henri De Vries, Eugen Rex, Paul Morgan, Carl Geppert.

Die Abenteuer eines Zehnmarkscheines [Deutsche Vereins-Film AG (Defa-Deutsche Fox)] D: *Berthold Viertel.* Mary Nolan, Werner Fuetterer, Oskar Homolka, Frieda Blumenthal, Hans Brausewetter, Renate Brausewetter, Maly Delschaft, Karl Etlinger, Walter Franck, Julius E. Herrmann, Margo Lion, Luise Morland, Agnes Mueller, Ressel Orla, Harald Paulsen, Vladimir Sokoloff, Francesco von Mendelssohn, Otto Wallburg, Iwa Wanja, Geza L. Weiss.

Die Königin des Weltbades (Alfred Sittzarz) D: *Victor Janson.* Mary Nolan, Walter Rilla, Livio Pavanelli, Camilla von Hollay, Ida Wüst, Gertrud Arnold, Ferdinand Hart, Lissy Arna, Eva Speyer, Alf Blutecher, Paul Morgan, Siegfried Berisch, Oreste Bilancia.

Das Panzergewölbe (Rex-Film GmbH) D: *Lupu Pick.* Ernst Reicher, Johannes Riemann, Mary Nolan, Heinrich George, Aud Egede Nissen, Sig Arno, Max Gülstorff, Hugo Fischer-Köppe, Julius E. Herrmann, Hadrian Maria Netto, Erich Kaiser-Titz, Paul Rehkopf, Fritz Rulard , Lewis Brody, Ernst Behmer.

1927

Die Mädchen von Paris D: *Victor Janson.* Mary Nolan, Livio Pavanelli.

Halloh–Caesar! (Reinhold Schünzel Film) D: *Reinhold Schünzel.* Reinhold Schünzel, Mary Nolan, Wilhelm Diegelmann, Julius Falkenstein, Ilka Grüning.

Erinnerungen einer Nonne [*(Münchner Lichtspielkunst AG (Emelka)*] D: *Arthur Bergen.* Georg John, Ellen Kürti, Mary Nolan, Werner Pittschau, Camilla von Hollay.

As Mary Nolan:

Sorrell and Son (Joseph M. Schenck Productions) D: *Herbert Brenon.* H.B. Warner, Anna Q. Nilsson, Mickey McBan, Carmel Myers, Lionel Belmore, Norman Trevor, Betsy Ann Hisle , Louis Wolheim, Paul McAllister, Alice Joyce, Nils Asther, Mary Nolan.

Topsy and Eva (United Artists) D: *Del Lord.* Rosetta Duncan, Vivian Duncan, Gibson Gowland, Noble Johnson, Marjorie Daw, Myrtle Ferguson, Nils Asther, Henry Victor, Lionel Belmore, Dot Farley, Carla Laemmle, Mary Nolan.

1928

Good Morning, Judge (Universal) D: *William A. Seiter.* Reginald Denny, Mary Nolan, Otis Harlan, Dorothy Gulliver, William B. Davidson, Bull Montana, William Worthington, Sailor Sharkey, Charles Coleman, William H. Tooker.

The Foreign Legion (Universal) D: *Edward Sloman.* Norman Kerry, Lewis Stone, Crauford Kent, Mary Nolan, June Marlowe, Walter Perry.

West of Zanzibar (M-G-M) D: *Tod Browning.* Lon Chaney, Lionel Barrymore, Mary Nolan, Warner Baxter, Jacqueline Gadsden, Tiny Ward, Kalla Pasha, Curtis Nero.

1929

Silks and Saddles aka *Thoroughbreds (Universal)* D: *Robert F. Hill.* Richard Walling, Marian Nixon, Sam De Grasse, Montagu Love, Mary Nolan, Otis Harlan, David Torrence, Claire McDowell, Johnny Fox, Hayden Stevenson.

Desert Nights aka *Thirst (M-G-M)* D: *William Nigh.* John Gilbert, Ernest Torrence, Mary Nolan, Claude King.

Eleven Who Where Loyal (UFA — German) Fritz Alberti, Rudolf Meinert, Mary Nolan, Grete Reinwald, Ernst Rückert, Gustav Adolf Semler, Albert Steinrück.

Charming Sinners aka *The Constant Wife (Paramount)* D: *Robert Milton.* Ruth Chatterton, Clive Brook, Mary Nolan, William Powell, Laura Hope Crews, Florence Eldridge, Montagu Love, Juliette Crosby, Lorraine MacLean, Claud Allister.

Shanghai Lady aka *Girl from China (Universal)* D: *John S. Robertson.* Mary Nolan, James Murray, Lydia Yeamans Titus, Wheeler Oakman, Anders Randolf, Yola d'Avril, Mona Rico, James B. Leong, Irma Lowe.

1930

Undertow (Universal) D: *Harry A. Pollard.* Mary Nolan, Robert Ellis, Johnny Mack Brown, Churchill Ross, Audrey Ferris.

Young Desire (Universal) D: *Lewis D. Collins.* Mary Nolan, William Janney, Ralf Harolde, Mae Busch, George Irving, Claire McDowell, Alice Lake, Gretchen Thomas.

Outside the Law (Universal) D: *Tod Browning.* Mary Nolan, Edward G. Robinson, Owen Moore, Eddie Sturgis, John George, Delmar Watson, DeWitt Jennings, Rockliffe Fellowes, Frederick Burt, Sidney Bracey.

1931

Enemies of the Law (Regal Talking Pictures Corp.) D: *Lawrence C. Windom.* Mary Nolan, Johnnie Walker, Lou Tellegen, Harold Healy, Alan Brooks, Dewey Robinson, John Dunsmuir, Danny Hardin, Bert West, Gordon Westcott, Doe Doe Green, Barry Townley.

X Marks the Spot (Tiffany) D: *Erle C. Kenton.* Lew Cody, Sally Blane, Fred Kohler, Wallace Ford, Mary Nolan, Virginia Lee Corbin, Helen Parrish, Joyce Coad, Charles Middleton, Clarence Muse, Richard Tucker.

The Big Shot aka *The Optimist (RKO Pathé Pictures)* D: *Ralph Murphy.* Eddie Quillan, Maureen O'Sullivan, Mary Nolan, Roscoe Ates, Belle Bennett, Arthur Stone, Louis John Bartels, Otis Harlan, William Eugene, Edward McWade, Harvey Clark, Edward Brophy, Frank Mayo

1932

Docks of San Francisco (Mayfair) D: *George B. Seitz.* Mary Nolan, Jason Robards Sr., Marjorie Beebe, John Davidson, William Haynes, Max Davidson.

The Midnight Patrol (Monogram) D: *Christy Cabanne.* Regis Toomey, Betty Bronson, Edwina Booth, Mary Nolan, Earle Foxe, Robert Elliott, Eddie Kane William Bailey, Mischa Auer, James J. Jeffries, 'Snub' Pollard, Ray Cooke, Franklin Pangborn, Jack Mower, J.C. Fowler, Wilfred Lucas, Barrie Oliver, Tod Sloan, Mack Swain.

1933

File 113 (Allied Pictures) D: *Chester M. Franklin.* Lew Cody, Mary Nolan, Clara Kimball Young, George E. Stone, William Collier Jr., June Clyde, Herbert Bunston, Roy D'Arcy, Irving Bacon, Harry Cording, Crauford Kent.

Marie Prevost signed this portrait for Lucille Ricksen during the filming of
The Married Flapper *(1922).* COURTESY OF THE RICKSEN FAMILY

MARIE PREVOST

Cast lists of 1930s films were littered with the names of Hollywood has-beens, pioneers of the business, who were now relics in an industry that had found its voice and moved on.

In "Sometimes They Do Come Back," *The New York Times* offered a glimmer of hope to those who had navigated the precarious curves of the film industry and found themselves desperate for a Hollywood handout.

"The former stars who have taken the arduous way back are getting speaking parts again. Some of them are, at least. Others are playing atmosphere. Still others are working behind the camera. Occasionally one of them acquires a screen credit, something he hasn't had since 1928. That may be much more important to him than the check he got from the studios. Troupers, one hears, are like that."[1]

In the fall of 1936, Marie Prevost, a trouper if there ever was one, felt she was one of the ones on her way back — finally. Warner Brothers, where she'd once been at the top of the heap, had recalled their former star to play bits and walk-ons.

Most at the studio, from the stars to the production crew, knew the name Marie Prevost. A famous Sennett bathing beauty of the 1910s, she shed her bathing suits for negligees in the early 20s and moved from the beaches to the boudoirs in some of the finest romantic comedies of the decade.

The tragic death of her mother and the failure of her marriage to actor Kenneth Harlan mid-decade sent Marie on a perilous and destructive course of crash dieting and alcohol. A heavier Marie made a successful transition to sound and became a favorite hardboiled gal, usually with a heart of gold.

A worsening weight problem all but ended her career in the mid-1930s. In 1936, she made a desperate attempt at a comeback. Warner Brothers heard her pleas and hired her for bits and walk-ons. Her life started looking up.

"Now that she is under contract she will work in numerous films, perhaps as many as five a week, depending on the number of sets on which she is needed," *The New York Times* article said of Marie. "She will be at the studio every day — regularly. A few more parts of a few lines each and the studio may find bigger and better things for her to do."[2]

But now, in late January 1937, life took another downward turn. Marie had weathered another lonely Christmas. Alone, except for Maxie, her dachshund, and a bottle of booze, which seemed to make life go down a little easier. She had also fought the battle of the bulge too long, now to the point of malnourishment. All for work in motion pictures.

For most of her adult life, she'd battled the bottle, but as 1937 got underway, there wasn't much battle to it. The amber-colored liquid kept her warm on cold nights and company when it seemed she had no friends left.

She was now out of touch with fellow bathing beauties Juanita Hansen and Phyllis Haver. Juanita was battling her own demons and Haver had married well and was living in retirement in New York. Her sister, Peg, had her own life in San Francisco, and Joan Crawford routinely helped her out financially, but was busy with her marriages and career.

Wednesday, January 20, seemed like any other day to Marie. President Roosevelt was being inaugurated, but the event meant little to her. She visited a local delicatessen around the corner from her Hollywood apartment, where she made good on a returned $2.50 check.

Back in her apartment, Marie turned up the bottle to the last drop, lit her portable gas heaters, changed into her silk pajamas, lay down on her rollaway bed, and drifted off.

The New York Times article was right. Sometimes they do come back. Then, again, sometimes they don't.

She was born Marie Bickford Dunn on November 8, 1896,[3] in Sarnia (Ontario), Canada. When she was a toddler, her father, Arthur (Teddy) Dunn, a railroad car conductor, was killed when gas seeped into the St. Clair Tunnel that ran from Sarnia to Port Huron, Michigan.

Later in the decade, Marie's mother, the former Hughlina Marion Bickford, married Frank Prevost, a mine inspector and surveyor. The three moved to Colorado, where, in April 1900, Marie's half-sister, Marjorie, was born.

The Prevosts rarely stayed in one place for any length of time. Frank Prevost, notorious among mining camps around the West, was either looking for a pot of gold or getting out of town.

In 1902, while living in Ogden, Utah, Frank was arrested for burglarizing a knitting factory and hauling away blankets and ladies' underwear.[4] In 1905, Frank told the *Ogden Standard* that he and his family, who had been in Los Angeles visiting relatives, would be making Zion, Utah, their permanent home. He also announced the development of a mine in Mexico that would one day makes its investors rich.[5]

The next year, however, the family moved to Reno, Nevada. The Prevosts had just moved into their new home when a tragic accident almost took their lives.

In an effort to tidy up the place, Marie was sent next door to ask the neighbors for a mop. When she returned without one, Frank suggested his wife check the cellar. When she lit a match and started to light a candle, the flame fell into a bag of powder on the table. The explosion seriously burned Marion and Marjorie. Marie escaped with only minor injuries.[6]

Two months later, Frank Prevost reported he had lost $43,000 in cash while on a visit to Denver. Prevost said he stepped off a train in Denver to "see a man or two." On his way from the Albany Hotel to the Windsor Baths, he apparently dropped his wallet. He told authorities he discovered the loss while disrobing and preparing for his bath.[7]

The Prevosts eventually moved to California, first to the Fresno area, then Los Angeles, where Marie attended Manual Arts High School. Her mother and Frank Prevost eventually divorced.[8]

In 1915, she was working as a secretary for a law firm that represented Keystone Film Company. One day, she was on official business at the studio when Ford Sterling asked her to play a scene in *His Father's Footsteps*, a Keystone comedy he was directing.

"Marie did what she was told," her sister said in an interview years later. "Nobody bothered to tell her the chair and table would collapse when she sat down. I saw the scene many months later and Marie just bubbled. All you could see when the chair and table gave way were her legs waving in the air. Sterling shouted that it was a good take and without saying another word stalked off to a nearby building. Marie, rather red-faced, brushed herself off and waited for Mack Sennett to see her."[9] She did her business with him and left.

The next day, back at work, the senior partner of the law firm told Marie that Sennett wanted her to return to the studio immediately. She jumped on a streetcar and headed for Edendale.

When she arrived at the studio, "I asked for Mr. Sennett and was ushered in right away," Marie later told *Motion Picture World*.[10] "He looked very stern as I walked into his office. I was ready to cry. Suddenly, he smiled. 'I want your signature today,' he said. 'Sign right here.' I suddenly realized the paper he pushed in front of me was a contract. I was to be one of his Sennett Bathing Beauties. Best of all I was to be paid $15 a week. I signed without reading a word. Fifteen dollars was a lot of money."

Not long after Marie started with Sennett, her best friend from high school, Phyllis O'Haver,[11] was signed as a bathing beauty.

Marie's initial work for Sennett called for her to do little more than stand around and look pretty. "We had a different part every day," Marie told *Motion Picture World*. "Usually we were just in the background, occasionally we were given small parts, but most of the time we were photographed romping around on the Venice Beach, which was near Edendale."[12]

Marie Prevost as a Sennett Bathing Beauty.

Marie wanted more than to simply pose for the camera. She wanted to be a comedienne. She tested the waters one afternoon when Sennett asked some of the beauties to do something funny for the camera.

"He was dressed in a swimming costume, making faces, and generally adding to the scene. As I was one of the few Bathing Beauties who could swim and dive, he asked me to pretend to fall off the pier and wave my arms and legs until I hit the water. That didn't sound too funny to me so I pretended to slip and pushed him off the pier instead."[13]

Rather than fire Marie for her stunt, as many onlookers thought he would, Sennett increased her salary to $25 a week and used her in more comedy scenes for Keystone.

The young beauty stood out from the rest of the girls. "Marie soon developed into a suave and skillful actress who could perform such deft scenes with a mere look or a slight gesture that she was obviously out of place among my roaring pie throwers," Mack Sennett later wrote.[14] She honed her acting skills, and in 1917, received her first screen credit with *Her Nature's Dance*.

On June 18, 1918, Marie married socialite Henry Charles "Sonny" Gerke. The two kept their nuptials secret.[15] Neither told their families and Marie certainly had no intentions of telling Sennett, for fear her marriage would dampen her budding career.

In an interview for this book, Gerke's daughter, Arden Keevers, said the marriage was during a time when her father flirted with the beauties of the silent screen.

"My father met Marie Prevost at a party," Keevers said in 2009. "He was a good looking youth, a feather weight boxer, who had enlisted in the Navy during World War I. The movie industry was new and it was a time when he moved through the social life of it."[16]

In the fall of 1919, William Randolph Hearst approached Marie about making films for his company, Cosmopolitan Pictures. She decided to stay with Sennett, who renegotiated her contract and signed her to a three-year deal at $195 a week.[17]

For the next two years, Marie appeared in two-reelers with some of the screen's top comedians: Ben Turpin, Chester Conklin, Heinie Conklin, Al Cooke, and others. She made several feature films: *Yankee Doodle in Berlin* (1919), *Down on the Farm* (1920), *Love, Honor, and Behave!* (1920), and *A Small Town Idol* (1921).

The circumstances that led to Marie's departure from Sennett in early 1921 are not entirely clear. Irving Thalberg, then working at Universal, reportedly took an interest in her, as did director King Baggot. It's also probable that Marie had simply outgrown Sennett comedies and was ready for more challenging material.

Marie later told *Photoplay* that "a lot of the fun had gone (at Sennett's). Now everything was ruled by money. Money was the bottom line and we no longer had the time to think up ideas or improvise. So, when King Baggot, by then a major director, convinced Universal to offer me a thousand-dollar-a-week deal, I went to Mr. Sennett and told him it was time for me to move on. He was very kind. 'All my stars leave me eventually,' he said, perhaps a little wistfully. 'But I wish you well.'"

A letter from Mack Sennett to Marie Prevost, dated February 21, 1921, however, suggests that Marie was fired. The letter points to the following clause in Marie's contract:

> The employee shall attend daily during established working hours (whether cast or not) for the performance of his duties herein required at the studio or studios of the employer or on location or other place as may be designated by the employer.

No excuse from work, duties or attendance at the studio or on location or in other place as required hereby shall be good or sufficient except it be in writing signed by an authorized agent of the employer. In no event shall a written excuse be good for an absence of more than one day. Inclement weather shall be no excuse for non-attendance hereunder. The employee agrees to abide by, obey and perform any and all orders, requests, requests, communications, rules and regulations of the employer. The employee's method, manner and way of acting, posing, and performing shall at all times be conducted and carried out as required by the employer.

The Sennett letter continues, "In as much as you did not put in an appearance at the studio on February 19th, 1921, as requested, your contract is hereby terminated as of this date."[18]

Whatever the circumstances, Marie joined Universal and was almost immediately elevated to star level. Her first item of business was to break with the past. She traveled to Coney Island, New York, where she ceremonially burned photos of herself as a bathing beauty, a one-piece swim suit, and several thousand feet of film of her in bathing scenes.[19]

Her first Universal role, under the direction of King Baggot, was as a flapper in *Moonlight Follies* (1921). *The New York Times*, in its analysis of Marie's move from bathing beauty to flapper, gave her performance a nod.

"Whether you accept her as an actress rather than a bathing beauty, depends upon your readiness to accept the Universal Company's assurances that she is an honest-to-goodness star. Miss Prevost herself does very little in the picture to convince the skeptical. She has a pout and a smile, pretty feet and a figure. Some people will probably call her cute. And when you come to think of it you must agree that she has as much as a good many others who are commonly accepted as photodramatic stars.

"So why not let her into the company? She's not conspicuous by her lack of qualifications, surely. The only people who are conspicuous by their unusualness on the screen today are those who can act. Decidedly, Miss Prevost is not conspicuous. She belongs to the great majority."[20]

During the year she was at Universal, Marie made eight features, all lighthearted comedies. Her final film at Universal was *The Married Flapper* (1922), in which she played the flirtatious and unsettled wife of Kenneth Harlan. Her playful ways are imitated by the adoring Lucille Ricksen, who played Harlan's niece.

It was while filming *The Married Flapper* that Marie fell in love with the newly-divorced Harlan. They were soon a serious item around town. The only hitch was that Marie was still secretly married to Sonny Gerke.

Jack Warner didn't know about Marie's marriage when he signed both Marie and Harlan to a Warner Brothers contract and starred them in *The Beautiful and Damned* (1922), based on F. Scott Fitzgerald's novel. The two

Marie Prevost and Kenneth Harlan on the set of The Married Flapper *(1922).* COURTESY OF THE RICKSEN FAMILY

lovebird stars, he boasted, would be married on the set. Their engagement, however, continued into 1923.

Marie and Harlan were perfect as Fitzgerald's jazz-age couple who goes through money like water. While critics and audiences were mostly favorable, Fitzgerald said the film adaptation was "by far the worst movie I've ever seen in my life — cheap, vulgar, ill-constructed and shoddy."[21]

Marie was teamed with popular leading man Monte Blue in *Brass* (1923), the first of ten films they starred in together. *Brass* centers on Marjorie (Marie), a frivolous city girl, who leaves her husband (Blue) and baby for a better life. The child is left in the care of a trained nurse

(Irene Rich), who falls in love with Blue. Marjorie returns to her senses and begs her husband to take her back. Her pleas are to no avail, as he is now in love with their child's nurse.

Variety gave kudos to both Marie and Irene Rich, "the outstanding feminine members, both because of the prominence of the characters they play and the caliber of their respective performances."[22]

An original advertisement for The Marriage Circle *(1924).*

By the fall of 1923, Marie had proven herself a capable dramatic actress. When director Ernst Lubitsch personally selected her for *The Marriage Circle* (1924), the first of his sex farces, there was no doubt her star had risen.

"Naturally, I enjoy dramatic work for more (than comedy), because it marks the reality of serious ambition," Marie said in August 1923, before filming began on *The Marriage Circle*. "Comedy work was very enjoyable because it was refreshing rather than fatiguing. And as a training school for development of acting ability there is nothing better. Comedy is fun from a girl's viewpoint; drama is hard work. To be selected by Mr. Lubitsch for such a role is to be considered a great compliment."[23]

Before filming could get underway, however, all hell broke loose with the film's star. On August 12, Sonny Gerke filed for divorce against his wife, Marie Gerke. It took no time for Mrs. Gerke to be identified as Marie

Prevost. Hollywood was in shock over the revelation that its new darling had been married for five years. Jack Warner was beyond shocked; he was livid.

When contacted by the *Los Angeles Times* for a comment, "Miss Prevost expressed no surprise and after a momentary hesitation admitted that she and Marie Gerke are one and the same." She refused further comment.[24]

A Melbourne Spurr portrait of Marie Prevost.

Three days later, a cornered Marie had little choice but to satisfy the public's hunger for details about her personal life. She sat down with the *Los Angeles Times* and told about her marriage.

"I knew he was going to sue," she admitted. "Nevertheless, I was surprised and — yes — frightened. Really, there isn't anything to tell. It was during the war and everybody was marrying, but immediately the ceremony was over and we both realized what a silly thing we had done. Mr. Gerke went to his home and I went to mine. Why, I never even realized I was married. We were just two foolish children who ran away and married and then separated immediately. And now it's all over."[25]

Marie said the two remained friends and often "dated." They talked about an annulment, but after a while, saw no reason to initiate the proceedings.

Gerke soon filed for divorce on the grounds of desertion. An "insurmountable barrier" to their domestic happiness, Gerke stated, was that Marie wanted to keep their marriage secret for fear it would damage her career.[26] Hoping to quietly put the bad publicity behind her, Marie offered no defense.[27]

"My father said very little about that marriage," Sonny Gerke's daughter said. "Marie, he did say, was very tempestuous and had a drinking problem during the time they were married."[28]

Working on *The Marriage Circle* under the expert direction of Lubitsch, Marie kept herself together. When filming began in September 1923, she put her troubles aside and threw herself into the role of Mizzi, the restless flapper wife of Adolphe Menjou.

"At first it seemed as though there wasn't any sense to it at all," Marie said of working with the famed director. "Then it began to dawn upon me what the art of acting was all about, and it seemed intolerably and impossibly difficult. Then I began to see it as he saw it... He deals in subtleties that I never dreamed of before."[29]

The film was universally praised for Lubitsch's direction and Marie's performance. "It is possibly the first time any director has had the nerve to put a farce comedy on the screen, play it legitimately and get laughs," noted *Variety*. "It is certainly the picture that gives Marie Prevost the chance of her life, and she assuredly makes the most of it, walking away with the honors. There is no question as to whom the picture belongs.[30]

It was Lubitsch himself who held the highest praise for his star. At an opening party for the picture, he boldly told studio chief Jack Warner and the other cast members (Adolphe Menjou and Florence Vidor), "it is unforgivable that she is (Marie) is not billed as the number one star of my film. Marie Prevost is one of the few actresses in Hollywood who knows how to underplay comedy to achieve the maximum effect. She stole every scene in my picture."[31]

Menjou and Vidor reportedly bristled at the comments. Warner, who had it in for Marie from the beginning of her Warner Brothers contract, told Lubitsch that he, and he alone, decided who were the stars of any Warner Brothers production.

A pouty Marie Prevost (1924).

Lubitsch later talked about his problems with Warner. "He threatened to fire me, fire Bern (Paul Bern, who worked on the script), fire everyone. It made me doubt his sanity when he announced he was going to burn every reel of the film. We talked him out of it, but he used to stand in the shadows of the set and if Marie made a good take he would send his secretary over to me to demand I shoot the scene again. I did what he said, of course, but it was always the best take I used. He had a wonderful star and he wanted to destroy her career."[32]

Warner may have had it in for Marie; however, her Warner Brothers years were her most productive and successful years on the screen. She worked with Lubitsch in two more films: *Three Women* (1924) and *Kiss Me Again* (1925). And, she had the good fortune to work with some of the industry's leading directors: William Beaudine, George Fitzmaurice, Harry Beaumont, Millard Webb, and Lewis Milestone.

In *Cornered*, a crime drama she made in 1924, Marie tackles a dual role: as a girl from the wrong side of the tracks and a wealthy heiress. Critics praised the film and her performance. It was one of Marie's personal favorites. *Cornered*, noted *Harrison's Reports*, "is a crook melodrama, the kind that holds the spectator breathless from start to finish, making him lean forward lest any details escape him."[33]

After Marie completed *The Dark Swan*, the last of the nine films she made in 1924, she took a much needed vacation. When boyfriend Kenneth Harlan finished his latest picture, the two tied the knot in a simple ceremony at Wilshire Presbyterian Church.[34]

Marie and her husband were teamed in *Bobbed Hair* (1925), only their second film together. In the film, she has two suitors: one likes bobbed hair, the other doesn't. The question in the narrative is whether her character has bobbed her hair. She keeps everyone guessing by wearing the attire of a convent sister. Her secret is revealed at the end. *The New York Times* said the actress is "just as attractive with her hair covered as when it is seen."[35]

In early 1926, Warner Brothers informed the Harlans that the studio would not be picking up their options. Marie's close friend Phyllis Haver later told a fan magazine she believed this rejection caused the first rift in the Harlan-Prevost marriage and was the trigger that led to Marie's decline into alcoholism.

No sooner had Warners dropped their bombshell on Marie when tragedy struck. Marie's mother, Hughlina, producer Al Christie, and actress Vera Stedman were traveling by car from Los Angeles to Palm Beach when a back wheel came apart, causing the automobile to veer out of control and overturn in rural New Mexico. Hughlina was crushed by the rear of the car and suffered a broken spine and fractured skull. She died at the scene.[36]

Stedman received bruises and lacerations on her face and lower limbs and Christie escaped with cuts on his arm and head. The next day, Stedman and Christie accompanied Hughlina Prevost's body back to Hollywood, where a devastated Marie waited.

Kenneth Harlan and Marie Prevost, newlyweds.

"Marie took this as just one more slap in the face from a cruel world," her sister, Peg Halliday, said.[37]

After her mother's funeral and burial at Forest Lawn, Marie threw herself into her work. She made a series of low-budget bedroom farces for Producers Distributing Corporation (PDC) in 1926 and early 1927.

An original advertisement for Up in Mabel's Room *(1926).*

In *Up in Mabel's Room* (1926), the most successful of Marie's seven films at PDC, she plays a newlywed who realizes she's made a mistake and tries to win back her former husband (Harrison Ford). "Marie Prevost demonstrates very capably that she is a clever comedienne," *Motion Picture Classic* said of her performance.[38]

Teamed again with Harrison Ford in *Almost a Lady*, Marie plays a model who uses the fancy clothes she wears to break into society. *Harrison's Reports* credited Marie's "long service under the directorial wing of Mack Sennett" with her "unquestionable comedy proficiency" in the film, noting, "She carries the stellar placement in this film handedly."[39]

Marie was equally successful in *For Wives Only*, *Man Bait*, *Getting Gertie's Garter*, and *The Night Bride*, in which she gives the "best portrayal of a petulant girl crying that has been seen on the screen for moons and moons," noted *The New York Times*.[40]

Two weeks before Christmas in 1926, Marie was driving home from dinner at a friend's house when a young girl walked out in front of her car.

The girl was only bruised, but the incident tormented Marie, bringing back images of her mother's death. "For a year she wouldn't drive," her sister said. "When she had to go to the studio she went by streetcar. Imagine, earning more than a thousand dollars a week, riding on a streetcar!"[41]

By the spring of 1927, the Harlan married had fallen apart. Marie left their home and took residence in a local hotel. "Yes, I've been staying here for more than a week," she told reporters, "but there is nothing to say. Mr. Harlan is at our home. I can't say more at this time."[42]

That summer, Marie went to work at Pathé and was teamed again with Harrison Ford in *The*

Marie Prevost on the cover of Photoplay.

Girl in the Pullman and *The Rush Hour*, both 1927 releases.

In October, she sued Kenneth Harlan for divorce, claiming extreme mental cruelty. On the witness stand, Marie claimed her husband was accustomed to spending his evenings at drinking parties.

"Almost every hour he would telephone me the details of the good time he was having," she told the judge. "My sleep was interrupted to such an extent that I was unfit for work the following days."[43]

Marie introduced a letter Harlan had written her during one of his absences: "Get back tonight and then the merry-go-round will start and I will not worry you again, honestly. Love from your bad boy who does bad things but doesn't mean to and is going to try and straighten out."[44]

Following her divorce from Harlan, Marie hardly missed a beat. She scored two more successes with *A Blonde for a Night* and *The Racket*, an underworld story of "nightsticks, bootleg, and bullets." Marie, *Photoplay* noted, is "marvelously hard-boiled."[45]

By the end of the decade, Marie saw her career slipping. She was putting on weight and drinking. With the added weight came depression and more alcohol abuse. Also, Marie had concerns about her voice and how she would fare in talkies.

Harrison Ford and Marie Prevost in A Blonde for the Night *(1928).*

Cecil B. DeMille came to her rescue. According to Marie's sister, DeMille called one afternoon and said he'd been looking for her. "I have a fine role for you in my new film. Are you available?"[46]

The film was *The Godless Girl*, which DeMille, under his direction, hoped would shed light on juvenile reform institutions and take on atheism and its propaganda among America's youth. Marie was delighted with the supporting role of Mame, a hard-boiled girl in a reform school. The lead was Lina Basquette, a friend of Marie's.

"For such an established star, the secondary role was a bitter pill to swallow," Basquette wrote in 1990. "'Aw, hell, that's the way it is,' she (Marie) said. 'But remember this, kid. Friendship ceases after the cameras start rolling. I'll be in there upstaging you every inch of the way, stealing every Goddamn scene I can!'"[47]

The first order of business was to change Marie's hair color. "DeMille ordered her to bleach her hair so she would be more of a contrast to me," Lina wrote. "Marie begged him to let her wear a wig. 'A wig will not do.' DeMille slapped his riding crop against his leather boot. 'Start bleaching your hair. I want it almost white within a week.'"[48]

While her performance in *The Godless Girl* was praised by most review-

Marie Prevost (L) and Lina Basquette in The Godless Girl *(1929).*

ers, *Harrison's Reports* was bewildered. "Prevost is notably confusing as a character. She is for the Bible, but in a smart-cracking, tough egg sort of way that is incongruous, to express it politely."[49]

As the new decade got underway, Marie, who had made a successful transition to talkies, had little trouble finding work. Although she was no longer the star of the picture, her supporting parts almost always stole the scene.

In the fall of 1930, Marie signed with M-G-M. The *Los Angeles Times* noted that Marie was "surprisingly svelte-like these days. She has lost considerable pounds, which may or may not have something to do with her reappearance on the film horizon."[50]

At M-G-M, she appeared in supporting roles in *Paid* with Joan Crawford, *War Nurse* with Anita Page, *Gentlemen's Fate* with Anita Page and John Gilbert, *It's a Wise Child* with Marion Davies, and *Sporting Blood* with Clark Gable and Madge Evans.

Marie worked steadily throughout the early 1930s. After 1933, work, however, came only sporadically. She waged an often public battle with her weight. Columbia put her on notice that her supporting role in *Parole Girl* (1933) was in jeopardy if she failed to trim down.

Marie Prevost in 1930.

"Give me two weeks," she told the studio, "and I'll be down to whatever you say. Lose 13 pounds? Alright!"[51] In two weeks, she returned and took a test. The part was hers.

Over the next couple of years, Marie drifted from public sight, except for a few odds mentions in the papers.

In 1933, her rebel-rousing stepfather died at age 73 surrounded by

Marie Prevost (R) with Joan Crawford (C) and Polly Moran in Paid *(1930).*

friends who had joined him in a week-long round of gaiety. "Warned by physicians that death was near, Prevost gathered a circle of friends at the Elks Club. For six days he played cards, laughed and joked. Today he walked into the club and sank into a chair. In a few minutes he was dead."[52] Marie was named beneficiary of his will.

The next year, Marie filed suit against actor Tom Gallery for cleaning bills she had to pay after he vacated her house after a six month tenancy. She maintained he kept a menagerie in the basement and that fleas had infested the house.[53]

Then, in October 1934, *The New York Times* reported that one Dr. Samuel Newman died of a heart attack while visiting Marie at the Roosevelt Hospital. [54]

Back in Hollywood, Marie tried for yet another comeback. Her diet called for no food and lots of booze. She managed to secure small parts in such films as *Tango, Cain and Mabel, Bengal Tiger, 13 Hours by Air,* and *Ten Laps to Go,* her final film. Her roles were little more than bits.

"I wrote her several times in 1936 but never got anything more than a brief postcard in reply," her sister, Peg, said. "She sent me a Christmas card with a note telling me to go and see her latest film, 13 Hours by Air. I did go, but was shocked to find she had only a tiny part as a waitress

The Aftonian Apartments in 2009.

in one scene. Not even a speaking part. I told my husband we should drive down to see her in the new year and I wrote asking when would be a good time."[55] They never received a reply.

On January 23, 1937, William Bogle, a houseboy at the Aftonian Apartments, was sent to Marie's apartment to check on the actress. It had been several days since anyone had seen her. Also, neighbors had been complaining about her barking dog.

Attached to Marie's door was a penciled note: "Please do not knock on this door more than once. It makes my dog bark. If I am in, I will hear you as I am not deaf."

Using his master key, Bogle entered the apartment and found Marie lying face down on her bed. Her dog, Maxie, sat whining on the floor. Her body showed teeth marks from Maxie, which apparently had tried to awaken her.[56] An empty whiskey bottle was found in the kitchen sink.[57]

Detectives estimated she had been dead for two days.

An autopsy showed she'd died of natural causes, induced by acute alcoholism. Dr. Frank Webb, deputy autopsy surgeon, said his examination showed a considerable amount of alcohol in the brain and other organs.[58]

It took no time for a sad composite of a lonely soul to emerge. Marie had been beset with financial worries and unable to keep up payments on grocery debts. She had existed on the kindness of friends for years. Among her belongings was an unsigned promissory note for $110 payable to Joan Crawford.

"We were good friends," Crawford said in a statement. "She had only to ask and I would gladly have given her help, money, or other assistance that she needed. She was a wonderful friend and a great comedy actress." Phyllis Haver, a life-long friend since their Sennett days, said she was "shocked and saddened. I had no inkling of her need. I am ashamed to say that after my marriage, I isolated myself from those who mattered most."[59]

Marie Prevost (L) and Phyllis Haver in happier times.

Kenneth Harlan, "upset and shocked" at Marie's death, said, "I was surprised to hear of the circumstances under which she died. We hadn't been in touch with each other for some time."[60]

The *Los Angeles Times* quoted Marie's sister as saying that the body of Marie's mother, who died in 1926, would be exhumed from Forest Lawn and cremated with the remains of her daughter. She gave no details about funeral arrangements, but said it would be a Christian Science service with no flowers.[61]

Years later, Peg Halliday said Marie's service and burial were at Hollywood Memorial Cemetery and that Joan Crawford paid for both the plot and the service. "I offered to pay," Peg said in 1968, "but she wouldn't consider it. She seemed to think she was in some way responsible for Marie's death and was inconsolable."[62]

Hollywood's elite attended the service, Marie's sister continued. "Joan, of course, and Barbara Stanwyck, Mack Sennett, King Baggot, Douglas Fairbanks Jr., Franklin Pangborn, Lewis Milestone, Wallace Beery, Clark Gable, Andy Devine, Ralph Bellamy, Fred MacMurray, Robert Young, Mervyn LeRoy, and so many more that I can't remember. But where were they when she needed them? And where was I?"[63]

Rex Lease, who appeared with Marie in her final film, *Ten Laps to Go*, felt that had Marie held on another month or so, the comeback she yearned for might have materialized.

"Miss Prevost was cast in a good part, a comedienne, and she made a splendid showing, stealing the show," he said. "She was in the same good form as her old days. I think she was ready for a comeback."[64]

The New York Times was correct in its assessment of old-time stars and their winding and sometimes treacherous road back to stardom. Sometimes they did come back. Most of the time, unfortunately, they didn't.

1. "Sometimes They Do Come Back," *The New York Times*, 26 July 1936.

2. Ibid.

3. The 1900 U.S. Federal Census lists 1896 as Marie's birth year. Her earliest publicity suggests November 8 as her birth date. Her death certificate lists November 6, 1899.

4. "Prevost Confesses," *Salt Lake City Tribune*, Salt Lake City, Utah, 7 January 1902.

5. "Prevost Chooses Zion," *Ogden Standard*, Ogden City, Utah, 24 April 1905.

6. "Powder Explodes Burning Three People," *Daily Nevada State Journal*, 27 June 1906.

7. "$42,000 Lost on Denver Street by Reno Citizen," Daily Nevada State Journal," Reno, Nevada, 12 August 1906.

8. Frank Prevost was charged with assault in 1917 when he drew a pistol on a San Francisco hotel manager. Prevost claimed only wanted to shoot rats that had invaded his room." "Rats! That's Why Prevost Drew Pistol," *Oakland Tribune*, 20 August 1917.

9. Foster, Charles, *Stardust and Shadows: Canadians in Early Hollywood*, Dundurn Press Ltd., 2000.

10. *Motion Picture World*, 1923.

11. The "O" was dropped from her name and she became Phyllis Haver.

12. *Motion Picture World*, 1923.

13. Ibid.

14. Sennett, Mack, *King of Comedy*, Pinnacle Books, 1954.

15. The 1920 U.S. Federal Census lists Marie as single and living with her mother and sister.

16. Arden Keevers to Michael G. Ankerich, February 2009.

17. Actor's contract between Mack Sennett and Marie Prevost, signed 15 September 1919. Academy of Motion Picture Arts and Sciences Library, Mack Sennett Special Collections. The contract stipulated that, if she remained with Sennett through September 1922, her weekly salary would increase to $500.

18. Letter from Mack Sennett to Marie Prevost, 21 February 1921. Academy of Motion Picture Arts and Sciences Library, Mack Sennett Special Collections.

19. "Marie Quits One-Piece," *Oakland Tribune*, Oakland, California, 5 June 1921.

20. *The New York Times*, 19 September 1921.

21. Mellow, James R., *Invented Lives: F. Scott & Zelda Fitzgerald*. Houghton Mifflin Company, 1984.

22. *Variety*, March 1923.

23. "Marie Prevost, Past and Present," *Los Angeles Times*, 12 August 1923.

24. "Marie Prevost Secretly Wed," *Los Angeles Times*, 12 August 1923.

25. "Star Tells of Marriage," Los Angeles Times, 15 August 1923.

26. "Husband Sues Marie Prevost," *Los Angeles Times*, 4 September 1923.

27. "Ignores Husband's Suit," New York Times, 5 September 1923.

28. Arden Keevers to Michael G. Ankerich, February 2009. Ms. Keevers said her father dated Virginia Fox after his marriage to Marie Prevost. After he married her mother, Ms. Keevers said he had no more to do with the film industry. "Knowing my father, I am sure he followed Marie's career and downfall, but he was very closed about it."

29. Golden, Eve, *Golden Images: 41 Essays on Silent Film Stars*, McFarland & Company, Inc., 2001.

30. *Variety*, 7 February 1924.

31. Foster, Charles, *Stardust and Shadows: Canadians in Early Hollywood*, Dundurn Press Ltd., 2000.

32. Ibid.

33. Harrison's Reports, 25 October 1924.

34. "Kenneth Harlan Weds Marie Prevost," *The New York Times*, 15 October 1924

35. *The New York Times*, 4 November 1925.

36. "Crash Kills Mother of Screen Star," *Oakland Tribune*, Oakland, California, 6 February 1926.

37. Foster, Charles, *Stardust and Shadows: Canadians in Early Hollywood*, Dundurn Press Ltd., 2000.

38. *Motion Picture Classic*, August 1926.

39. *Harrison's Reports*, 29 September 1926.

40. *The New York Times*, 30 March 1927.

41. Foster, Charles, *Stardust and Shadows: Canadians in Early Hollywood*, Dundurn Press Ltd., 2000.

42. "'Perfect Pair' of Films Part," *Modesto News-Herald*, Modesto, California, 27 May 1927.

43. "Film Star to Divorce Spouse," *Ogden Standard-Examiner*, Ogden, Utah, 17 November 1927.

44. Ibid.

45. *Photoplay*, August 1928.

46. Foster, Charles, *Stardust and Shadows: Canadians in Early Hollywood*, Dundurn Press Ltd., 2000.

47. Basquette, Lina, *DeMille's Godless Girl*, Denlinger's Publishing, 1990.

48. Ibid.

49. *Harrison's Reports*, 3 April 1929.

50. "Marie Prevost Gets Contract," *Los Angeles Times*, 3 September 1930.

DANGEROUS CURVES ATOP HOLLYWOOD HEELS

51. "Marie Prevost Wins Role By Losing Pounds," *Portsmouth Times*, Portsmouth, Ohio, 21 March 1933.

52. "Week of Gaiety Planned When he Sees Death Near," *Nevada State Journal*, Reno, Nevada, 29 September 1933.

53. "Zasu's Former Hubby Denies Flees in House," 12 April 1934.

54. "Dentist Succumbs on Visit to Marie Prevost, Actress," *The New York Times*, 23 October 1934.

55. Foster, Charles, *Stardust and Shadows: Canadians in Early Hollywood*, Dundurn Press Ltd., 2000.

57. "Marie Prevost Found Dead in Hollywood," *Los Angeles Times*, 24 January 1937.

58. "Death of Film Star Laid to Alcoholism," 25 January 1937. In addition, her death certificate lists acute alcoholism as the cause of death.

59. Foster, Charles, *Stardust and Shadows: Canadians in Early Hollywood*, Dundurn Press Ltd., 2000.

60. Marie Prevost and Mother to be Cremated Together," *Los Angeles Times*, 25 January 1927.

61. Ibid.

62. Foster, Charles, *Stardust and Shadows: Canadians in Early Hollywood*, Dundurn Press Ltd., 2000.

63. Ibid.

64. Marie Prevost Autopsy Held," *Hammond Times*, Hammond, Indiana, 25 January 1937.

FILMOGRAPHY

1915

Those Bitter Sweets (short) (Keystone) D: *F. Richard Jones.* Bobby Dunn, Virginia Fox, Phyllis Haver, Dell Henderson, Evelyn Lynn, Harry McCoy, Marie Prevost, Al St. John, Slim Summerville, Mack Swain.

His Father's Footsteps (short) (Keystone) D: *Charley Chase and Ford Sterling.* Charley Chase, Alice Davenport, May Emory, Cecille Evans, Virginia Fox, Polly Moran, Marie Prevost, Fritz Schade, Ford Sterling, Bobby Vernon, Guy Woodward.

1916

Better Late Than Never (short) (Keystone) D: *Frank Griffin.* William Collier Sr., Mae Busch, Joseph Belmont, Frank Opperman, Marie Prevost, Josef Swickard.

Unto Those Who Sin (Selig Polyscope) D: *William Robert Daly.* Fritzi Brunette.

Al W. Filson, Lillian Hayward, Marion Warner, Edward J. Piel, Earle Foxe, George Larkin, William Sheerer, George Hernandez, Louise Sothern, Marie Prevost, Jack Albert.

Sunshine (short) (Keystone) D: *Edward F. Cline.* Jack Cooper, Hank Mann, Bobby Dunn, Viola Barry, Marie Prevost, Phyllis Haver, Gloria Swanson, Cecille Evans.

A Scoundrel's Toll (short) (Keystone) D: *Glen Cavender.* Raymond Griffith, Mary Thurman, Gene Rogers, Edgar Kennedy, Dale Fuller, Albert T. Gillespie, Frank Hayes, Marie Prevost.

1917

Her Nature's Dance (short) (Keystone) D: *Edward F. Cline.* Cecile Arnold, Alice Lake, Roxana McGowan, Marie Prevost, Gene Rogers, Fritz Schade, Eva Thatcher.

Secrets of a Beauty Parlor (short) (Keystone) D: *Harry Williams.* Hugh Fay, Bobby Dunn, Marie Prevost, Alice Davenport, Jay Dwiggins, Sylvia Ashton, Elinor Field, Earle Rodney.

Two Crooks (short) (Keystone) Joseph Belmont, Bobby Dunn, Harry Gribbon, Tom Kennedy, Laura La Varnie, Alice Maison, Marie Prevost, Caroline Rankin, Gene Rogers.

1918

His Hidden Purpose (short) (Mack Sennett Comedies) D: *Edward F. Cline.* Chester Conklin, Marie Prevost, Gene Rogers, Neal Burns, Cliff Bowes, George Binns, Slim Summerville, Jack Cooper, Laura La Varnie.

Those Athletic Girls (short) (Mack Sennett Comedies) D: *Edward F. Cline.* Louise Fazenda, Jack Cooper, Laura La Varnie, Glen Cavender, Ethel Teare, Phyllis Haver, Vera Steadman, Marvel Rea, Roxana McGowan, Josephine Banks, Edith Valk, Lillian Biron, Virginia Nightingale, Elinor Field, Marie Prevost, Slim Summerville.

Friend Husband (short) (Mack Sennett Comedies) D: *Walter Wright.* Charles Murray, Wayland Trask, Mary Thurman, Gene Rogers, Harry Gribbon, Erle C. Kenton, Laura La Varnie, Davy Lee, James Donnelly, Alice Maison, Marie Prevost, Marvel Rea, Eva Thatcher.

His Smothered Love (short) (Mack Sennett Comedies) D: *Edward F. Cline.* Chester Conklin, Harry Gribbon, Marie Prevost, Jack Cooper, Laura La Varnie, Larry McGrath, Alice Maison, Paddy McGuire, Wayland Trask, Ben Turpin, Marvel Rea, Phyllis Haver, Vera Steadman, Josephine Banks, Slim Summerville.

Her Screen Idol (short) (Mack Sennett Comedies) D: *Edward F. Cline.* Louise Fazenda, Ford Sterling, Marvel Rea, Edgar Kennedy, Glen Cavender, Jack Cooper, Gene Rogers, Roxana McGowan, Laura La Varnie, Ben Turpin, Heinie Conklin, Marie Prevost.

She Loved Him Plenty (short) (Mack Sennett Comedies) D: *Hampton Del Ruth and F. Richard Jones.* Ben Turpin, Heinie Conklin, Polly Moran, Gonda Durand, Harriet Hammond, Phyllis Haver, Patrick Kelly, Edgar Kennedy, Roxana McGowan, Paddy McGuire, Marie Prevost, Eva Thatcher.

Whose Little Wife Are You? (short) (Mack Sennett Comedies) D: *Edward F. Cline.* Joseph Belmont, Heinie Conklin, Harriet Hammond, Phyllis Haver, Tom Kennedy, Alice Lake, Laura La Varnie, Myrtle Lind, Paddy McGuire, Charles Murray, Marie Prevost, Gene Rogers, Vera Steadman, Eva Thatcher, Mary Thurman, Wayland Trask, Ben Turpin.

Hide and Seek, Detectives (short) (Mack Sennett Comedies) D: *Edward F. Cline.* Heinie Conklin, Tom Kennedy, Paddy McGuire, Al McKinnon, Charles Murray, Marie Prevost, Ben Turpin.

The Village Chestnut (short) (Mack Sennett Comedies) D: *Raymond Griffith and Walter Wright.* Chester Conklin, Louise Fazenda, Myrtle Lind, Paddy McGuire, Eva Thatcher, Al McKinnon, George Gray, Hughie Mack, Pearl Elmore, Raymond Griffith, Harriet Hammond, Phyllis Haver, Patrick Kelly, Marie Prevost, Gene Rogers.

1919

Never Too Old (short) (Mack Sennett Comedies) D: *F. Richard Jones.* Charles Murray, Eva Thatcher, Joseph Belmont, Bert Roach, Phyllis Haver, Marie Prevost, James Finlayson, Tom Kennedy, Louise Fazenda, Billy Armstrong.

East Lynne With Variations (short) (Mack Sennett Comedies) D: *Edward F. Cline.* Ben Turpin, Heinie Conklin, Marie Prevost, Bobby Dunn, Tom Kennedy, Alice Lake, Marvel Rea, Bert Roach, Ford Sterling.

Yankee Doodle in Berlin (Mack Sennett Comedies) D: *Richard Jones.* Bothwell Browne, Ford Sterling, Mal St. Clair, Bert Roach, Ben Turpin, Charles Murray, Marie Prevost, Eva Thatcher, Baldy Belmont, Chester Conklin, Charles Lynn.

Reilly's Wash Day (short) (Mack Sennett Comedies) D: *F. Richard Jones.* Russ Powell, Joseph Belmont, Robert Finlay, Eddie Gribbon, Charles Murray, Marie Prevost, Eva Thatcher.

Why Beaches are Popular? *(short) (Mack Sennett Comedies)* D: *Richard Jones.* Marvel Rea, Malcolm St. Clair, Phyllis Haver, Bert Roach, Myrtle Lind, Harriet Hammond, Marie Prevost, Ford Sterling, Alice Maison, Louise Fazenda.

When Love is Blind (short) (Mack Sennett Comedies) D: *Edward F. Cline.* Heinie Conklin, Chester Conklin, Phyllis Haver, Erle C. Kenton, Al McKinnon, Charles Murray, Kalla Pasha, Marie Prevost, John Rand, Marvel Rea, Gene Rogers, Ben Turpin.

Love's False Faces (short) (Mack Sennett Comedies) D: *F. Richard Jones.* Chester Conklin, Marie Prevost, James Finlayson, Charlotte Mineau, Kalla Pasha, Billy Armstrong, Heinie Conklin, Ben Turpin, Edgar Kennedy, Eddie Gribbon.

The Dentist (short) (Mack Sennett Comedies) D: *F. Richard Jones.* Charles Murray,.

Charlotte Mineau, James Finlayson, Fanny Kelly, Marie Prevost, Kalla Pasha, Eddie Gribbon, Joseph Belmont, Hughie Mack, Ben Turpin, Harry Gribbon, Phyllis Haver, Patrick Kelly.

Sleuths (short) (Mack Sennett Comedies) D: *F. Richard Jones.* Ben Turpin, Chester Conklin, Heinie Conklin, Patrick Kelly, Tom Kennedy, Dutch Meyer, Marie Prevost, Bert Roach, Eva Thatcher.

Uncle Tom Without a Cabin (short) (Mack Sennett Comedies) D: *F. Richard Jones.* Ben Turpin, Chester Conklin, Marie Prevost, Billy Bevan, Eddie Gribbon, Isabelle Keith, Kathryn McGuire, Charles Murray, Kalla Pasha, Ford Sterling, Eva Thatcher, Gladys Whitfield.

Salome vs. Shenandoah (short) (Mack Sennett Comedies) D: *Ray Grey and Ray Hunt.* Ben Turpin, Marie Prevost, Billy Bevan, Heinie Conklin, Al Cooke, Annette DeGandis, Louise Fazenda, Eddie Gribbon, Harry Gribbon, Harriet Hammond, Phyllis Haver, Fanny Kelly, Alice Maison, Kathryn McGuire, Charles Murray, Sybil Seely, Ford Sterling, Eva Thatcher, Gladys Whitfield.

The Speakeasy (short) (Mack Sennett Comedies) D: *F. Richard Jones.* Charles Murray, Marie Prevost, Eddie Gribbon, Kalla Pasha, Patrick Kelly, Fanny Kelly.

1920

A Kitchen Cinderella (short) (Mack Sennett Comedies) D: *Malcolm St. Clair.* Marie Prevost, George O'Hara, Renne Galian, Carolyn Ashley, Julia Rand, Fanny Kelly.

Down on the Farm (Mack Sennett Comedies) D: *Ray Grey and F. Richard Jones.* Louise Fazenda, Harry Gribbon, Bert Roach, Eva Thatcher, James Finlayson, Billy Armstrong, Don Marion, Phyllis Haver, Marie Prevost, Mildred June, Harriet Hammond, Ben Turpin, Jane Allen, Thelma Bates, Joseph Belmont, Elva Diltz, Frank Earle, Virginia Fox, Eddie Gribbon, Fanny Kelly, Patrick Kelly, Kathryn McGuire, Charles Murray, Kalla Pasha, Sybil Seely.

Fresh from the City (short) (Mack Sennett Comedies) D: *Walter Wright.* Ford Sterling, Marie Prevost, Bert Roach, Gordon Lewis, Kalla Pasha, Virginia Fox, Eddie Gribbon, Patrick Kelly, Billy Armstrong, Billy Bevan, Jack Ackroyd, Eva Thatcher.

You Wouldn't Believe It (short) (Mack Sennett Comedies) D: *Erle C. Kenton.* Jane Allen, Gladys Atkins, Thelma Bates, Harry Bowen, Chester Conklin, Louise Fazenda, James Finlayson, Eddie Gribbon, Charlotte Mineau, Marie Prevost, Bert Roach, Ben Turpin.

His Youthful Fancy (short) (Mack Sennett Comedies) D: *Erle C. Kenton.* Charles Murray, Marie Prevost, Ford Sterling, Charlotte Mineau, George O'Hara, Fanny Kelly, Eddie Gribbon.

Movie Fans (short) (Mack Sennett Comedies) D: *Erle C. Kenton.* Gordon Lewis, Lige Conley, Charlotte Mineau, Eva Thatcher, Garry O'Dell, Harriet Hammond, Mildred June, Fanny Kelly, Kalla Pasha, Jane Allen, Thelma Bates, Billy Bevan, Al Cooke, Virginia Fox, Phyllis Haver, Patrick Kelly, Kathryn McGuire, Charles Murray, George O'Hara, Marie Prevost, John Rand, Jack Richardson, Sybil Seely, Ford Sterling, Tiny Ward, Gladys Whitfield.

Love, Honor and Behave (Mack Sennett Comedies) D: *Richard Jones.* Charles Murray, Ford Sterling, Phyllis Haver, Marie Prevost, George O'Hara, Charlotte Mineau,.

Billy Bevan, Kalla Pasha, Eddie Gribbon, Fanny Kelly, Billy Armstrong, Baldy Belmont, Eva Thatcher.

1921

Dabbling in Art (short) (Mack Sennett Comedies) D: *Erle C. Kenton.* George O'Hara, Marie Prevost, Harriet Hammond, Jack Richardson, Al Cooke, William Sloan, Lige Conley, Gordon Lewis, Tiny Ward, Billy Bevan, Fanny Kelly, Patrick Kelly, Mary Mayberry, Kathryn McGuire.

A Small Town Idol (Mack Sennett Productions) D: *Erle Kenton and Mack Sennett.* Ben Turpin, James Finlayson, Phyllis Haver, Bert Roach, Al Cooke, Charles Murray, Marie Prevost, Dot Farley, Eddie Gribbon, Kalla Pasha, Billy Bevan, George O'Hara.

Wedding Bells Out of Tune (short) (Mack Sennett Productions) D: *Malcolm St. Clair.* Louise Fazenda, Lige Conley, Kathryn McGuire, Whitney Raymond, Garry O'Dell, Fanny Kelly, Marie Prevost.

She Sighed by the Seaside (short) (Mack Sennett Productions) D: *Erle C. Kenton.* Ben Turpin, Marie Prevost, Heinie Conklin, James Finlayson, Bert Roach, Charlotte Mineau, Tiny Ward, Lige Conley, Jane Allen, Thelma Bates, Elva Diltz, Virginia Fox, Isabelle Keith, Kathryn McGuire, Irene Tiver, Gladys Whitfield.

Call a Cop (short) (Mack Sennett Productions) D: *Malcolm St. Clair.* Marie Prevost, George O'Hara, Patrick Kelly, Jack Richardson, Eddie Gribbon, Eddie Fitzgerald, John Rand, Tiny Ward, Fanny Kelly, Sam Bernard, Kalla Pasha.

Moonlight Follies (Universal) D: *King Baggot.* Marie Prevost, Lionel Belmore, Marie Crisp, George Fisher, George Fillmore.

Nobody's Fool (Universal) D: *King Baggot.* Marie Prevost, Helen Harris, Vernon Snively, R. Henry Guy, Percy Challenger, Harry Myers, George Kuwa, Lucretia Harris, Lydia Yeamans Titus.

A Parisian Scandal (Universal) D: *George L. Cox.* George Periolat, Lillian Lawrence, Marie Prevost, Bertram Grassby, George Fisher, Lillian Rambeau, Tom Gallery, Mae Busch, Rose Dione.

1922

Don't Get Personal (Universal) D: *Clarence C. Badger.* Marie Prevost, George Nichols, Daisy Robinson, Roy Atwell, T. Roy Barnes, G. Del Lorice, Sadie Gordon, Alida B. Jones, Ralph McCullough.

The Dangerous Little Demon (Universal) D: *Clarence C. Badger.* Marie Prevost, Jack Perrin, Robert Ellis, Anderson Smith, Fontaine La Rue, Edward Martindel, Lydia Knott, Herbert Prior.

The Crossroads of New York (Mack Sennett) D: *F. Richard Jones.* George O'Hara, Noah Beery, Ethel Grey Terry, Ben Deeley, Billy Bevan, Herbert Standing, Dot Farley, Eddie Gribbon, Kathryn McGuire, Robert Cain, Mildred June, Raymond Griffith, Charles Murray, James Finlayson, Al Cooke, Jack Cooper, Floy Guinn, Patrick Kelly, Daphne Pollard, Marie Prevost.

Kissed (Universal) D: *King Baggot.* Marie Prevost, Lloyd Whitlock, Lillian Langdon, J. Frank Glendon, Arthur Hoyt, Percy Challenger, Harold Miller, Marie Crisp, Harold Goodwin.

Her Night of Nights (Universal) D: *Hobart Henley.* Marie Prevost, Edward Hearn, Hal Cooley, Betty Francisco, Charles Arling, Jane Starr, George B. Williams, William Robert Daly, Richard Daniels.

The Married Flapper (Universal) D: *Stuart Paton.* Marie Prevost, Kenneth Harlan, Philo McCullough, Frank Kingsley, Lucille Ricksen, Kathleen O'Connor, Hazel Keener, Tom McGuire, Burton Wilson, William Quinn, Lydia Titus, Martha Mattox.

The Beautiful and Damned (Warner Brothers) D: *William A. Seiter.* Marie Prevost, Kenneth Harlan, Harry Myers, Tully Marshall, Louise Fazenda, Cleo Ridgely, Emmett King, Walter Long, Clarence Burton, Parker McConnell, Charles McHugh, Kathleen Key, George Kuwa.

Heroes of the Street (Warner Brothers) D: *William Beaudine.* Wesley Barry, Marie Prevost, Jack Mulhall, Philo McCullough, Will Walling, Aggie Herring, Wilfred Lucas, Wedgewood Nowell, Phil Ford, "Peaches" Jackson, Joe Butterworth, Lillian Leeds, Billie Beaudine Jr.

1923

Brass (Warner Brothers) D: *Sidney A. Franklin.* Monte Blue, Marie Prevost, Harry Myers, Irene Rich, Frank Keenan, Helen Ferguson, Miss Du Pont, Cyril Chadwick, Margaret Seddon, Pat O'Malley, Edward Jobson, Vera Lewis, Harvey Clark, Gertrude Bennett, Ethel Grey Terry, Bruce Puerin.

Red Lights (Goldwyn) D: *Clarence C. Badger*. Marie Prevost, Raymond Griffith, Johnny Walker, Alice Lake, Dagmar Godowsky, William Worthington, Frank Elliott, Lionel Belmore, Jean Hersholt, George Reed.

The Wanters (Associated First National Pictures) D: *John M. Stahl*. Marie Prevost, Robert Ellis, Norma Shearer, Gertrude Astor, Huntley Gordon, Lincoln Stedman, Lillian Langdon, Louise Fazenda, Hank Mann, Lydia Yeamans Titus, Vernon Steele, Harold Goodwin, William Buckley.

1924

Daughters of Pleasure (Principal Pictures) D: *William Beaudine*. Marie Prevost, Monte Blue, Clara Bow, Edythe Chapman, Wilfred Lucas.

The Marriage Circle (Warner Brothers) D: *Ernst Lubitsch*. Florence Vidor, Monte Blue, Marie Prevost, Creighton Hale, Adolphe Menjou, Harry Myers, Dale Fuller, Esther Ralston.

How to Educate a Wife (Warner Brothers) D: *Monta Bell*. Marie Prevost, Monte Blue, Claude Gillingwater, Vera Lewis, Betty Francisco, Creighton Hale, Edward Earle, Nellie Bly Baker.

Being Respectable (Warner Brothers) D: *Philip Rosen*. Marie Prevost, Monte Blue, Louise Fazenda, Irene Rich, Theodore von Eltz, Frank Currier, Eulalie Jensen, Lila Leslie, Sidney Bracey.

Cornered (Warner Brothers) D: *William Beaudine*. Marie Prevost, Rockliffe Fellowes, Raymond Hatton, John Roche, Cissy Fitzgerald, Vera Lewis, George Pearce, Bartine Burkett, Billy Fletcher, Ruth Dwyer, Bertram Johns, Wilfred Lucas.

Tarnish (Goldwyn) D: *George Fitzmaurice*. May McAvoy, Ronald Colman, Marie Prevost, Albert Gran, Mrs. Russ Whytall, Priscilla Bonner, Harry Myers, Kay Deslys, Lydia Yeamans Titus, William Boyd.

Three Women (Warner Brothers) D: *Ernst Lubitsch*. May McAvoy, Pauline Frederick, Lew Cody, Marie Prevost, Willard Louis, Raymond McKee, Pierre Gendron, Mary Carr.

The Lover of Camille (Warner Brothers) D: *Harry Beaumont*. Monte Blue, Marie Prevost, Willard Louis, Pierre Gendron, Pat Moore, Carlton Miller, Winifred Bryson, Brandon Hurst, Rose Dione, Trilby Clark.

The Dark Swan (Warner Brothers) D: *Millard Webb.* Marie Prevost, Monte Blue, Helene Chadwick, John Patrick, Lilyan Tashman, Vera Lewis, Carlton Miller, Mary MacLaren, Arthur Rankin.

1925

Recompense (Warner Brothers) D: *Harry Beaumont.* Marie Prevost, Monte Blue, John Roche, George Siegmann, Charles Stevens, Virginia Brown Faire, William B. Davidson, Katherine Lewis.

Kiss Me Again (Warner Brothers) D: *Ernst Lubitsch.* Marie Prevost, Monte Blue, John Roche, Clara Bow, Willard Louis.

Bobbed Hair (Warner Brothers) D: *Alan Crosland.* Marie Prevost, Kenneth Harlan, Louise Fazenda, John Roche, Emily Fitzroy, Reed Howes, Pat Hartigan, Walter Long, Francis McDonald, Tom Ricketts, Otto Hoffman, Kate Toncray.

Seven Sinners (Warner Brothers) D: *Lewis Milestone.* Marie Prevost, Clive Brook, John Patrick, Charles Conklin, Claude Gillingwater, Mathilde Brundage, Dan Mason, Fred Kelsey.

1926

His Jazz Bride (Warner Brothers) D: *Herman C. Raymaker.* Marie Prevost, Matt Moore, Gayne Whitman, John Patrick, Mabel Julienne Scott, Stanley Wayburn, Don Alvarado, Helen Dunbar, George Irving, George Seddon.

The Caveman (Warner Brothers) D: *Lewis Milestone.* Matt Moore, Marie Prevost, John Patrick, Myrna Loy, Phyllis Haver, Hedda Hopper.

Other Women's Husbands (Warner Brothers) D: *Erle C. Kenton.* Monte Blue, Marie Prevost, Huntley Gordon, Phyllis Haver, Marjorie Gay, John Patrick.

Up in Mabel's Room (Producers Distributing Corp.) D: *E. Mason Hopper.* Marie Prevost, Harrison Ford, Phyllis Haver, Harry Myers, Sylvia Breamer, Paul Nicholson, Carl Gerard, Maude Truax, William Orlamond, Arthur Hoyt.

Almost a Lady (Producers Distributing Corp.) D: *E. Mason Hopper.* Marie Prevost, Harrison Ford, George K. Arthur, Trixie Friganza, John Miljan, Barney Gilmore.

For Wives Only (Producers Distributing Corp.) D: *Victor Heerman.*
Marie Prevost, Victor Varconi, Charles Gerrard, Arthur Hoyt, Claude
Gillingwater, Josephine Crowell, Dorothy Cumming, William
Courtright.

1927

Man Bait (Producers Distributing Corp.) D: *Donald Crisp.* Marie Prevost,
Kenneth Thomson, Douglas Fairbanks Jr., Louis Natheaux , Eddie
Gribbon, Betty Francisco, Adda Gleason, Sally Rand, Fritzi Ridgeway.

Getting Gertie's Garter (Producers Distributing Corp.) D: *E. Mason
Hopper.* Marie Prevost, Charles Ray, Harry Myers, Sally Rand, William
Orlamond ,Fritzi Ridgeway, Franklin Pangborn, Del Henderson, Lila
Leslie.

The Night Bride (Producers Distributing Corp.) D: *E. Mason Hopper.*
Marie Prevost, Harrison Ford, Franklin Pangborn, Robert Edeson,
Constance Howard, Richard Crawford, George Kuwa.

The Girl in the Pullman (Pathé) D: *Erle Kenton.* Marie Prevost, Harrison
Ford, Franklin Pangborn, Kathryn McGuire, Ethel Wales, Harry
Myers.

The Rush Hour (Pathé) D: *E. Mason Hopper.* Marie Prevost, Harrison
Ford, Seena Owen, David Butler, Ward Crane.

1928

On to Reno (Pathé) D: *James Cruze.* Marie Prevost, Cullen Landis, Ethel
Wales, Ned Sparks, Jane Keckley.

A Blonde for a Night (Pathé) D: *E. Mason Hopper.* Marie Prevost,
Franklin Pangborn, Harrison Ford, T. Roy Barnes, Lucien Littlefield.

The Racket (Paramount) D: *Lewis Milestone.* Thomas Meighan, Louis
Wolheim, Marie Prevost, Pat Collins, Henry Sedley, George Stone,
Sam De Grasse, Skeets Gallagher, Lee Moran, John Darrow, Lucien
Prival, Dan Wolheim, Tony Marlo, Burr McIntosh.

The Sideshow (Columbia) D: *Erle C. Kenton.* Marie Prevost, Ralph
Graves, Little Billy, Alan Roscoe, Pat Harmon, Texas Madesen, Martha
McGruger, Steve Clemento, Janet Ford, Paul Dismute, Bert Price,
Chester Morton, Jacques Ray.

1929

The Godless Girl (Pathé) D: *Cecil B. DeMille.* Lina Basquette, Marie Prevost, George Duryea, Noah Beery, Eddie Quillan, Mary Jane Irving, Clarence Burton, Dick Alexander, Kate Price, Hedwig Reicher, Julia Faye, Viola Louie, Emily Barrye, Jimmy Aldine, Vivian Bay, Elaine Bennett, Wade Boteler, Betty Boyd, Julia Brown, Archie Burke, Colin Chase, Cameron Coffey, Cecilia DeMille, Jacqueline Dyris, George Ellis, Anielka Elter, James Farley, Larry Fisher, Evelyn Francisco, May Giraci, Grace Gordon, Milton Holmes, William Humphrey, George Irving, Peaches Jackson, Dolores Johnson, Jane Keckley, Nora Kildare, Richard Lapan, Ida McKenzie, Don Marion, Edith May, Mary Mayberry, Collette Merton, Buddy Messinger, Pat Moore, Jack Murphy, Pat Palmer, Janice Peters, Hortense Petra, Gertrude Quality, Rae Randall, Billie Van Avery, Dorothy Wax.

The Flying Fool (Pathé) D: *Tay Garnett.* William Boyd, Marie Prevost, Russell Gleason, Tom O'Brien.

Divorce Made Easy (Paramount) D: *Neal Burns.* Douglas MacLean, Marie Prevost, Johnny Arthur, Frances Lee, Dot Farley, Jack Duffy, Buddy Wattles, Hal Wilson.

1930

Party Girl (Tiffany) D: *Victor Halperin.* Douglas Fairbanks Jr., Jeannette Loff, Judith Barrie, Marie Prevost, John St. Polis, Sammy Blum, Harry Northrup, Almeda Fowler, Hal Price, Charles Giblyn, Sidney D'Albrook, Lucien Prival, Florence Dudley, Earl Burtnett's Biltmore Orchestra and Trio.

Ladies of Leisure (Columbia) D: *Frank Capra.* Barbara Stanwyck, Ralph Graves, Lowell Sherman, Marie Prevost, Nance O'Neil, George Fawcett, Johnnie Walker, Juliette Compton, Charles Butterworth.

Sweethearts on Parade (Columbia) D: *Marshall Neilan.* Alice White, Lloyd Hughes, Marie Prevost, Kenneth Thomson.

War Nurse (M-G-M) D: *Edgar Selwyn.* Robert Montgomery, Anita Page, Robert Ames, June Walker, ZaSu Pitts, Marie Prevost, Helen Jerome Eddy, Hedda Hopper, Edward Nugent, Martha Sleeper.

Paid (M-G-M) D: *Sam Wood.* Joan Crawford, Robert Armstrong, Marie Prevost, Kent Douglass, John Miljan, Hale Hamilton, Polly Moran, William Bakewell, Gwen Lee.

1931

Gentleman's Fate (M-G-M) D: *Mervyn LeRoy.* John Gilbert, Louis Wolheim, Leila Hyams, Anita Page, Marie Prevost, John Miljan, George Cooper, Ralph Ince.

It's a Wise Child (M-G-M) D: *Robert Z. Leonard.* Marion Davies, Sidney Blackmer, James Gleason, Polly Moran, Lester Vail, Clara Blandick, Ben Alexander, Emily Fitzroy.

The Good Bad Girl (Columbia) D: *R. William Neill.* Mae Clarke, James Hall, Marie Prevost, Robert Ellis, Nance O'Neil, Paul Porcasi, Wheeler Oakman.

Call of the Rockies (Road Show Pictures). D: *Raymond K. Johnson.* Ben Lyon, Marie Prevost, Gladys Johnston, Anders Randolf, Russell Simpson, James Mason.

Sporting Blood (M-G-M) D: *Charles Brabin.* Clark Gable, Ernest Torrence, Madge Evans, Lew Cody, Marie Prevost, Hallam Cooley, J. Farrell MacDonald, John Larkin, Eugene Jackson.

The Runaround (RKO) D: *William James Craft.* Geoffrey Kerr, Mary Brian, Johnny Hines, Marie Prevost, Joseph Cawthorn.

Reckless Living (Universal) D: *Cyril Gardner.* Ricardo Cortez, Marie Prevost, George "Slim" Summerville, Robert Emmett O'Connor, Thomas E. Jackson, Louis Natheaux, Murray Kinnell, Russell Hopton, Perry Ivins, Brooks Benedict, Frank Hagney, Louise Beavers.

The Sin of Madelon Claudet (M-G-M) D: *Edgar Selwyn.* Helen Hayes, Neil Hamilton, Robert Young, Cliff Edwards, Jean Hersholt, Marie Prevost, Karen Morley.

1932

Hell Divers (M-G-M) D: *George Hill.* Clark Gable, Wallace Beery, Conrad Nagel, Dorothy Jordan, Marjorie Rambeau, Cliff Edwards, John Miljan, Landers Stevens, Reed Howes, Alan Roscoe, Frank Conroy.

Three Wise Girls (Columbia) D: *William Beaudine.* Jean Harlow, Mae Clarke, Walter Byron, Marie Prevost, Andy Devine, Natalie Moorhead.

Carnival Boat (RKO) D: *Albert S. Rogell.* William Boyd, Ginger Rogers, Fred Kohler, Hobart Bosworth, Marie Prevost, Edgar Kennedy, Harry Sweet, Charles Sellon, Eddy Chandler, Walter Percival.

Slightly Married (Chesterfield) D: *Richard Thorpe.* Evalyn Knapp, Walter Byron, Marie Prevost, Jason Robards Sr., Robert Ellis, Dorothy Christy, Clarissa Selwynne, Phillips Smalley, Herbert Evans, Lloyd Ingraham, Mary Foy.

Hesitating Love (short) (Universal) D: *James W. Horne.* Louise Fazenda, Bert Roach, Marie Prevost, Gertrude Astor, Louise Beavers, Vince Barnett.

1933

Rock-a-Bye Cowboy (short) (Universal) D: *George Stevens.* James Gleason, Vince Barnett, Raymond Hatton, Marie Prevost.

Parole Girl (Columbia) D: Edward F. Cline. Mae Clarke, Ralph Bellamy, Marie Prevost, Hale Hamilton, Ferdinand Gottschalk.

The Eleventh Commandment (Allied Pictures) D: *George Melford.* Marian Marsh, Theodore von Eltz, Alan Hale, Marie Prevost, Gloria Shea.

Pick Me Up (short) (Universal) D: *George W. Horne.* Marie Prevost, Henry Armetta.

Only Yesterday (Universal) D: *John M. Stahl.* Margaret Sullavan,
John Boles, Edna May Oliver, Billie Burke, Jimmy Butler, Benita
Hume, Reginald Denny, George Meeker, Jimmy Butler, Noel Francis,
Bramwell Fletcher, June Clyde, Jane Darwell, Oscar Apfel, Robert
McWade, Onslow Stevens, Huntley Gordon, Edmund Breese, Jay
Whidden, Astrid Allwyn, Leon Ames, Marion Clayton Anderson,
King Baggot, Ben Bard, Frank Beal, Louise Beavers, Betty Blythe,
Robert Bolder, Sidney Bracey, Sheila Bromley, Ralph Brooks, Marion
Byron, Julie Carter, Walter Catlett, Lita Chevret, Dorothy Christy,
Berton Churchill, Harvey Clark, Ruth Clifford, Sammy Cohen, Joyce
Compton, Tommy Conlon, Herbert Corthell, Lynn Cowan, Ida
Darling, Jean Darling, William B. Davidson, Mary Doran, Robert
Ellis, Julia Faye, Hans Fuerberg, Dorothy Granger, Creighton Hale,
Jeanne Hart, Otto Hoffman, Virginia Howell, Arthur Hoyt, George
Irving, Eddie Kane, Crauford Kent, Natalie Kingston, Florence Lake,
Caryl Lincoln, Alphonse Martell, Sam McDaniel, Matt McHugh,
Lafe McKee, Natalie Moorhead, Barry Norton, Vivien Oakland, Tom
O'Brien, William H. O'Brien, Dennis O'Keefe, Franklin Pangborn,
Marie Prevost, Craig Reynolds, Jack Richardson, Bert Roach, Jason
Robards Sr., Grady Sutton.

1935

Keystone Hotel (short) (Warner Brothers). D: *Ralph Staub.* Ford Sterling,
Ben Turpin, Chester Conklin, Hank Mann, Marie Prevost, Vivien
Oakland, Dewey Robinson, Bert Roach, Leo White, Jack Duffy,
Keystone Kops.

Hands Across the Table (Paramount) D: *Mitchell Leisen.* Carole Lombard,
Fred MacMurray, Ralph Bellamy, Astrid Allwyn, Ruth Donnelly,
Marie Prevost.

1936

Tango (Chesterfield) D: *Phil Rosen.* Marian Nixon, Chick Chandler,
Marie Prevost, Matty Kemp, Warren Hymer, Herman Bing, George
Meeker, Virginia Howell, Franklin Pangborn, Kathryn Sheldon.

13 Hours by Air (Paramount) D: *Mitchell Leisen*. Fred MacMurray, Joan Bennett, ZaSu Pitts, Alan Baxter, Fred Keating, Brian Donlevy, John Howard, Adrienne Marden, Ruth Donnelly, Benny Bartlett, Grace Bradley, Dean Jagger, Jack Mulhall, Granville Bates, Arthur Singley, Clyde Dilson, Mildred Stone, Dennis O'Keefe, Henry Arthur, Paul Barrett, Edward Biby, John Juettner, Marie Prevost, Ed Schaefer.

Cain and Mabel (Cosmopolitan) D: *Lloyd Bacon*. Marion Davies, Clark Gable, Allen Jenkins, Roscoe Karns, Walter Catlett, Robert Paige, Hobart Cavanaugh, Ruth Donnelly, Pert Kelton, William Collier Sr., Sammy White, E.E. Clive, Allen Pomeroy, Robert Middlemass, Joseph Crehan, Charles Teske, Eily Malyon, John T. Murray, Mary Treen, Emmett Vogan, Josephine Allen, Bill Archer, William Arnold, Herbert Ashley, Earl Askam, Curtis Benton, George Beranger, Jack Bergman, Georgie Billings, Harry C. Bradley, Victor Briedis, Tex Brodus, George Bruggeman, Billy Coe, Joe Cunningham, Virginia Dabney, Dick Dennis, Don Downen, Ralph Dunn, Robert Eberhardt, Jerry Fletcher, Dick French, Peter Gowland, Harry Harvey, Stuart Holmes, Delos Jewkes, Milton Kibbee, Joe King, Lillian Lawrence, John Lince, Miriam Marlin, Rosalind Marquis, John Marsden, Leona McGenty, Tom McGuire, Martha Merrill, Bert Moorhouse, Hal Neiman, Spec O'Donnell, Ted O'Shea, George Ovey, Paul Panzer, Bob Perry, Lee Phelps, Marie Prevost, George Riley.

Bengal Tiger (Warner Brothers) D: *Louis King*. Barton MacLane, June Travis, Warren Hull, Paul Graetz, Joseph Crehan, Dick Purcell, Carlyle Moore Jr., John Aasen, Richard Alexander, Don Barclay, Joseph Belmont, Glen Cavender, Jack A. Goodrich, Sol Gorss, Willard Hall, Gordon Hart, Jolly Lee Harvey, Jack Holmes, Stuart Holmes, Clara Horton, Milton Kibbee, Paul Panzer, Marie Prevost, 'Little Billy' Rhodes, Houseley Stevenson, Charlotte V. Sullivan, Lucille Ward, Carol Wines, Jane Wyman.

Ten Laps to Go (Fanchon Royer Films) D: Elmer Clifton. Rex Lease, Muriel Evans, Duncan Renaldo, Tom Moore, Charles Delaney, Yakima Canutt, Barney Smith, Eddie Davis, Lloyd Ingraham, Walter McGrail, Gay Seabrook, Lester Dorr.

A Melbourne Spurr portrait of Lucille Ricksen. COURTESY OF THE
RICKSEN FAMILY

LUCILLE RICKSEN

There was always something mysterious about little Lucille Ricksen, the teenage actress who went from playing childhood to leading lady roles almost overnight.

"She is the surprise package of Filmland," wrote Albert Dorris in 1924, "the strangest conglomeration of contradictions and possibilities ever incorporated into one little body. Perhaps she is the reincarnation of the Sphinx. That antique pile of rocks carelessly left out in the desert for a flock of centuries is just about as unexplainable as Lucille."

Another writer sent to interview Lucille concluded, "She is young and she is old, and accomplished it all at once. Mentally, she is trying to gobble up life in huge mouthfuls, and thank goodness, indigestion hasn't yet set in."

But, something did go horribly wrong with Lucille Ricksen. Her story is one of profound loss, a mysterious illness in 1924, followed by her death a year later, just as she was achieving the fame she — and her mother — worked so hard for.

In the spring of 2009, her nephews (the sons of her brother, Marshall) and grandnephew invited me out to San Francisco to study Lucille's scrapbooks to see if any answers to her sudden illness and death lay between the crumbling pages. No concrete answers, but certainly, there are clues.

Lucille took great care in the first years of her career to thoroughly document her experience in films. She clipped and pasted newspaper clippings and publicity photos into her scrapbook, and underneath each photo, wrote captions in white ink about her feelings as her career developed. She seemed to save everything from her roles in the *Edgar* comedies in the early 1920s, her subsequent publicity campaign across the country, and her return to Hollywood, where roles awaited her.

She took care to clip and arrange the announcement of her being named a Wampas Baby Star of 1924 and the headlines that year announcing she was being elevated at age 16 to playing adult roles and given the title, "The Youngest Leading Lady in Pictures." In truth, she was not 16 as the publicity insisted, but 13, barely a teenager.

Her attention to her scrapbook diminished as the direction of her career changed. She did indeed continue in leading roles, but fewer and fewer articles were saved, and when they were, they appeared to be torn from their source, their edges left jagged. They were no longer pasted with pride and care into her memory book.

What the movie-going public didn't know was that, while she was learning to become a woman in the movie studios of Hollywood under the direction of Marshall Neilan and with such actors as Sydney Chaplin and Jack Pickford and working harder than most adults twice her age, the teenager was also battling for her life, after contracting a mysterious illness. Being the sole breadwinner in her family, she continued working, but eventually became bedridden and unable to go to the studio.

Then, mother Ingeborg Ricksen, exhausted over caring for little Lucille, collapsed in death over her daughter's sick body in February 1925. Less than a month later, Lucille followed her mother.

Whatever the reason, Lucille Ricksen's death is one of the saddest — and mysterious — tales to come out of Hollywood.

Her age was always a source of speculation. We know she was born Lucille Erickson, in Chicago, Illinois, on August 22. Her year of birth is questionable. In Hollywood, three to four years was typically added to her age to fit her emerging image as a leading lady. Some publicity lists 1906 as her year of birth. Her death certificate states 1909. The most likely year is 1910, as indicated by the 1910 U.S. Federal Census.[1]

Her parents, Soren (Samuel), a salesman, and Ingeborg Neilsen were born in Denmark and immigrated to the United States in the late 1800s. Their first child, Marshall, was born in 1907.

Lucille had anything but a normal childhood. First, this beautiful little baby with golden curls worked as a professional model from the time she was a toddler. Then, she worked for about a year on the legitimate Chicago stage. In 1915, Ingeborg carried little Lucille to the Essanay Studios on Argyle Street and registered the five-year-old for work.

Going to the studio was one of Lucille's first recollections. "A man my mother talked to picked me up and put me on a table," she wrote. "He pulled my curls and asked if he could have one. I shook my head, no, and then he said, 'Well, I'll be nicer to you than that. I am going to give you a part."[2]

They gave Lucille the role of a cupid in a Henry B. Walthall drama. Lucille had started her life's work.

For the next three years, she worked in small roles at Essanay and Selig Polyscope, where she was cast as Baby Ericksen in a Grace Darmond film, *The Millionaire Baby* (1915).

By 1918, the Erickson marriage was on the rocks. With filmmaking in Chicago also on the downswing, Ingeborg divorced her husband and journeyed west with Marshall and eight-year-old Lucille. Ingeborg hoped

Even in her modeling work, it seemed they were always trying to make Lucille Ricksen appear older than she was. COURTESY OF THE RICKSEN FAMILY

they could all work in the movies. There's no doubt, however, that she had big plans for her little Lucille.

Not long after the Ericksons were in Los Angeles, they met theatre mogul F. A. Rothapfel, who assured Ingeborg that little Lucille had what it took to be successful in Hollywood. The Ericksons met with Rothapfel a second time in Chicago. Shortly thereafter, Lucille's Hollywood career was launched.

Lucille Ricksen with her mother, Ingeborg, and brother, Marshall.
COURTESY OF THE RICKSEN FAMILY

Producer Samuel Goldwyn signed Lucille to appear as the dainty sweetheart of Johnny Jones in Booth Tarkington's *Edgar* comedy series.

The three Ericksons settled first at an apartment house on Washington Boulevard in Culver City so Lucille could be near the Goldwyn Studios.[3] At the recommendation of the studio, the Ericksons dropped the "E" from their name and changed the "O" to "E." Ricksen became the new family name.

E. Mason Hopper directed the first film in the series: *Edgar and the Teacher's Pet* (1920). Lucille, ever diligent and enthusiastic in her work, praised Hopper. "I am very glad I got to play the leading part of the girl and I hope I can make you very proud of me," the 10-year old wrote in her neat cursive handwriting. "I think you are the most patient child's director I have ever known." She signed the note, "Lovingly, your little leading lady."

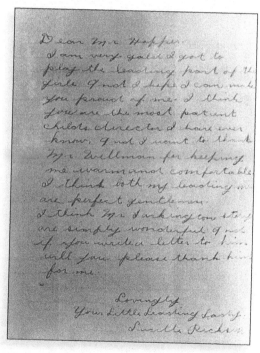

The letter Lucille wrote to her director, E. Mason Hopper.
COURTESY OF THE RICKSEN FAMILY

Lucille made quite an impression on studio heads with her naturalness, spunk and ability to handle herself in any scene. The series was also wildly popular with kids across the country. Lucille, as Alice Littlefield, is mischievous and rambunctious in most of the shorts, but sentimental and sweet when the scene called for a change.

When the cameras stopped rolling for the day, Lucille carried on her screen personality and loved playing jokes on her friends. While wandering around the wardrobe department at Goldwyn one afternoon, the little actress "spied a pair of silver slippers with French heels." She put them on and found they fit perfectly. She located a pair of silver stockings and a blue silk dress. She ran to the hairdresser and asked her to pin up her

Lucille Ricksen at the time she worked in the Edgar *comedies and* The Old Nest. COURTESY OF THE RICKSEN FAMILY

curls. All dressed up, Lucille returned to the lot. "I asked someone if they had seen my sister, Lucille Ricksen, and they said no — Lucille finished work a while ago and went home. I nearly died laughing. I wish I could have a day like that every day!"[4]

In the spring of 1921, Lucille and Marshall went to Goldwyn Studios to test, along with hoards of other young hopefuls, for roles in *The Old Nest*, which was to be based on a story published several years before by author and director Rupert Hughes, uncle of Howard.

The sentimental story told of the married life of a kind and giving mother (Mary Alden), the wife of a country doctor, whose children grow up, marry, and neglect their mother as they live their own lives. Most of the principal players from the *Edgar* comedy series, including Lucille, were given roles in the picture. Marshall was also cast.[5]

During the production of *The Old Nest*, Rupert Hughes quickly became a close family friend of the Ricksens and would soon play an important role in Marshall's life as the years unfolded.

When work was completed on *The Old Nest*, Lucille and her family embarked on a mid-Western publicity tour to capitalize on the popularity of the *Edgar*

Lucille Ricksen clowns around for the camera while on tour in Duluth, Minnesota. COURTESY OF THE RICKSEN FAMILY

comedy series. In her scrapbooks, Lucille meticulously documented the summer and early fall events of 1921. She gave interviews, appeared at theaters, posed with local dignitaries, was honored at receptions and department stores, and participated in a number of publicity gimmicks.

The Superior Telegram (Michigan) newspaper sponsored a contest to see who could guess Lucille's real age. "I think she is 27 years old and five months and 10 days old," one entry read. "A person who can talk and act and travel all over like Lucille does has to be grown up." One entry said she was two years old; another, age 30. The newspaper was vague. "She's too old to sit on her mother's lap and not old enough to put her yellow curls up.⁶"

In Duluth, a look-a-like contest for Johnny Jones (as *Edgar*) was held. All boys were urged to submit their photo for the judging. Lucille selected the winner.

Lucille Ricksen sits in Jimmie Murphy's racecar on her publicity trip to Indianapolis. COURTESY OF THE RICKSEN FAMILY

When she appeared at a theater (once in the afternoon and twice in the evening), Lucille's routine was usually the same. In her act, "Scenes from Studio Land," she told about life in a movie studio and going to school four hours a day on the lot. She closed her routine with a rendition of "I Love You Truly," "An Old-Fashioned Garden," and "I'm A-Wearying for You."

The experience was exhausting, yes, but Lucille told *The Superior Telegram*, "I like spending my vacation this way. It's hard work, but I have my mother with me and she always sees that I am comfy.⁷"

Lucille devoted most of her scrapbook to her visit to Indianapolis in September 1921. There are candid photographs pasted to the pages with captions in Lucille's handwriting. In addition to her stage routine, Lucille posed at the wheel of a touring car and at the racetrack with drivers Eddie Heame and Jimmie Murphy.

She also paid a visit to the home of Booth Tarkington, the author of the Edgar stories, but found no one home. The local newspaper covered the scene of a disappointed Lucille sitting alone on Tarkington's front steps.

Ralph W. Lieber, business manager of the Circle Theater in Indianapolis, was quite taken with the young star. In a letter given to Lucille before she left the city, he wrote, "Of course, being an old 'bach' myself, it

Lucille Ricksen (R) with Marie Prevost and Kenneth Harlan on the set of The Married Flapper *(1922).* COURTESY OF THE RICKSEN FAMILY

wouldn't do for me to say that your beautiful curls, that winning, million-dollar smile, and your charming self have not only won me completely, but all of us."[8] In her "Friends O' Mine" autograph book, he wrote, "The biggest vamp that ever came to this city. Watch your step."

Back in Hollywood in the fall of 1921, Lucille had high expectations for herself. In *The Married Flapper* (1922), Lucille, as the niece of Kenneth Harlan, idolizes and immolates his flapper wife, Marie Prevost. In *The Girl Who Ran Wild*, Lucille is a school girl who catches the eye of her school master (Vernon Steele). She had a small role in *Forsaking All Others* with Colleen Moore and Cullen Landis.

She was happy to be reunited with Rupert Hughes at Goldwyn when he directed *Remembrance*, a family melodrama about a father (Claude

Gillingwater) who suffers a nervous breakdown trying to provide for his family. He directed her again in a small role as a street urchin in *Look Your Best* (1923).

In a form letter to her fans while she was working in her final picture for Hughes, Lucille explained she was too busy to answer each letter personally. "I'm often asked this question: Do I find my work hard? No,

An original advertisement for Judgment of the Storm *(1923).*
COURTESY OF THE RICKSEN FAMILY

indeed, it is not hard for me. Because I enjoy doing it. I can be no happier than when I am working before the camera." She also expressed praise for Hughes. "If I was to write in this little letter how much I love Rupert Hughes, it would take pages and pages."[9]

After working with Hughes a final time, Lucille had a small role in *Human Wreckage* (1923), a film that exposed the destruction caused by drug addiction. Mrs. Wallace Reid (Dorothy Davenport) headed the cast and made a powerful statement to movie audiences who were still grieving over the death of her husband, film star Wallace Reid, who, earlier in the year, succumbed to morphine addiction.

In the spring of 1923, while she was still 12 years old, Lucille was cast in her first adult role, the sweetheart of Lloyd Hughes in *Judgment of the*

Storm. The film, including Lucille's performance, garnered the praise of movie critics.

Producer Thomas H. Ince, impressed with Lucille's strong performance, signed the young girl to a contract. Then, in the summer of 1923, she was sent to Goldwyn Studios to make a test for the leading lady in *The Rendezvous* (1924). Much to the surprise of many in the industry, especially to the scores of older actresses who had tested for the role, Marshall Neilan selected Lucille for the honor.

The publicity machines went into overload proclaiming Lucille the "youngest leading lady in movies." Overnight, three years were added to her age. Although she was not quite 13 years old, the studio and press declared her to be 16. Before she realized what was happening, she was off to San Francisco to film waterfront scenes for the film.

For this young hopeful, playing the part of a peasant during the Russian Revolution was the dream of a lifetime. Not only was Neilan at the height of his career as a director, the accomplished cast consisted of Conrad Nagel, Richard Travers, Sydney Chaplin, Kate Lester, and Lucien Littlefield.

In the film, Vera (Lucille) is an orphaned girl who turns out to be a Russian princess. Exiled to Siberia, she establishes a growing friendship with an American lieutenant, Stanford (Nagel), who promises to return for her. She is left in the care of a friend of the lieutenant, a British sergeant (Sydney Chaplin). In the meantime, the evil governor of the province, Godunoff (Elmo Lincoln), throws the sergeant in jail and forces marriage on the girl. She faints and the marriage is not completed. In the final reel, Vera unknowingly locks Godunoff in a tomb and seals his fate for eternity. She sails to America with Stanford.

One reporter visiting her on the Goldwyn lot was stunned at her maturity and the grasp she had on such an emotional role. "It (*The Rendezvous*) is so dramatic. I'm a little Russian girl and I grow up to marry a horrid man who beats and misuses me and all that sort of thing. Oh, it's wonderful," exclaimed Lucille. The interviewer came away feeling that Lucille had been "born under the shadow of a Lillian Gish complex and that nothing is too intense for her."[10]

The interviewer surmised that Lucille's work on the *Edgar* series might have been the only time the young actress had experienced her childhood. "That makes her different," the interviewer wrote. "It is almost uncanny how different she is. It makes you sorry and it makes you glad."

Lucille, by her own admission, said she felt more comfortable around adults than those her own age. "They never say or do anything interesting or worthwhile," she explained. "I do have such good times playing with the folks here (at the studio)."

While Conrad Nagel became a close family friend, Lucille was more smitten with her director (Neilan) and Sydney Chaplin. "Mr. Neilan is simply wonderful," she gushed to an interviewer. "He's my best friend. Syd Chaplin and I had a perfectly screaming time the other day between scenes imitating people. Oh, what fun!"

Lucille Ricksen on the cover of Picture Play. COURTESY OF THE RICKSEN FAMILY

Perhaps reporters had cause to worry about little Lucille and her developing friendships in Hollywood. There has been some speculation over the years about her relationship with Sydney Chaplin. Around the time *The Rendezvous* was released, an item in *The Billboard* suggested the two were married in the fall of 1923.[11] It seems implausible, given Lucille's age and the tight reign Ingeborg held on her daughter. When asked about the possibility today, Lucille's family expressed doubt the marriage ever happened. There's nothing in her scrapbooks or papers to suggest such a union.

Variety gave a nod to Lucille's performance in *The Rendezvous.* "Lucille Ricksen, the feminine contingent, is alleged to have been around the studios for some time, but it looks as if this vehicle can be designated as her first instance of an empathetic bid for attention, and it should lead to further prominence."[12]

Further publicity was afforded Lucille when she was named one of the 1924 Wampas Baby Stars.[13] In writing about her selection as a Baby star, Albert Dorris wrote, "This kiddie is like a wonderful violin; fairly attractive to look at when not in use, but when called upon to deliver, there springs into existence that gloriously fascinating something which all players should have, but which seldom ever comes except with generous maturity. She is a finished actress, yet a mere child, and the more a person, or the Wampas, or the whole world, tries to fathom the professional cross-currents or solve the riddle of her future through analysis, the more will all be compelled to sit back and marvel at this adorable, dancing sunbeam which can degenerate into anything human or female if called upon to do so by a motion picture characterization."[14]

As 1924 dawned, it seemed Lucille had it all — youth, beauty, talent, and ambition. The other necessity for Lucille, Dorris prophetically noted,

Lucille Ricksen about the time she appeared in The Galloping Fish *(1924).*
COURTESY OF THE RICKSEN FAMILY

was the physical stamina to keep herself together and on track. "All she requires is her health, for she is about to embark on a career so full of opportunities that a stream shovel will be required to keep her pathway clear of attractive offers."[15]

For much of 1924, Lucille went from picture to picture at an alarming pace. After her appearance in *The Rendezvous*, Lucille was again teamed with Sydney Chaplin in *The Galloping Fish* (1924), a farce about a seal who outshines the actors in a vaudeville show. *Harrison's Reports* called the picture a "comedy of the Keystone type" and assured audiences they would "laugh until tears come down their cheeks."[16]

Lucille plays a carefree mountain girl who marries Jack Pickford after rescuing him from drowning in *The Hill Billy* (1924). According to early publicity for the film, the story was a reworking of one of Mary Pickford's earlier films. Pickford selected Lucille for the role and spent hours working on her costume and make-up.[17]

In *Behind the Curtain*, a murder mystery with a bit of clairvoyance, Lucille stood out among the cast, which included Johnny Harron and Winifred Bryson. *Variety* said, "Lucille Ricksen is her usual superlatively sweet self, quite enough to win her a raft of new admirers."[18] *Harrison's Reports* proclaimed that the film "holds the interest well at all times by virtue of fast action, colorful atmosphere, good direction and good acting."[19]

Harrison's Reports also thought Lucille's acting notable in *Vanity's Price*, a vehicle for Anna Q. Nilsson. "Lucille Ricksen, a newcomer and a really young one, gives a performance that again gives much promise for her future."[20]

Lucille's fans had seen a lot of her on the screen in 1924. She completed an astonishing 10 feature films in a little over seven months. By the time *Vanity's Price* was released in September, Lucille, unbeknownst to her public, had collapsed and was fighting for her life.

With her physical and emotional health wrecked, Lucille was confined to her bed and in seclusion at the family's apartment on North Gardner Avenue in Hollywood. The Ricksens kept the secret for months, hoping rest would make her better than ever. Toward the end of the year, word leaked out that Lucille's dream of stardom was being delayed while she recovered for exhaustion brought on by a nervous breakdown in June.

Calls from the studios continued coming with offers. Ingeborg held them off as long as she could. Then, she had to come clean. "Nervous breakdown — that's all," she assured the producers and directors who called for Lucille. "No, she can't think of working now — not for months at least." She must have rest — lots of it. After that — perhaps."[21]

Ingeborg gave Lucille's doctor, J.F. McKitrick, permission to speak about her daughter's illness and chances for recovery. He immediately blamed her condition on overwork. He said, "Miss Ricksen is a high-strung, enthusiastic girl, full of ambition and energy. She crowded too much work into too short a time, and overtaxed her capacities. Other youthful stars have done the same thing. The result is that she has had a

Lucille Ricksen's Hollywood home (Gardner Drive) in 2009.

complete physical and nervous collapse — so complete that she has not rallied from it as she should. It will be several months, at least, I should say, before there is any chance of her returning to her work."[22]

With no money coming in, Marshall, Lucille's brother, quit high school and found work to support his family. Ingeborg and a nurse stayed by Lucille's side. One morning before daylight in February 1925, Ingeborg, who slept on a sofa near Lucille's bed, thought she heard Lucille call her. She awoke and went to her side. As she was speaking to Lucille and tucking in the covers, Ingeborg collapsed over her fragile daughter's body.

Marshall, sleeping next door, heard Lucille's screams and rushed into the room. As they tried to lift their mother from the bed, she turned to Lucille and uttered her final words, "Take care of yourself, dear."[23] She was two days away from her 45th birthday.[24]

Lucille slipped further into the dark shadows of her illness. While services were being held for her mother at the W.A. Brown chapel in Hollywood, Lucille "buried her face in her pillow, sobbed once and sank into a coma."[25]

The film community rallied around Lucille and her brother. Paul Bern, known for his generosity to those in trouble, paid for around-the-clock nursing care. Lois Wilson sat by her bed for hours at a time. Lois remembered Lucille telling her how tired she was and that she had "supported her family with her acting since she was four years old." Their father, Soren Erickson, who lived in the area, reappeared to offer comfort to his children.

Lucille and her brother, Marshall, in a Melbourne Spurr photograph.
COURTESY OF THE RICKSEN FAMILY

Shortly after their mother died, Lucille and Marshall asked Conrad Nagel and Rupert Hughes to become their guardians. Nagel and Hughes filed a petition for guardianship.

With her illness worsening and the loss of her mother unbearable, Lucille knew the end was near. "I've known for the last two days that I'm going I'm going — fast, and somehow, I'm not afraid," she told her nurse.[26]

Early in the morning of Friday, March 13, Lucille could fight her illness and broken heart no longer. With Lois Wilson, Soren, and Marshall by her side, Lucille breathed her last breath and joined her mother in death.

"I have never known anyone so full of joy," Lois sobbed to the press. "Confined to her little bed, the sweet child would always welcome us with a smile. 'This is my sunshine room,' she would say, 'and I love the sunshine so much. Please won't you all be so happy. I know I will be well soon.'"[27]

Two days later, Episcopal services were conducted for Lucille by the Rev. Neal Dodd, rector of the Little Church around the Corner on Highland Avenue. Paul Bern, Lois Wilson, Rupert Hughes, and Dr. J.J. McKitrick (Lucille's physician) were among the mourners.

The ashes of Lucille and her mother were placed in a bronze urn and interned in the Columbarium of Hope at Forest Lawn (Glendale).

A few days after she died, it was revealed that Lucille, whose finances were thought to be dire, left a $50,000 life insurance policy. Her father, Soren, was the sole beneficiary. She intended the money be used for her brother's education.

Guardianship over Marshall ended up in court later in the month when Soren contested the earlier request that Rupert Hughes and Conrad Nagel be named guardians for the Ricksen children. Attorneys for Marshall's father, in opposing the Hughes-Nagel application for guardianship papers, cited a magazine article recently written by Hughes, "Why I Quit Going to Church," and argued that Nagel was too busy to act as guardian.

Lucille signed this portrait for her father. COURTESY OF THE RICKSEN FAMILY

The article proved, the attorneys said, that Hughes "is an atheist and not a fit person to control the education of a minor."[28]

In its decision, the court named Marshall's father administrator of Lucille's $50,000 estate, and named Hughes and Nagel as joint guardians of Marshall.

The 18-year-old, though devastated over the loss of his mother and

Lucille Ricksen's death made headlines around the country.
COURTESY OF THE RICKSEN FAMILY

sister, worked through his grief and enrolled in the University of California, determined to move forward with his life. He majored in law and became a successful attorney in the Oakland area.

In 1930, Marshall married Bertha (Boopie) Clymer. Their twin sons were born in 1932. They had intended to name their child, Rupert, after Rupert Hughes, in recognition of his unfailing support of Marshall. When twin boys were born, the parents tossed a coin to see which would be named for Hughes. The other son, they named John.

Rupert and John Ricksen remained close to Rupert Hughes until his death in 1956. The twins studied law together at the University of California at Berkeley and became successful attorneys.

The Ricksen twins grew up knowing very little about their Aunt Lucille, as their father never talked about the devastating losses of his mother and sister at such as early age in his life.[29] The sons and the Ricksen family are left not knowing what (or who) ruined and eventually took the life a 14-year-old child who was on the cusp of stardom in Hollywood.

They have the same questions that journalists asked over 80 years ago. The obituaries reporting Lucille's death attributed a nervous breakdown brought on by overwork. One article mentioned anemia and a lung condition. Her death certificate gives pulmonary tuberculosis as the cause of death.[30] Contemporary references have cited a botched abortion as the contributing factor.

Her death reignited the concerns many felt about parents who put their children to work in the movies. "The child, at best, is a frail little being. When should it ever be used for profit? Many parents sin unwittingly by pushing their children too hard because they want to show

Lucille Ricksen, the youngest leading lady in motion pictures. COURTESY OF THE RICKSEN FAMILY

how bright they are or that they have special talent. But when it comes to exploitation, the evil is more than sin. Maybe the death of Lucille Ricksen will turn our attention once more to the transgressions against child life that we still allow."[31]

A look at her filmography confirms that Lucille was a hard worker. Daisy Dean, in her "News Notes from Movieland," noted that some become movie stars by winning beauty contests; some register emotional talent when they are given an interview by a director or producer; some graduated from the Follies or the stage. "Then, there are those who grow up in the light of the kliegs and win their stardom by hard, grinding work. Among those latter is Lucille Ricksen."[32]

Writer Harry Carr dismissed the idea that overwork was the culprit. "It's all nonsense, of course, to say that her health was wrecked by her work. Girls at that age who act for the screen don't feel much of the emotion they portray. Not really deep down in their hearts. It is merely an instinctive imitation."[33]

At this late date, we'll probably never know definitively what dangerous curve derailed the career and life of Lucille Ricksen. All those who could answer the question or be held accountable are long gone. Was it a nervous breakdown? Was it really tuberculosis? Or, did this overworked teenager, billed "The Youngest Leading Lady in Pictures," suffer the ramifications of being forced both on *and* off the screen into becoming an adult, with all its pressures, temptations, and demands?

1. The 1910 U.S. Federal Census, which was taken April 15, 1910, shows only three in the Erickson household: Samuel (father), Ingeborg (mother), and Marshall (son). The information shows that Ingeborg and Samuel had been married for five years and that she was the mother of *only* one child (Marshall).

2. "Dolls and Curls," *Movie Weekly*, undated article.

3. The 1920 U.S. Federal Census shows the apartment building at 126 Washington Boulevard as the home to numerous film players and directors. Ingeborg seems to have reinvented herself for the census. In her entry, her name is Irene, she is widowed, and she is two years younger than her true age. She also lists Ohio as her place of birth and actress as her occupation. Marshall, who did some work in films, is listed as an actor.

4. "How I Grew Up In An Hour," Unknown newspaper clipping.

5. While Marshall may have been an extra in some of the *Edgar* comedies, *The Old Nest* was his only feature film appearance.

6. "Two, Thirteen, Thirty — - How Old Do You Think Lucille Can Be?," *The Superior Telegram*, September 1921.

7. "Lucille Promises to Visit Superior Friends When She Comes Again," *The Superior Telegram*, August 24, 1921.

8. Letter from Ralph W. Lieber to Lucille Ricksen, 24 September 1921.

9. Letter from Lucille Ricksen to her fans, c. 1922

10. The interview is cut and pasted in Lucille's scrapbook. The title of the article and writer are not known.

11. *The Billboard*, 8 December 1923. Also, there is no marriage certificate on file in Los Angeles County for Sydney Chaplin and Lucille Ricksen.

12. *Variety*, 10 January 1924.

13. The other 1924 Wampas Babies were: Clara Bow, Elinor Fair, Carmelita Geraghty, Gloria Grey, Ruth Hiatt, Julanne Johnston, Hazel Keener, Dorothy Mackaill, Blanche Mehaffey, Margaret Morris, Marian Nixon, and Alberta Vaughn.

14. "Little Lucille is Too Versatile to Classify," by Albert Dorris, undated.

15. *Ibid.*

16. *Harrison's Reports*, 25 April 1924.

17. "On the Camera Coast," undated or credited.

18. *Variety*, 30 July 1924.

19. *Harrison's Reports*, 5 July 1924

20. *Harrison's Reports*, 13 September 1924.

21. "Light of 'Baby Star' Dimmed," unknown newspaper clipping from Lucille's scrapbook.

22. Ibid.

23. Driscoll, Marjorie, "Death Takes Mother in Lucille Ricksen's Arms," *Los Angeles Times*, 22 February 1925.

24. Ingeborg Ricksen's death certificate indicates pulmonary hemorrhage and pulmonary tuberculosis (contributing) as the cause of death. County of Los Angeles, Registrar/Recorder/County Clerk, Death Certificate, no. 1993, 24 February 1925.

25. "Lucille Near Death of Grief," newspaper clipping from Lucille Ricksen's scrapbook.

26. "Lois Wilson at Bedside as Tragic Career of Lucille Ricksen Ends," newspaper clipping from Lucille Ricksen's scrapbook.

27 " Wampas Baby Star Dies," *Los Angeles Times*, 14 March 1925.

28. "Rupert Hughes Named Guardian for Youth," *New York Times*, 18 April 1925.

29. Marshall Ricksen died in 1975.

30. County of Los Angeles, Registrar/Recorder/County Clerk, Death Certificate, no. 2703, March 1925.

31. "A Child Star," *The Port Arthur News*, 21 March 1925.

32. "News Notes From Movieland," Clipping from Lucille's scrapbook.

33. "The Lancer," by Harry Carr. Clipping from Lucille's scrapbook.

FILMOGRAPHY

1915

Unknown Essanay film that starred Henry B. Walthall.

The Millionaire Baby *(Selig Polyscope)* D: *Lawrence Marston*. Grace Darmond, Harry Mestayer Mrs. A. C. Marston, John Charles, Frederick Hand, Charlotte Stevens, Charles Siddon, Robert Sherwood, Baby Erickson *(Lucille Ricksen)*.

1920

Edgar and the Teacher's Pet *(short) (Goldwyn)* D: *E. Mason Hopper*. Edward Peil Jr. *(Johnny Jones)*, Cordelia Callahan, Nick Cogley, John Cossar, Marie Dunn, Kenneth Earl, Lucretia Harris, Arthur H. Little, Virginia Madison, Ellison Manners, Buddy Messinger, Frederick Moore, Lucille Ricksen.

Edgar's Hamlet *(short) (Goldwyn)* D: *E. Mason Hopper*. Edward Peil Jr. *(Johnny Jones)*, Cordelia Callahan, Nick Cogley, John Cossar, Marie Dunn, Kenneth Earl, Lucretia Harris, Arthur H. Little, Virginia Madison, Ellison Manners, Buddy Messinger, Frederick Moore, Lucille Ricksen.

Edgar's Jonah Day *(short) (Goldwyn)*. Edward Peil Jr. *(Johnny Jones)*, Cordelia Callahan, Nick Cogley, John Cossar, Marie Dunn, Kenneth Earl, Lucretia Harris, Virginia Madison, Buddy Messinger, Frederick Moore, Lucille Ricksen.

Edgar Takes the Cake *(short) (Goldwyn)* Edward Peil Jr. *(Johnny Jones)*, Cordelia Callahan, Nick Cogley, John Cossar, Marie Dunn, Kenneth Earl, Lucretia Harris, Virginia Madison, Buddy Messinger, Frederick Moore, Lucille Ricksen.

Edgar's Sunday Courtship (short) (Goldwyn) Edward Peil Jr. *(Johnny Jones)*, Cordelia Callahan, Nick Cogley, John Cossar, Marie Dunn, Kenneth Earl, Lucretia Harris, Virginia Madison, Buddy Messinger, Frederick Moore, Lucille Ricksen.

Edgar Camps Out (short) (Goldwyn) D: *E. Mason Hopper.* Edward Peil Jr. *(Johnny Jones)*, Cordelia Callahan, Nick Cogley, John Cossar, Marie Dunn, Kenneth Earl, Lucretia Harris, Virginia Madison, Ellison Manners, Arthur H. Little, Buddy Messinger, Frederick Moore, Lucille Ricksen.

Edgar's Little Saw (short) (Goldwyn) D: *E. Mason Hopper.* Edward Peil Jr. *(Johnny Jones)*, Cordelia Callahan, Nick Cogley, John Cossar, Marie Dunn, Kenneth Earl, Lucretia Harris, Virginia Madison, Ellison Manners, Arthur H. Little, Buddy Messinger, Frederick Moore, Lucille Ricksen.

Edgar, the Explorer (short) (Goldwyn) D: *Mason N. Litson.* Edward Peil Jr. *(Johnny Jones)*, Cordelia Callahan, John Cossar, Marie Dunn, Kenneth Earl, Lucretia Harris, Virginia Madison, Ellison Manners, Arthur H. Little, Buddy Messinger, Frederick Moore, Lucille Ricksen.

1921

Edgar's Country Cousin (short) (Goldwyn) D: *Mason N. Litson.* Edward Peil Jr. *(Johnny Jones)*, Cordelia Callahan, John Cossar, Marie Dunn, Kenneth Earl, Lucretia Harris, Virginia Madison, Buddy Messinger, Frederick Moore, Lucille Ricksen.

Edgar's Feast Day (short) (Goldwyn) D: *Mason N. Litson.* Edward Peil Jr. *(Johnny Jones)*, Cordelia Callahan, John Cossar, Marie Dunn, Kenneth Earl, Lucretia Harris, Virginia Madison, Buddy Messinger, Frederick Moore, Lucille Ricksen.

Edgar, the Detective (short) (Goldwyn) D: *Paul Bern.* Edward Peil Jr. *(Johnny Jones)*, Cordelia Callahan, Nick Cogley, John Cossar, Marie Dunn, Kenneth Earl, Lucretia Harris, Virginia Madison, Buddy Messinger, Frederick Moore, Lucille Ricksen.

The Old Nest (Goldwyn) D: *Reginald Barker.* Dwight Crittenden, Mary Alden, Nick Cogley, Fanny Stockbridge, Laura La Varnie, Johnny Jones, Richard Tucker, Marshall Ricksen, Buddy Messinger, Cullen Landis, Lucille Ricksen, Louise Lovely, Robert De Vilbiss, J. Parks Jones, Marie Moorehouse, Billie Cotton, Helene Chadwick, Theodore von Eltz, Molly Malone, Maurice B. Flynn, Roland Rushton.

1922

The Married Flapper (Universal) D: *Stuart Paton*. Marie Prevost, Kenneth Harlan, Philo McCullough, Frank Kingsley, Lucille Ricksen, Kathleen O'Connor, Hazel Keener, Tom McGuire, Burton Wilson, William Quinn, Lydia Titus, Martha Mattox.

Remembrance (Goldwyn) D: *Rupert Hughes*. Claude Gillingwater, Kate Lester, Patsy Ruth Miller, Cullen Landis, Max Davidson, Richard Tucker, Dana Todd, Nell Craig, Esther Ralston, Helen Hayward, Lucille Ricksen, Arthur Trimble, William A. Carroll, Guinn 'Big Boy' Williams.

The Girl Who Ran Wild (Universal) D: *Rupert Julian*. Gladys Walton, Marc Robbins, Vernon Steele, Joseph Dowling, William Burress, Al Hart, Nelson McDowell, Lloyd Whitlock, Lucille Ricksen.

Forsaking All Others (Universal) D: *Emile Chautard*. Colleen Moore, Cullen Landis, Irene Wallace, Sam De Grasse, June Elvidge, David Torrence, Melbourne MacDowell, Elinor Hancock, Lucille Ricksen.

Stranger's Banquet (Goldwyn) D: *Marshall Neilan*. Hobart Bosworth, Claire Windsor, Rockliffe Fellowes, Ford Sterling, Eleanor Boardman, Thomas Holding, Eugenie Besserer, Nigel Barrie, Stuart Holmes, Claude Gillingwater, Margaret Loomis, Tom Guise, Lillian Langdon, William Humphrey, Edward McWade, Lorimer Johnson, James Marcus, Edward W. Borman, Jack Curtis, Brinsley Shaw, Arthur Hoyt, Aileen Pringle, Virginia Ruggles, Cyril Chadwick, Philo McCullough, Jean Hersholt, Lucille Ricksen, Dagmar Godowsky, Hayford Hobbs, Violet Joy.

1923

The Social Buccaneer (Universal) D: *Roy F. Hill*. Jack Mulhall, Margaret Livingston, William Welsh, Harry De Vere, Wade Boteler, Percy Challenger, Lucille Ricksen, Robert Anderson, Buck Connors, Tom London, Sidney Bracey, Tote Du Crow, Fontaine La Rue, William T. Horne, Scott Pembroke.

One of Three (short) (Universal) D: *Duke Worne*. Roy Stewart, Hayden Stevenson, Jack Perrin, Lucille Ricksen, Carol Holloway, Fontaine La Rue.

Under Secret Orders (short) (Universal) D: *Duke Worne.* Roy Stewart, Esther Ralston, Jack Perrin, William Welsh, Hayden Stevenson, Fontaine La Rue, Lucille Ricksen.

Trimmed in Scarlet (Universal) D: Jack Conway. Kathlyn Williams, Roy Stewart, Lucille Rickson, Robert Agnew, David Torrence, Phillips Smalley, Eve Southern, Bert Sprotte, Grace Carlyle, Gerrard Grassby, Raymond Hatton, Philo McCullough.

The Secret Code (short) (Universal) D: *Duke Worne.* Roy Stewart, Hayden Stevenson, Jack Perrin, Ethel Ritchie, Lucille Ricksen, Fontaine La Rue.

The Radio Active Bomb (short) (Universal) D: *Duke Worne.* Roy Stewart, Hayden Stevenson, Jack Perrin, Lucille Ricksen, Fontaine La Rue, Sylvia Breamer, Burton Law.

The Showdown (short) (Universal) D: *Duke Worne.* Roy Stewart, Hayden Stevenson, Jack Perrin, Lucille Ricksen, Fontaine La Rue.

Human Wreckage (FBO) D: *John Griffith Wray.* Mrs. Wallace Reid, James Kirkwood, Bessie Love, George Hackathorne, Claire McDowell, Robert McKim, Harry Northrup, Victory Bateman, Eric Mayne, Otto Hoffman, Philip Sleeman, George Clark, Lucille Ricksen.

The Rendezvous (Goldwyn) D: *Marshall Neilan.* Conrad Nagel, Lucille Ricksen, Richard Travers, Kathleen Key, Emmett Corrigan, Elmo Lincoln, Sydney Chaplin, Kate Lester, Cecil Holland, Lucien Littlefield, Max Davidson, Eugenie Besserer, R. O. Pennell.

The Judgment of the Storm (FBO) D: *Del Andrews.* Lloyd Hughes, Lucille Ricksen, George Hackathorne, Myrtle Stedman, Claire McDowell, Philo McCullough, Bruce Gordon, Frankie Darro, Fay McKenzie.

Galloping Fish (Associated First National Pictures) D: *Del Andrews.* Louise Fazenda, Sydney Chaplin, Ford Sterling, Chester Conklin, Lucille Ricksen, John Steppling, "Freddie".

The Hill Billy (Allied Producers and Distributors) D: George Hill. Jack Pickford, Lucille Ricksen, Frank Leigh, Ralph Yearsley, Jane Keckley, Snitz Edwards, Malcolm Waite, Maine Geary, Margaret Caldwell Shotwell, Alphie James, Madame de Bodamere.

Those Who Dance (Associated First National Pictures) D: *Lambert Hillyer.* Blanche Sweet, Bessie Love, Warner Baxter, Robert Agnew, John Sainpolis, Lucille Ricksen, Matthew Betz, Lydia Knott, Charles Delaney, W. S. McDonough, Jack Perrin, Frank Campeau.

Young Ideas (Universal) D: *Robert F. Hill.* Laura La Plante, T. Roy Barnes, Lucille Ricksen, James O. Barrows, Lydia Yeamans Titus, Jennie Lee, Rolfe Sedan, Buddy Messinger, Brownie.

Behind the Curtain (Universal) D: *Chester M. Franklin.* Lucille Ricksen, Johnny Harron, Winifred Bryson, Charles Clary, Eric Mayne, George Cooper, Clarence Geldert, Pat Harmon.

Vanity's Price (FBO) D: *R. William Neill.* Anna Q. Nilsson, Stuart Holmes, Wyndham Standing, Arthur Rankin, Lucille Rickson, Robert Bolder, Cissy FitzGerald, Dot Farley, Charles Newton.

1924

The Painted Lady (Fox) D: *Chester Bennett.* George O'Brien, Dorothy Mackaill, Harry T. Morey, Lucille Hutton, Lucille Ricksen, Margaret McWade, John Miljan, Frank Elliott, Lucien Littlefield.

Idle Tongues (First National) D: *Lambert Hillyer.* Percy Marmont, Doris Kenyon, Claude Gillingwater, Lucille Ricksen, David Torrence, Malcolm McGregor, Vivia Ogden, Marguerite Clayton, Ruby Lafayette, Dan Mason, Mark Hamilton.

1925

The Denial (Metro Goldwyn Pictures) D: *Hobart Henley.* Claire Windsor, Bert Roach, William Haines, Lucille Rickson, Robert Agnew, Emily Fitzroy, William Eugene, Estelle Clark, Vivia Ogden.

EVE SOUTHERN

We know more about Eve Southern's past lives than we do about her life in the 20th century and her Hollywood film career. That's because she gave so few interviews in Hollywood, and her most extensive talk with a reporter was about her past life as Mary Queen of Scots.[1] Puzzling, yes, but this mysterious figure from the silent film era *was* once known as "Hollywood's mystic."

Okay, so what if she was once Mary Queen of Scots? History tells us about this figure from our past. What about Eve Southern, the actress from the silent film days? Who was she? More importantly, what happened to her? No one ever really knew, except her family and close friends.

First, the actress was a woman of unusual beauty. She was almost supernatural in appearance. One writer described her as creepy in appearance. Arguably, she had the most enormous eyes, made bigger by long, dark eyelashes, than any actress of her day. They were, without a doubt, her greatest asset.

Second, her career was nothing special, a series of false starts and dead ends, followed by disappointment. She'd been in films for 10 years, having been discovered by director D.W. Griffith and brought to Hollywood in the mid-1910s, before she got her chance to shine with Douglas Fairbanks in *The Gaucho* (1928).

Eve had three strikes during those 10 years, but was far from being out. First, she thought her breakthrough would be as a Griffith actress in the same vein as Mae Marsh or Lillian Gish. Not so! He temporarily retired and left his discovery adrift. In the early 1920s, director Rupert Hughes was to use her in a prominent role. He left Goldwyn Studios, where she was working, before he fulfilled his promise. Then, Charlie Chaplin gave Eve a big role in *A Woman of the Sea*, a film he never finished or released.

Between these series of disappointments, many of Eve's parts were spliced and sliced. In 1927, she was described in the film colony as "the face on the cutting room floor." "The worst part of it is that the saying was true," Eve said at the time. "I never seemed to have any difficulty getting parts I wanted, but almost invariably they ended up on the cutting-room floor instead of on the screen."[2]

When Douglas Fairbanks hired Eve for a prominent role in *The Gaucho*, her luck turned around. Under a Tiffany-Stahl contract, Eve played leading roles opposite Walter Pidgeon and Malcolm McGregor. The road opened up for her and she made a successful transition to talkies. Then, dangerous curves appear out of nowhere. First, a car accident kept her out of work for two months. Then, a toboggan mishap put an end to her career and almost her life. She disappeared from the screen.

Piecing together Eve Southern's sojourn through Hollywood was a daunting task. Had any film personality dropped so completely and permanently out of sight that no one knew where they were or what became of them? Few had left a trail this cold. Film books and internet references, when they mentioned her, provided her date of birth and a few facts. Her date of death was unknown, a question mark.

I traced Eve during most of 2008 using census records, city directories, and newspaper clippings. Using old-fashioned detective work, I pieced her story together and went after living relatives, who verified my theory that they were Eve Southern's kin. By the way, her relatives were amused, but doubtful, that they were also related, through reincarnation, to Mary Queen of Scots.

Nevertheless, in her 1929 interview, Eve explained how her own life in the 20th century was being influenced by having once been the Scottish queen.

"The life that I remember best," she told Dorothy Donnell, "was when I was Mary (Queen of Scots), a queen who was cruel to her people. I am sure that I am paying in this life for the cruelty and pride of that queen. My struggle to succeed in Hollywood has been payment in kind."[3]

She was born Elva Lucille McDowell on August 23, 1900, in Ranger, Texas. When she was still very young, she and her parents, William Watson and Sydney Lucille, relocated to Fort Worth, Texas. Her brother, Wallace Watson, was born in 1908.

It was in Fort Worth that 16-year-old Elva was discovered by director D.W. Griffith and offered a chance in the movies. "Her parents told Elva she could go on one condition: that they go with her," said William McDowell, Elva's nephew, son of her brother, Wallace. "At 16, she was too young to sign a contract herself, and knowing my grandfather, Elva's dad,

I'm sure he wouldn't have picked up the family and moved to California without a contract in hand."[4]

The McDowells left Texas for California in 1916 and settled in a large rental house on 23rd Street, not far from where Griffith was erecting his massive sets for *Intolerance* (1916). Griffith's first matter of business was to change her age and name. "They wouldn't use Elva, so they gave her a

An early portrait of Eve Southern. COURTESY OF WILLIAM MCDOWELL

short name, Eve, and he chose Southern because she was from the South,"
McDowell said. Elva McDowell became Eve Southern.[5] Griffith also
added two years to her age, making her 18.[6]

The pioneer director used Eve twice in his films. One of her roles was
in the famous orgy scene in *Intolerance* (1916) with Mildred Harris, Pauline Starke, Carmel Myers, Jewel Carmen, Natalie Talmadge, and Carol
Dempster. He predicted a great future for his young discovery.

Intolerance, however, was a box-office failure. In March 1917, Griffith
sailed for Europe to publicize the film and, according to his passport
application, "exploit motion picture photoplays."[7]

Eve felt she had been left by the side of the road. Later publicity suggested that Eve and her family returned to Texas so she could "cultivate"
her voice.[8] Her nephew, however, said the McDowells bought the "mansion" they were living in on 23rd Street from their landlord and stayed
close to the studios so that Eve could continue working.

"Elva's mother couldn't drive, neither could Elva at that time, so her dad
drove her to the studio and acted as her chauffeur and bodyguard," Eve's
nephew said. "After all, she was a beautiful 16-year-old running around in
Hollywood and, according to my dad (her brother), she was pretty wild."[9]

At Triangle in 1917, Eve appeared in one-reel shorts and a feature film,
A Matrimonial Accident. Also, that year, a newspaper clipping announced
that Eve, "southern in name, northern in inclinations, westerner by
work — Eve Southern, coming back to the subject, has been cast for
a part in Gladys Brockwell's new drama, *Conscience*, and came east to
make the film."

In the first part of Eve's career, from 1918 to the mid-1920s, her roles
were small and undistinguished. At a variety of studios, she played chorus
girls, vamps, and the "other woman" in such minor melodramas as *Broadway Love* (1918), a Dorothy Phillips vehicle; *After the Show* (1921) with
Jack Holt and Lila Lee; *Nice People* (1922) with Wallace Reid and Bebe
Daniels; and *The Rage of Paris* (1921) and *The Golden Gallows* (1922), two
Universal films starring Miss Dupont.

It was in *The Golden Gallows* that Eve received her first positive press
reviews. "In support of Miss Dupont is a girl whose work has earned the
admiration of a number of directors. Eve Southern is her name and she
handles the role of the heroine's chum who later becomes her maid in
a country home. Miss Southern took a big step forward by her work in
The Golden Gallows."

As the "other woman" in *The Girl in his Room* (1922), Eve was singled
out for her portrayal of Elinor, who informs the heroine (Alice Calhoun)

that she is engaged to the hero (Warner Baxter). "Eve Southern is a decided contrast to Miss Calhoun in every respect, noted *The Atlanta Constitution*. "She appears in but a few scenes but does her work remarkably well and those scenes stand out in bold relief."[10]

Eve's second opportunity to showcase herself came when she was working at Goldwyn Studios. She played the part of Velma Slade in

Conrad Nagel and Eve Southern in Nice People *(1922)*. COURTESY OF WILLIAM MCDOWELL

Souls for Sale (1923), a comedy-melodrama based on the novel by Rupert Hughes. The film centers on a young hopeful's (Eleanor Boardman) rise to fame in Hollywood. Hughes, who also directed the film, hoped to give to movie-going audiences another side of Hollywood than the queasiness left over by a string of scandals in the movie industry.

Goldwyn signed Eve for a major part in an upcoming film that Hughes was to direct. What happened next is uncertain. One story is that the deal was off for Eve when Hughes left M-G-M in 1925. Another source suggests that Eve was released from the contract after the producer realized she wasn't suited for the part. However it played out, Eve was devastated.

Before she showed him the door, Eve shredded the contract in front of the studio representative who'd been sent to break the news.

"I knew that mother had a package of rat poison in the pantry," Eve remembered. "When he (the studio messenger) was gone, I decided I would go back there and take some."

When the man was gone, Eve walked through the dining room to get to the pantry.

"As I entered the dining room, my eye was caught by a movement," Eve said. "A hand, a beautiful hand, was placing a small bunch of forget-me-nots on the table. There was no arm to the hand. As I stood there looking at it, the hand vanished. The flowers remained for a time and then vanished in their turn." Eve, believing the vision was sent to save her life, gave up her suicide intention.

Eve was named the Golden Rule Girl by a committee for Near East Relief in 1924. The group conducted a nationwide search for "an American girl" whose beauty symbolized the spirit of their campaign. Eve's photograph appeared in papers around the country in connection with International Golden Rule Day (December 7).

In June 1925, Eve married Robert E. Shepherd. Newspaper clippings referred to Shepherd as an architect. Eve's nephew said he was a car salesman.

"When they were dating," McDowell explained, "Shepherd would arrive in a different car every time, so she thought he was rich. It turned out that he sold cars for a living." The marriage was rocky from the start.

When director Josef von Sternberg was casting a supporting role in *The Sea Gull*, Eve, still a newlywed, was eager to meet him. Charlie Chaplin, who produced and sponsored the film, hoped it would serve as a comeback for his former leading lady, Edna Purviance. Eve hoped it would pave her way to fame.

Von Sternberg was looking for a type — she must be tall, willowy, ethereal, brooding, beautiful — and different! He found what he was looking for in Eve Southern. She was hired on the spot.

Filming took place in 1926 over a three-month period in the Los Angeles area. Outdoor scenes were filmed on location in the Monterey and Carmel coastal areas of California.

Eve figured prominently in the film and with Chaplin's involvement and von Sternberg's expert direction, she believed her long struggle in the film industry would pay off.

Disappointment struck again, however, after von Sternberg screened the film, which had been re-titled *A Woman of the Sea*. The director addressed the subject of the ill-fated picture in his autobiography, *Fun in a Chinese Laundry*.

After the screening, "the film was promptly returned to Mr. Chaplin's vaults and no one has ever seen it again. We spent many idle hours with each other, before, during, and after the making of this film, but not once was this work of mine discussed, nor have I ever broached the subject of

Edwin Carewe and Eve Southern on the set of Resurrection *(1927).*
COURTESY OF WILLIAM MCDOWELL

its fate to him."[11] Eve's hopes were dashed again.

In 1927, director Edwin Carewe cast Eve as Princess Sonia in *Resurrection* (1927), based on Leo Tolstoy's novel of the same name. Carewe was so impressed with Eve's performance that he also signed her to a personal contract. Eve believed her role, the sweetheart of Dimitri, played by Rod La Rocque, would finally bring her the success she had long craved.

When filming was complete, however, the director realized the 200,000 feet of film would have to be trimmed to no more than 9,000 feet. Consequently, much of Eve's role, if not all, was cut and ended up on the infamous cutting room floor. Her role was the great unseen.

Eve was crushed. Although she had suffered career setbacks over the years, Eve said the elimination of her part in *Resurrection* was her greatest disappointment. "I could not help but believe that Fate never meant for me to succeed in pictures. It seemed so hopeless. So, I prayed. It was the only thing I could do. I prayed all night, prayed for a chance, prayed that all my hard work, all my experience, all my disappointments of 10 years might not all go for nothing."[12]

Edwin Carewe had the same hopes for Eve. One afternoon during lunch, Douglas Fairbanks told Carewe that he had two important feminine roles in his upcoming film, *The Gaucho* (1928). He had already cast Lupe Velez as an untamed mountain native in one of the roles and was searching for an actress of opposite character and looks. Carewe took Fairbanks by the arm and led him into the projection room, where he screened Eve's test for *Resurrection*.

Southern as she appeared in The Gaucho *(1928).*

Fairbanks, impressed with the 26-year-old actress, directed her in a screen test.[13] He realized he had found his other feminine lead, the deeply religious and sympathetic "miracle girl." Eve, after 10 years of struggle, had arrived.

Winning the role of the Miracle Girl gave Eve the biggest publicity treatment of her career. Her climb to fame was touted as a 10-year struggle to make a name for herself on the screen. There were headlines such as "Eve Wins out After Ten Years of Ill Luck," "Two Gals Who Got the Breaks: Eve Southern Waited 10 Years," and "Turning Point".

In *The Gaucho*, Eve survives a fall from a cliff in the Argentine Alps and is rewarded with healing powers. A shrine and town grow up around site of the miraculous event. Pilgrims traveling to the site over the years have made the town wealthy. Its riches catch the eye of the greedy Ruiz (Gustav von Seyffertitz), who intends to rob the city of its riches. The

Gaucho, a tanned, chain-smoking Fairbanks, intercedes and saves the city from tyranny and terrorism.

Lupe Velez plays the hot blooded and fiery mountain girl whom the Gaucho picks up along the way. She is enraged with jealousy when the Gaucho begins paying attention to the Miracle Girl, and at one point, attacks her with a knife when she finds her alone with him.

Eve Southern and Lupe Velez in The Gaucho *(1928).* COURTESY OF WILLIAM MCDOWELL

The Gaucho, made when Fairbanks was at the crest of his fame, was met with mixed reviews. *Variety* gave high accolades to Lupe Velez, who was making her second film appearance. "When it comes to acting she does not have to step aside for anyone." The reviewer also touted Eve as a "standout" as the Miracle Girl.[14]

A review in the *Sheboygan Press* noted that "Eve Southern, as the girl of the shrine, is perhaps the most beautiful actress that could have been chosen for this ethereal part, and is splendidly cast, giving credence to parts in the picture that might otherwise be lacking."[15] Another reviewer wrote, the character of the Miracle Girl is "symbolic of that which is good. Miss Southern has one great asset — her eyes. They are big and soft —

Belle Bennett, Eve Southern, and Anita Stewart in Wild Geese *(1927).*

and make her look like a woman who has never known anything but good."

Fairbanks was also pleased with Eve's work in *The Gaucho*. A friendship developed between the two. "My dad (Eve's brother) always told me it was more than a friendship. It became romantic, and Fairbanks promised to use her again in his pictures."[16]

On the merits of her appearance in *The Gaucho*, Eve was cast by Tiffany-Stahl as a farm girl in *Wild Geese* (1927), a family drama that revolves around an ever-suffering mother (Belle Bennett) and her domineering husband (Russell Simpson). Amelia (Bennett) plows through life assuring that her children (Eve plays a daughter) will survive the brutality of their father. The clan is liberated in the final reel when the father sinks in quicksand to his long-awaited death.

Reviewers were generally positive in their comments about *Wild Geese* and its cast, one exception being *Variety*, which called attention to Eve's "blonde tresses" as "poor wig outfitting."[17] With *Wild Geese*, *Photoplay* noted, "Eve Southern establishes herself as one of the most striking, unusual types on the screen."[18]

After *Wild Geese*, Tiffany-Stahl signed Eve to a contract. In early 1928, she appeared in *Clothes Make the Woman* as the long lost Anastasia, last of the Romanoffs. By the time the picture was released in May, Eve's

Malcolm McGregor and Eve Southern in Stormy Waters *(1928).*

marriage had fallen apart. She sued Shepherd for divorce.

On the stand, Eve told the judge that Shepherd had "choked her nearly into insensibility" until she "established a non-stop crying record of 18 hours." Her mother, corroborating Eve's testimony, told of finding her daughter almost unconscious after an episode with Shepherd.[19] Eve moved in with her parents and vowed she was finished with marriage. She concentrated on her work at Tiffany-Stahl.

In *Stormy Waters*, Lola (Eve) is a seductress who turns her lustful eyes on every man in the picture. First, she weaves her web around David (Malcolm McGregor), a ship crewman, in a bar in Buenos Aires. Even though he has a fiancée in New York, she returns with him to the States, against the better judgment of his brother, Angus, the captain of the ship. When she plans to runaway with a boxing champ, Angus sails her back to Argentina, puts her overboard into a lifeboat, and points her toward the shore and back to the dive she came from.

Variety, while not wild about *Stormy Waters*, raved over the wild Lola. "Miss Southern gets enough sensuousness into the role to make it stand up in a loose-hipped characterization under the world's longest eyelashes, which demonstrates how the femmes turn on the s.a. (sex appeal) for better

Eve Southern turns on the sex appeal for Malcolm McCregor in Stormy Waters. COURTESY OF WILLIAM MCDOWELL

or worse. And, this being a drama, she's out for no good." The film, the review continued, "Figures to kill an hour passably, but can't claim it will be remembered, unless for the round-eyed Miss Southern gone deck-walker."[20]

Eve was next cast in *Naughty Duchess* (1928) as a shady lady who tries to escape the law by boarding a train and posing as the wife of a duke (H.B. Warner). *Picture Play* wrote that Eve, "aloof, tall, dark, and dreamy is seen at excellent advantage" as the impostor.[21]

Later in the year, Eve was loaned to First National, where she appeared as a sleepwalker in *The Haunted House* (1928), a parody of *The Cat and the Canary* and *The Bat*. Two songs, performed by Eve, were inserted after the picture was completed. *Variety* noted that the synchronization was handled poorly, with Eve and the song out of kilter. "Either Eve Southern, as the girl, just moved her lips or sang another number than the one recorded."[22]

Back at Tiffany-Stahl, Eve was reteamed with Malcolm McGregor in *Whispering Winds* and with Walter Pidgeon in *The Voice Within*. Eve made her talkie debut in *Whispering Winds* as an ambitious songstress who leaves her village along coastal Maine and her love (McGregor) to search for fame in New York.

Just before the release of *The Voice Within*, Eve was driving through an intersection in Los Angeles when her Rolls Royce was struck by another car, driven by Carl Kearnzinger. He was arrested and charged with reckless driving. Eve's car overturned and she suffered a fractured right hip and broken back. Surgeons who operated on the actress told the press that Eve would be rehabilitating for several months.[23] While she was lying flat on her back in the hospital, fans sent their good wishes. Five fans sent her Bibles.[24]

As it turns out, her nephew said, Eve's 1918 Rolls Royce was a total loss. She later sold the wreck to the studio to use as a prop in a war movie.

The accident not only left her car a wreck and her body broken, it also knocked the wind from her career. She was cast as one of six gold-digging dames, or "lilies", in *Lilies of the Field*, a Corinne Griffith picture for First National.[25] She worked in small roles with Gary Cooper in *Morocco* (1930) and *Fighting Caravans* (1931). At Monogram, she was Sally Blane's sister in *Law of the Sea* (1931).

In March 1932, Eve, ever the adventuress, was riding in a toboggan in the San Bernardino Mountains when the sled went out of control and threw her to the ground. Her back was broken a second time. By the time they got her to the hospital, she was in serious condition. Several days later, surgeons performed a delicate spinal operation and wrapped her in a plaster cast.[26]

"That accident did her in," her nephew said. "It seems to me that after breaking her back in that 1929 accident, she wouldn't have been riding in a toboggan, but that was Elva for you. She was quite a character."[27]

Eve made few films after her second accident. Following her long recovery, she appeared in a small role as a psychic in *The Ghost Walks* (1934), and director Josef von Sternberg, with whom she'd worked in *The Sea Gull*, used her in *The King Steps Out* (1936).

After she could no longer work as an actress, Eve disappeared behind the camera and became a retoucher in the photography department of a movie studio. She dropped completely out of sight from her fans.

Eve continued to live with her father and mother in the house they bought when they first settled in California. Her brother, Wallace, married and had two children, William and Evelyn. The family remained close.

By the time William (Eve's nephew) was old enough to remember Eve, she had mostly recovered from her injuries in the toboggan accident. "Elva was in my dad's garage[28] one day and I asked her why she didn't

Eve Southern and Gary Cooper in Morocco *(1930).*

go back into pictures. She was still a very beautiful woman. She said she couldn't stand for too long and the work was too strenuous. She still had nagging back pain."

When the family would go waterskiing, Eve would often accompany the family, but never hooked herself up to skies. "Elva was very protective of her skin," her nephew said. "She stayed out of the water and the sun.

Eve Southern's grave marker in Valhalla Cemetery.

She was lots of fun to be around, very outgoing. She wasn't one to keep things to herself. You knew exactly what she was thinking."[29]

While Eve had many female friends, after her failed marriage in 1928, she was never much interested in the opposite sex. Her time was filed with her work at the studio and with writing music and playing the piano.

After Eve's father died, she was often scraped for cash. Her brother kept an eye on her and made sure she had everything she needed. The siblings had been close over the years, much closer than Eve had been to her father.

"Elva and her dad never really got along," her nephew explained, "partially because she was a lavish spender and her dad was very frugal, the opposite of Elva. She made a lot of money in her day, but I'm guessing she squandered it early in her life."

In her fifties, Eve, like her mother, developed Parkinson's disease. In her later years, she lived on Earl Street in the Silver Lake district of Los Angeles. At age 70 and in failing health, she left her home and moved to a nursing home in Santa Monica. She died there on November 29, 1972, from arteriosclerosis and the ravages of Parkinson's.[30] She was buried beside her mother in Valhalla Cemetery in Burbank, not far from where Mae Murray, another hard-luck girl of the silent screen, rests.

One hot May afternoon in 2009, I ventured out to Valhalla to pay my respects to this hard-luck girl. A receptionist looked through her directory, highlighted the plot on a map, and sent me on my way. Under the roar of jets landing and taking off from Burbank Airport, I found Eve Southern's final resting place, a bronze marker sitting in the dry, parched earth. The deafening roar of those jet engines harkened back to something Eve's nephew told me as he summed up his aunt's life.

"Aunt Elva was a pretty wild girl," he said. "After all, she was 20 in 1920. Those were the Roaring Twenties and she was roaring with the best of them."

1   Donnell, Dorothy, "Before They Were Born, Who Were They?" *Motion Picture*, June 1929.

2   Thomas, Dan, "Eve Wins Out After Ten Years of Ill Luck," *Ogden Standard Examiner*, 1927.

3   Donnell, Dorothy, "Before They Were Born, Who Were They?" *Motion Picture*, June 1929.

4   William McDowell to Michael G. Ankerich, October 2008.

5   Sothern, a variation of Southern, has also been as Eve's last name.

6   Eve later reclaimed those years (and more) when her break came 10 years later. She gave 1903 as her year of birth.

7   Department of State passport, dated March 3, 1917.

8   "Two Girls Who Got the Breaks," *Photoplay*, September 1927.

9   William McDowell to Michael G. Ankerich, October 2008.

10 *The Atlanta Constitution*, June 6, 1924.

11 Von Sternberg, Josef. *Fun in a Chinese Laundry*, 1965.

12 "Two Girls Who Got the Breaks," *Photoplay*, September 1927.

13 Douglas Fairbanks Jr., currently out of work, was hired to film Eve's screen test.

14 *Variety*, 9 November 1927.

15 *The Sheboygan Press*, 29 May 1928.

16 William McDowell to Michael G. Ankerich, October 2008.

17 *Variety*, 7 December 1927.

18 *Photoplay*, January 1928.

19 "Eve Southern, Film Actress, Gets Divorce," *Oakland Tribune*, 4 May 1928.

20 *Variety*, 4 July 1928.

21 *Picture Play*, July 1929.

22 *Variety*, 19 December 1928.

23 "Eve Southern Seriously Hurt in Auto Crash," *Fresno Bee*, 5 April 1929.

24 *Hamilton Evening Journal*, 15 June 1929.

25 The "lilies," who teach Corinne Griffith how to become a showgirl, were selected from various studios: Eve from Tiffany-Stahl; Jean Bary from Fox; Rita Le Roy from R-K-O; Betty Boyd from Warner Brothers; and Virginia Bruce from Paramount.

26 "Actress has her Spine Corrected," *Oakland Tribune*, 18 March 1932.

27 William McDowell to Michael G. Ankerich, October 2008.

28 Wallace McDowell owned a car repair shop.

29 William McDowell to Michael G. Ankerich, October 2008.

30 County of Los Angeles, Registrar/Recorder/County Clerk, Death Certificate, no.7097-048262, 30 November 1972.

FILMOGRAPHY

1916

Intolerance (D. W. Griffith; Wark Producing Corp.) D: *D.W. Griffith* Lillian Gish, Lillian Langdon, Olga Grey, Baron Von Ritzau, Count Von Stroheim, Bessie Love, George Walsh, Howard Gaye, William Brown, Margery Wilson, Spottiswoode Aitken, Ruth Handforth, Eugene Pallette, A. D. Sears, Frank Bennett, Maxfield Stanley, Josephine Crowell, Georgia Pearce, W. E. Lawrence, Joseph Henabery, Louis Romaine, Morris Levy, Howard Gaye, Raymond Wells, George James, Louis Ritz, John Bragdon, Constance Talmadge, Elmer Clifton, Alfred Paget, Seena Owen, Loyola O'Connor, Carl Stockdale, Tully Marshall, George Siegmann, Elmo Lincoln, Robert Lawler, Grace Wilson, Lotta Clifton, George Beranger, Ah Singh, Ranji Singh, James Curley, Ed Burns, James Burns, Kate Bruce, Pauline Stark, Mildred Harris, Winifred Westover, Martin Landry, Howard Scott, Arthur Meyer, Alma Rubens, Ruth Darling, Margaret Mooney, Charles Eagle Eye, William Dark Cloud, Charles Van Cortland, Jack Cosgrove, Ethel Terry, Mae Marsh, Fred Turner, Robert Harron, Sam de Grasse, Clyde Hopkins, Vera Lewis, Mary Alden, Luray Huntley, Lucille Brown, Eleanor Washington, Pearl Elmore, Mrs. Arthur Mackley, Miriam Cooper, Walter Long, Tom Wilson, Ralph Lewis, A. W. McClure, Edward Dillon, Lloyd Ingraham, William Brown, Max Davidson, Alberta Lee, Frank Brownlee, Barney Bernard, Marguerite Marsh, Tod Browning, Kate Bruce.

1917

Conscience (Fox) D: *Bertram Bracken*. Gladys Brockwell, Marjorie Daw, Eugenie Forde, Eve Southern, Genevieve Blinn, Douglas Gerrard, Edward Cecil, Harry G. Lonsdale, Colin Chase, Bertram Grassby.

1918

Broadway Love (Bluebird Photoplays) D: *Ida Mae Park*. Dorothy Phillips, Juanita Hansen, William Stowell, Harry Von Meter, Lon Chaney, Gladys Tennyson, Eve Southern.

1921

After the Show (Paramount) D: *William DeMille*. Jack Holt, Lila Lee, Charles Ogle, Eve Southern, Shannon Day, Carlton King, Stella Seager, Ethel Wales .

Greater Than Love (Associated Producers) D: *Fred Niblo*. Louise Glaum, Patricia Palmer, Rose Cade, Eve Southern, Willie May Carson, Betty Francisco, Mahlon Hamilton, Donald MacDonald, Edward Martindel, Gertrude Claire, Stanhope Wheatcroft.

The Rage of Paris (Universal) D: *Jack Conway*. Miss Du Pont, Elinor Hancock, Jack Perrin, Leo White, Ramsey Wallace, Freeman Wood, Eve Southern, Mathilde Brundage, J. J. Lanoe.

The Golden Gallows (Universal) D: *Paul Scardon*. Miss Du Pont, Edwin Stevens, Eve Southern, Jack Mower, George B. Williams, Douglas Gerrard, Elinor Hancock, Barbara Tennant.

1922

The Girl in His Room (Vitagraph) D: *Edward Jose´*. Alice Calhoun, Warner Baxter, Robert Anderson, Faye O'Neill, Eve Southern.

Nice People (Paramount) D: *William DeMille*. Wallace Reid, Bebe Daniels, Conrad Nagel, Julia Faye, Claire McDowell, Edward Martindel, Eve Southern, Bertram Jones, William Boyd, Ethel Wales.

1923

Souls for Sale *(Goldwyn)* D: Rupert Hughes. Eleanor Boardman, Mae Busch, Barbara La Marr, Richard Dix, Lew Cody, Arthur Hoyt, David Imboden, Roy Atwell, William Orlamond, Forrest Robinson, Edith Yorke, Dale Fuller, Snitz Edwards, Jack Richardson, Aileen Pringle, Eve Southern, May Milloy, Sylvia Ashton, Margaret Bourne, Fred Kelsey, Jed Prouty, Yale Boss, William Haines, George Morgan, Auld Thomas, Leo Willis, Walter Perry, Sam Damen, R. H. Johnson, Rush Hughes, L. J. O'Connor, Charles Murphy, Hugo Ballin, Mabel Ballin, T. Roy Barnes, Barbara Bedford, Hobart Bosworth, Charles Chaplin, Chester Conklin, William H. Crane, Elliott Dexter, Robert Edeson, Claude Gillingwater, Dagmar Godowsky, Raymond Griffith, Elaine Hammerstein, Jean Haskell, Alice Lake, Bessie Love, June Mathis, Patsy Ruth Miller, Marshall Neilan, Fred Niblo, Anna Q. Nilsson, ZaSu Pitts, John Sainpolis, Milton Sills, Anita Stewart, Erich von Stroheim, Blanche Sweet, Florence Vidor, King Vidor, Johnny Walker, George Walsh, Kathlyn Williams, Claire Windsor.

Burning Words (Universal) D: *Stuart Paton*. Roy Stewart, Laura La Plante, Harold Goodwin, Edith Yorke, Alfred Fisher, William Welsh, Noble Johnson, Eve Southern, Harry Carter, George McDaniels.

Trimmed in Scarlet (Universal) D: *Jack Conway*. Kathlyn Williams, Roy Stewart, Lucille Rickson, Robert Agnew, David Torrence, Phillips Smalley, Eve Southern, Bert Sprotte, Grace Carlyle, Gerrard Grassby, Raymond Hatton, Philo McCullough.

1923

The Dangerous Blonde (Universal) D: *Ralph F. Hill*. Laura La Plante, Edward Hearn, Arthur Hoyt, Philo McCullough, Rolfe Sedan, Eve Southern, Margaret Campbell, Dick Sutherland, Frederick Cole.

1924

Chorus Lady (Regal Pictures) D: *Ralph Ince*. Margaret Livingston, Alan Roscoe, Virginia Lee Corbin, Lillian Elliott, Lloyd Ingraham, Philo McCullough, Eve Southern, Mervyn LeRoy.

1926

A Woman of the Sea D: *Josef von Sternberg, Charlie Chaplin*. Edna Purviance, Eve Southern, Gayne Whitman.

1927

Resurrection (United Artists) D: *Edwin Carewe.* Dolores Del Rio, Marc MacDermott, Lucy Beaumont, Vera Lewis, Clarissa Selwynne, Eve Southern, Count Ilya Tolstoy.

Wild Geese (Tiffany Stahl) D: *Phil Stone.* Belle Bennett, Russell Simpson, Eve Southern, Donald Keith, Jason Robards, Anita Stewart, Wesley Barry, Rada Rae, Austin Jewel, Evelyn Selbie, D'Arcy Corrigan, Jack Gardner, James Mack, Bert Sprotte, Bodil Rosing, Bert Starkey.

1928

The Gaucho (United Artists) D: *F. Richard Jones.* Douglas Fairbanks, Lupe Velez, Geraine Greear, Eve Southern, Gustav von Seyffertitz, Michael Vavitch, Charles Stevens, Nigel De Brulier, Albert MacQuarrie, Mary Pickford.

Stormy Waters (Tiffany-Stahl) D: *Edgar Lewis.* Eve Southern, Malcolm McGregor, Roy Stewart, Shirley Palmer, Olin Francis, Norbert Myles, Bert Apling.

Naughty Duchess (Tiffany-Stahl) D: *Tom Terriss.* Eve Southern, H. B. Warner, Duncan Renaldo, Maude Turner Gordon, Gertrude Astor, Martha Mattox, Herbert Evans.

Clothes Make the Woman (Tiffany-Stahl) D: *Tom Terriss.* Eve Southern, Walter Pidgeon, Charles Byer, George E. Stone, Adolph Millar, Duncan Renaldo, Gordon Begg, Catherine Wallace, Corliss Palmer, Margaret Selby, H. D. Pennell.

The Haunted House (First National) D: *Benjamin Christensen.* Larry Kent, Thelma Todd, Edmund Breese, Sidney Bracy, Barbara Bedford, Flora Finch, Chester Conklin, William V. Mong, Montague Love, Eve Southern, Johnny Gough.

The Voice Within (Tiffany) D: *George Archainbaud.* Eve Southern, Walter Pidgeon, Montagu Love, J. Barney Sherry.

1929

Whispering Winds (Tiffany-Stahl) D: *James Flood.* Patsy Ruth Miller, Malcolm McGregor, Eve Southern, Eugénie Besserer, James Marcus.

Morocco (Paramount) D: *Josef von Sternberg.* Gary Cooper, Marlene Dietrich, Adolphe Menjou, Rich Haupt, Juliette Compton, Francis McDonald, Albert Conti, Eve Southern, Michael Visaroff, Paul Porcasi, Theresa Harris.

1930

Lilies of the Field (First National) D: *Alexander Korda.* Corinne Griffith , Ralph Forbes, John Loder, Eve Southern, Jean Bary, Tyler Brooke, Freeman Wood, Ann Schaeffer, Clarissa Selwynne, Patsy Page, André Beranger, Douglas Gerrard, Rita LeRoy, Betty Boyd, May Boley, Virginia Bruce, Charles Mailes, Ray Largay, Joe Bernard, Tenen Holtz, Wilfred Noy, Alice Moe.

Fighting Caravans (Paramount) D: *Otto Brower, David Burton.* Gary Cooper, Lily Damita, Ernest Torrence, Fred Kohler, Tully Marshall, Eugene Pallette, Roy Stewart, Mae Boley, James Farley, James Marcus, Eve Southern, Donald Mackenzie, Syd Saylor, Frank Campeau, Charles Winninger, Jane Darwell, Irving Bacon, Iron Eyes Cody.

1931

Law of the Sea (Monogram) D: *Otto Brower.* William Farnum, Priscilla Dean, Wally Albright, Rex Bell, Ralph Ince, Sally Blane, Eve Southern.

1932

The Ghost Walks (Chesterfield) D: *Frank R. Strayer.* John Miljan, June Collyer, Richard Carle, Henry Kolker, Spencer Charters, Johnny Arthur, Donald Kirke, Eve Southern, Douglas Gerrard, Wilson Benge, Jack Shutta, Harry Strang.

1936

The King Steps Out (Columbia) D: *Josef von Sternberg.* Grace Moore, Franchot Tone, Walter Connolly, Elisabeth Risdon, Nana Bryant, Victor Jory, Frieda Inescourt, Thurston Hall, Herman Bing, George Hassell, John Arthur, E.E. Clive, Eve Southern, Sidney Bracy.

ALBERTA VAUGHN

To the delight — and embarrassment — of those watching, she insisted on redoing the scene. In the arms of cops, she twisted and turned so the camera would get her best side, her most dazzling smile, her zaniest expression. One more pose and that was it. There was no "cut" or "that's a take."

It turns out that her jig wasn't the Charleston, but a drunken swagger; she was not on a movie set, but in a police station; these guys weren't Keystone Cops, but authorities from the Van Nuys Police Department. It was not 1926, when she was one of the brightest comediennes, but 1946, and she was being arrested.

Police had earlier responded to a disorderly conduct call about an apparently drunken, middle-aged woman, dressed in men's long-johns dancing on the side of a local highway before a group of GIs from an adjacent camp.

By the time they brought her to the station, they were astonished to learn the woman was Alberta Vaughn, a popular actress from the silent film days, who was now, without question, on the down side of fame.

Call it one of those Norma Desmond moments, but when a photographer from the *Los Angeles Examiner* arrived at the station, Alberta insisted on repeating her dance.

Poor Alberta! How had it come to this? All this drama — or comedy — for a few cigarettes.

The Vaughns came from Ashland, Kentucky. Adamae was the first Vaughn born to Charles and Martha Shephard Vaughn on November 8, 1900.[1] Her sister, Alberta, came along on June 27, 1904[2].

Somewhere along the way, Charles, a coalminer and later a brakeman for the railroad, vanished from the scene. Martha married Frank Bruce Preston, a self-employed merchant.

How the family made their way from the hills of Kentucky to Hollywood is unclear. Early publicity suggests that a promoter came to town and announced he was going to make a motion picture in Ashland and would choose the entire cast from among the locals. Alberta was selected to play the leading role. While the production was an amateurish effort, Alberta's work was so impressive that the promoter advised her to try her luck in Hollywood.[3]

Another source has Alberta the victim of a plot engineered by envious chlorines, who appeared with her on Broadway in the ensemble of Irving Berlin's first *Music Box Revue*. They entered the photograph in a funny face contest, sponsored by a New York newspaper, but the gag backfired when Alberta won first prize, which included a trip to Hollywood and a flattering film offer.

Her obituary states it simply: "Miss Vaughn came to Hollywood after being named the 'prettiest girl in Kentucky.'"

It seems likely that Alberta and her family arrived in Hollywood in 1919. She first worked for director William Desmond Taylor in an unbilled role in *The Furnace* (1920), followed by a bit part in *The Son of Wallingford* (1921). Her sister, Adamae, also worked in small, unbilled roles, typically in two-reel comedies.

Alberta got her break into comedy when she was cast as Lupino Lane's ex-bathing beauty wife in *A Friendly Husband* (1923). In the picture, packed with five reels of slapstick, Lane must patiently contend with his in-laws on a camping trip, which was intended to be a vacation for the newlyweds.

Variety was reserved in its review of the picture. "It has falls, somersaults, trick props and speedy action. It is the busiest comedy since Harold Lloyd's early efforts." They found Lupino Lane, a star of two-reelers, "devoid of screen personality. Everything is overdone, of course, except by Miss Vaughan, who really puts some human moments into her absurd positions as a lollipop to a lunatic."[4]

Following her work in *A Friendly Husband*, comic Buster Keaton, sensing a comedic talent in the young actress, introduced Alberta to producer Mack Sennett, who, in November 1922, signed the 18-year-old to a one-year contract at $100 a week.[5]

Throughout 1923, Alberta worked in comedy shorts at Sennett's studios with such comedians as Harry Langdon, Andy Clyde, Mack Swain, and Billy Bevan.

Following her strong showing in *A Friendly Husband* and in anticipation of her bright future ahead, Alberta was named one of the Wampas Baby Stars of 1924, along with two other hard-luck girls profiled in this book: Lucille Ricksen and Elinor Fair.[6]

After her contract with Sennett ended in late 1923, Alberta was hired by FBO (Film Bookings Offices of America) to star in *The Telegraph Girl* comedy series, many of which were directed by Malcolm "Mal" St. Clair. In the series of two-reelers, Alberta plays Gladys Murgatroyd, a telegraph girl who, with her best friend, Sadie (Gertrude Short), takes a trip to France, where they become actresses for a film company that eventually goes broke and leaves the girls stranded.

Alberta Vaughn in 1924.

After *The Telegraph Girl* movies, FBO teamed Alberta with George O'Hara in *The Go-Getter* comedy series. The two-reelers were spoofs of some of the popular dramatic films of the day: *In the Knicker Time*, *A Kick for Cinderella*, *A Miss in the Dark*, *The Sleeping Cutie*, and *The Way of a Maid*.

During the filming of *And Never the Trains Shall Meet*, the third film of the series, writer Harry Carr interviewed the pair about their work. "We

Alberta Vaughn and George O'Hara.

are playing in some railroad pictures now," O'Hara related. Alberta piped in, "And, I'm always getting rescued from villains. I'm always a young lady telegraph operator out in the great open spaces. I'll never see another girl telegraph operator without wanting to tell her to look behind the chair for lurking villains."[7]

Carr questioned Alberta about her recent work with Mack Sennett. "I liked Sennett's studio," she sighed. "That's the trouble with me. I always like them all. The ambition of my life is to be able to leave a studio without crying. I always cry."[8]

Asked whether she hoped to settle down with a husband someday, she exclaimed, "Well, I s'pose so. You have to have them, don't you? It's usual, isn't it?"[9]

The series was so popular that FBO planned another series for the duo: *The Pacemakers* (1925). Each comedy, directed by Wesley Ruggles, stood on its own — there was no one continuing storyline. Also, each short was named for a popular dramatic film: *He Who Gets Rapped, Merton of the Goofies; The Great Decide; The Covered Flagon, Madam Sans Gin; What Price Gloria?*, for example. Clark Gable is said to have been an extra in at least one of the shorts.[10]

Following *The Pacemaker* series, Alberta played Mazie in *The Adventures of Mazie* (1925-1926) comedy series. The titles of some of the shorts hint at some of her character's escapades: *Amazing Mazie, Mazie Won't Tell, So's Your Old Man, High, But Not Handsome,* and *Mazie's Married.*

It was on the set of her next series of comedies, *Fighting Hearts*, that Alberta fell for Grant Withers, an actor just starting in films. Withers, also under contract to FBO, appeared in at least two of the comedies: *Smoldering Tires* and *All's Swell That Ends Swell.*[11] The two were soon engaged.

To capitalize on Alberta's growing popularity in comedy, FBO featured Alberta and Donald Keith in a feature film, *Collegiate*, directed by Del Andrews, with whom she worked in the *Go-Getter* series. The story about love on a college campus amid study, play, and exams, was written especially for Alberta. She didn't disappoint.

Alberta "gives a characterization of collegiate youth, peppy, versatile, and humorous, that is beyond improvement. As the poor little rich girl manicuring dishes to avoid the fell consequences of wealth, she enlivens the time by impromptu dancing exhibitions among the dishes." The film promised to "shock the audiences into peals of laughter."[12]

In *The Adorable Deceiver* (1926), an FBO comedy feature, Alberta plays an exiled princess forced to flee her country during a revolution. *Variety* was puzzled by the selection of Alberta for the role. "When they picked Alberta Vaughan to play a hoyden heroine, with all the coquettish mannerisms of a Betty Bronson, they hung a heavy handicap on the piece. Miss Vaughan is by disposition and by established reputation a low comedienne, a lady clown given to the custard pie school of humor." In the picture, they concluded, Alberta could not decide whether she is a "polite comedienne or a slapstick lady clown."[13]

Adamae Vaughn, beat Alberta to the altar when she married Los Angeles contractor Albert R. Lindman in May 1926. Like Alberta, Adamae was trying to make a name for herself in films, but she wasn't developing as successfully as her younger sister. On their rollercoaster relationship, Adamae and Lindman divorced after a couple of months. Soon after the judge set them free, the couple, realizing they couldn't live without one another, remarried.

Adamae's fledgling career was given a boost, albeit a small tug, when she was named a Wampas Baby Star in 1927. Overcome with emotion, the young hopeful fainted at the award ceremonies.

An original advertisement for The Adorable Deceiver *(1926).*

After Alberta's appearances in *Uneasy Payments* and *Ain't Love Funny?*, both 1927 FBO releases, *Motion Picture* magazine announced that she had left FBO. "It is understood that she is dissatisfied with the parts being given her and the company claims to have no place for her on next year's program."[14]

Following her departure from FBO, Alberta had prominent roles in two independent films: *Sinews of Steel* (Gotham) and *Backstage* (Tiffany), both 1927 releases. She was a showgirl in one and a love interest in the other. Neither were comedies, nor did they advance her career.

Alberta rounded out 1927 in *The Romantic Age*, as the romantic interest of two brothers, and *The Dropkick*, in which the female leads went to Dorothy Revier and Barbara Kent. *Variety* told readers that Alberta was used for a "few necking scenes."[15]

In 1928, Alberta had supporting roles in *Old Age Handicap*, *Skyscraper*, and *Forbidden Hours*, a Ramon Novarro and Renee Adoree comedy. Later in the year, with her roles in features becoming less substantial, Alberta returned to two-reel comedies. For the next year or so, she appeared with Al Cooke in the *Racing Blood* and *Record Breakers* series, R-K-O and Standard Photoplay Company productions, respectively.

An autographed photo of Alberta Vaughn at the height of her career.

In early 1928, Alberta met multi-millionaire William Tait Jr., a member of a prominent steel family from Pittsburgh. They were both smitten. In August, with a 10-carat diamond on her hand, Alberta announced their engagement and plans for a Christmas wedding. She cooed that the two would marry at his Pasadena home and live in a new Beverly Hills home they would build together[16].

Adamae (L) and Alberta Vaughn in Show of Shows *(1929).*

As their plans unfolded that fall, however, Tiffany-Stahl cast Alberta in a featured role in *Molly and Me,* a showbiz comedy with Joe E. Brown and Belle Bennett. Most of the film was silent and filmed in Hollywood. In December, however, the cast was sent to New York to record talking sequences. Alberta's Christmas wedding was postponed until she returned to Hollywood.

Alberta assured Tait that her trip to New York was strictly for business. She agreed not to enjoy nights on the town with anyone. He checked on her by placing frequent calls at varying times during the afternoon and evening.

One evening, she was out and Tait failed to reach his bride to be. The next night, he also failed to make contact. The third evening, she answered and said she'd been to various nightclubs with friends. A heated discussion ensued. Alberta was not used to answering to anyone. Was this what married life was all about? Through angry tears, the comedienne cancelled the engagement.

By the time she returned to the West coast, her grief over Tait was history. She boasted to friends of her intention to marry Charles Feldman.[17] That relationship ended without much fanfare.

Her other 1929 appearances did little to further her career. In fact, they were a testament that her career was skidding. At Warner Brothers, she danced with Adamae, who was making one of her final film appearances, in *Show of Shows.* She was part of a second-string vaudevillian family in *Noisy Neighbors* and a heroine in her first Western, *Points West,* with Hoot Gibson.

In late 1930, Alberta was bankrupt, declaring that she had no assets and over $5,000 in liabilities.[18] She and Adamae moved in with their mother and stepfather (now an automobile salesman) in a house he was renting on Stanley Avenue in Hollywood.[19] Like many silent film personalities of their day, the Vaughn sisters were yesterday's story.

She struggled to find work. Back in Gower Gulch, Alberta appeared with Hoot Gibson in *Wild Horse* (1931) and with Tim McCoy in *Daring Danger* (1932). Alberta was teamed with another silent film player on the skids, Harrison Ford, in a low budget comedy-thriller, *Love in High Gear* (1932).[20]

In September 1932, Alberta was cast with Madge Bellamy and Judith Voselli in a play, *Intermission*, a light farcical comedy. She traveled with the cast to San Francisco, where they rehearsed for 10 days at the Geary Theatre. A man sitting beside Madge's mother leaned over and exclaimed, "She (Madge) can't act her way out of a paper bag."

The play closed after a week.[21]

Back in Hollywood, Alberta continued to work sporadically in whatever films came her way. There were *Dance Hall Hostess, Alimony Madness,* and an uncredited role in *Emergency Call*, all 1933 releases.

On May 14, 1933, Alberta was a passenger in a car driven by Joseph Egli, an assistant casting director for Paramount. Somewhere along Ventura Boulevard in Sherman Oaks, Alberta lunged forward into the dash when Egli applied the breaks. Two months later, Alberta filed a $5,750 suit against Egli, claiming that the accident broke her teeth and caused face lacerations that prevented her from securing work on the screen.

In a strange twist of events, Alberta forgot her injuries and became Mrs. Joseph Egli on April 8, 1935. Few knew the couple had eloped to Yuma, Arizona. "They hadn't said a word about being married," Martha, her mother, told the press. "They left here Saturday and intimated that they were going to a show, but if my girl is happy, it's perfectly alright with me."

On hearing of the union between the plaintiff and defendant, the judge dismissed the case, citing "good and sufficient cause."[22]

In June, sister Adamae took another stab at matrimony by wedding her long-time love, Joseph Valentine d'Auvray, rumored to be of nobility. The two had been engaged since 1929.

Marital bliss lasted a little over a year for Joseph and Alberta Egli. In her November 1935 divorce suit, Alberta described her husband as being "quarrelsome, boisterous, jealous, and intemperate." In addition, she continued, he was a gambler.[23] She asked for half of his $850 monthly salary and $1,500 for attorney fees.

After riding the range with cowboys John Wayne in *Randy Rides Alone* (1934) and Tom Tyler in *The Laramie Kid* (1935) and following an appearance with stuntman Richard Talmadge in *Live Wire* (1935), Alberta called an end to her film career.

She spent the rest of the decade making up — and breaking up — with Egli. He was, after all, a source of income. In October 1942, she was back in court, declaring that their attempt at reconciliation had failed for the final time. She asked for all community property, which included two cars and a bicycle, and $400 a month support.[24] The divorce was final in August 1943.[25]

A month after her divorce, tragedy struck the Vaughn family. Adamae entered Hollywood Hospital in early September with an intestinal obstruction caused by multiple adhesions left over from surgery she'd had in the late 1930s. Her condition worsened, and after 10 days of suffering, Adamae died at age 42.[26]

It was in January of 1945 that Alberta's life spun publicly out of control. Two Van Nuys police officers were called to the side of a highway where a drunken woman was parading in men's underwear in front a group of GIs.

One of the officers on the scene said it best. "Like a woodland nymph she was — dancin' and cavortin' in a two-piece suit of G.I. long woolies decorated with posies and leaves!"[27]

Later that evening, Alberta was booked at Lincoln Heights jail on a drunken charge under Alberta Egli. She insisted to the officers that she saw nothing wrong with her antic.

"What's all the excitement about?" she asked. "I only wanted some cigarettes. After all, a girl's gotta smoke!"

Later that year, a drunken Alberta was driving down Ventura Boulevard not far from her home on Woodbridge Street, when she collided with another vehicle. Several people were injured. She pled guilty to the charges and was sentenced to five years probation and ordered to refrain from drinking alcohol.

Columnist Jimmie Fidler wrote that perhaps the attention paid to the case was a bit excessive. "Ethically, of course, the unusual amount of publicity given her offense is unfair, and I presume she is bitterly resentful." He suggested that perhaps Alberta should consider the headlines from another viewpoint. That is, if it prevented others from "mixing gasoline and alcohol", the attention might result in a positive outcome. "If so, Miss Vaughn is entitled to the dubious consolation of being a valuable example."[28]

In June of 1948, Alberta, now working as a waitress at a local inn, married roofer John R. Thomas. Instead of a bridal gown, she wore yellow slacks, a brown-striped tee shirt and a suit coat, "only because it was so sudden," she claimed.

Alberta was so consumed by her honeymoon that she neglected to report to a meeting with her probation officer. When her officer finally made

Alberta Vaughn, when taken to the police station after publicly parading around in men's underwear, struck a similar pose (left) she had perfected as a Hollywood darling 20 years before (right).

contact, it was clear she had violated her agreement not to drink. She was arrested in a Lankersham Boulevard motel where she'd been living and ordered to serve a one-year jail sentence.[29] Her husband issued a strong appeal to the court. "She has settled down," he said.

Alberta seemed relieved to have the matter behind her. She told reporters, "Now I can serve my time and leave here without violating any probation."[30]

From her jail cell, Alberta filed for divorce, claiming Thomas caused her "great anguish and suffering" making her "ill in mind and body."

She was released in February 1949 after serving eight months of her sentence. Five days later, Alberta was arrested for drunkenness in Pasadena and charged a $25 fine. She insisted she was only celebrating her release from jail.[31] Rather than pay the fine, Alberta chose to return to jail. She was given a 12-day sentence and faced the possibility of serving out the remainder for her previous conviction.

"If I have to do those four months," she told reporters, "a few extra days won't matter."[32]

On a Saturday night in early August, police answered a disturbance of the peace call at the Vaughn home on Woodbridge Street. Alberta and mother Martha wanted Alberta's husband arrested. The officers explained they would have to make a request in person at the city attorney's office. According to the police report, Alberta and her mother followed the officers into the street, cursing them. Police arrested the three for public drunkenness. They plead not guilty.[33]

In May 1953, Alberta and her mother failed to revive 38-year-old Harry Reese, a man they claimed to be a servant at their Woodbridge Street home. They explained they had found him earlier in the day and nursed him until nightfall. Police said the man had been dead 24 hours.

Alberta made her first personal appearance in years when she joined other old-timers (Phyllis Haver, Sally Eilers, Louise Fazenda, and others) in a salute to her old boss, Mack Sennett, in an episode of *This is Your Life*.

After reliving the old days with Sennett, Alberta seemed to drop from sight. Her mother died at age 85 in October 1968. Silent film historian Roi Uselton reached out successfully to Alberta in the 1970s and 80s. They corresponded sporadically. Former vaudevillians, Andy and Dolores Albin, neighbors of Alberta, were acquaintances. Otherwise, the former silent film actress lived in seclusion in a guest house on the main property on Woodbridge Street. She rented the main house, built as a farm house in the 1920s, to tenants. Over the years, both houses fell into disrepair.

Michael Laskin moved across the street in 1986, but never saw his eccentric neighbor nor had any personal interaction with her. "She was a recluse," he said. "I am not certain if she simply withdrew from society or had health problems that confined her to her home."[34]

Alberta died of a heart attack at her residence on August 26, 1992. She was also suffering from cancer of the mouth and tongue. She was 87.[35]

"About a week after her death, I was coming down the block to my house when I saw a tow-truck dragging a very old and moss-encrusted Cadillac convertible out from the back yard of her home," Laskin remembered. "I had never seen the car before. I assume it was her last car, and it looked like it had been sitting for decades, acquiring its appearance of having been grown over by moss and vines. It was a rather spooky sight, and not unlike images from the great film *Sunset Boulevard*."[36]

After the estate was settled, the house was sold and refurbished. The estate might have been settled, but, according to future residents of the house, Alberta was not at rest.

"There was a lot of talk about a ghost in the house — her ghost," said actor Richard Cox, another neighbor.[37]

"The ghost idea would not surprise me," Laskin said. "The whole place looked and seemed decrepit and strange. Ghost sightings would be par for the course."[38]

Not only was the house said to be haunted, but Cox said there were rumors that the house had once been a brothel. He suggested I contact actor Keith Szarabajka, who owned the house in the 1990s.

"Most definitely, the stories I heard was that it was a brothel in the 1960s and 70s and that Ms. Vaughn was the madam," Szarabajka said in a telephone interview. As far as the ghost rumors, "my youngest child, who was four at the time, said he saw her ghost, but I never saw it myself."[39]

Sharon Lane, who bought the house from Szarabajka, said she was aware of the ghost stories when she bought the house. As part of the deal, she was required to sign papers acknowledging that she had been informed that the house could be haunted.

Upon moving into the house, Lane said one of the first items of business was to confront the ghost. She sat and addressed the spirit. "Okay, if you are here, that's fine." Lane explained that there would be parties and lots of drinking and smoking going on from time to time. "I guess that pleased her," Lane said, "because I've never seen a ghost."[40]

If Alberta Vaughn, the gifted silent film comedienne, still roams the halls of her long-time home on Woodbridge Street in Studio City, the question is — why? Could it be that the former hard-luck gal is looking for a couple of cigarettes? After all, she once said, "a girl's gotta smoke!"

1. Adamae Vaughn's death certificate states she was born in 1905. The 1910 U.S. Federal Census suggests 1900 as the year of birth.

2. Alberta Vaughn's death certificate also states that she was born in 1905. The 1910 U.S. Federal Census suggests she was born in 1904. Early publicity gives 1906.

3. *Stars of the Photoplay*, Photoplay Publishing Company, 1924.

4. *Variety*, 14 June 1923.

5. Contract between Mack Sennett and Alberta Vaughn, signed in November 1922, is among Sennett's papers at the Motion Picture Academy of Arts and Sciences Library.

6. Clara Bow was the most prominent actress to come out of the 1924 group of Wampas (Western Association of Motion Picture Advertisers) babies. The other actresses that year were Carmelita Geraghty, Gloria Grey, Ruth Hiatt, Julanne Johnston, Hazel Keener, Dorothy Mackaill, Blanche Mehaffey, Margaret Morris, and Marian (Marion) Nixon.

7. Carr, Harry, "Dining with George and Alberta," *Motion Picture Classic*, December 1924.

8. *Ibid.*

9. *Ibid.*

10. Wayne, Jane Ellen, *Gable's Women*, New York: Prentice Hall Press, 1987.

11. Grant Withers (1904-1959), a former newspaper reporter, was the first husband of Loretta Young. He went on to appear in over 200 films.

12. "Alberta Vaughn Sparkles in Brilliant College Comedy," unknown publication, 1927.

13. *Variety*, 22 December 1926.

14. *Motion Picture*, 1927

15. *Variety*, 21 September 1927.

16. "Actress to Wed Rich Pittsburgher," *Chronicle Telegram*, Elyria, Ohio, 25 August 1928.

17. "She Says it's Off," *Oelwein Daily Register*, Oelwein, Ohio, 12 January 1929.

18. "Alberta Vaughn is Broke," November 1930.

19. 1920 U.S. Federal Census.

20. *Love in High Gear* was Harrison Ford's final film.

21. Bellamy, Madge, *A Darling of the Twenties*, Vestal Press, 1989.

22. "Actress Settles by Marrying Defendant," 23 August 1934.

23. "Wampas Girl Asks Divorce, Alimony," November 1935.

24. "Film Star Sues for Maintenance," 28 October 1942.

25. "Actress Divorced," 11 August 1943.

26. County of Los Angeles, Registrar/Recorder/County Clerk, Death Certificate, no. 13598, September 1943. The death certificate states that she was divorced from d'Auvray and living with her mother, Martha, on Carpenter Avenue in Studio City. Adamae Vaughn was buried at Forest Lawn Memorial Park in Glendale.

27. "Alberta Vaughn, in GI Woolies, Dances on Road," *Los Angeles Examiner*, 12 January 1945.

28. "Jimmie Fidler in Hollywood," *Joplin Globe*, Joplin, Missouri, 23 May 1946.

29. "Alberta Vaughn, Former Silent Actress, Jailed," *Los Angeles Times*, 1 July 1948.

30. Ibid.

31. "Silent Screen Actress is a Real Celebrator," 17 February 1949.

32. "Former Silent Film Star Alberta Vaughn is Jailed on Intoxication Charge," 3 March 1949.

33. "Actress Gives Innocent Plea in Drunk Case," Los Angeles Times, 9 August 1949.

34. Michael Laskin to Michael G. Ankerich, June 2009.

35. County of Los Angeles, Registrar/Recorder/County Clerk, Death Certificate, no. 39219019316, 28 August 1992.

36. Michael Laskin to Michael G. Ankerich, June 2009.

37. Richard Cox to Michael G. Ankerich, June 2009.

38. Michael Laskin to Michael G. Ankerich, June 2009.

39. Keith Szarabajka to Michael G. Ankerich, June 2009.

40. Sharon Lane to Michael G. Ankerich, June 2009.

FILMOGRAPHY

1921

Stop Kidding (short) (Pathe) D: *Nicholas T. Barrows, Robert P. Kerr.* Eddie Boland, Ethel Broadhurst, Alberta Vaughn, Adamae Vaughn.

1922

A Friendly Husband (Fox) D: *John Blystone.* Lupino Lane, Alberta Vaughn, Eva Thatcher.

Women First (short) (Century Film) D: *Frank Hackert.* Lee Moran, Alberta Vaughn.

1923

The Adorable Deceiver (Robertson-Cole) D: *Phil Rosen.* Alberta Vaughn, Cora Williams, Daniel Makarenko, Jane Thomas.

Flip Flops (short) (Sennett) D: *Roy Del Ruth.* Alberta Vaughn, Lewis Sargent, Jack Cooper, Andy Clyde, Billy Armstrong, Cecille Evans, Elsie Tarron.

Down to the Sea in Shoes (Sennett) D: *Del Lord.* Billy Bevan, Harry Gribbon, Margaret Cloud, Jack Cooper, Cecille Evans, Sunshine Hart, Elsie Tarron, Gladys Tennyson, Alberta Vaughn.

Skylarking (short) (Sennett) D: *Roy Del Ruth.* Harry Gribbon, Lila Leslie, Kewpie Morgan, Alberta Vaughn, Josephine Adair, Jackie Lucas.

Nip and Tuck (short) (Sennett). D: *Roy Del Ruth.* Billy Bevan, Harry Gribbon, Kewpie Morgan, Alberta Vaughn, Mildred June, Cameo the Dog.

A Friendly Husband (Fox) D: *John G. Blystone.* Lupino Lane, Alberta Vaughn, Eva Thatcher.

Rough and Ready (short) (Sennett) D: *William Campbell.* Jackie Lucas, Mack Swain, Andy Clyde, Alberta Vaughn, Jack Cooper, Alice Waldron.

1924

Go-Getters *(series) (FBO)* D: *Del Andrews.* Alberta Vaughn, George O'Hara *(Who's Hooligan?, The Going of Cumming, A Miss in the Dark, Fire When Ready, A Kick for Cinderella, And Never the Trains Shall Meet, In the Knicker Time, Getting Going, The Way of a Maid, Ain't Love Grand?, The Sleeping Cutie, Playing with Fire).*

The Telephone Girl (series) (FBO) Alberta Vaughn, Al Cooke. *Julius Sees Her, When Knighthood Was in Tower, Money to Burns, King Leary, William Tells, Sherlock's Home, For the Love of Mike, Never Say Never, Faster Foster, Love and Learn, Bee's Knees, Square Sex.*

Smile Please *(short) (Sennett)* D: *Roy Del Ruth.* Alberta Vaughn, Harry Langdon, Jack Cooper, Madeline Hurlock, Tiny Ward, Jackie Lucas,.

Picking Peaches (short) Sennett. D: *Erle C. Kenton.* Harry Langdon, Alberta Vaughn, Ethel Teare, Dot Farley, Kewpie Morgan, Vernon Dent, Mary Akin, Andy Clyde, Jack Cooper, Alice Day, Marceline Day, Dorothy Dorr, Cecille Evans, Evelyn Francisco, Eugenia Gilbert, Thelma Hill, Si Jenks, Leo Sulky, Elsie Tarron.

1925

The Sleuth (short) (Joe Rock Comedies) D: *Harry Sweet, Joe Rock.* Stan Laurel, Glen Cavender, Alberta Vaughn, Anita Garvin.

Twins (short) (Joe Rock Comedies) D: *Scott Pembroke, Joe Rock.* Stan Laurel, Julie Leonard, Alberta Vaughn.

The Adventures of Mazie (series) (FBO) D: *Ralph Ceder, Jimmy Wilkinson.* Alberta Vaughn. *Amazing Mazie, The Constant Simp, Or What Have You, Mazie Won't Tell, So's Your Old Man, Pike's Pique, The Vanishing Armenian, Tea for Toomey, High, But Not Handsome, Little Andy Looney, A Snitch in Time, Mazie's Married.*

The Pacemakers (series) (FBO) D: *Wesley Ruggles.* Alberta Vaughn, George O'Hara. *(Welcome Granger, He Who Gets Rapped, Merton of the Goofies, The Great Decide, The Fast Male, The Covered Flagon, Madam Sans Gin, Three Bases East, The Merry Kiddo, What Price Gloria?, Don Coo-Coo, Miss Me Again, Barbara Snitches).*

1926

Ain't Love Funny? (Robertson-Cole) D: *Del Andrews*. Alberta Vaughn, Syd Crossley, Babe London, Johnny Gough, Charles Hill Mailes.

Collegiate (FBO) D: *Del Andrews*. Alberta Vaughn, Donald Keith, John Steppling, Alys Murrell, William Austin , Frankie Adams, Charles Cruz .

Fighting Heart (series): *Twelve Smiles Out, When Sally's Irish Rose, All's Swell That Ends Swell Up and Wooing, The Big Charade, The Lightning Slider, Whiskering Chorus, Smouldering Tires, Sock Me to Sleep, Plane Jane, It's a Buoy, Roll Your Own.*

1927

Backstage (Tiffany) D: *Phil Stone*. William Collier Jr., Barbara Bedford, Alberta Vaughn, Eileen Percy, Shirley O'Hara, Gayne Whitman, Jocelyn Lee, Guinn Williams, Jimmy Harrison, Brooks Benedict, Lincoln Plummer, Marcia Harris, Louise Carver, John Batten.

Romantic Age (Columbia) D: *Robert Florey*. Alberta Vaughn, Eugene O'Brien, Stanley Taylor.

Uneasy Payments (FBO) D: *David Kirkland*. Alberta Vaughn, Jack Luden, Gino Corrado, Gene Stone, Victor Potel, Betty Francisco, Amber Norman.

The Dropkick (First National) D: *Millard Webb*. Richard Barthelmess, Barbara Kent, Dorothy Revier, Eugene Strong, Alberta Vaughn.

Sinews of Steel (Gotham Productions) D: *Frank O'Connor*. Alberta Vaughn, Gaston Glass, Anders Randolf, Paul Weigel, Greta von Rue, Nora Hayden, Charles Wellesley, John H. Gardener, Bobby Gordon.

Forbidden Hours (M-G-M) D: *Harry Beaumont*. Ramon Novarro, Renée Adorée, Dorothy Cumming, Edward Connelly, Alberta Vaughn.

1928

Old Age Handicap (Trinity Pictures) D: *Frank S. Mattison*. Alberta Vaughn, Gareth Hughes, Vivian Rich, Olaf Hytten, Alberta Vaughn, Gareth Hughes, Vivian Rich, Olaf Hytten, Mavis Villiers, Robert "Buddy" Shaw, Jimmy Humes, Carolyn Wethall, Robert Rodman, Frank Mattison Jr., Ford Jessen, Hall Cline, Edna Hearn, Arthur Hotaling, White Star.

Skyscraper (Pathé) D: *Howard Higgin.* William "Hopalong" Boyd, Alan Hale, Sue Carol, Alberta Vaughn.

Molly and Me (Tiffany-Stahl) D: *Albert Ray.* Belle Bennett, Alberta Vaughn, Charles Byer.

Racing Blood (series): *Broadway Ladies; The Naughty Forties; The Six Best Fellows; That Wild Irish Pose; Mild But She Satisfies; Watch Your Pep; The Sweet Buy and Buy; Ruth Is Stranger Than Fiction; The Arabian Fights; You Just Know She Dares 'Em; The Wages of Synthetic.*

1929

Noisy Neighbors (Pathé) D: *Charles Reisner.* Alberta Vaughn, Theodore Roberts, Eddie Quillan, Jane Keckley, Joseph Quillan, Marie Quillan, Theodore Roberts, Ray Hallor, Russell Simpson, Bob Perry, Mike Donlin, Billy Gilbert.

Show of Shows (Warner Brothers) D: *John G. Adolphi.* Frank Fay, William Courtenay, H.B. Warner, Hobart Bosworth, Marian Nixon, Sally O'Neil, Myrna Loy, Alice Day, Patsy Ruth Miller, Ben Turpin, Heinie Conklin, Lupino Lane, Lee Moran, Bert Roach, Lloyd Hamilton, Noah Beery, Tully Marshall, Wheeler Oakman, Carmel Myers, Ruth Clifford, Sally Eilers, Viola Dana, Shirley Mason, Ethlyne Clair, Frances Lee, Julanne Johnston, Douglas Fairbanks Jr., Chester Conklin, Chester Morris, William Bakewell, Lois Wilson, Gertrude Olmstead, Pauline Garon, Edna Murphy, Jacqueline Logan, Monte Blue, Albert Gran, Dolores Costello, Helene Costello, Molly O'Day, Alberta Vaughn, Adamae Vaughn, Alice White, Loretta Young.

Points West (Universal) D: *Arthur Rosson.* Hoot Gibson, Alberta Vaughn, Frank Campeau, Jack Raymond.

1930

The Record Breakers (series) As You Mike It, Meet the Quince, Love's Labor Found, They Shall Not Pass Out, The Captain of His Roll, The Sleeping Cutie, Lost and Foundered, Old Vamps for New, The Setting Son, The Dear Slayer, Cash and Marry, , Land of the Sky Blue Daughters, Eventually, But Not Now.

1931

Wild Horse (Allied) D: *Richard Thorpe, Sidney Algier.* Hoot Gibson, Alberta Vaughn, Stepin Fetchit, Neal Hart, Edmund Cobb, Joe Rickson.

Speed (short) (Sennett) D: *Mack Sennett.* Andy Clyde, Marjorie Beebe, Alberta Vaughn, Frank Eastman, Cyril Chadwick, Walter Weems, Marion Sayers, Roger Moore, George Gray, Tom Dempsey, Anna Dodge, Aaron Edwards, Julia Griffith, Pat Harmon, Barney Hellum, Ted Stroback.

The Love Bargain (short) (Educational Film Exchanges) D: *Arvid E. Gillstrom.* Robert Agnew, Alberta Vaughn, Tyler Brooke, Margaret Clark, George MacFarlane.

Dancers in the Dark (Paramount) D: David Burton. Miriam Hopkins, Jack Oakie, William Collier, Jr., Eugene Pallette, Lyda Roberti, George Raft, Alberta Vaughn, Paul Fix.

Spell of the Circus (series) (Universal) D: *Robert F. Hill.* Ralph Bushman, Alberta Vaughn, Tom London, Walter Shumway, Charles Murphy.

Working Girls (Paramount) D: *Dorothy Arzner.* Judith Wood, Dorothy Hall, Charles 'Buddy' Rogers, Paul Lukas, Stuart Erwin, Frances Dee, Mary Forbes, Frances Moffett, Claire Dodd, Dorothy Stickney, Alberta Vaughn.

1932

Daring Danger (Columbia) D: *D. Ross Lederman.* Tim McCoy, Alberta Vaughn, Wallace McDonald, Robert Ellis, Richard Alexander, Murdock MacQuarrie, Edward J. Le Saint, Bobby Nelson.

Love in High Gear (Mayfair) D: *Frank Strayer.* Harrison Ford, Alberta Vaughn, Tyrell Davis, Arthur Hoyt, Ethel Wales.

Midnight Morals (Mayfair) D: *E. Mason Hopper.* Beryl Mercer, De Witt Jennings, Charles Delaney, Alberta Vaughn, Gwen Lee, Rex Lease.

Emergency Call (RKO) D: *Edward Cahn.* Bill Boyd, Wynne Gibson, William Gargan, George E. Stone, Betty Furness, Reginald Mason, Edwin Maxwell, Merna Kennedy, Jane Darwell, Alberta Vaughn, Helen Lynch, Gertrude Sutton, Paul Fix, Arthur Hoyt.

1933

Dance Hall Hostess (Mayfair) D: *Breezy Eason*. Helen Chandler, Jason Robards, Sr., Eddie Nugent, Natalie Moorhead, Alberta Vaughn.

Alimony Madness (Mayfair) D: *Breezy Eason*. Helen Chandler, Edward Earle, Charlotte Merriam, Leon Waycoff, Blanche Friderici, Alberta Vaughn.

Randy Rides Alone (Monogram) D: *Harry Fraser*. John Wayne, Alberta Vaughn, George Hayes, Yakima Canutt, Earl Dwire.

1934

The Laramie Kid (Reliable) D: *Harry S. Webb*. Tom Tyler, Alberta Vaughn, Al Ferguson. Murdock MacQuarrie, George Chesebro, Snub Pollard, Steve Clark.

1935

The Live Wire (Reliable) D: *Harry S. Webb*. Richard Talmadge, Alberta Vaughn, George Walsh, Charles K. French, Martin Turner, George Chesebro.

INDEX

Michael G. Ankerich (R) with Donald Gallery (the son of Barbara La Marr) and actress Sherri Snyder.

ABOUT THE AUTHOR

Michael G. Ankerich admits there have always been stars going around in his head. While still in college, he began interviewing country music stars as a way to meet his favorites. He considers his best conversations to have been with Loretta Lynn, Dolly Parton, and Tammy Wynette, whom he calls the "holy trinity" of country music queens.

He later became interested in silent films and interviewed many of the remaining actors and actresses from that era. His efforts were published in two books: *Broken Silence: Conversations with 23 Silent Film Stars* and *The Sound of Silence: Conversations with 16 Film and Stage Personalities Who Bridged the Gap Between Silents and Talkies*.

His most recent book, *The Real Joyce Compton: Behind the Dumb Blonde Movie Image*, was released in 2009.

He is currently working on a biography of silent film actress Mae Murray.

A former newspaper reporter, Ankerich has written extensively for *Classic Images, Films of the Golden Age,* and *Hollywood Studio Magazine*, which featured his interview with Butterfly McQueen (Prissy) on the 50th anniversary of the release of *Gone With The Wind*.

Ankerich lives with his partner, Charlie, and their three girls, MaeBelle, Ms. Taylor, and Tallulah, in Georgia. Contract Ankerich through his website, *michaelgankerich.com*.

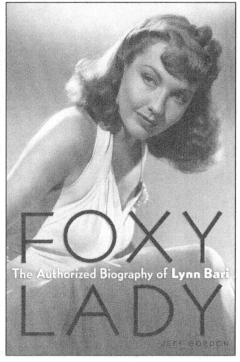

Made in the USA
Coppell, TX
05 February 2023

12199930R10226